COMPENDIA

Computer-Generated Aids
to Literary and Linguistic Research
General Editor: R. A. WISBEY

VOLUME 4

A COMPLETE CONCORDANCE TO THE
SONGS OF THE EARLY TUDOR COURT

A COMPLETE CONCORDANCE

TO THE

SONGS OF THE EARLY TUDOR COURT

MICHAEL J. PRESTON

Temple Buell College
and Co-ordinator, Center for Computer Research in
the Humanities at the University of Colorado

W. S. MANEY AND SON LTD

1972

© Michael J. Preston
PRINTED BY W. S. MANEY AND SON LTD LEEDS ENGLAND

CONTENTS

Preface vii

Index of First Lines 1

Index of First Lines (Original Order) 7

Concordance of English Graphic Forms 13

Concordance of Foreign Graphic Forms 327

Reverse Index of English Graphic Forms 335

Reverse Index of Foreign Graphic Forms 353

Index of Rhymes 355

Ranking List of Frequencies 423

Ranking List of Foreign Forms 433

PREFACE

This concordance to BM Add. Ms. 5665 (*Ritson's MS*), BM Add. Ms. 5465 (*The Fayrfax MS*), and BM Add. Ms. 31922 (*Henry VIII's MS*) is based on the edition by John Stevens.[1] These three manuscripts contain virtually all that is known of early Tudor song. Two are associated with the court circle; the third, Ritson's, appears to be from the west. The exact reproduction of Stevens's edition on a line-for-line basis has been my aim throughout. For clarity I repeat his summary of his editorial practice:

Throughout the English texts I have modernized capitals, punctuation, and word-division and stanza arrangement. The letters *u, v, i, j, þ,* and *ȝ* have been replaced by their modern equivalents; *ff* is printed as *F* or *f*; roman numerals are spelt out. When a word in the MS ends in an ambiguous flourish, I have added or omitted the conjectural *e* to accord with present-day spelling. Manuscript contractions and abbreviations have been silently expanded.[2]

Rather than make use of a series of unfamiliar 'short titles', I have relied upon Stevens's system of alphabetic and numeric characters to identify manuscript, poem, and stanza. Thus H33b refers to the burden ('Grene growith the holy') of Henry VIII's popular lyric, the thirty-third in BM Add. Ms. 31922; H33.1 refers to the first stanza of the same poem. To facilitate identification of these poems, and to make the volume useful to those who do not have Stevens's edition, two indices of first lines precede the body of the concordance: the first is based on the standard alphabetic arrangement of first lines (first lines beginning with an article are entered under that article, and the first lines of burdens are underlined); the second is ordered on the sequence in which the poems occur in the manuscripts. It is hoped that, in this fashion, any user may find his way into the concordance and out as well.

The body of this concordance appears exactly as it was sorted by computer. Variant forms of the same word are not grouped together, and distinctions are not made among homographs. Although

---

[1] John Stevens, 'Appendix A', *Music & Poetry in the Early Tudor Court* (London: Methuen & Co. Ltd, 1961), pp. 337–425. My thanks are due both to the editor and to the publisher for permission to use this text for the present concordance.

[2] Stevens, p. 337.

at one time I did consider following the practice of Kottler and Markman in their *A Concordance to Five Middle English Poems*[1] (in fact, programs were written to do just this), I decided that it would be more useful to refrain from re-sorting and re-arranging the text in any way. Alphabetic arrangement usually places variants in close succession within a few lines or, at most, within a few pages. This is especially true because of Stevens's slight modernization of the text. In addition, I consider that homographs should not be too hastily separated, for word-play of various kinds has always been one of the features of our language, and distinctions made in a concordance tend to make differences in meaning too clear-cut and, often, too permanent.

Appendixes appear at the end of this volume as has become traditional with computer-produced concordances. First of all, the foreign words appear in a little concordance, so to speak, of their own. Although the state of the language in the early sixteenth century occasionally makes the identification of particular items difficult, it seemed better to isolate the relatively few foreign forms in this fashion rather than to allow them to become lost among the mass of English forms. The latter were picked out by supplying a list of foreign words which were sorted separately, but because of the usual problem of homographs, for example the Latin *sum* and the English *sum*, it is perhaps more efficient to code such words in the text. Reverse indexes of English and foreign forms follow; they are the product of re-sorting the headwords.

One of the more problematic sections of this volume was the Index of Rhymes. This is, of course, based on a sorting of the individual elements of a rhyme-group reverse alphabetically, i.e. from back to front. If similar spellings in English denoted similar sounds, and if the rhyme were always contained only in the final syllable or final vowel, this would be sufficient. However a glance at the Reverse Index of Graphic Forms will indicate just what distance would separate the rhyme words *be* and *we*. As a result, I ordered the entries according to the spelling of the rhyme syllable(s) as is common in most rhyme dictionaries, giving cross-references to other endings which occur in the rhyme scheme, as well as frequencies of rhyme-endings and rhyme words. By this arrangement I do not

---

[1] Barnet Kottler and Alan M. Markman, *A Concordance to Five Middle English Poems* (Pittsburgh: University of Pittsburgh Press, 1966).

mean to imply that all pronunciations of an identical syllable are the same, just as in the body of the concordance I do not mean that all words spelled the same are equivalent. In fact, *lamentable* rhymes with *hely* and *rufully* in F36.4 5, 6, 7; this pronunciation of *-able* is certainly far from usual. The cross-reference to the *-y* endings which follows the *-able* heading is intended to point out this rare pronunciation at a glance. On the whole, the conventional method of arranging rhymes is employed simply because it is convenient. From a literary point of view some interesting, though not surprising, observations may be made. For example, the frequent appearance of rhymes like *hart-smart-depart* and *moan-alone* shows a quite similar mental reaction on the part of the various poets in that one word brings the other immediately to mind.

The ranking lists of frequencies come last. Although these may be somewhat misleading for certain purposes because of variants and homographs, it is certainly noteworthy that the most frequently occurring word is *I*. (The alternative form *Y*, although it appears almost exclusively in the western *Ritson's MS*, also occurs many times.) Whether popular, secular, courtly or religious — and to describe the early Tudor lyric would be virtually to indicate the range of the Middle English lyric — most of these poems manifest the personal qualities of the love lyric. It is not surprising, therefore, that *my*, *me*, *her*, and *love* are among the most frequently occurring forms.

In compiling a work of this nature, especially when it is the first among those produced by a research group to reach publication, one receives help from many people. This volume was produced through the facilities of the Center for Computer Research in the Humanities at the University of Colorado in Boulder, and the Director of the Center, Dean H. Lewis Sawin, deserves special thanks, as does the Center's programmer, Samuel S. Coleman. On a more literary level, Constance Wright offered many suggestions which were incorporated; Donald C. Baker was a continual source of information as well as of personal encouragement. Roy Wisbey, whose first visit to the University of Colorado resulted in the establishment of the Center, spent five weeks of the summer of 1969 again in Colorado and his experience was invaluable. Finally I must acknowledge gratefully a Faculty research grant from Temple Buell College which defrayed a large portion of the expense of this volume; Charles Rich and others saw to it that I received as much aid as the College could afford. To all of these, and particularly to my wife Katie who endured it all, and helped perhaps more than she really wished, I owe most profound thanks.

LONGMONT, COLORADO, August 1971   M.J.P.

INDEX OF FIRST LINES

F2	A, a, my herte, I knowe you well;
F37	A blessid Jhesu, hough fortunyd this?
F34b	'A, gentill Jhesu!'
F48	A, man, I have yevyn and made a graunt
F30b	'A, my dere, a, my dere Son,'
F38	A myn hart, remembir the well
F38b	A, myn hert, remembir the well,
H49	A Robyn, gentyl Robyn,
H27	A the syghes that cum from my hart
H103	A thorne hath percyd my hart ryght sore
H17	Aboffe all thynge!
R4	Absens of you causeth me to sygh and complayne
H68	Adew, adew, le company,
H16	Adew, adew, my hartis lust!
H38	Adew, corage, adew;
F32b	Affraid, alas, and whi so sodenli?
H96	Ageynst the Frenchmen in the feld to fyght
H30	Alac, alac, what shall I do,
F22	Alas, for lak of her presens,
F14	Alas, it is I that wote nott what to say,
H12	Alas, what shall I do for love?
R10	Alone, alone,
R14	Alone, alone,
F29b	Alone, alone, alone, alone,
H14	Alone I leffe, alone,
H101	And I war a maydyn,
F29	As I me walkyd this endurs day
H33	As the holy grouth grene
F41	Ay, besherewe yow! Be my fay
F48b	Be hit knowyn to all that byn here
R3	'Be pes, ye make me spille my ale!'
F49	'Beholde', he saide, 'my creature,
F33	Beholde me, I pray the, with all thi hole reson,
F12	Benedicite! Whate dremyd I this nyght?
H35b	Blow thi horne, hunter, and blow thi horn on hye!
F17	But why am I so abusyd?
R16b	Come over the burne, Besse,
F28	Complayne I may wherevyr I go,
F31	Crist, that was of infynyt myght,
H74	Deme the best of every dowt
F6	Demyd wrongfully
H56	Departure is my chef payne;
H18	Downbery down!
F47b	Enforce yourselfe as Goddis knyght
H96b	Englond, be glad! Pluk up thy lusty hart!
R9	Fayre and discrete, fresche wommanly figure,
H63	Farewell, my joy, and my swete hart!
F44b	From stormy wyndis and grevous wethir,
H33b	Grene growith the holy,
R19	Hay how the mavys on a brere!
H31b	Hey nony nony nony nony no,
H109b	Hey troly loly lo!
H75	Hey troly loly loly!
F40	Hit is so praty in every degre;

3

R20b	How shall Y plece a creature uncerteyne?
F43b	Hoyda, hoyda, joly rutterkin!
H65b	I am a joly foster
F15	I am he that hath you dayly servyd,
H62	I have bene a foster
F27	'I love a flour of swete odour'
F27b	'I love, I love, and whom love ye?'
F21	I love, loved, and loved wolde I be
H40	I love trewly withowt feynyng;
H108	I love unloved; suche is myn aventure,
F16	[I pray daily ther paynys to asswage]
H44	If love now reynyd as it hath bene
H29	Iff I had wytt for to endyght
F45	In a glorius garden grene
F49b	In a slumbir late as I was,
H20	In May, that lusty sesoun
R15	In wyldernes
F31b	Jhesu, mercy, how may this be,
F40b	Jhoone is sike and ill at ease;
H82	Let not us that yong men be
F8	Lett serch your myndis ye of hie consideracion!
F9	Love fayne wolde I;
F46	Love is naturall to every wyght,
H92	Lusti yough shuld us ensue,
F25	Madam, defrayne!
H67	Madame d'amours,
F39b	Margaret meke
F20	Most clere of colour and rote of stedfastness,
F36b	My feerfull dreme nevyr forgete can I:
R11	My herte ys yn grete mournyng,
H102	My lady hath me in that grace
H25	My love sche morneth
H50	My soverayne lorde for my poure sake
H106	My thought oppressed, my mynd in trouble,
F5	My wofull hart in paynfull weryness,
R2	My wofull hert of all gladnesse baryeyne
R8	Now helpe, Fortune, of thy godenesse,
H109	Now yn this medow fayer and grene
F10	Nowe the lawe is led be clere conciens
R6	O blessed lord, how may this be
F44	O blessed Lord of hevin celestiall,
F7	O my desyre, what eylyth the,
H15	O my hart and O my hart!
F26	O rote of trouth, o princess to my pay,
R12	Passetyme with good cumpanye
H97	Pray we to God that all may gyde
H105b	Quid petis, o fily?
F43	Rutterkyn is com unto oure towne
F32	Sith it concludid was in the Trinite
F46b	Smale pathis to the grenewode,
F4	So fer I trow from remedy,
R13	So put yn fere I dare not speke;
H35	Sore this dere strykyn ys,
F47	Soverayn lorde, in erthe most excellent,

4

F24	Sumwhat musyng
H107	Sumwhat musyng
F39	That goodly las,
F23	That was my joy is now my woo and payne;
F11	That was my woo is nowe my most gladness;
R16	The burne ys this worlde blynde
F1	The farther I go, the more behynde;
R5	The hye desire that Y have for to se
H41	The knyght knockett at the castell gate;
H105	The moder full manerly and mekly as a mayd,
H24	The thowghtes within my brest,
H23	The tyme of youthe is to be spent;
F45b	This day day dawes,
F30	This endurs nyght
H31	This other day
H66	Though sum saith that yough rulyth me,
R7	Thow man, envired with temptacion,
H51	Thow that men do call it dotage,
F19	Thus musyng in my mynd, gretly mervelyng
F36	To Calvery he bare his cross with doulfull payne,
F13	To complayne me, alas, why shulde I so?
H39	Trolly lolly loly lo,
R18	Up Y arose in verno tempore
F34	Uppon the cross nailid I was for the,
F3	What causyth me wofull thoughtis to thynk
H103b	What remedy, what remedy?
H104b	Wher be ye
H65	Wherfore shuld I hang up my bow
H47	Wherto shuld I expresse
H50b	Whilles lyve or breth is in my brest
H102b	Why shall not I?
F42	Who shall have my fayre lady?
H34	Whoso that wyll all feattes optayne,
H79	Whoso that wyll for grace sew,
H22	Whoso that wyll hymselff applye
H28	With sorowfull syghs and grevos payne
H64	Withowt dyscord
F33b	Woffully araid,
R1	Y have ben a foster long and meney day;
R20	Your light grevans shall not me constrayne
H41b	Yow and I and Amyas,
H104	Yower company
F18	Yowre counturfetyng

INDEX OF FIRST LINES
(ORIGINAL ORDER)

R1	Y have ben a foster long and meney day;
R2	My wofull hert of all gladnesse baryeyne
R3	'Be pes, ye make me spille my ale!'
R4	Absens of you causeth me to sygh and complayne
R5	The hye desire that Y have for to se
R6	O blessed lord, how may this be
R7	Thow man, envired with temptacion,
R8	Now helpe, Fortune, of thy godenesse,
R9	Fayre and discrete, fresche wommanly figure,
R10	Alone, alone,
R11	My herte ys yn grete mournyng,
R12	Passetyme with good cumpanye
R13	So put yn fere I dare not speke;
R14	Alone, alone,
R15	In wyldernes
R16b	Come over the burne, Besse,
R16	The burne ys this worlde blynde
R18	Up Y arose in verno tempore
R19	Hay how the mavys on a brere!
R20b	How shall Y plece a creature uncerteyne?
R20	Your light grevans shall not me constrayne
F1	The farther I go, the more behynde;
F2	A, a, my herte, I knowe yow well;
F3	What causyth me wofull thoughtis to thynk
F4	So fer I trow from remedy,
F5	My wofull hart in paynfull weryness,
F6	Demyd wrongfully
F7	O my desyre, what eylyth the,
F8	Lett serch your myndis ye of hie consideracion!
F9	Love fayne wolde I;
F10	Nowe the lawe is led be clere conciens
F11	That was my woo is nowe my most gladness;
F12	Benedicite! What dremyd I this nyght?
F13	To complayne me, alas, why shulde I so?
F14	Alas, it is I that wote nott what to say,
F15	I am he that hath you dayly servyd,
F16	[I pray daily ther paynys to asswage]
F17	But why am I so abusyd?
F18	Yowre counturfetyng
F19	Thus musyng in my mind, gretly mervelyng
F20	Most clere of colour and rote of stedfastness,
F21	I love, loved, and loved wolde I be
F22	Alas, for lak of her presens,
F23	That was my joy is now my woo and payne;
F24	Sumwhat musyng
F25	Madam, defrayne!
F26	O rote of trouth, o princess to my pay
F27b	'I love, I love, and whom love ye?'
F27	'I love a flour of swete odour'
F28	Complayne I may wherevyr I go,
F29b	Alone, alone, alone, alone,
F29	As I me walkyd this endurs day
F30b	'A, my dere, a, my dere Son,'
F30	This endurs nyght

9

F31b	Jhesu, mercy, how may this be,
F31	Christ, that was of infynyt myght,
F32b	Affraid, alas, and whi so sodenli?
F32	Sith it concludid was in the Trinite
F33b	Woffully araid,
F33	Beholde me, I pray the, with all thi hole reson.
F34b	'A, gentill Jhesu!'
F34	Uppon the cross nailid I was for the,
F36b	My feerfull dreme nevyr forgete can I:
F36	To Calvery he bare his cross with doulfull payne,
F37	A blessid Jhesu, hough fortunyd this?
F38b	A, myn hert, remembir the well,
F38	A myn hart, remembir the well
F39b	Margaret meke
F39	That goodly las,
F40b	Jhoone is sike and ill at ease;
F40	Hit is so praty in every degre;
F41	Ay, besherewe yow! Be my fay
F42	Who shall have my fayre lady?
F43b	Hoyda, hoyda, joly rutterkin!
F43	Rutterkyn is com unto oure towne
F44b	From stormy wyndis and grevous wethir,
F44	O blessed Lord of hevin celestiall,
F45b	This day day dawes,
F45	In a glorius garden grene
F46b	Smale pathis to the grenewode,
F46	Love is naturall to every wyght,
F47b	Enforce yourselfe as Goddis knyght
F47	Soverayn lorde, in erthe most excellent,
F48b	Be hit knowyn to all that byn here
F48	A, man, I have yevyn and made a graunt
F49b	In a slumbir late as I was,
F49	'Beholde', he saide, 'my creature,
H12	Alas, what shall I do for love?
H14	Alone I leffe, alone,
H15	O my hart and O my hart!
H16	Adew, adew, my hartis lust!
H17	Aboffe all thynge!
H18	Downbery down!
H20	In May, that lusty sesoun
H22	Whoso that wyll hymselff applye
H23	The tyme of youthe is to be spent;
H24	The thowghtes within my brest,
H25	My love sche morneth
H27	A the syghes that cum from my hart
H28	With sorowfull syghs and grevos payne
H29	Iff I had wytt for to endyght
H30	Alac, alac, what shall I do,
H31b	Hey nony nony nony nony no,
H31	This other day
H33b	Grene growith the holy,
H33	As the holy grouth grene
H34	Whoso that wyll all feattes optayne,
H35b	Blow thi horne, hunter, and blow thi horn on hye!

H35	Sore this dere strykyn ys,
H38	Adew, corage, adew;
H39	Trolly lolly loly lo,
H40	I love trewly withowt feynyng;
H41b	Yow and I and Amyas,
H41	The knyght knockett at the castell gate;
H44	If love now reynyd as it hath bene
H47	Wherto shuld I expresse
H49	A Robyn, gentyl Robyn,
H50b	Whilles lyve or breth is in my brest
H50	My soverayne lorde for my poure sake
H51	Thow that men do call it dotage,
H56	Departure is my chef payne;
H62	I have bene a foster
H63	Farewell, my joy, and my swete hart!
H64	Withowt dyscord
H65b	I am a joly foster
H65	Wherfore shuld I hang up my bow
H66	Though sum saith that yough rulyth me,
H67	Madame d'amours,
H68	Adew, adew, le company,
H74	Deme the best of every dowt
H75	Hey troly loly loly!
H79	Whoso that wyll for grace sew,
H82	Let not us that yong men be
H92	Lusti yough shuld us ensue,
H96b	Englond, be glad! Pluk up thy lusty hart!
H96	Ageynst the Frenchmen in the feld to fyght
H97	Pray we to God that all may gyde
H101	And I war a maydyn,
H102b	Why shall not I?
H102	My lady hath me in that grace
H103b	What remedy, what remedy?
H103	A thorne hath percyd my hart ryght sore
H104b	Wher be ye
H104	Yower company
H105b	Quid petis, o fily?
H105	The moder full manerly and mekly as a mayd,
H106	My thought oppressed, my mynd in trouble,
H107	Sumwhat musyng
H108	I love unloved; suche is myn aventure,
H109b	Hey troly loly lo!
H109	Now yn this medow fayer and grene

CONCORDANCE OF
ENGLISH GRAPHIC FORMS

A (136)

R1.1	1	Y have ben a foster long and meney day;
R1.2	3	I shall bygge me a boure atte the wodes ende,
R3.1	2	Now thyngke ye this ys a fayre ray?
R3.1	4	Leff werke a twenty-a-devell away!
R3.1	8	Ye will not make to huge a waste.
R3.2	4	A, kan ye that? Nou, gode, go hens!
R9	6	Unly to yeure swete grace a thousande sithe
R10.2	2	A lover trewly,
R10.4	5	Takyn yn a snare
R11.3	1	Such a mastras I may calle
R14.1	3	With a dulfull chere here I make my mone,
R14.2	3	With a dulfull chere [here I make my mone,
R15.2	2	'Y was a mayde
R15.3	1	A wanton chyld
R15.5	2	Withoute a frynd
R15.5	6	A mayde agayn.
R15.6	3	"Go wach a byrde!
R18.1	2	And found a maydyn sub quadam arbore,
R19.1	1	Hay how the mavys on a brere!
R19.2	2	And stop a tyde;
R19.2	4	To a forest wyde
R20b	1	How shall Y plece a creature uncerteyne?
R20.1	4	How sholde Y [plece a creature uncerteyne?]
R20.2	4	How sholde Y plece a creature oncertayne?
R20.3	4	How sholde Y plece a creature oncerteyne?
R20.4	4	How sholde Y plece a creature oncertayne?
F1	6	Thoo I go lose, yet am I teyd with a lyne:
F2	1	A, a, my herte, I knowe yow well;
F8	6	A rose most riall with levis fressh of hew,
F9	5	A lady fre,
F9	8	So long a space.
F17	4	Yet moreovyr a gretter payne,
F18.1	6	Hath such a demyng
F18.1	7	To make a belevyng:
F19	7	Wherfore I hope to fynd a speciall remedy
F27b	2	'I love a floure of fressh beaute;'
F27.1	1	'I love a flour of swete odour'
F27.2	1	'Ther is a floure where so he be,
F27.4	1	'I chese a floure fresshist of face.'
F27.4b	2	'I love a floure of fressh beaute.'
F27.5	1	'The rose it is a ryall floure.'
F29.2	2	I sawe a maide fayre inow;
F29.2	3	A childe she hoppid; she song, she lough;
F30b	1	'A, my dere, a, my dere Son,
F30b	2	Seyd Mary, 'A, my dere;
F30b	4	With a lawghyng chere.'
F30.1	2	I sawe a syght
F30.1	16	My Sone, a Kyng
F30.2	11	Many a wownd
F30.2	18	Uppon a tre.'
F31.3	1	A Jhesu, whi suffyrd thou such entretyng,
F31.3	3	Drawne like a theffe, and for payne swetyng
F33.2	9	Was like a lombe offerd in sacrifice:

15

A (cont.)

F33.3	1	Off sharpe thorne I have worne a crowne on my hede,
F34b	1	'A, gentill Jhesu!'
F34b	3	'I, a synner that offt doth fall.'
F34b	10	'A, I will, I will, gentyll Jhesu'.
F36b	2	Methought a maydynys childe causless shulde dye.
F36.1	3	A crowne of thorne as nedill sharpe shyfft in his brayne
F36.3	8	As a woman terrestriall
F37.1	1	A blessid Jhesu, hough fortunyd this?
F37.1	3	Nature of aquayntance ys turned to a gest,
F37.1	4	So shortly am I bydyn to a grevus fest,
F38b	1	A, myn hert, remembir the well,
F38.1	1	A myn hart, remembir the well
F38.1	3	Thou thynkyst on hym nevir a dele
F40.1	2	Good Lord, who may a goodlyer be
F40.3	4	I-wis, she will not gyve me a bone:
F40.4	2	Be lost so sone? I am a fole:
F41.2	1	'Be Gad, ye be a prety pode,
F41.2	5	Go watch a bole, your bak is brode.
F43b	2	Like a rutterkin, hoyda!
F43.1	2	In a cloke withoute cote or gowne,
F43.1	3	Save a raggid hode to kover his crowne,
F43.1	4	Like a rutter:
F43.2	4	Like a rutter:
F43.3	2	A stoupe of bere up at a pluk,
F43.3	3	Till his brayne be as wise as a duk;
F43.3	4	Like a rutter:
F43.4	2	He will piss a galon-pot full at twise
F43.4	4	Like a rutter:
F45.1	1	In a glorius garden grene
F45.1	2	Sawe I syttyng a comly quene
F45.1	4	She gaderd a floure and set betwene;
F48.1	1	A, man, I have yevyn and made a graunt
F48.1	6	But a lovyng and a contrite hart,
F49b	1	In a slumbir late as I was,
F49b	2	I harde a voice lowde call and crye
H17	5	A bud is spryngynge
H25.7	5	Halff in a swone,
H27.1	1	A the syghes that cum from my hart
H31.1	2	I hard a may
H31.2	6	Forsake me for a new.
H31.3	2	Hath chosen a new
H31.4	2	In no maner a way
H31.6	3	To be a lady's pere!'
H35b	2	Ther ys a do in yonder wode; in faith, she woll not dy
H35.2	1	As I stod under a bank
H35.3	3	And yf ye lust to have a shott,
H41.3	1	The portres was a lady bryght;
H41.6	1	He was cownselled to breffe a byll
H49.1	1	A Robyn, gentyl Robyn,
H50.2	2	As the chefteyne of a waryowere,
H50.3	2	Above all other as a kyng,

A (cont.)

H50.3	4	But of a trewth he worthyest
H50.5	5	A vengeance on them that loveth nott best
H62.1	1	I have bene a foster
H62.1	2	Long and many a day;
H62.1	5	Yet have I bene a foster.
H62.2	5	Yet have I [bene a foster.]
H62.3	5	Yet have [I bene a foster.]
H62.4	5	Yet have I bene [a foster.]
H62.5	5	Yet have [I bene a foster.]
H62.6	5	Yet have [I bene a foster.]
H63.1	3	Frome yow a whyle must I depart;
H65b	1	I am a joly foster
H65b	2	And have ben many a day,
H65.1	3	I cane bend and draw a bow
H65.1	5	I am a joly foster.
H65.2	5	I am [a joly foster.]
H65.3	3	I can blow the deth of a dere
H65.3	5	I am [a joly foster.]
H65.4	3	I can luge and make a sute
H65.4	5	I am [a joly foster.]
H66.2	4	Therin a wager lay dar I:
H79.2	3	But love us a thyng gevyn by God;
H101.1	1	And I war a maydyn,
H101.2	1	When I was a wanton wench
H103.1	1	A thorne hath percyd my hart ryght sore
H105.1	1	The moder full manerly and mekly as a mayd,
H106.3	5	A payne it is, hens to depart,

ABAK (1)

H62.5	3	Thay stand abak and make it strange;

ABATTYTH (1)

H34.4	2	Dysdayne abattyth and makith hym colde.

ABLE (1)

F38.2	3	I will axe grace while I am able,

ABOFFE (1)

H17	1	Aboffe all thynge

ABOVE (5)

F5	6	That I am bownde above all erthly thyng
F38.2	2	To God above I call and crye;
H25.4	4	The Gode above
H50.3	2	Above all other as a kyng,
H104.4	4	And God above

ABOWTE (2)

F30.1	8	Full fast abowte
F43.2	3	Besmerde with grece abowte his disshe,

ABSENCE (3)

H25.2	3	Of absence nedes must be,

ABSENCE (cont.)
H27.2   3 And now absence to be in place
H104.2   2 With your absence

ABSENS (2)
R4   1 Absens of you causeth me to sygh and complayne
F22   4 Absens it is that wolde me wrong;

ABSENT (1)
F6.1   2 In absent,

ABUSYD (2)
F14   2 For why I stond as he that is abusyd;
F17   1 But why am I so abusyd?

ABYDE (2)
R3.1   6 Abyde awhile! What have ye haste?
R19.2   1 I bade her abyde

ABYDYNG (1)
R13.1   7 Abydyng your grace yn hope of mercy.

ACHEFFE (1)
H97   4 He may acheffe this gret viage:

ACORDE (1)
H64.1   2 And bothe acorde

ACTYVENESSE (1)
H23.4   2 Wherby actyvenesse oon may utter.

ADEW (23)
R18.2   1 Adew, plesers _antiquo_ _tempore_!
H16   1 Adew, adew, my hartis lust!
H16   2 Adew, my joy and my solace!
H17   4 Adew mornyng,
H31.4   6 Myne owne swet hart, adew.
H31.5   1 Adew, derlyng,
H31.5   2 Adew, swettyng,
H31.5   3 Adew, all my welfare!
H31.5   4 Adew, all thyng
H31.6   1 Adew, full swete,
H31.6   2 Adew, ryght mete
H31.6   6 She said, 'Adew my dere!'
H31.7   1 Adew, farewell,
H31.7   2 Adew la bell,
H31.7   3 Adew, bothe frend and foo!
H33.4   1 Adew, myne owne lady,
H33.4   2 Adew, my specyall,
H38   1 Adew, corage, adew;
H38   4 Adew, corage, adew, adew.
H109.4   4 Adew, farewell and kysse me now!

ADOWNE (1)
  F34.3   4   He put his handes depe in my syde adowne.

ADRADDE (1)
  F32.2   4   Thi son was doughti, the fende was adradde;

ADULACION (1)
  F10   7   Men may fynd day ne nyght adulacion

ADVENTURE (2)
  H103.2   1   Bewayll I may myn adventure
  H108   7   And love unloved; such ys myne adventure.

ADVERSITE (1)
  R8   2   And onse withdrawe thy adversite

ADVERSYTE (1)
  F16   4   Withoute disease or adversyte.

AFECCION (1)
  F34.5   2   Thy deth remembryng of humble afeccion,

AFFORMYTH (1)
  H51.5   2   But mynd afformyth with full consent.

AFFRAID (1)
  F32b   1   Affraid, alas, and whi so sodenli?

AFFRAIDE (4)
  F32.1   8   Affraide.
  F32.2   9   Affraide.]
  F32.3   9   [Affraide.]
  F34.4   8   Be thou not affraide sith I am merciable.

AFFTER (1)
  F46.2   2   Affter my reason and jugement,

AFORE (3)
  F19   6   As I of aquayntance had never byn afore;
  F34.4   6   Afore thi hart hang this litell table,
  H35.4   2   But he ran fast afore;

AFRAY (1)
  R3.1   7   Y trow for all youre gret afray

AFRAYDE (1)
  R15.2   5   Y was afrayde

AFTER (3)
  R3.2   1   After asay then may ye wette;
  R7   5   And say after me, and be noght unkynde:
  H39   4   Now after wyll I go;

AGANE (1)
H56   2 I trust ryght wel of retorn agane.

AGAST (1)
F36.4 11 And of my dreme was sore agast.

AGAYN (2)
R10.5 7 Not lovyd agayn,
R15.5 6 A mayde agayn.

AGAYNE (11)
R20.3 3 But light credens turnyth your love agayne:
F5   5 Is nowe be hym so comfortide agayne
F32.1 5 Oure sowlis comfort cam agayne;
F34.4 1 Thynk agayne, pride, on my humilite;
F48b   8 And for I wolde have thyne heritage agayne,
F48.2 1 If any man will say here agayne
H28   3 Alas, pour hart, tyl that we mete agayne,
H47.1 4 Tyl that we mete agayne.
H47.5 4 Tyll that we mete agayne.
H105.3 4 Now, gracious God and goode swete babe, yet ons
              this game agayne
H109.2 3 Syth I love you, love me agayne;

AGE (6)
H62.5 4 Lo, age ys cause of this;
H66.1 2 I trust in age to tarry;
H82.1 3 Thow that age with gret dysdayne
H101.2 2 Of twelve yere of age,
H101.3 2 The age of fifteen yere,
H109.2 1 Ye be so nyce and so mete of age

AGED (1)
H66.2 1 I pray you all that aged be,

AGENSTE (1)
R3.3   3 Ye herte my legge agenste the walle;

AGEYNST (1)
H96.1 1 Ageynst the Frenchmen in the feld to fyght

AGRE (4)
F27b   5 Yff we three can agre in on.'
F27.4b 5 Yff we three can agre in oon.'
H47.3 3 It may in no wyse agre
H51.4 1 Wyth ee and mynd doth both agre;

AGREDE (1)
F27.6b 5 That we three be agrede in oon.'

ALAC (3)
H30   1 Alac, alac, what shall I do,
H49.2 2 Alac, why is she so?

ALAK (5)
```
F40b       3   Alak, good Jhoane, what may you please?
F40.1      5   Alak, good Jhoone, [what may you please?
F40.2      5   Alak, good [Jhoone, what may you please?
F40.3      5   Alak, good Jhoan, [what may you please?
F40.4      5   Alak, good Jhoan, [what may you please?
```

ALAS (35)
```
R10.1      4   Alas, why so?
R10.3      5   Alas, with thought
R11.1      3   Alas, alas, what remedy?
R11.2      3   Alas, alas, what remedy?
R11.3      3   Alas, alas, [what remedy?
R11.4      3   Alas, alas, what remedy?
R15.2      1   'Alas,' she seyd,
R15.8      1   Alas, that he
F13        1   To complayne me, alas, why shulde I so?
F14        1   Alas, it is I that wote nott what to say,
F22        1   Alas, for lak of her presens,
F29b       2   Here I sytt alone, alas, alone!
F32b       1   Affraid, alas, and whi so sodenli?
F36.1      7   Alas, all for my gilt,
F37.4      4   Alas, to dye thou makyst me sure; yet then, good
                   Lord, do thou thi cure
F38.1      5   Alas, for sorow myne hart doth blede
F39.1      3   Alas, alas,
F40.4      1   Alas, good Jhoan, shall all my mone
H12        1   Alas, what shall I do for love?
H16        4   Untyl I dye, alas, alas!
H25.1      4   Alas, pour hart,
H25.5      1   Alas, thought I,
H27.2      4   Alas, for wo I dye, I dye.
H28        3   Alas, pour hart, tyl that we mete agayne,
H31.2      1   Sshe said, alas,
H41b       3   To the grenewode must we go, alas!
H102.2     3   Alas, alas, what word ys this?
H106.2     7   Endure, alas, withowt hope of recure.
```

ALASSE (2)
```
H12        2   For love, alasse, what shall I do,
H12        6   Alasse!
```

ALE (6)
```
R3.1       1   'Be pes, ye make me spille my ale!'
F41.1      7   With manerly Margery, milk and ale.
F41.2      7   With manerly [Margery, milk and ale.]
F41.3      7   With manerly Margery, [milke and ale.]
F41.4      7   With manerly Margery, milke and ale;
F41.4      9   With manerly Margery, [milke and ale.]
```

ALEGEAUNCE (1)
```
F11        4   That was my grefe is now my alegeaunce.
```

ALIAUNCE (1)
F44.1   5   Which of aliaunce

ALL (107)
R1.2   1   All the whiles that Y may my bowe bende
R2.1   1   My wofull hert of all gladnesse baryeyne
R2.1   7   For yet Y am all drowned in the lake
R2.2   1   For sche weche ys of all godely the best
R3.1   7   Y trow for all youre gret afray
R3.3   5   Take to gev all, and be stille than!
R4   5   All for youre sake, til God me so avaunce
R6   4   Ever to plese hym with all myghth,
R8   4   Of sorwe and all hevenesse.
R10.1   3   And all for one;
R10.4   1   All lovers beware,
R11.3   2   Dame Petyles yn every place over all;
R12.1   8   All godely sport
R12.2   4   All thoftes and fantyses to dygest.
R12.2   7   Of vices all;
R12.2   10 Ys best of all?
R13.3   6   And all othyr for hyr sake to eschew,
R15.7   3   And all for oone;
F2   4   Thoo that all this yet in vayne be,
F4   2   And from all hope so fer banysshid
F5   6   That I am bownde above all erthly thyng
F7.2   3   Sum tyme is lost and all in vayne
F7.2   6   And all be folissh fantasy
F8   7   All myrthis to maynten, all sorous to subdewe.
F20   6   Which that all men knowith, both more and less;
F24.4   7   All contrary
F25.3   8   All other to esshewe.
F26   3   In whom all vertu is knytt withouten varyaunce,
F27.2   4   He pass them all in his degre;
F27.5   4   All on they be;
F29.1   3   And all hevyness to put away,
F29.5   3   For thou art he that hath all wrought,
F30.1   3   All in my slepe:
F30.1   17 That made all thyng
F31.4   2   Gladly suffyrd I all this.'
F32.3   4   All was on red blod withoute any shirt;
F32.4   2   Lay downe all thi wepyng, let no more be sene!
F33.1   1   Beholde me, I pray the, with all thi hole reson,
F33.2   6   Thus wrappid all in woo,
F34.4   4   My blode all spent by distillacion.
F34.5   1   Lord, on all synfull here knelyng on kne,
F34.5   6   May washe us all from surfettes reprovable.
F36.1   7   Alas, all for my gilt,
F36.2   3   Beholdyng ther his lymmys all to-rent and tore,
F36.3   1   Saynt Jhon than said, 'Feere not, Mary; his
                 paynys all
F36.4   3   His vaynys all and synowis to-raff and brast;
F37.2   3   My tast disordyrd all reson far passyng,
F37.4   5   With all good sowlis to cause me lyve in rest.
F38.2   6   Fo all my lyff-daies I have myspend:

22

F40.4	1	Alas, good Jhoan, shall all my mone
F41.4	4	Yet for his love that all hath wrought
F43.2	2	His tong rennyth all on buttyrd fyssh,
F43.3	1	Rutterkyn shall bryng you all good luk;
F44.3	1	Now, good Lady among thi sayntes all,
F44.3	4	Be thi servaunt with all his hart so fre.
F47.1	6	Enforcyng yourselfe with all your myght
F47.2	3	All mysdone thynges to redress,
F47.2	6	In your person all ther hope is pyght
F48b	1	Be hit knowyn to all that byn here
F48b	2	And to all that here-afftir
F48b	9	Therefore I suffird all this payne.
F48.1	5	Not covetyng more for all my smert
F48.2	4	Yet wold Y eft be all to-torne.]
F48.3	2	Witness, stonys that all to-brake,
H17	1	Aboffe all thynge
H25.6	4	Yet for all that
H25.10	3	From all other that be,
H25.11	3	All lovers that trew be,
H25.11	5	From jebardyse all
H29.5	1	Lernyng it war for women all
H31.5	3	Adew, all my welfare!
H31.5	4	Adew, all thyng
H31.5	6	Cryst kepe yow frome all care.
H33.2	2	With ive all alone
H33.3	3	Frome all other only
H34.1	1	Whoso that wyll all feattes optayne,
H34.2	1	For love enforcyth all nobyle kynd,
H34.2	2	And dysdayne dyscorages all gentyl mynd.
H44.2	2	All ways wherby thay myght it rech;
H50.1	5	And of all other for to love best
H50.3	2	Above all other as a kyng,
H50.3	5	To have the prayse of all the best;
H50.6	1	The soverayne lorde that is of all,
H50.6	5	Off all gode fortunes to send hym best;
H51.7	1	Love maynteynyth all noble courage;
H51.7	2	Who love dysdaynyth ys all of the village.
H63.2	2	And leve me all alone,
H66.2	1	I pray you all that aged be,
H66.4	3	That all amend; and here an end,
H67.1	2	All tymes or ours
H67.1	5	In all socours
H92.1	2	Hys mery hart shall sure all rew;
H92.2	2	And all mery company for to dysdayne;
H92.2	4	But follow hys mynd in all that we may.
H92.3	2	But all dysdaynares for to refuse?
H92.4	4	All only reches to purchase.
H96.1	4	Bowys and arows to put them all to flyght:
H97	1	Pray we to God that all may gyde
H97	5	Now let us syng this rownd all thre;
H101.1	3	For all the golde in England
H101.3	3	In all this lond, nowther fre nor bond,
H104.1	3	From care and from all mone;

ALL (cont.)
H106.3   4   Of all the sorowes within my hart;
H106.4   2   My chance contrarious from all plesure,
H106.4   3   From all plesure to gret penance;
H107.4   7   All contrary

ALLMOST (1)
R10.6   7   Allmost owt of mynde;

ALLSO (1)
R15.4   5   With sorow allso,

ALLWAY (10)
F13   6   And lett me not allway be guerdonless,
F17   3   And my service allway refusyd,
F39b   8   She delis allway.
F39.1   12   She delis allway.]
F39.2   12   She delis allway.]
F39.3   12   She delis allway.]
F41.1   2   This wanton clarkis be nyse allway.
H29.3   3   But allway trew I do her fynd;
H29.4   3   For she to me ys allway kynd;
H31.1   4   She sayd allway

ALONE (39)
R10.1   1   Alone, alone,
R10.1   2   Mornyng alone,
R10.1   6   For on alone
R10.6   8   Alone ys no cumfort.
R14.1   1   Alone, alone,
R14.1   2   Here Y am mysylf alone;
R14.1   4   Pyteusly, my own sylf alone.
R14.2   4   Pyteusly, my own sylf alone.]
R15.1   3   Secret, alone,
R15.3   3   To me alone,
R15.8   3   Mysylf alone,
R19.3   2   And Y alone,
F6.4   2   Of one alone
F29b   1   Alone, alone, alone, alone,
F29b   2   Here I sytt alone, alas, alone!
F29.1   4   Myself alone;
F29.2   4   That childe wepid alone.
F29.3   4   But be still alone.'
F29.4   4   Therfor I cum hyther alone.'
F29.5   4   And I, thy modir, alone.'
F37.4   2   Nature hath forsakyn me, and lefft me thus alone.
F40.3   3   Yff she and I were together alone,
H14   1   Alone I leffe, alone,
H31.9   6   In wyldernes alone.
H33.2   2   With ive all alone
H63.2   2   And leve me all alone,
H64.1   4   Bothe hartes alone
H104b   6   Yt is but you, my love, alone.
H104.1   6   But you, my love, alone.

24

ALONE (cont.)

H104.2	6	But you, my love, alone.
H104.3	6	But yow, my love, alone.
H104.4	6	For you have myne alone.

ALSO (5)

R11.1	2	My mynd also gretly waylyng;
F12	4	The see also drownyd both towre and towne.
F31.2	2	That made both paynys and joy also,
F47.1	4	Of marshiall power and also hye dygnite,
H34.5	2	To woman also, I thynk, the same.

AM (50)

R2.1	7	For yet Y am all drowned in the lake
R6	2	That Y am thus in heviness?
R10.4	2	For Y am bare
R10.6	5	I am put behynd,
R14.1	2	Here Y am mysylf alone;
R20.3	2	Y am right glad, tristyng hit woll remanyne;
F1	6	Thoo I go lose, yet am I teyd with a lyne:
F5	6	That I am bownde above all erthly thyng
F6.2	3	Assuryd am I;
F11	6	Wherfor I am and shal be tyll I dye
F15	1	I am he that hath you dayly servyd,
F17	1	But why am I so abusyd?
F17	7	When that they knowe I am sory.
F24.4	2	Bounden am I
F25.3	5	I am content
F33.2	1	Thus nakyd am I nailid, O man, for thy sake;
F34.1	6	Be not dispayryd, for I am not vengeable;
F34.1	8	Whi art thou froward, syth I am mercyable?
F34.2	8	Why art thou froward sith I am merciable?
F34.3	6	Syth I am kynd, why are thou unstable?
F34.3	8	Be thou not froward syth I am merciable.
F34.4	8	Be thou not affraide sith I am merciable.
F36.3	4	'O frend,' she said, 'I am sure he is inmortall.'
F37.1	4	So shortly am I bydyn to a grevus fest,
F37.1	5	Whereas I am ybid with bodily rest;
F37.1	6	Thus trobled am I yet I trust it shalbe for the best
F37.2	6	Thus trobled am I [yet I trust it shalbe for the best
F37.3	6	Thus trobled am I [yet I trust it shalbe for the best
F37.4	6	Thus trobled am I [yet I trust it shalbe for the best
F38.2	3	I will axe grace while I am able,
F39.3	4	Woffull am I.
F40b	2	I am full sory for Jhoon's disease.
F40.4	2	Be lost so sone? I am a fole:
F41.2	4	I am no hakney for your rode;
F48.1	4	As long as I am Lord and Kyng,
F48.1	10	That am the cheffe lorde of the fee.
F48.2	6	In the awter I am offerd my Fader beforne;

AM (cont.)
```
H18       2   Now am I exild my lady fro
H33.1     3   So I am, ever hath bene,
H40       3   To love her sure whill I am levyng,
H51.6     1   Thus am I fyxed withowt gruge,
H65b      1   I am a joly foster
H65.1     5   I am a joly foster.
H65.2     5   I am [a joly foster.]
H65.3     5   I am [a joly foster.]
H65.4     5   I am [a joly foster.]
H103.1    3   Thus withowt comfort I am forlore;
H104b     4   I am so sad;
H106.2    4   Begyled am I, and cannot refrayne;
H107.4    2   Bowndon am I
```

AMEN (1)
```
H64.2    12   God yt amen.
```

AMEND (6)
```
F30.2     2   Amend your chere,
F38.1     7   I crye God mercy, I will amend.
F38.2     5   Me to amend I will me hye
F38.2     7   I crye God mercy, I will amend.
H66.4     3   That all amend; and here an end,
H92.7     3   And that we may ower fauttes amend,
```

AMENDE (2)
```
R2.2      7   For till she amende Y shall have noght truly
F49b      3   'Amende the, man, of thi trespace,
```

AMONG (5)
```
R19.1     5   The greves among.
F44.3     1   Now, good Lady among thi sayntes all,
F45.1     3   Among the flouris that fressh byn.
H20       9   Among the thornys kene.
H66.3     1   Pastymes of yough sumtyme among,
```

AMORUS (1)
```
H101.2    3   Thes cowrtyers with ther amorus
```

AMYAS (3)
```
H41b      1   Yow and I and Amyas,
H41b      2   Amyas and yow and I,
H41b      4   Yow and I, my lyff, and Amyas.
```

AMYSSE (1)
```
H101.1    4   I wold not do amysse.
```

AN (12)
```
R20.4     1   An olde seyde saw: hasty men sone slayne;
F24.5     2   To an entent;
F31.3     4   Both water and blode, ye, crucified an hevy case?
F40.1     4   But it were an angell of the Trinite?
F40.2     4   Myght wel be calde an conjuracion.
```

AN (cont.)

F41.2	2	And I love you an hole cart-lode.'
H25.11	1	Thus here an ende;
H27.2	2	Was wont to cast an nye;
H35.7	1	Here I leve and mak an end,
H66.4	3	That all amend; and here an end,
H92.7	4	An blysse opteyne at ower last end. Amen.
H107.5	2	To an entent;

AND (347)

R1.1	1	Y have ben a foster long and meney day;
R2.1	8	Of sorfull joye and paynefull plesaunce.
R2.2	2	To myn entent, and so sayeth mo then I,
R2.2	5	Now Y pray God and that righth hertily
R2.2	8	But sorfull joy and paynefull plesaunce.
R3.3	5	Take to gev all, and be stille than!
R4	1	Absens of you causeth me to sygh and complayne
R4	3	And thogh Y wolde, Y koude me noght refrayne
R5	2	The godely and wommanly bewte
R5	6	And only to be putte to yeure rememoraunce.
R6	3	And yet Y have do my besynesse
R6	5	Both erly, late, by day and by nyghth.
R7	4	This lyon and lambe was, causyng pyte;
R7	5	And say after me, and be noght unkynde:
R8	2	And onse withdrawe thy adversite
R8	4	Of sorwe and all hevenesse.
R9	1	Fayre and discrete, fresche wommanly figure,
R9	2	That with yeure beute and fresche plesaunce pure
R9	5	My lyves ladi and my hertis cure,
R9	9	Thorffe with yeur beute that Y most love and prise.
R10.1	3	And all for one;
R10.2	3	And now, fy, fy,
R10.3	2	And love dere bought
R11.4	2	Iff my sorow and woe she knew:
R12.1	2	I love and shall unto I dye;
R12.1	6	Hunte, syng and daunce;
R12.2	4	All thoftes and fantyses to dygest.
R12.3	2	Ys vertu, and vyce to flee;
R13.1	6	And so shall contynew tyll I dye,
R13.2	5	And no help but Fortunys whele,
R13.2	6	And only she which my wound begunne;
R13.3	2	And geve me salfe unto my sore?
R13.3	5	Myn hert and love; what wyll she more?
R13.3	6	And all othyr for hyr sake to eschew,
R13.3	7	And never to chaunge hyr for no new.
R15.2	4	And at-a-brayde
R15.3	4	And me begylyd,
R15.3	6	And now ys gone.
R15.4	4	And let hym goo,
R15.4	6	And play the wyse.
R15.6	2	Yn sport and play,
R15.7	3	And all for oone;
R16.1	2	And Besse ys mankynde;
R16.1	4	She daunces and she lepys,

AND (cont.)

R16.1	5	And Crist stondes and clepys;
R18.1	2	And found a maydyn sub quadam arbore,
R18.3	4	And me sore chast coram omnibus.
R19.1	2	She satt and sang with notes clere;
R19.1	8	And seyd, 'No nere!
R19.2	2	And stop a tyde;
R19.2	7	And flo her way;
R19.3	2	And Y alone,
R20.2	3	With hert Y wyll you plece and your love attayne:
R20.3	1	When Y fynde you stedfast and certayne,
R20.4	2	Love me lytell and longe; hot love doth not reyne;
F3	6	And yet mythynkyth hit grevith me moche more
F4	2	And from all hope so fer banysshid
F5	4	Saffe helpe and grace of my lord and soverayne,
F5	7	To love and dred hym as my lord and kyng.
F6.1	3	And wote not why
F7.2	3	Sum tyme is lost and all in vayne
F7.2	6	And all be folissh fantasy
F11	6	Wherfor I am and shal be tyll I dye
F11	7	Your trewe servant with thought, hart and body.
F12	3	The son, the moone, had lost ther force and light;
F12	4	The see also drownyd both towre and towne:
F13	6	And lett me not allway be guerdonless,
F14	4	And no cause gevyn to be so refusyd;
F15	3	And mervell I have syth I not deservid
F16	3	And sone to sende where they faynest wolde be,
F17	2	Syth worde and dede is take in vayne,
F17	3	And my service allway refusyd,
F18.1	4	And wote ye why?
F18.2	7	And thynk the contrary:
F19	4	And so sodenly will chaunge in every degre;
F19	8	To lett itt over pass, and thynk theron no more.
F20	1	Most clere of colour and rote of stedfastness,
F20	4	Of her bounte, beaute and womanhode;
F20	5	The bryghtest myrrour and floure of goodlyhed,
F20	6	Which that all men knowith, both more and less;
F21	1	I love, loved, and loved wolde I be
F21	2	In stedfast fayth and trouth with assuraunce;
F22	2	Whom I serve and shall as long,
F22	5	And thus is the tyme of his song;
F23.1	1	That was my joy is now my woo and payne;
F23.1	7	That hath byn your fayre lady and mastress.
F23.2	4	And with pite have me in remembraunce
F23.2	7	Have but yourselfe, fayre lady and mastres.
F24.1	2	And more morenyng
F24.2	7	And no redress
F24.3	3	And no suraunce
F24.4	3	And that gretly
F26	2	Endewid with vertu and goodly plesaunce,
F26	4	With welth and wordly joy long to endure,
F27b	1	'I love, I love, and whom love ye?'
F27.2	2	And shall not yet be namyd for me;
F27.4b	1	'Now have I lovyd, and whom love ye?'

F27.5	3	'Both be full swete and of lyke savoure;
F27.6	1	'I love the rose, both red and white.'
F27.6	5	Oure prince to se, and rosys thre.'
F27.6b	1	'Nowe have we lovyd, and love will we
F28	3	To love her best and no mo
F28	4	And she me takyth in gret disdayne:
F29.1	3	And all hevynesse to put away,
F29.5	4	And I, thy modir, alone.'
F30.1	6	And sore did wepe.
F30.2	3	And now be styll;
F31.1	4	And wolde so take mortalite!
F31.2	2	That made both paynys and joy also,
F31.2	3	And suffyr wolde payne as sorowfull thought,
F31.3	3	Drawne like a theffe, and for payne swetyng
F31.3	4	Both water and blode, ye, crucified an hevy case?
F31.4	3	And why, good Lord? Express thi mynd!
F31.4	4	'The to purchace both joy and bliss.'
F32b	1	Affraid, alas, and whi so sodenli?
F32.4	4	Thi dere sone is past his trobill and his tene;
F33b	5	My body bloo and wan,
F33.1	2	And be not hard-hartid, and for this encheson
F33.1	4	Begylde and betraide by Judas' fals treson;
F33.2	5	Thus toggid to and fro,
F33.3	5	My fete and handis sore
F34b	9	And thynk on this lesson that now I teche the.
F34.2	2	Loke on them well, and have compassion;
F34.2	4	Percide hand and fote of indignacion,
F34.3	1	I hade on Petur and Mawdlen pyte
F36.1	2	And theruppon straynyd he was in every vayne;
F36.1	4	His modir dere tendirly wept and cowde not
		refrayne
F36.1	5	Myn hart can yerne and mylt
F36.1	8	Tho I wept and sore did complayne
F36.1	11	So ripe and endles was her payne.
F36.2	1	His grevous deth and her morenyng grevid me sore;
F36.2	3	Beholdyng ther his lymmys all to-rent and tore,
F36.2	4	That with dispaire for feer and dred I was nere
		forlore
F36.3	10	And yet verely I know in myn hart
F36.4	1	Unto the cross, handes and feete, nailid he was;
F36.4	3	His vaynys all and synowis to-raff and brast;
F36.4	8	Wepyng and wrang her handes fast.
F36.4	11	And of my dreme was sore agast.
F37.4	2	Nature hath forsakyn me, and lefft me thus alone.
F38b	2	And thynk on the paynys that byn in hell.
F38.2	2	To God above I call and crye;
F39.2	5	Both Cate and Bes,
F39.2	6	Mawde and Anes,
F39.3	7	And let us daunce
F40b	1	Jhoone is sike and ill at ease;
F40.1	3	In favoure and in facion (lo, will ye se?)
F40.3	3	Yff she and I were together alone,
F41.1	7	With manerly Margery, milk and ale.

F41.2	2	And I love you an hole cart-lode.'
F41.2	7	With manerly [Margery, milk and ale.]
F41.3	3	'What, and ye shal be my piggesnye?'
F41.3	7	With manerly Margery, [milke and ale.]
F41.4	7	With manerly Margery, milke and ale;
F41.4	9	With manerly Margery, [milke and ale.]
F43.4	3	And the overplus undir the table of the newe gyse;
F44b	1	From stormy wyndis and grevous wethir,
F44.1	4	In honor to rayne, Lord, graunt hym tyme and space,
F44.1	8	Of Ynglond and Fraunce
F44.2	8	Of Castell and Spayne,
F44.3	3	For this yong prince, which is and daily shal
F44.3	8	To the we crye and call,
F45b	4	And I must home gone.
F45.1	4	She gaderd a floure and set betwene;
F45.1	7	And ever she sang:
F45.2	4	And said, 'The white rose is most trewe
F45.2	7	And evyr she sang:
F46b	2	Will I love and shall I love,
F46b	3	Will I love and shall I love
F46.2	2	Affter my reason and jugement,
F46.2	3	Consideryng dyvers fayrer and fetter,
F46.2	4	Plesaunt, buxum, and ever obedient,
F46.3	5	And love her only whereever she gone:
F47.1	3	With gyfftes grete and evydent
F47.1	4	Of marshiall power and also hye dygnite,
F47.2	2	Wisdome with strenkyth and soveraynte
F47.2	4	And specially hurtis of thi commynalte,
F47.2	5	Which crye and call unto your Majeste.
F48b	2	And to all that here-afftir
F48b	3	To me shal be leffe and dere,
F48b	8	And for I wolde have thyne heritage agayne,
F48.1	1	A, man, I have yevyn and made a graunt
F48.1	2	To the, and thou wilt be repentant;
F48.1	4	As long as I am Lord and Kyng,
F48.1	6	But a lovyng and a contrite hart,
F48.1	7	And that thou be in charite;
F48.3	4	And othir wittness, many one;
F48.3	7	And, man, for the more sykyrnesse,
F49b	2	I harde a voice lowde call and crye
F49b	4	And aske forgeveness or evyr thou dye.'
H14	2	And sore I sygh for one.
H15	1	O my hart and O my hart!
H15	4	And know no cause wherefore.
H16	2	Adew, my joy and my solace!
H17	3	Both day and nyght,
H17	6	Of the red rose and the whyght.
H18	3	And no cause gevyn therto:
H18	7	And never more to remayne.
H22	4	Of lusty bloddys and chevalry.
H23.2	2	Whych one may use, and vice denye;
H23.3	1	And they be plesant to God and man,
H23.4	1	As featys of armys, and suche other

AND (cont.)

H25.2	6	And morne no more for me.
H25.3	3	But anguysch and pete,
H25.3	6	And morne no more for me.
H25.5	6	To helpe my love and me.
H25.7	3	And sett her on my knee:
H25.8	4	And her smalle waste
H25.8	6	And sayd sche morned for me.
H25.9	3	And prayd her to be ble,
H25.9	6	And morne no more for me.
H25.10	4	In well and wo
H25.11	4	And in especyall
H27.2	3	And now absence to be in place
H27.3	2	And take in armys twayne;
H27.3	3	And now with syghs manyfold,
H27.3	4	Farewell, my joe, and welcom payne.
H27.4	1	And I thynk I se her yet,
H28	1	With sorowfull syghs and grevos payne
H29.1	2	Of my lady, both fayre and fre,
H29.2	1	I love her well with hart and mynd;
H29.6	1	My hart she hath and ever shall
H30	3	And trew love lokked therto?
H31.3	3	And thynkes with her to rest,
H31.3	4	And will not rew,
H31.3	5	And I so trew,
H31.4	1	And now I may
H31.4	4	So ever and ay
H31.6	5	And yes replete
H31.7	3	Adew, bothe frend and foo!
H31.8	4	And saide, 'Goode mayde,
H31.9	3	In voydyng care and mone
H33.1	2	And never chaungyth hew,
H33.2	4	And grenewode levys be gone.
H33.4	4	Be suere, and ever shall.
H34.2	2	And dysdayne dyscorages all gentyl mynd.
H34.3	1	Wherfor to love and be not loved
H34.4	1	Love encoragith and makyth on bold;
H34.4	2	Dysdayne abattyth and makith hym colde.
H34.5	1	Love ys gevyn to God and man;
H34.6	1	But dysdayne ys vice and shuld be refused;
H34.7	2	With dysdayne bothe falce and subtell.
H35b	1	Blow thi horne, hunter, and blow thi horne on hye!
H35b	3	Now blow thi horne, hunter, and blow thi horne, joly hunter
H35.1	2	And yet she bledes no whytt;
H35.3	3	And yf ye lust to have a shott,
H35.4	1	He to go and I to go,
H35.4	3	I bad hym shott and strik the do,
H35.5	3	And arrow in her hanch she hent;
H35.7	1	Here I leve and mak an end,
H38	2	Hope and trust,
H41b	1	Yow and I and Amyas,
H41b	2	Amyas and yow and I,
H41b	4	Yow and I, my lyff, and Amyas.

H41.6	2	And shew my lady hys oune wyll.
H41.7	2	And Pyte said she wold be ther.
H41.8	2	We left them ther and went ower way.
H44.1	2	And war rewardit as it hath sene,
H44.3	2	And causith lovers owtwardly to refrayne,
H44.4	1	Which puttes them to more and more
H44.4	2	Inwardly most grevous and sore:
H44.7	1	And unto them which doth it know
H47.4	2	The violett wan and blo;
H47.4	4	I love you and no mo.
H47.5	1	I make you fast and sure;
H49.1	3	And thow shal know of myne.
H49.2	4	And yet she will say no.
H50.1	5	And of all other for to love best
H50.2	3	With spere and swerd at the barryoure
H50.4	4	Next God but he and ever prest
H50.4	5	With hart and body to love best
H50.5	3	Beholde his favor and his face,
H50.6	3	He hath my hart and ever shall.
H51.2	1	And whosoever may love gete,
H51.3	2	And she to hym most seme most fayre.
H51.4	1	Wyth ee and mynd doth both agre;
H51.5	1	The ee doth loke and represent;
H62.1	2	Long and many a day;
H62.5	3	Thay stand abak and make it strange;
H62.6	2	For and my santes booke,
H62.6	3	And pray I wyll for them that may,
H63.1	1	Farewell, my joy, and my swete hart!
H63.2	2	And leve me all alone,
H64.1	2	And bothe acorde
H64.1	12	And love to optayne.
H65b	2	And have ben many a day,
H65b	3	And foster will I be styll
H65.1	3	I cane bend and draw a bow
H65.1	4	And shot well enough:
H65.2	4	And kyll bothe hart and hynd:
H65.4	3	I can luge and make a sute
H66.1	3	God and my ryght and my dewtye,
H66.4	2	Pray we to God and Seynt Mary
H66.4	3	That all amend; and here an end,
H67.2	1	And make you sure
H67.2	8	Loyall and playne.
H75	2	My love is lusty, plesant and demure
H75	9	And thus I wyll endure;
H79.1	3	And love her in hart and dede,
H79.2	5	But perfite in dede and betwene two.
H82.2	2	And wold then have goten grace,
H92.2	2	And all mery company for to dysdayne;
H92.5	1	With goode order, councell and equite,
H92.6	1	For yough ys frayle and prompt to doo,
H92.6	4	And vertuus pastaunce must be theryn usyd.
H92.7	3	And that we may ower fauttes amend,
H96b	2	Help now thi kyng, thi kyng, and take his part!

AND (cont.)

H96.1	2	In the quarell of the church and in the ryght,
H96.1	3	With spers and sheldys on goodly horsys lyght,
H96.1	4	Bowys and arows to put them all to flyght:
H96.1	5	Help now thi king [and take his part!]
H101.1	1	And I war a maydyn,
H103.1	2	Which dayly encressith more and more;
H104b	3	And where be ye gone?
H104.1	3	From care and from all mone;
H104.2	3	My myrth and joy is gone;
H104.4	4	And God above
H105.1	1	The moder full manerly and mekly as a mayd,
H105.1	4	Full softly and full soberly unto her swet son she saide
H105.3	4	Now, gracious God and goode swete babe, yet ons this game agayne
H106.2	4	Begyled am I, and cannot refrayne;
H106.3	7	That deth is plesur and nothyng noyus.
H107.1	2	And more mornyng
H107.2	7	And no redresse
H107.3	3	And no surance
H107.4	3	And that gretly
H108	2	And cannot cesse tyl I sore smart,
H108	7	And love unloved; such ys myne adventure.
H109b	5	To gather the flowres both fayer and swete.
H109.1	1	Now yn this medow fayer and grene
H109.1	2	We may us sport and not be sene;
H109.1	3	And yf ye wyll, I shall consent;
H109.2	1	Ye be so nyce and so mete of age
H109.3	3	And graunte me here your maydynhed,
H109.4	4	Adew, farewell and kysse me now!

ANE (1)

| R10.4 | 6 | As carles doth ane hare, |

ANES (1)

| F39.2 | 6 | Mawde and Anes, |

ANGELL (1)

| F40.1 | 4 | But it were an angell of the Trinite? |

ANGUYSCH (1)

| H25.3 | 3 | But anguysch and pete, |

ANON (4)

F27b	4	'Than shal be provid here anon
F27.4b	4	'Than shall be provid here anon
F27.6b	4	Than may be provid here anon
F36.4	10	Wherwith sodenly anon I awoke,

ANOTHER (2)

| F27b | 3 | 'I love another as well as ye.' |
| H49.2 | 3 | She lovyth another better than me |

ANOTHIR (1)
F40.4   3   Leve this array! Anothir day

ANOTHYR (1)
F27.4b 3   'I love anothyr as well as ye.'

ANY (4)
F32.3   4   All was on red blod withoute any shirt;
F48.2   1   If any man will say here agayne
H65.3   4   As well as any that ever I see:
H65.4   4   As well as any in May:

APAIDE (1)
F32b   4   Or otherwise evyll apaide?

APAYD (1)
H105.1 3   So pretyly, so pertly, so passingly well apayd,

APEYLE (1)
R13.2   7   Ther of right I apeyle hyr to be my surgyon.

APON (1)
R10.2   4   Apon fals love!

APPETITE (1)
F27.6   2   'Is that your pure perfytt appetite?'

APPLYE (3)
F21   6   Yet will I me trust to fortune applye;
F25.2   5   For to applye
H22   1   Whoso that wyll hymselff applye

AQUAYNTANCE (2)
F19   6   As I of aquayntance had never byn afore;
F37.1   3   Nature of aquayntance ys turned to a gest,

AR (2)
F40.4   4   We shall both play, when we ar sole:
H47.4   3   Ye ar not varyable;

ARAID (3)
F33b   1   Woffully araid,
F33.1 10   Woffully araid.
F36.2   7   With wondis sore araid,

ARAIDE (2)
F33b   6   Woffully araide.
F33.3 10   Woffully araide.

ARAYD (1)
F33.2 10   Woffully arayd.

ARE (3)
F34.3   6   Syth I am kynd, why are thou unstable?

ARE (cont.)
F36.2   9   'Yet thou are unkynd, which sleith myn hert,'
H25.5   3   Venus, to blame are ye.

ARESTED (1)
R9   3   Arested hathe my herte in sodeyn wise,

ARMYS (3)
H23.4   1   As featys of armys, and suche other
H27.3   2   And take in armys twayne;
H31.9   1   In armys he hent

AROSE (1)
R18.1   1   Up Y arose _in verno tempore_

AROW (1)
H62.3   2   Myne arow ny worne ys;

AROWS (1)
H96.1   4   Bowys and arows to put them all to flyght:

ARRAY (1)
F40.4   3   Leve this array! Anothir day

ARROW (2)
H35.5   3   And arrow in her hanch she hent;
H65.2   1   Wherfor shuld I hang up myne arrow

ART (5)
F29.5   3   For thou art he that hath all wrought,
F34.1   8   Whi art thou froward, syth I am mercyable?
F34.2   8   Why art thou froward sith I am merciable?
F37.2   1   Where art thou, Nature, that wont were me to store
F38.1   2   Howgh gretly thou art bownd indeed;

ARTHUR (1)
F44.1   3   Arthur oure prynce to us here terrestriall,

ARYSE (1)
F36.3   11   From deth to lyff he aryse shall.'

AS (64)
R10.4   6   As carles doth ane hare,
R10.6   3   Turnyng as the wynd,
R10.6   6   As man that ys blynd,
R15.2   3   As others be,
R16.1   3   So propyr I can none fynde as she;
R19.3   6   'Such on as she,
F5   7   To love and dred hym as my lord and kyng.
F14   2   For why I stond as he that is abusyd;
F14   3   Ther as I trusted I was late cast away,
F19   5   As solen, as stately, as strange toward me,
F19   6   As I of aquayntance had never byn afore;
F22   2   Whom I serve and shall as long,

35

AS (cont.)

F27b	3	'I love another as well as ye.'
F27.4b	3	'I love anothyr as well as ye.'
F27.6b	3	Most worthy it is, as thynkyth me.
F29.1	1	As I me walkyd this endurs day
F29.2	1	As I walkyd undir the grenewode bowe
F30.2	10	As it is fownde,
F31.2	3	And suffyr wolde payne as sorowfull thought,
F31.3	2	As betyng, bobbyng, ye, spettyng on thi face?
F33.1	9	Condemp to deth, as thou maist se;
F36.1	3	A crowne of thorne as nedill sharpe shyfft in his brayne
F36.3	8	As a woman terrestriall
F43.3	3	Till his brayne be as wise as a duk;
F46.1	4	As fortune fallyth, I yow ensure;
F46.3	1	But I will do as I saide furst,
F46.3	2	So it is best, as thynkyth me,
F47b	1	Enforce yourselfe as Goddis knyght
F48.1	4	As long as I am Lord and Kyng,
F48.1	8	Love thi neyboure as I love the!
F49b	1	In a slumbir late as I was,
H23.4	1	As featys of armys, and suche other
H25.9	1	Then as I ought
H27.4	2	As wol to God I cowld,
H27.4	4	Unto my hart as now she shuld.
H29.3	1	She doth not waver as the wynde,
H33.1	1	As the holy grouth grene
H33.2	1	As the holy grouth grene
H35.2	1	As I stod under a bank
H41.5	2	He said, 'Madame, as your prisoner.'
H44.1	1	If love now reynyd as it hath bene
H44.1	4	And war rewardit as it hath sene,
H50.2	2	As the chefteyne of a waryowere,
H50.2	4	As hardy with the hardyest,
H50.3	2	Above all other as a kyng,
H65.3	4	As well as any that ever I see:
H65.4	4	As well as any in May:
H67.1	7	To be as yours
H75	5	As the hauke to the lure,
H92.3	3	Yough has as chef assurans
H92.6	2	As well vices as vertuus to ensew;
H101.1	2	As many one ys,
H102.1	2	She takes me as her howne;
H105.1	1	The moder full manerly and mekly as a mayd,
H106.1	4	My lyffe as one that dye would fayne;

ASAY (1)

R3.2	1	After asay then may ye wette;

ASK (1)

H50.6	4	Of God I ask for hym request,

ASKE (1)

F49b	4	And aske forgeveness or evyr thou dye.'

ASKED (1)
  H41.4   1   She asked hym what was his name;

ASSAY (1)
  R19.2   8   She wolde assay

ASSURANS (1)
  H92.3   3   Yough has as chef assurans

ASSURAUNCE (2)
  F21   2   In stedfast fayth and trouth with assuraunce;
  F23.2   2   My hart is yours with gret assuraunce.

ASSURYD (1)
  F6.2   3   Assuryd am I;

ASSWAGE (1)
  F16   2   I pray daily ther paynys to asswage

AT (13)
  R10.3   3   Settyth me at nought,
  F32.3   2   The crowne on his hed, the spere at his hart,
  F34.5   8   At hir request be to us merciable.
  F38.1   4   That helpis the ever at thi most nede.
  F40b   1   Jhoone is sike and ill at ease;
  F43.3   2   A stoupe of bere up at a pluk,
  F43.4   2   He will piss a galon-pot full at twise
  H25.7   1   At last sche wept;
  H41.1   1   The knyght knokett at the castell gate;
  H50.1   2   Six coursys at the ryng dyd make,
  H50.2   3   With spere and swerd at the barryoure
  H92.7   4   An blysse opteyne at ower last end. Amen.
  H109b   4   Than at the medow I wyll you mete

AT-A-BRAYDE (1)
  R15.2   4   And at-a-brayde

AT-ABRAYDE (1)
  H31.8   2   But at-abrayde

ATTAYNE (1)
  R20.2   3   With hert Y wyll you plece and your love attayne:

ATTE (1)
  R1.2   3   I shall bygge me a boure atte the wodes ende,

AVAILE (1)
  F4   7   But them to tell cannott availe.

AVANCE (1)
  H107.2   8   Me doth avance

AVAUNCE (4)
  R4   5   All for yeure sake, til God me so avaunce

37

AVAUNCE (cont.)
F24.2   8   Me doth avaunce
F39.3   6   Your chere avaunce,
H22   3   Avaunce hym to the companye

AVAYLE (1)
F7.2   2   Cannot avayle, it shal be sayd;

AVAYLYTH (1)   •
F18.1   3   Avaylyth nothyng;

AVENT (2)
F41.1   3   Avent, avent, my popagay!

AVENTURE (4)
R9   8   Sum love comaundes me this aventure,
H106.4   4   Right suere to have no good aventure,
H106.4   5   Good aventure in me to have place:
H108   1   I love unloved; suche is myn aventure,

AVOYDE (1)
R20.1   2   To avoyde your custumabyll disdayne;

AWAKE (1)
F33.2   2   I love the, then love me; why slepist thou? Awake!

AWAY (5)
R3.1   4   Leff werke a twenty-a-devell away!
R14.2   2   Takyn away from me bycause of hevynes;
R19.3   7   That away woll flee,
F14   3   Ther as I trusted I was late cast away,
F29.1   3   And all hevyness to put away,

AWHILE (1)
R3.1   6   Abyde awhile! What have ye haste?

AWOKE (1)
F36.4   10   Wherwith sodenly anon I awoke,

AWTER (1)
F48.2   6   In the awter I am offerd my Fader beforne;

AXE (2)
F38.2   3   I will axe grace while I am able,
F48.1   9   This is that I axe of the,

AY (2)
F41.1   1   Ay, besherewe yow! Be my fay
H31.4   4   So ever and ay

AYE (1)
F32.4   3   Remembir thi joys that joyfull aye byn!

AYEN (1)
F8   5   Through whose swete showris now sprong ther is ayen

AYLYTH (1)
F7.2   8   O my desyre, what aylyth the?

BABE (1)
H105.3   4   Now, gracious God and goode swete babe, yet ons
                    this game agayne

BAD (1)
H35.4   3   I bad hym shott and strik the do,

BADE (1)
R19.2   1   I bade her abyde

BAK (1)
F41.2   5   Go watch a bole, your bak is brode.

BANK (1)
H35.2   1   As I stod under a bank

BANYSHT (1)
H82.1   2   Frome Venus' ways banysht to be;

BANYSSHID (1)
F4   2   And from all hope so fer banysshid

BARE (2)
R10.4   2   For Y am bare
F36.1   1   To Calvery he bare his cross with doulfull payne,

BARKE (1)
R20.4   3   Speke or ye smyte, barke or ye byte; holde yowre
                    hondes twane

BARRAYNE (1)
H35.3   4   I warrant her barrayne.

BARRYOURE (1)
H50.2   3   With spere and swerd at the barryoure

BARYEYNE (1)
R2.1   1   My wofull hert of all gladnesse baryeyne

BAS (1)
F39.1   2   When she me bas,

BAWME (1)
F34.4   7   Swetter than bawme gayne gostly poyson:

BE (197)
R1.1   4   Foster woll Y be no more.
R2.2   6   That she be voyded owte of the grete grevaunce;

39

BE (cont.)

R3.1	1	'Be pes, ye make me spille my ale!'
R3.3	1	Cum kys me! 'Nay!' Be God, ye shall!
R3.3	2	'Be Criste, Y nelle, what ses the man?
R3.3	5	Take to gev all, and be stille than!
R3.3	8	Be Criste, Y wolde have schytte the dore!'
R5	6	And only to be putte to yeure rememoraunce.
R6	1	O blessed lord, how may this be
R7	5	And say after me, and be noght unkynde:
R11.2	2	So onkyndly thus to be slayn;
R12.1	4	So God be plecyd, this lyve woll I;
R12.3	7	My mynde shall be;
R13.1	5	Of my pore hert she may be sure,
R13.2	7	Ther of right I apeyle hyr to be my surgyon.
R15.2	3	As others be,
R15.5	5	Men wene I be
R15.6	5	When clothis be downe
R15.7	6	Thof he be gon.
R19.3	9	Wherever she be
F2	4	Thoo that all this yet in vayne be,
F2	6	Or else I thynke to be content
F2	7	With my desyre tyll I be spent:
F2	8	Wherefor, my hart, lett be, lett be!
F3	4	Then be it they that doth me trobill so
F3	5	That be won thought my rest from me doth go.
F4	5	Cannot be well for to be wisht:
F5	5	Is nowe be hym so comfortide agayne
F6.3	7	To be demyd wrongfully.
F7.1	3	In willfullness so for to be,
F7.1	7	Butt yff hit be to wissh for one:
F7.2	2	Cannot avayle, it shal be sayd;
F7.2	4	Thynkyth my hart can be well payd
F7.2	6	And all be folissh fantasy
F9	7	Her man to be
F10	1	Nowe the lawe is led be clere conciens
F11	6	Wherfor I am and shal be tyll I dye
F12	7	Thi lady hath forgoten to be kynd.'
F13	3	But be constraynt, now must I shew my woo
F13	6	And lett me not allway be guerdonless,
F14	4	And no cause gevyn to be so refusyd;
F14	5	But pite it is that trust shulde be mysusyd
F14	7	Wher that is usyd can be no surance.
F15	2	Thow I be lytyll in your remembraunce;
F15	4	To be put owte of your good governaunce . . .
F16	3	And sone to sende where they faynest wolde be,
F17	6	For where I shulde, they be mery,
F19	2	Houghevyr such dyversite in on person may be,
F21	1	I love, loved, and loved wolde I be
F21	5	Lest that mysaventure myght fall be chaunce;
F24.4	4	To be content,
F24.5	6	Thus to be shent;
F25.3	7	Thowe I be shent,
F27b	4	'Than shal be provid here anon
F27.1	4	'Nay, nay, let be;

F27.2	1	'Ther is a floure where so he be,
F27.2	2	And shall not yet be namyd for me;
F27.4b	4	'Than shall be provid here anon
F27.5	3	'Both be full swete and of lyke savoure;
F27.5	4	All on they be;
F27.6	4	Joyed may we be
F27.6b	4	Than may be provid here anon
F27.6b	5	That we three be agrede in oon.'
F28	7	Lest cause in me be fownd of offens.
F29.3	4	But be still alone.'
F29.5	1	'Sone', she sayd, 'let it be in thy thought,
F30.2	3	And now be styll;
F30.2	15	Ther shall I be,
F31b	1	Jhesu, mercy, how may this be,
F31b	5	Jhesu, mercy, how may this be?
F31.1	5	Jhesu, mercy, [how may this be?]
F31.2	5	Jhesu, mercy, [how may this be?]
F31.3	5	Jhesu, mercy, [how may this be?]
F31.4	5	[Jhesu, mercy, how may this be?]
F32b	3	Whi shuld she hevy be?
F32.1	3	Though deth be bewaylid by waies of pite,
F32.1	6	Therfore, though deth be nevyr so sore,
F32.2	1	Methynkyth in my reson thou owfte to be gladd
F32.2	7	Therfor, thowe deth be never so sore,
F32.3	5	But blessid be that oure,
F32.3	7	Therfore though deth be never so sore,
F32.4	2	Lay downe all thi wepyng, let no more be sene!
F32.4	7	Therefore, though deth be nevir so sore,
F33b	4	It may not be naid;
F33.1	2	And be not hard-hartid, and for this encheson
F34.1	4	Be repentant; make playne confession.
F34.1	6	Be not dispayryd, for I am not vengeable;
F34.2	1	My blody wowndes downe railyng be this tre,
F34.2	6	Lett now us twayne in this thyng be tretable:
F34.2	7	Love for love be just convencion;
F34.3	8	Be thou not froward syth I am merciable.
F34.4	8	Be thou not affraide sith I am merciable.
F34.5	8	At hir request be to us merciable.
F36.3	7	I must nedis wofull be,
F37.3	2	My slepis be so feerfull, I thynk then sure to dye;
F40b	4	I shal bere the cost, be swete Sent Denys!
F40.1	2	Good Lord, who may a goodlyer be
F40.1	6	I shal bere the cost, be swete Sent Denys!]
F40.2	4	Myght wel be calde conjuracion.
F40.2	6	I shal bere the cost, be swete Sent Denys!]
F40.3	6	I shal bere the cost, be swete Sent Denys!]
F40.4	2	Be lost so sone? I am a fole:
F40.4	6	I shal bere the cost, be swete Sent Denys!]
F41.1	1	Ay, besherewe yow! Be my fay
F41.1	2	This wanton clarkis be nyse allway.
F41.1	5	Tully, valy, strawe, let be I say!
F41.2	1	'Be Gad, ye be a prety pode,
F41.3	3	'What, and ye shal be my piggesnye?'

F41.3	4	Be Crist, ye shal not! No, no, hardely!
F41.3	5	I will not be japed bodely.
F43.3	3	Till his brayne be as wise as a duk;
F44.1	7	Be inerytaunce
F44.1	9	Ryght eyre for to be;
F44.2	3	In every case be his preservacion,
F44.2	9	Ryght eyre for to be;
F44.3	4	Be thi servaunt with all his hart so fre.
F44.3	9	His savegard to be;
F45.2	1	In that garden be flouris of hewe:
F45.2	5	This garden to rule be ryghtwis lawe.'
F46.3	4	Forever yff she will trew be,
F47.1	2	Whom God hath chose oure gyde to be,
F47.1	5	Sith it is so, now let your labour be
F48b	1	Be hit knowyn to all that byn here
F48b	3	To me shal be leffe and dere,
F48.1	2	To the, and thou wilt be repentant;
F48.1	7	And that thou be in charite;
F48.2	3	[Rather then manne sholde be forlorne
F48.2	4	Yet wold Y eft be all to-torne.]
F48.2	5	Yet, man, that thou sholdest not be lorne,
H18	6	Sone shal be slayne
H23.1	1	The tyme of youthe is to be spent;
H23.1	2	But vice in it shuld be forfent.
H23.2	1	Pastymes ther be I nought treulye
H23.3	1	And they be plesant to God and man,
H23.5	1	Comparysons in them may lawfully be sett,
H24	3	That I cannot be prest
H25.2	3	Of absence nedes must be,
H25.9	3	And prayd her to be ble,
H25.10	3	From all other that be,
H25.11	3	All lovers that trew be,
H27.2	3	And now absence to be in place
H28	4	Joy shall I never ye may be sure.
H29.4	2	Pytte it war that I shuld be,
H29.5	2	Unto ther lovers trew for to be;
H29.6	2	To by deth departed we be;
H31.6	3	To be a lady's pere!'
H31.8	5	Be not dysmayd,
H33.2	3	When flowerys cannot be sene,
H33.2	4	And grenewode levys be gone.
H33.4	4	Be suere, and ever shall.
H34.1	2	In love he must be withowt dysdayne,
H34.3	1	Wherfor to love and be not loved
H34.3	2	Is wors then deth? Let it be proved!
H34.6	1	But dysdayne ys vice and shuld be refused;
H40	4	My hart with her ever shall be.
H41.7	2	And Pyte said she wold be ther.
H47.3	4	That I shuld be unkynde.
H50.4	3	My hart with joe that I be hete
H51.4	2	There is no bote; ther must it be.
H51.9	2	Thay hynder lovers that wolde be trew.
H51.10	2	Chaunge who so wyll, I wyll be none.

BE (cont.)

H62.1	3	Foster wyl I be no more
H64.1	3	Now let us be;
H64.2	2	That lovers be
H65b	3	And foster will I be styll
H66.2	1	I pray you all that aged be,
H67.1	7	To be as yours
H67.2	6	Ye may be sure,
H74	2	Tyll the trowth be tryed owt.
H79.1	2	Hys entent must nedys be trew,
H79.1	6	But those be thay which can no skyll:
H79.2	4	In that therfor can be non odde,
H82.1	1	Let not us that yong men be
H82.1	2	Frome Venus' ways banysht to be;
H92.5	2	Goode Lord, graunt us our mancyon to be!
H92.6	3	Wherfor be thes he must be gydyd
H92.6	4	And vertuus pastaunce must be theryn usyd.
H92.7	2	That this rude play may well be take,
H96b	1	Englond, be glad! Pluk up thy lusty hart!
H102b	3	Why shall I not be trew?
H102.2	2	No love that can be lost;
H104b	1	Wher be ye
H104b	3	And where be ye gone?
H104.2	1	When ye be hens,
H107.4	4	To be content;
H107.5	6	Thus to be shent;
H109b	6	Nay, God forbede! That may not be -
H109.1	2	We may us sport and nqt be sene;
H109.1	4	How sey ye, mayde? Be ye content?
H109.1b	5	Nay, God forbede! That may not be;
H109.2	1	Ye be so nyce and so mete of age
H109.2	4	Let us make one, though we be twayne!
H109.3	4	Or elles I shall for you be ded.

BEAUTE (5)

F20	4	Of her bounte, beaute and womanhode;
F27b	2	'I love a floure of fressh beaute;'
F27.4b	2	'I love a floure of fressh beaute.'
F27.6b	2	This fayre fressh floure full of beaute;
F39.2	4	In her beaute;

BEAWTE (1)

| H25.6 | 3 | I dyspraysed her beawte; |

BEAWTYE (1)

| H62.4 | 4 | That beawtye ys my foo; |

BECAUSE (1)

| H79.2 | 1 | Or else because they may not opteyne, |

BEDES (1)

| H62.6 | 1 | Now will I take to me my bedes |

BEFORE (1)
F36.2   2   With pale visage tremlyng she stode her child
                 before

BEFORNE (1)
F48.2   6   In the awter I am offerd my Fader beforne;

BEGUNNE (1)
R13.2   6   And only she which my wound begunne;

BEGYLDE (1)
F33.1   4   Begylde and betraide by Judas' fals treson;

BEGYLED (2)
H106.2   3   My payne with hope hath me begyled;
H106.2   4   Begyled am I, and cannot refrayne;

BEGYLYD (1)
R15.3   4   And me begylyd,

BEGYN (1)
F46.2   5   Tyll sum of them begyn to grone:

BEHAVYNG (1)
F19   3   So goodly, so curtesly, so gentill in behavyng;

BEHOLD (1)
H27.3   1   I was wont her to behold,

BEHOLDE (4)
F8   2   Beholde the soveren sede of this rosis twayn,
F33.1   1   Beholde me, I pray the, with all thi hole reson,
F49.1   1   'Beholde', he saide, 'my creature,
H50.5   3   Beholde his favor and his face,

BEHOLDYNG (1)
F36.2   3   Beholdyng ther his lymmys all to-rent and tore,

BEHYND (1)
R10.6   5   I am put behynd,

BEHYNDE (2)
F1   1   The farther I go, the more behynde;
F1   2   The more behynde, the nere my wayes ende;

BELEVYNG (1)
F18.1   7   To make a belevyng:

BEN (3)
R1.1   1   Y have ben a foster long and meney day;
R1.1   2   My lockes ben hore.
H65b   2   And have ben many a day,

44

BEND (1)
H65.1   3   I cane bend and draw a bow

BENDE (1)
R1.2   1   All the whiles that Y may my bowe bende

BENE (9)
H33.1   3   So I am, ever hath bene,
H44.1   1   If love now reynyd as it hath bene
H62.1   1   I have bene a foster
H62.1   5   Yet have I bene a foster.
H62.2   5   Yet have I [bene a foster.]
H62.3   5   Yet have [I bene a foster.]
H62.4   5   Yet have I bene [a foster.]
H62.5   5   Yet have [I bene a foster.]
H62.6   5   Yet have [I bene a foster.]

BENEDICITE (1)
F12   1   Benedicite! Whate dremyd I this nyght?

BENIGNITE (1)
F34.5   3   O Jhesu, graunt of thi benignite

BEQWEST (1)
H50.1   4   Wherfor my hart I hym beqwest,

BERD (1)
H62.5   1   My berd ys so hard, God wote,

BERE (8)
F12   6   Of onys voice sayyng, 'Bere in thy mynd,
F40b   4   I shal bere the cost, be swete Sent Denys!
F40.1   6   I shal bere the cost, be swete Sent Denys!]
F40.2   6   I shal bere the cost, be swete Sent Denys!]
F40.3   6   I shal bere the cost, be swete Sent Denys!]
F40.4   6   I shal bere the cost, be swete Sent Denys!]
F43.3   2   A stoupe of bere up at a pluk,
H41.7   1   Kyndnes said she wold yt bere,

BES (1)
F39.2   5   Both Cate and Bes,

BESECHYNG (1)
R9   7   Besechyng yeure excuse, ther Y supprise;

BESHEREWE (1)
F41.1   1   Ay, besherewe yow! Be my fay

BESMERDE (1)
F43.2   3   Besmerde with grece abowte his disshe,

BESSE (6)
R15.1   2   Ther founde I Besse
R16b   1   Come over the burne, Besse,

45

BESSE (cont.)

R16b	2	Thou lytyll, prety Besse,
R16b	3	Come over the burne, Besse, to me!
R16.1	2	And Besse ys mankynde;
R16.1	6	Cum over the burne, Besse, to me!

BEST (26)

R2.2	1	For sche weche ys of all godely the best
R12.2	3	Company me thynckyth then best
R12.2	10	Ys best of all?
R12.3	5	The best insew,
F27.2	5	That best lykyth me.'
F27.4	5	In hart so fre, that best lykyth me.'
F28	3	To love her best and no mo
F34.3	7	My blode best triacle for thi transgression;
F37.1	6	Thus trobled am I yet I trust it shalbe for the best
F37.2	6	Thus trobled am I [yet I trust it shalbe for the best
F37.3	6	Thus trobled am I [yet I trust it shalbe for the best
F37.4	6	Thus trobled am I [yet I trust it shalbe for the best
F41.4	3	The best chepe flessh that evyr I bought.'
F42.2	1	The fayrest man that best love can,
F46.3	2	So it is best, as thynkyth me,
H50b	2	My soverayne lord I shall love best.
H50.1	5	And of all other for to love best
H50.2	5	He provith hymselfe that I sey best,
H50.3	5	To have the prayse of all the best;
H50.4	5	With hart and body to love best
H50.5	5	A vengeance on them that loveth nott best
H50.6	5	Off all gode fortunes to send hym best;
H64.1	6	Best semyth me.
H74	1	Deme the best of every dowt
H92.3	1	How shuld yough hymselfe best use
H103.3	1	O my swet hart, whome I love best,

BESY (1)

| F28 | 2 | Syth I have done my besy payne |

BESYNESSE (1)

| R6 | 3 | And yet Y have do my besynesse |

BET (1)

| F32.2 | 3 | They bet him for oure gilt, though he no syn hadd; |

BETAKE (1)

| H33.3 | 4 | To her I me betake. |

BETE (1)

| R18.3 | 3 | They wyll me bete cum virgis ac fustibus |

BETHOUGHT (1)
  H25.9   2   I me bethought

BETRAIDE (2)
  F33.1   4   Begylde and betraide by Judas' fals treson;
  F36.2   6   Her Son was so betraide,

BETRAYD (1)
  F7.2   5   So for to se ye betrayd,

BETTER (2)
  H44.7   2   Better than do I, I thynk it so.
  H49.2   3   She lovyth another better than me

BETTYR (1)
  F46.2   1   One is good, but mo were bettyr

BETWENE (2)
  F45.1   4   She gaderd a floure and set betwene;
  H79.2   5   But perfite in dede and betwene two.

BETYNG (2)
  F31.3   2   As betyng, bobbyng, ye, spettyng on thi face?
  F32.3   3   They betyng they broysyng, or liff did depart;

BEUTE (2)
  R9   2   That with yeure beute and fresche plesaunce pure
  R9   9   Thorffe with yeur beute that Y most love and prise.

BEWARE (2)
  R10.4   1   All lovers beware,
  H109.4   2   But the nexte tyme ye must beware

BEWAYLID (1)
  F32.1   3   Though deth be bewaylid by waies of pite,

BEWAYLL (1)
  H103.2   1   Bewayll I may myn adventure

BEWTE (1)
  R5   2   The godely and wommanly bewte

BEYNG (2)
  F24.1   5   This wordle beyng
  H107.1   5   This world beyng

BLAME (2)
  R3.2   2   Why blame ye me withoute offence?
  H25.5   3   Venus, to blame are ye.

BLASTYS (1)
  H33b   3   Thow wynter blastys blow never so hye,

47

BLE (1)
H25.9   3   And prayd her to be ble,

BLEDE (1)
F38.1   5   Alas, for sorow myne hart doth blede

BLEDES (1)
H35.1   2   And yet she bledes no whytt;

BLESSED (2)
R6   1   O blessed lord, how may this be
F44.1   1   O blessed Lord of hevyn celestiall,

BLESSID (6)
F32.1   7   Now blessid Lady, wepe no more:
F32.2   8   Now, blessid Lady, wepe [no more:
F32.3   5   But blessid be that oure,
F32.3   8   Now, blessid Lady, wepe no more:
F32.4   8   Now blessid Lady, wepe no more:
F37.1   1   A blessid Jhesu, hough fortunyd this?

BLISS (3)
F23.1   2   That was my bliss is now my displesaunce;
F31.4   4   'The to purchace both joy and bliss.'
F48.1   3   Hevyn bliss thyn eritage withoute endyng

BLO (1)
H47.4   2   The violett wan and blo;

BLOD (1)
F32.3   4   All was on red blod withoute any shirt;

BLODDYS (1)
H22   4   Of lusty bloddys and chevalry.

BLODE (6)
F31.3   4   Both water and blode, ye, crucified an hevy case?
F32.4   6   He bought us with his precious blode:
F33b   2   My blode, man,
F33.3   4   Onfaynyd, not deynyd, my blode for to shede:
F34.3   7   My blode best triacle for thi transgression;
F34.4   4   My blode all spent by distillacion.

BLODY (1)
F34.2   1   My blody wowndes downe railyng be this tre,

BLOO (1)
F33b   5   My body bloo and wan,

BLOSSUM (1)
R14.2   1   My blossum bright ys gone,

BLOW (6)
H33b   3   Thow wynter blastys blow never so hye,

BLOW (cont.)
H35b   1   Blow thi horne, hunter, and blow thi horne on hye!
H35b   3   Now blow thi horne, hunter, and blow thi horne,
                          joly hunter
H65.3   3   I can blow the deth of a dere

BLYN (1)
H41.2   1   To call the porter he wold not blyn;

BLYND (1)
R10.6   6   As man that ys blynd,

BLYNDE (1)
R16.1   1   The burne ys this worlde blynde

BLYSSE (1)
H92.7   4   An blysse opteyne at ower last end. Amen.

BOBBID (1)
F33.3   3   Thus bobbid, thus robbid, thus for thi love ded;

BOBBYNG (1)
F31.3   2   As betyng, bobbyng, ye, spettyng on thi face?

BODELY (1)
F41.3   5   I will not be japed bodely.

BODIES (1)
F48.2 10   Witness, the bodies that rose from deth to lyve.

BODILY (1)
F37.1   5   Whereas I am ybid with bodily rest;

BODY (5)
F11   7   Your trewe servant with thought, hart and body.
F25.2   6   With hart, body,
F33b   5   My body bloo and wan,
H50.4   5   With hart and body to love best
H106.1 2   My body languisshyng, my hart in payn;

BOISTUSLY (1)
F36.4   2   Full boistusly in the mortess he was downe cast;

BOLD (1)
H34.4   1   Love encoragith and makyth on bold;

BOLE (1)
F41.2   5   Go watch a bole, your bak is brode.

BOLT (1)
H35.7   4   Hys bolt may fle no more.

BOND (2)
F39.1   6   I thynk me bond,

49

BOND (cont.)
H101.3 3 In all this lond, nowther fre nor bond,

BONE (1)
F40.3 4 I-wis, she will not gyve me a bone:

BOOKE (1)
H62.6 2 For and my santes booke,

BOOTE (1)
H25.3 1 It is no boote

BORAGE (1)
F27.3 3 Camamyll, borage, or savery?'

BORDE (1)
F43.4 1 When rutterkyn from borde will ryse

BORE (1)
F33.3 6 The sturdy nailis bore;

BORNE (1)
F29.3 1 'Son,' she sayd, 'I have the borne

BOTE (2)
H51.4 2 There is no bote; ther must it be.
H63.1 4 Ther ys none other bote.

BOTH (14)
R6   5 Both erly, late, by day and by nyghth.
F12   4 The see also drownyd both towre and towne:
F20   6 Which that all men knowith, both more and less;
F27.5 3 'Both be full swete and of lyke savoure;
F27.6 1 'I love the rose, both red and white.'
F31.2 2 That made both paynys and joy also,
F31.3 4 Both water and blode, ye, crucified an hevy case?
F31.4 4 'The to purchace both joy and bliss.'
F39.2 5 Both Cate and Bes,
F40.4 4 We shall both play, when we ar sole:
H17   3 Both day and nyght,
H29.1 2 Of my lady, both fayre and fre,
H51.4 1 Wyth ee and mynd doth both agre;
H109b 5 To gather the flowres both fayer and swete.

BOTHE (6)
H31.7 3 Adew, bothe frend and foo!
H34.7 2 With dysdayne bothe falce and subtell.
H35.5 1 To the covert bothe thay went,
H64.1 2 And bothe acorde
H64.1 4 Bothe hartes alone
H65.2 4 And kyll bothe hart and hynd:

BOUGH (2)
H62.2 2 Upon the grenewod bough,

BOUGH (cont.)
H65.1   2   Upon the grenwod bough?

BOUGHT (3)
R10.3   2   And love dere bought
F32.4   6   He bought us with his precious blode:
F41.4   3   the best chepe flessh that evyr I bought.'

BOUNDEN (2)
F24.4   2   Bounden am I
F25.2   2   Bounden were I

BOUNTE (1)
F20   4   Of her bounte, beaute and womanhode;

BOURE (1)
R1.2   3   I shall bygge me a boure atte the wodes ende,

BOW (4)
H35.7   3   I thynk his bow ys well unbent,
H62.2   1   Hange I wyl my nobyl bow
H65.1   1   Wherfore shuld I hang up my bow
H65.1   3   I cane bend and draw a bow

BOWE (3)
R1.2   1   All the whiles that Y may my bowe bende
F29.2   1   As I walkyd undir the grenewode bowe
H62.3   1   Every bowe for me ys to bygge;

BOWND (1)
F38.1   2   Howgh gretly thou art bownd indede;

BOWNDE (1)
F5   6   That I am bownde above all erthly thyng

BOWNDEN (1)
F21   3   Then bownden were I such on faythfully

BOWNDON (1)
H107.4   2   Bowndon am I

BOWYS (1)
H96.1   4   Bowys and arows to put them all to flyght:

BRAKE (1)
F33.2   3   Remembir my tendir hart-rote for the brake,

BRAST (1)
F36.4   3   His vaynys all and synowis to-raff and brast;

BRAUGHT (1)
R10.3   6   My hert ys braught

51

BRAY (1)
H35.5   4   For faynte she myght nott bray.

BRAYNE (2)
F36.1   3   A crowne of thorne as nedill sharpe shyfft in his
                  brayne
F43.3   3   Till his brayne be as wise as a duk;

BREFFE (1)
H41.6   1   He was cownselled to breffe a byll

BRERE (1)
R19.1   1   Hay how the mavys on a brere!

BREST (4)
H24   1   The thowghtes within my brest,
H31.3   6   Wherfore my hart will brest.
H50b   1   Whilles lyve or breth is in my brest
H103.3   3   For which my hart is lyk to brest,

BRETH (2)
F41.4   6   Gup, Cristian Clowte, your breth is stale,
H50b   1   Whilles lyve or breth is in my brest

BRIGHT (1)
R14.2   1   My blossum bright ys gone,

BRODE (1)
F41.2   5   Go watch a bole, your bak is brode.

BROYSYNG (1)
F32.3   3   They betyng they broysyng, or liff did depart;

BRYGHT (1)
H41.3   1   The portres was a lady bryght;

BRYGHTEST (1)
F20   5   The bryghtest myrrour and floure of goodlyhed,

BRYNG (2)
R4   7   That myght my herte in more ese bryng.
F43.3   1   Rutterkyn shall bryng you all good luk;

BRYTAYNE (1)
F44.2   7   This eyre of Brytayne,

BUD (1)
H17   5   A bud is spryngynge

BURNE (4)
R16b   1   Come over the burne, Besse,
R16b   3   Come over the burne, Besse, to me!
R16.1   1   The burne ys this worlde blynde
R16.1   6   Cum over the burne, Besse, to me!

BUT (62)

R2.2	3	Ys full but late oute of hur kyndely rest
R2.2	8	But sorfull joy and paynefull plesaunce.
R3.3	7	But hadde Y wyste when ye bygan,
R12.1	3	Grugge so woll, but noon denye;
R12.2	9	But passe-the-day
R12.3	4	But every man hath hys frewyll.
R13.2	5	And no help but Fortunys whele,
R15.7	2	But soore Y wepe
R18.2	3	But for my mysse <u>michi deridere</u>;
R20.3	3	But light credens turnyth your love agayne:
F4	7	But them to tell cannott availe.
F6.4	6	But everychone
F10	6	The pore pepull no tyme hath but ryght
F13	3	But be constraynt, now must I shew my woo
F14	5	But pite it is that trust shulde be mysusyd
F17	1	But why am I so abusyd?
F23.1	5	What causyth this but only yowre plesaunce
F23.2	7	Have but yourselfe, fayre lady and mastres.
F24.5	7	But she it ment,
F29.3	4	But be still alone.'
F32.3	5	But blessid be that oure,
F40.1	4	But it were an angell of the Trinite?
F41.1	4	What, will ye do nothing but play?
F42.1	2	Who but I, who but I, who but I,
F46b	4	No mo maydyns but one.
F46.2	1	One is good, but mo were bettyr
F46.3	1	But I will do as I saide furst,
F48.1	6	But a lovyng and a contrite hart,
H23.1	2	But vice in it shuld be forfent.
H25.3	3	But anguysch and pete,
H25.4	6	But styll to morne for me.
H25.10	2	But suere retaylle
H29.3	3	But allway trew I do her fynd;
H31.8	2	But at-abrayde
H34.6	1	But dysdayne ys vice and shuld be refused;
H35.2	4	But yet she was not dede.
H35.4	2	But he ran fast afore;
H44.5	2	But let them tell which love doth gett.
H50.3	4	But of a trewth he worthyest
H50.4	4	Next God but he and ever prest
H51.5	2	But mynd afformyth with full consent.
H62.6	4	For I may nowght but loke;
H64.2	9	But condyscend;
H66.3	2	None can sey but necessary;
H67.2	5	But to endure
H79.1	6	But those be thay which can no skyll:
H79.2	3	But love us a thyng gevyn by God;
H79.2	5	But perfite in dede and betwene two.
H92.2	3	But I wyll not so whatsoever thay say,
H92.2	4	But follow hys mynd in all that we may.
H92.3	2	But all dysdaynares for to refuse?
H104b	6	Yt is but you, my love, alone.
H104.1	4	But when ye mysse,

BUT (cont.)
H104.1 6 But you, my love, alone.
H104.2 6 But you, my love, alone.
H104.3 6 But yow, my love, alone.
H107.5 7 But she it ment,
H108 3 But love my fo, that fervent creature
H108 6 But leve in payne whyls I endure
H109.4 2 But the nexte tyme ye must beware

BUTT (3)
F7.1 7 Butt yff hit be to wissh for one:
H44.3 1 Butt envy reynyth with such dysdayne,
H51.10 1 For whoso lovith shuld love butt oone;

BUTTYRD (1)
F43.2 2 His tong rennyth all on buttyrd fyssh,

BUXUM (1)
F46.2 4 Plesaunt, buxum, and ever obedient,

BY (17)
R1.1   3 Y shall hong up my horne by the grenewode spray;
R6   5 Both erly, late, by day and by nyghth.
F6.4   3 That I must sett by;
F8   4 By dropys of grace that on them down doth rayn;
F14   6 Other by colour or by fals semblaunce;
F32.1 3 Though deth be bewaylid by waies of pite,
F33.1 4 Begylde and betraide by Judas' fals treson;
F34.4 4 My blode all spent by distillacion.
F34.5 5 Callid thi fyve wondes by computacion,
F36.3 9 Is by nature constraynyd to smert,
F37.2 5 Thou, Nature, hast lefft me; by the fynd I no rest:
H20   3 By the medows grene;
H29.6 2 To by deth departed we be;
H79.2 3 But love us a thyng gevyn by God;
H105.2 1 I mene this by Mary, our Maker's moder of myght,

BYCAUSE (2)
R14.2 2 Takyn away from me bycause of hevynes;
R18.3 2 Bycause Y lay with quidam clericus?

BYDYN (1)
F37.1 4 So shortly am I bydyn to a grevus fest,

BYGAN (1)
R3.3   7 But hadde Y wyste when ye bygan,

BYGGE (2)
R1.2   3 I shall bygge me a boure atte the wodes ende,
H62.3 1 Every bowe for me ys to bygge;

BYLL (1)
H41.6 1 He was cownselled to breffe a byll

54

BYN (9)
F3   2   Syn thoughtis byn cheff causers of my woo;
F5   2   Which hath byn long plongyng with thought unseyne,
F19   6   As I of aquayntance had never byn afore;
F20   7   Thes vertues byn pryntyd in her doutless.
F23.1   7   That hath byn your fayre lady and mastress.
F32.4   3   Remembir thi joys that joyfull aye byn!
F38b   2   And thynk on the paynys that byn in hell.
F45.1   3   Among the flouris that fressh byn.
F48b   1   Be hit knowyn to all that byn here

BYND (1)
H29.2   3   My hart to have she doth me bynd;

BYNDE (1)
F9   6   I wolde bynde me

BYRDE (1)
R15.6   3   "Go wach a byrde!

BYRDYS (1)
H20   4   The byrdys sang on every syde

BYTE (1)
R20.4   3   Speke or ye smyte, barke or ye byte; holde yowre
                 hondes twane

CACE (1)
H44.6   1   To lovers I put now suer this cace -

CALDE (1)
F40.2   4   Myght wel be calde an conjuracion.

CALL (10)
R13.2   1   The sterre of Venus which I call her ye,
F34b   2   Who is that that dothe me call?
F34b   7   'Ye, my maker I call the.'
F38.2   2   To God above I call and crye;
F44.3   8   To the we crye and call,
F47.2   5   Which crye and call unto your Majeste.
F49b   2   I harde a voice lowde call and crye
H41.2   1   To call the porter he wold not blyn;
H51.1   1   Thow that men do call it dotage,
H106.3 1   Oftyme for death forsoth I call

CALLE (1)
R11.3   1   Such a mastras I may calle

CALLID (1)
F34.5   5   Callid thi fyve wondes by computacion,

CALVARY (1)
F48.3   9   Iyevyn upon the mownt of Calvary,

CALVERY (3)
R7   2   Unto Calvery caste thy mynde.
F30.2   13   On Calvery,
F36.1   1   To Calvery he bare his cross with doulfull payne,

CAM (3)
R3.2   8   My moder cam in, or that ye wende.'
R19.1   6   When Y cam ther
F32.1   5   Oure sowlis comfort cam agayne;

CAMAMYLL (1)
F27.3   3   Camamyll, borage, or savery?'

CAMPARYNG (1)
H50.3   3   In that he doth no camparyng

CAN (23)
R3.3   4   Ys this the gentery that ye can?'
R12.2   8   Than who can say
R16.1   3   So propyr I can none fynde as she;
F1   3   The more I sech, the wers can I fynde;
F3   7   That no thought can reless me of my sore.
F7.1   6   Yet other grace can ye gett non
F7.2   4   Thynkyth my hart can be well payd
F14   7   Wher that is usyd can be no surance.
F27b   5   Yff we three can agre in on.'
F27.4b   5   Yff we three can agre in oon.'
F36b   1   My feerfull dreme nevyr forgete can I:
F36.1   5   Myn hart can yerne and mylt
F42.2   1   The fayrest man that best love can,
F43.2   1   Rutterkyn can speke no Englissh;
H23.3   2   Those shuld we covit wyn who can;
H47.1   3   No myrth can make me fayn
H65.3   3   I can blow the deth of a dere
H65.4   3   I can luge and make a sute
H66.3   2   None can sey but necessary;
H79.1   6   But those be thay which can no skyll:
H79.2   4   In that therfor can be non odde,
H102.2   2   No love that can be lost;
H108   5   From her love nothinge can me revert

CANE (1)
H65.1   3   I cane bend and draw a bow

CANNOT (11)
R15.7   1   I cannot kepe
F4   5   Cannot be well for to be wisht:
F7.2   2   Cannot avayle, it shal be sayd;
F39.3   2   I cannot mete
H24   3   That I cannot be prest
H33.2   3   When flowerys cannot be sene,
H41.8   1   Thus how thay dyd we cannot say -
H44.5   1   The faut in whome I cannot sett;
H49.3   1   I cannot thynk such doubylnes

CANNOT (cont.)
H106.2   4   Begyled am I, and cannot refrayne;
H108   2   And cannot cesse tyl I sore smart,

CANNOTT (3)
F4   7   But them to tell cannott availe.
H31.7   4   I cannott tell
H62.2   3   For I cannott shote in playne

CARE (6)
R10.4   3   Of yoy, yn care
H30   2   For care is cast into my hart,
H31.5   6   Cryst kepe yow frome all care.
H31.9   3   In voydyng care and mone
H104.1   3   From care and from all mone;
H104.4   1   Thus with my care

CARLES (1)
R10.4   6   As carles doth ane hare,

CARRY (1)
H66.2   2   How well dyd ye your yough carry?

CART-LODE (1)
F41.2   2   And I love you an hole cart-lode.'

CASE (4)
F10   5   Ther is trewly in every case consolacion
F31.3   4   Both water and blode, ye, crucified an hevy case?
F44.2   3   In every case be his preservacion,
H82.2   1   For yf thay war in lyk case

CAST (5)
F14   3   Ther as I trusted I was late cast away,
F36.4   2   Full boistusly in the mortess he was downe cast;
F36.4   9   Uppon her he cast his dedly loke,
H27.2   2   Was wont to cast an nye;
H30   2   For care is cast into my hart,

CASTE (1)
R7   2   Unto Calvery caste thy mynde.

CASTELL (3)
R19.3   10   Yn castell strong.'
F44.2   8   Of Castell and Spayne,
H41.1   1   The knyght knokett at the castell gate;

CATE (1)
F39.2   5   Both Cate and Bes,

CAUSE (8)
R18.2   4   With right goed cause _incipeo flere._
R20.2   2   Withowt cause, Gode knowyth; Y do not fayne.
F14   4   And no cause gevyn to be so refusyd;

CAUSE (cont.)
F28   7   Lest cause in me be fownd of offens.
F37.4   5   With all good sowlis to cause me lyve in rest.
H15   4   And know no cause wherefore.
H18   3   And no cause gevyn therto:
H62.5   4   Lo, age ys cause of this;

CAUSERS (1)
F3   2   Syn thoughtis byn cheff causers of my woo;

CAUSETH (1)
R4   1   Absens of you causeth me to sygh and complayne

CAUSITH (1)
H44.3   2   And causith lovers owtwardly to refrayne,

CAUSLESS (1)
F36b   2   Methought a maydynys childe causless shulde dye.

CAUSYNG (1)
R7   4   This lyon and lambe was, causyng pyte;

CAUSYTH (3)
R10.1   7   Whych causyth my mone;
F3   1   What causyth me wofull thoughtis to thynk
F23.1   5   What causyth this but only yowre plesaunce

CELESTIALL (2)
F44.1   1   O blessed Lord of hevyn celestiall,
F44.3   5   O celestiall

CERTAYNE (1)
R20.3   1   When Y fynde you stedfast and certayne,

CERTENLY (1)
F27.3   4   'Nay certenly;

CESE (1)
H107.2 3   Is now to cese

CESS (1)
F24.2   3   Is now to cess

CESSE (1)
H108   2   And cannot cesse tyl I sore smart,

CHANCE (5)
F39.3   5   'Leve, love, this chance,
H106.4 1   Thus may ye se my wofull chance,
H106.4 2   My chance contrarious from all plesure,
H107.2 4   My wofull chance;
H107.3 7   Such is my chance

CHANGE (1)
H49.3   4   She will change for no new.

CHANGID (1)
F37.1   2   My mode is changid in every wise,

CHARITE (1)
F48.1   7   And that thou be in charite;

CHARYTE (1)
F34.4   3   Gayne fals envy thynk on my charyte,

CHAST (1)
R18.3   4   And me sore chast <u>coram</u> <u>omnibus</u>.

CHAUNCE (6)
R10.3   4   This ys my chaunce;
F11   2   That was my payne is nowe my joyus chaunce;
F21   5   Lest that mysaventure myght fall be chaunce;
F24.2   4   My wofull chaunce;
F46.1   5   So rennyth the chaunce from one to one:
H25.2   2   Syth that oure chaunce

CHAUNGE (5)
R13.3   7   And never to chaunge hyr for no new.
F13   5   Trustyng sumtyme that she will chaunge her mode
F19   4   And so sodenly will chaunge in every degre;
H29.3   2   Nor for no new me chaunge doth she,
H51.10   2   Chaunge who so wyll, I wyll be none.

CHAUNGYNG (1)
F46.1   3   Chaungyng his course, now hevy, now lyght,

CHAUNGYTH (1)
H33.1   2   And never chaungyth hew,

CHEF (2)
H56   1   Departure is my chef payne;
H92.3   3   Yough has as chef assurans

CHEFF (2)
R12.2   6   Ys cheff mastres
F3   2   Syn thoughtis byn cheff causers of my woo;

CHEFFE (1)
F48.1   10   That am the cheffe lorde of the fee.

CHEFTEYNE (1)
H50.2   2   As the chefteyne of a waryowere,

CHEPE (1)
F41.4   3   The best chepe flessh that evyr I bought.'

CHERE (7)

R14.1	3	With a dulfull chere here I make my mone,
R14.2	3	With a dulfull chere [here I make my mone,
R19.1	4	To se her chere
F30b	4	With a lawghyng chere.'
F30.2	2	Amend your chere,
F39.2	1	Her lusty chere,
F39.3	6	Your chere avaunce,

CHERFULL (1)

| H50.4 | 2 | His cherfull contenance doth replete |

CHESE (1)

| F27.4 | 1 | 'I chese a floure fresshist of face.' |

CHEVALRY (1)

| H22 | 4 | Of lusty bloddys and chevalry. |

CHILD (3)

R15.3	5	Goten with child
R18.4	1	With the seid child, _quid faciam_?
F36.2	2	With pale visage tremlyng she stode her child before

CHILDE (3)

F29.2	3	A childe she hoppid; she song, she lough;
F29.2	4	That childe wepid alone.
F36b	2	Methought a maydynys childe causeless shulde dye.

CHOSE (1)

| F47.1 | 2 | Whom God hath chose oure gyde to be, |

CHOSEN (2)

| F27.4 | 2 | 'What is his name that thou chosen has? |
| H31.3 | 2 | Hath chosen a new |

CHURCH (1)

| H96.1 | 2 | In the quarell of the church and in the ryght, |

CHYLD (1)

| R15.3 | 1 | A wanton chyld |

CLARKIS (1)

| F41.1 | 2 | This wanton clarkis be nyse allway. |

CLENE (2)

| H20 | 6 | They toyned so clene; |
| H106.2 | 1 | My hope frome me is clene exiled, |

CLEPYS (1)

| R16.1 | 5 | And Crist stondes and clepys; |

CLERE (4)

| R19.1 | 2 | She satt and sang with notes clere; |

CLERE (cont.)
```
F10     1   Nowe the lawe is led be clere conciens
F20     1   Most clere of colour and rote of stedfastness,
F39.2   2   Her yes most clere,
```

CLOKE (1)
```
F43.1   2   In a cloke withoute cote or gowne,
```

CLOTHIS (1)
```
R15.6   5   When clothis be downe
```

CLOWTE (5)
```
F41.1   6   Gup, Cristian Clowte, gup, Jak of the Vale,
F41.2   6   Gup, Cristian Clowte, gup, Jak of the Vale,
F41.3   6   Gup, Cristian Clowte, gup, Jak of the Vale,
F41.4   6   Gup, Cristian Clowte, your breth is stale,
F41.4   8   Gup, Cristian Clowte, gup, Jak of the Vale,
```

COLDE (2)
```
F30.1   9   Her Son from colde;
H34.4   2   Dysdayne abattyth and makith hym colde.
```

COLOUR (3)
```
F14     6   Other by colour or by fals semblaunce;
F20     1   Most clere of colour and rote of stedfastness,
F27.5   2   'The red or the white? Shewe his colour!'
```

COLUMBYNE (1)
```
F27.1   3   Columbyne goldis of swete flavour?'
```

COM (3)
```
R2.1    5   Till gode tydinges com my sorwe to slake
F43.1   1   Rutterkyn is com unto oure towne
H41.2   2   The lady said he shuld not com in.
```

COMAUNDES (1)
```
R9      8   Sum love comaundes me this aventure,
```

COME (3)
```
R16b    1   Come over the burne, Besse,
R16b    3   Come over the burne, Besse, to me!
H101.3  1   When I was come to
```

COMFORT (6)
```
F32.1   5   Oure sowlis comfort cam agayne;
F39.1   8   To comfort her:
H25.9   4   To take comfort
H103.1  3   Thus withowt comfort I am forlore;
H104.2  4   Me to comfort
H106.1  7   Withowte hope or comfort off redresse.
```

COMFORTIDE (1)
```
F5      5   Is nowe be hym so comfortide agayne
```

61

COMFORTING (1)
H104.3 5 No comforting

COMFORTT (1)
H109.1b 3 Why, wyll ye nott geve me no comfortt,

COMLY (1)
F45.1 2 Sawe I syttyng a comly quene

COMMAUNDYD (1)
H62.4 1 Lady Venus hath commaundyd me

COMMYNALTE (1)
F47.2 4 And specially hurtis of thi commynalte,

COMPANY (3)
R12.2 3 Company me thynckyth then best
H92.2 2 And all mery company for to dysdayne;
H104.1 1 Yower company

COMPANYE (1)
H22 3 Avaunce hym to the companye

COMPARE (1)
H27.4 3 Ther myght no joys compare with it

COMPARYSONS (1)
H23.5 1 Comparysons in them may lawfully be sett,

COMPASSION (1)
F34.2 2 Loke on them well, and have compassion;

COMPELL (1)
H34.7 1 Grett pyte it ware, love for to compell

COMPLAYN (3)
F17 5 I wote nott where I may complayn;
H16 3 Wyth dowbyl sorow complayn I must
H18 4 Wherfor to her I me complayn, hey now!

COMPLAYNE (11)
R4 1 Absens of you causeth me to sygh and complayne
R18.1 3 That dyd complayne in suo pectore,
F4 6 To thynk my sorows, well may I complayne;
F6.1 5 To complayne
F13 1 To complayne me, alas, why shulde I so?
F23.2 3 Wherfore of ryght ye shuld my greffe complayne,
F25.1 6 To you complayne,
F28 1 Complayne I may wherevyr I go,
F28 5 I-wiss yet will I not me complayne
F36.1 8 Tho I wept and sore did complayne
H31.1 3 Ryght peteusly complayne;

COMPLAYNTE (1)
R2.1   2   Enforsed me this complaynte for to make,

COMPLAYNTES (1)
F13   2   For my complayntes it dyd me nevir good;

COMPUTACION (1)
F34.5   5   Callid thi fyve wondes by computacion,

COMYNS (2)
F47b   2   To strenkyth your comyns in ther ryght.
F47.1   7   To strenkyth your comyns in ther ryght.

CONCIENS (1)
F10   1   Nowe the lawe is led be clere conciens

CONCLUDID (1)
F32.1   1   Sith it concludid was in the Trinite

CONDEMP (1)
F33.1   9   Condemp to deth, as thou maist se;

CONDYSCEND (1)
H64.2   9   But condyscend;

CONFESSION (1)
F34.1   4   Be repentant; make playne confession.

CONJURACION (1)
F40.2   4   Myght wel be calde an conjuracion.

CONNYNG (1)
F20   2   With vertu connyng her maner is lede,

CONSENT (2)
H51.5   2   But mynd afformyth with full consent.
H109.1 3   And yf ye wyll, I shall consent;

CONSIDERACION (1)
F8   1   Lett serch your myndis ye of hie consideracion!

CONSIDERYNG (1)
F46.2   3   Consideryng dyvers fayrer and fetter,

CONSISTETH (1)
H92.4   1   For in them consisteth gret honor,

CONSOLACION (2)
F8   3   Renewde of God for owre consolacion
F10   5   Ther is trewly in every case consolacion

CONSTAUNCE (1)
F23.2   5   Much the rathir sith my suryd constaunce

CONSTRAYNE (1)
R20.1   1   Your light grevans shall not me constrayne

CONSTRAYNT (1)
F13   3   But be constraynt, now must I shew my woo

CONSTRAYNYD (2)
F33.2   4   With paynys my vaynys constraynyd to crake;
F36.3   9   Is by nature constraynyd to smert,

CONSTRUCCYON (1)
H35.6   3   Now the construccyon of the same -

CONSYDER (1)
H82.1   5   In ther myndes consyder thei must

CONTENANCE (1)
H50.4   2   His cherfull contenance doth replete

CONTENT (5)
F2   6   Or else I thynke to be content
F24.4   4   To be content,
F25.3   5   I am content
H107.4 4   To be content;
H109.1 4   How sey ye, mayde? Be ye content?

CONTRARIOUS (1)
H106.4 2   My chance contrarious from all plesure,

CONTRARY (3)
F18.2   7   And thynk the contrary:
F24.4   7   All contrary
H107.4 7   All contrary

CONTRARYE (1)
H64.2 10   Yf contrarye,

CONTRARYNG (1)
H107.1 7   My contraryng,

CONTRARYYNG (1)
F24.1   7   Me contraryyng;

CONTRICION (1)
F34.3   2   For-thi contrite of thy contricion;

CONTRITE (2)
F34.3   2   For-thi contrite of thy contricion;
F48.1   6   But a lovyng and a contrite hart,

CONTRYTE (1)
F34.1   5   To contryte hartes I do remission;

CONTYNAUNCE (1)
F40.2   1   Her contynaunce with her lynyacion,

CONTYNEW (1)
R13.1   6   And so shall contynew tyll I dye,

CONVENCION (1)
F34.2   7   Love for love be just convencion;

CORAGE (7)
H23.5   2   For therby corage is suerly owt fett:
H38   1   Adew, corage, adew;
H38   4   Adew, corage, adew, adew.
H51.1   2   Who lovyth not wantith corage.
H97   3   To send hym power to hys corage
H101.2 4   They kyndyld my corage.
H109.2 2   That ye gretly move my corage.

CORDE (1)
F33.1   6   With sharpe corde sore fretid,

COST (6)
F40b   4   I shal bere the cost, be swete Sent Denys!
F40.1   6   I shal bere the cost, be swete Sent Denys!]
F40.2   6   I shal bere the cost, be swete Sent Denys!]
F40.3   6   I shal bere the cost, be swete Sent Denys!]
F40.4   6   I shal bere the cost, be swete Sent Denys!]
F41.4   1   'Walke forthe your way, ye cost me nought;

COTE (1)
F43.1   2   In a cloke withoute cote or gowne,

COUDE (1)
F9   2   Yff I coude spye

COUNCELL (1)
H92.5   1   With goode order, councell and equite,

COUNTURFETYNG (1)
F18.1   1   Yowre counturfetyng

COURAGE (1)
H51.7   1   Love maynteynyth all noble courage;

COURSE (1)
F46.1   3   Chaungyng his course, now hevy, now lyght,

COURSYS (1)
H50.1   2   Six coursys at the ryng dyd make,

COURTE (1)
H62.4   2   Owt of her courte to go;

65

COVERT (1)
H35.5   1 To the covert bothe thay went,

COVETISE (1)
F10   2 Full sylde covetise hath dominacion

COVETYNG (1)
F48.1   5 Not covetyng more for all my smert

COVIT (1)
H23.3   2 Those shuld we covit wyn who can;

COW (3)
H109b   3 I go to the medowe to mylke my cow.
H109.1b 2 I pray you, sir, lett me go mylke my cow!
H109.4   3 How in the medow ye mylke your cow.

COWDE (5)
F18.2   4 That cowde nott tell,
F23.2   1 Nor nought cowde have, wolde I nevyr so fayne!
F36.1   4 His modir dere tendirly wept and cowde not
                 refrayne
F36.2   11 Unneth on worde cowde she speke more.
H35.1   3 She lay so fayre, I cowde nott mys;

COWLD (1)
H27.4   2 As wol to God I cowld,

COWNSELLED (1)
H41.6   1 He was cownselled to breffe a byll

COWRTYERS (1)
H101.2   3 Thes cowrtyers with ther amorus

CRAKE (1)
F33.2   4 With paynys my vaynys constraynyd to crake;

CRAVE (1)
F34b   5 'Mercy, Lord, of the I crave.'

CREACION (1)
F44.2   1 Wherfore, good Lord, syth of thi creacion

CREATUR (1)
H67.2   2 No creatur

CREATURE (9)
R20b   1 How shall Y plece a creature uncerteyne?
R20.1   4 How sholde Y [plece a creature uncerteyne?]
R20.2   4 How sholde Y plece a creature oncertayne?
R20.3   4 How sholde Y plece a creature oncerteyne?
R20.4   4 How sholde Y plece a creature oncertayne?
F37.4   3 'Remembir the, my creature, thou must nedis dye,
                 I the ensure.

66

CREATURE (cont.)
F46.1   2   Indyfferent to every creature,
F49.1   1   'Beholde', he saide, 'my creature,
H108   3   But love my fo, that fervent creature

CREDENS (1)
R20.3   3   But light credens turnyth your love agayne:

CRIED (1)
F36.4   6   Cried, 'Hely, hely, hely!'

CRIST (4)
R16.1   5   And Crist stondes and clepys;
F31.1   1   Crist, that was of infynyt myght,
F41.3   4   Be Crist, ye shal not! No, no, hardely!
H104.4 3   Crist kepe you from your fone;

CRISTE (2)
R3.3   2   'Be Criste, Y nelle, what ses the man?
R3.3   8   Be Criste, Y wolde have schytte the dore!'

CRISTIAN (5)
F41.1   6   Gup, Cristian Clowte, gup, Jak of the Vale,
F41.2   6   Gup, Cristian Clowte, gup, Jak of the Vale,
F41.3   6   Gup, Cristian Clowte, gup, Jak of the Vale,
F41.4   6   Gup, Cristian Clowte, your breth is stale,
F41.4   8   Gup, Cristian Clowte, gup, Jak of the Vale,

CROSS (4)
F34.1   1   Uppon the cross nailid I was for the,
F36.1   1   To Calvery he bare his cross with doulfull payne,
F36.4   1   Unto the cross, handes and feete, nailid he was;
F49.1   5   Upon the cross with naylis thre

CROSSE (1)
F48b   6   Upon the crosse with woundis smert

CROWNE (5)
F32.3   2   The crowne on his hed, the spere at his hart,
F33.3   1   Off sharpe thorne I have worne a crowne on my hede,
F34.2   3   The crowne of thorne, the spere, the nailis thre,
F36.1   3   A crowne of thorne as nedill sharpe shyfft in his
                 brayne
F43.1   3   Save a raggid hode to kover his crowne,

CRUCIFIED (1)
F31.3   4   Both water and blode, ye, crucified an hevy case?

CRUDELITE (1)
F34.3   3   Saynt Tomas of Indes, in crudelite

CRUELL (1)
F33.2   8   Entretid, thus in most cruell wise

67

CRYE (6)
F38.1   7   I crye God mercy, I will amend.
F38.2   2   To God above I call and crye;
F38.2   7   I crye God mercy, I will amend.
F44.3   8   To the we crye and call,
F47.2   5   Which crye and call unto your Majeste.
F49b   2   I harde a voice lowde call and crye

CRYST (1)
H31.5   6   Cryst kepe yow frome all care.

CUM (8)
R3.3   1   Cum kys me! 'Nay!' Be God, ye shall!
R16.1   6   Cum over the burne, Besse, to me!
F2   5   Sum other grace may cum, perde;
F28   6   Tyll that I cum tyll her presens,
F29.4   4   Therfor I cum hyther alone.'
F33.3   9   Cum when thou lyst, welcum to me!
F34.4   2   Cum to scole; record well this lesson:
H27.1   1   A the syghes that cum from my hart

CUMFORT (2)
R10.6   8   Alone ys no cumfort.
R12.1   9   To my cumfort:

CUMPANY (2)
R12.3   1   Cumpany with honeste
R12.3   3   Cumpany ys gode or yll,

CUMPANYE (1)
R12.1   1   Passetyme with good cumpanye

CUNTRE (1)
R15.5   4   In ferre cuntre

CURE (3)
R9   5   My lyves ladi and my hertis cure,
F37.4   4   Alas, to dye thou makyst me sure; yet then, good
              Lord, do thou thi cure
H75   3   That hath my hart in cure;

CURTESLY (5)
F19   3   So goodly, so curtesly, so gentill in behavyng;
F39b   6   So curtesly
F39.1   10   [So curtesly
F39.2   10   [So curtesly
F39.3   10   [So curtesly

CUSTUMABYLL (1)
R20.1   2   To avoyde your custumabyll disdayne;

DAILY (2)
F16   2   I pray daily ther paynys to asswage
F44.3   3   For this yong prince, which is and daily shall

DAISE (1)
H47.4   1   The daise delectable,

DALYAUNCE (1)
R12.2   1   Yowth woll have nedes dalyaunce,

DAME (1)
R11.3   2   Dame Petyles yn every place over all;

DAN (1)
F42.2   2   Dandirly, dandirly, dandirly dan,

DANDIRLY (3)
F42.2   2   Dandirly, dandirly, dandirly dan,

DAR (1)
H66.2   4   Therin a wager lay dar I:

DARE (2)
R13.1   1   So put yn fere I dare not speke;
F39b   4   I dare well say,

DARK (1)
F36.4   4   The erth quakyd, the son was dark, whos lyght was
                    past

DASLYNG (1)
F37.2   4   My face disfygurid, myn yes full daslyng;

DAUNCE (6)
R10.3   8   Yn lovys daunce.
R12.1   6   Hunte, syng and daunce;
F24.3   7   Such is my daunce
F39.3   7   And let us daunce
H25.2   1   In lovys daunce
H104.3   2   To daunce or syng,

DAUNCES (1)
R16.1   4   She daunces and she lepys,

DAWES (3)
F45b   1   This day day dawes,
F45b   2   This gentill day day dawes,
F45b   3   This gentill day dawes,

DAWNCE (1)
F21   4   To love, thowe I do fere to trace that dawnce,

DAY (16)
R1.1   1   Y have ben a foster long and meney day;
R6   5   Both erly, late, by day and by nyghth.
F10   7   Men may fynd day ne nyght adulacion
F27.5   5   That day to se it lykyth well me.'
F29.1   1   As I me walkyd this endurs day

69

DAY (cont.)
F40.4   3   Leve this array! Anothir day
F45b   1   This day day dawes,
F45b   2   This gentill day day dawes,
F45b   3   This gentill day dawes,
H17   3   Both day and nyght,
H31.1   1   This other day
H31.9   4   That day they spent
H62.1   2   Long and many a day;
H65b   2   And have ben many a day,

DAYE (2)
F48.2   7   Witness, the daye turnyd to nyghth,
F48.3   10   The grete daye of mannys mercy.

DAYLY (2)
F15   1   I am he that hath you dayly servyd,
H103.1   2   Which dayly encressith more and more;

DAYSY (1)
F27.2   3   Prymeros, violet, or fressh daysy,

DEATH (2)
H106.3   1   Oftyme for death forsoth I call
H106.3   3   For death ys endar principall

DED (2)
F33.3   3   Thus bobbid, thus robbid, thus for thi love ded;
H109.3   4   Or elles I shall for you be ded.

DEDE (4)
F17   2   Syth worde and dede is take in vayne,
H35.2   4   But yet she was not dede.
H79.1   3   And love her in hart and dede,
H79.2   5   But perfite in dede and betwene two.

DEDLY (1)
F36.4   9   Uppon her he cast his dedly loke,

DEFFEND (1)
H25.11   2   Goode Lorde, deffend

DEFRAYNE (1)
F25.1   1   Madam, defrayne!

DEGRE (4)
F19   4   And so sodenly will chaunge in every degre;
F27.2   4   He pass them all in his degre;
F40.1   1   Hit is so praty in every degre;
H66.2   3   I thynk sum wars of yche degre;

DEITE (1)
F31.1   2   Egall to the Fathir in deite,

70

DELE (3)
  R13.3   3   Or els yn feyth unkyndly she doth dele,
  F38.1   3   Thou thynkyst on hym nevir a dele
  F41.3   1   I-wiss, ye dele uncurtesly;

DELECTABLE (1)
  H47.4   1   The daise delectable,

DELIS (4)
  F39b   8   She delis allway.
  F39.1 12   She delis allway.]
  F39.2 12   She delis allway.]
  F39.3 12   She delis allway.]

DELITE (1)
  F27.6   3   'To here talke of them is my delite.

DELYNG (1)
  F18.1   2   With doubyll delyng

DEME (1)
  H74   1   Deme the best of every dowt

DEMURE (1)
  H75   2   My love is lusty, plesant and demure

DEMYD (8)
  F6.1   1   Demyd wrongfully
  F6.1   7   Demyd wrongfully.
  F6.2   1   Demyd wrongfully
  F6.2   7   Demyd wrongfully.
  F6.3   1   Demyd wrongfully
  F6.3   7   To be demyd wrongfully.
  F6.4   1   Demyd wrongfully
  F6.4   7   Demyd wrongfully.

DEMYNG (1)
  F18.1   6   Hath such a demyng

DENAY (3)
  H31.1   5   Withowt denay
  H31.4   5   Withowt denay,
  H64.2   6   Withowt denay.

DENY (1)
  R10.2   5   Love I deny;

DENYE (2)
  R12.1   3   Grugge so woll, but noon denye;
  H23.2   2   Whych one may use, and vice denye;

DENYS (5)
  F40b   4   I shal bere the cost, be swete Sent Denys!
  F40.1   6   I shal bere the cost, be swete Sent Denys!]

71

DENYS (cont.)
F40.2   6   I shal bere the cost, be swete Sent Denys!]
F40.3   6   I shal bere the cost, be swete Sent Denys!]
F40.4   6   I shal bere the cost, be swete Sent Denys!]

DEPART (7)
F32.3   3   They betyng they broysyng, or liff did depart;
H15   3   Sens I must nedys from my love depart
H25.1   5   Sen we depart
H27.1   3   Sen ye must nedes from me depart,
H63.1   3   Frome yow a whyle must I depart;
H63.2   1   Thowgh you depart now thus me fro,
H106.3 5   A payne it is, hens to depart,

DEPARTE (1)
F22   3   Tyll deth my lyff departe from hens!

DEPARTED (1)
H29.6   2   To by deth departed we be;

DEPARTURE (1)
H56   1   Departure is my chef payne;

DEPE (3)
R13.2   3   So depe hath thrylled my hert ynwardly
F34.3   4   He put his handes depe in my syde adowne.
F36.3   5   'Why than so depe morne ye?

DERE (17)
R4   4   For yeu, dere hert, thoff Y suffere penaunce
R10.3   2   And love dere bought
F30b   1   'A, my dere, a, my dere Son,'
F30b   2   Seyd Mary, 'A, my dere;
F30.2   1   'My moder dere,
F32.4   4   Thi dere sone is past his trobill and his tene;
F36.1   4   His modir dere tendirly wept and cowde not
                refrayne
F48b   3   To me shal be leffe and dere,
H31.2   3   Her dere hart was untrew;
H31.6   6   She said, 'Adew my dere!'
H31.8   3   Her dere hart was full nere
H31.8   6   My love, my derlyng dere.'
H35.1   1   Sore this dere strykyn ys,
H35.2   2   The dere shoffe on the mede;
H47.2   1   Do way, dere hart, not so.
H65.3   3   I can blow the deth of a dere

DERISION (1)
F30.2   7   Derision,

DERLYNG (2)
H31.5   1   Adew, derlyng,
H31.8   6   My love, my derlyng dere.'

72

```
DESERT (1)
 F7.1    2   Whan that desert lakkyth remedy,

DESERVID (1)
 F15     3   And mervell I have syth I not deservid

DESIRE (1)
 R5      1   The hye desire that Y have for to se

DESYRE (6)
 F2      7   With my desyre tyll I be spent:
 F7.1    1   O my desyre, what eylyth the,
 F7.1    8   O my desyre, what eylyth the?
 F7.2    8   O my desyre, what aylyth the?
 H41.4   2   He said, 'Desyre, your man, madame.'
 H41.5   1   She said, 'Desyre, what do ye here?'

DETH (19)
 F22     3   Tyll deth my lyff departe from hens!
 F32.1   3   Though deth be bewaylid by waies of pite,
 F32.1   6   Therfore, though deth be nevyr so sore,
 F32.2   2   When Jewis with treson to deth thi son ladde;
 F32.2   7   Therfor, thowe deth be never so sore,
 F32.3   7   Therfore though deth be never so sore,
 F32.4   5   His deth was swete, hit did us goode;
 F32.4   7   Therefore, though deth be nevir so sore,
 F33.1   9   Condemp to deth, as thou maist se;
 F34.1   2   Suffyrd deth to pay thi rawnsum;
 F34.5   2   Thy deth remembryng of humble afeccion,
 F36.2   1   His grevous deth and her morenyng grevid me sore;
 F36.3  11   From deth to lyff he aryse shall.'
 F48b    5   For thi love, man, have suffyrd deth
 F48.2  10   Witness, the bodies that rose from deth to lyve.
 H29.6   2   To by deth departed we be;
 H34.3   2   Is wors then deth? Let it be proved!
 H65.3   3   I can blow the deth of a dere
 H106.3  7   That deth is plesur and nothyng noyus.

DEVYSE (1)
 R15.4   3   With gode devyse,

DEW (1)
 F44.2   4   With joy to rejose his dew enerytaunce,

DEWTYE (1)
 H66.1   3   God and my ryght and my dewtye,

DEYNYD (1)
 F33.3   4   Onfaynyd, not deynyd, my blode for to shede:

DID (9)
 F30.1   6   And sore did wepe.
 F32.3   3   They betyng they broysyng, or liff did depart;
 F32.4   5   His deth was swete, hit did us goode;
```

73

DID (cont.)
```
F34.4   5  Whi did I this? To save the from prison.
F36.1   8  Tho I wept and sore did complayne
F45.2   3  The floure-de-luce she did on rewe,
F48.2   9  Witness, the vale that then did ryve,
F48.3   1  Witness, the erthe that did quake,
F49.1   2  Whome I did make so lyke unto me,
```

DISCOMFORT (1)
```
F2      2  Ye thynk for to discomfort me.
```

DISCRETE (1)
```
R9      1  Fayre and discrete, fresche wommanly figure,
```

DISDAYNE (2)
```
R20.1   2  To avoyde your custumabyll disdayne;
F28     4  And she me takyth in gret disdayne:
```

DISEASE (2)
```
F16     4  Withoute disease or adversyte.
F40b    2  I am full sory for Jhoon's disease.
```

DISFYGURID (1)
```
F37.2   4  My face disfygurid, myn yes full daslyng;
```

DISMAID (1)
```
F32b    2  Whi so dismaid?
```

DISORDYRD (1)
```
F37.2   3  My tast disordyrd all reson far passyng,
```

DISPAIRE (1)
```
F36.2   4  That with dispaire for feer and dred I was nere
                 forlore
```

DISPAYRYD (1)
```
F34.1   6  Be not dispayryd, for I am not vengeable;
```

DISPLESAUNCE (2)
```
F23.1   2  That was my bliss is now my displesaunce;
F24.3   1  With displesaunce
```

DISSHE (1)
```
F43.2   3  Besmerde with grece abowte his disshe,
```

DISTILLACION (1)
```
F34.4   4  My blode all spent by distillacion.
```

DO (34)
```
R3.2    5  What do ye here within oure spence?
R6      3  And yet Y have do my besynesse
R10.2   8  This do I prove.
R13.1   2  Thus under sylens I do endure,
R20.2   2  Withowt cause, Gode knowyth; Y do not fayne.
```

DO (cont.)
F18.2	5	When that ye do lye,
F21	4	To love, thowe I do fere to trace that dawnce,
F34.1	5	To contryte hartes I do remission;
F37.4	4	Alas, to dye thou makyst me sure; yet then, good
		Lord, do thou thi cure
F41.1	4	What, will ye do nothing but play?
F46.3	1	But I will do as I saide furst,
H12	1	Alas, what shall I do for love?
H12	2	For love, alasse, what shall I do,
H12	4	I do yow fynde
H25.2	5	Your love do way
H29.2	2	She ys right trew, I do it se.
H29.3	3	But allway trew I do her fynd;
H30	1	Alac, alac, what shall I do,
H31.4	3	Optayne that I do sew,
H35b	2	Ther ys a do in yonder wode; in faith, she woll
		not dy
H35.4	3	I bad hym shott and strik the do,
H35.6	4	What do yow meane or thynk?
H41.5	1	She said, 'Desyre, what do ye here?'
H44.7	2	Better than do I, I thynk it so.
H47.2	1	Do way, dere hart, not so.
H51.1	1	Thow that men do call it dotage,
H51.9	1	For often tymes wher they do sewe
H63.2	4	For yow do I mone.
H66.3	3	I hurt no man, I do no wrong;
H75	8	Glad to do her plesure
H92.1	3	For whatsoever they do hym tell,
H92.4	3	For they do sew to get them grace
H101.1	4	I wold not do amysse.

DOLE (2)
| H64.1 | 8 | Ys in the dole |
| H67.1 | 3 | From dole dolours |

DOLOURS (1)
| H67.1 | 3 | From dole dolours |

DOMINACION (1)
| F10 | 2 | Full sylde covetise hath dominacion |

DONE (2)
| F28 | 2 | Syth I have done my besy payne |
| F33.3 | 8 | Than I have done, O man, for the? |

DOO (1)
| H92.6 | 1 | For yough ys frayle and prompt to doo, |

DORE (1)
| R3.3 | 8 | Be Criste, Y wolde have schytte the dore!' |

DOTAGE (1)
| H51.1 | 1 | Thow that men do call it dotage, |

DOTH (29)

R10.4	6	As carles doth ane hare,
R10.5	6	Love doth refrayn,
R13.3	3	Or els yn feyth unkyndly she doth dele,
R20.4	2	Love me lytell and longe; hot love doth not reyne;
F3	4	Then be it they that doth me trobill so
F3	5	That be won thought my rest from me doth go.
F8	4	By dropys of grace that on them down doth rayn;
F24.2	8	Me doth avaunce
F24.4	6	Fortune doth wry
F34b	3	'I, a synner that offt doth fall.'
F36.3	2	He willfully doth suffir for love speciall
F37.3	4	Grete mowntens fallyng over me, thus slepe doth I
		yn feere
F38.1	5	Alas, for sorow myne hart doth blede
H29.2	3	My hart to have she doth me bynd;
H29.3	1	She doth not waver as the wynde,
H29.3	2	Nor for no new me chaunge doth she,
H33b	2	So doth the ive,
H44.5	2	But let them tell which love doth gett.
H44.6	2	Which of ther loves doth get them grace?
H44.7	1	And unto them which doth it know
H49.1	2	Tel me how thy lemman doth,
H50.3	3	In that he doth no camparyng
H50.4	2	His cherfull contenance doth replete
H51.4	1	Wyth ee and mynd doth both agre;
H51.5	1	The ee doth loke and represent;
H51.6	2	Myne ey with hart doth me so juge.
H106.1	5	Myn yes for sorow salt ters doth rayne:
H107.2	8	Me doth avance
H107.4	6	Fortune doth wry

DOTHE (2)

F34b	2	Who is that that dothe me call?
H23.6	2	In goode dysporttys whych it dothe fend.

DOUBYLL (1)

F18.1	2	With doubyll delyng

DOUBYLNES (1)

H49.3	1	I cannot thynk such doubylnes

DOUGHTI (1)

F32.2	4	Thi son was doughti, the fende was adradde;

DOULFULL (1)

F36.1	1	To Calvery he bare his cross with doulfull payne,

DOUTLES (1)

H107.2	1	I fere doutles

DOUTLESS (2)

F20	7	Thes vertues byn pryntyd in her doutless.
F24.2	1	I fere doutless

76

DOWBLE (1)
  H106.1 3 My joyes, dystres; my sorows dowble;

DOWBYL (1)
  H16   3 Wyth dowbyl sorow complayn I must

DOWN (4)
  F8   4 By dropys of grace that on them down doth rayn;
  H18   1 Downbery down!
  H20   2 To geder the flours down
  H25.7   4 The terys ran down

DOWNBERY (1)
  H18   1 Downbery down!

DOWNE (7)
  R15.6   5 When clothis be downe
  F12   2 Methought the worlde was turnyd up so downe,
  F32.4   2 Lay downe all thi wepyng, let no more be sene!
  F34.2   1 My blody wowndes downe railyng be this tre,
  F36.2 10 Wherewith she fell downe with paynys so smert;
  F36.4   2 Full boistusly in the mortess he was downe cast;
  H35.2   3 I stroke her so that downe she sanke,

DOWT (1)
  H74   1 Deme the best of every dowt

DOYST (1)
  R19.1   9 What doyst thou here?

DRAW (1)
  H65.1   3 I cane bend and draw a bow

DRAWNE (1)
  F31.3   3 Drawne like a theffe, and for payne swetyng

DRED (3)
  F4   4 So mekyll dred, so lytyll trust
  F5   7 To love and dred hym as my lord and kyng.
  F36.2   4 That with dispaire for feer and dred I was nere
                    forlore

DREME (3)
  F36b   1 My feerfull dreme nevyr forgete can I:
  F36.4 11 And of my dreme was sore agast.
  F37.3   3 My dreme is so mervelous, serpentis semyth me to
                    tere

DREMYD (1)
  F12   1 Benedicite! Whate dremyd I this nyght?

DREW (1)
  R19.1   3 I drew me nere

77

DROPYS (1)
F8   4   By dropys of grace that on them down doth rayn;

DROWNE (1)
F5   3   Full lyk to drowne in wavis of dystres,

DROWNED (1)
R2.1   7   For yet Y am all drowned in the lake

DROWNYD (1)
F12   4   The see also drownyd both towre and towne:

DRYNK (1)
H35.6   2   I went to tavern to drynk;

DUK (1)
F43.3   3   Till his brayne be as wise as a duk;

DULFULL (2)
R14.1   3   With a dulfull chere here I make my mone,
R14.2   3   With a dulfull chere [here I make my mone,

DWELL (1)
H31.7   5   Wher I shall dwell,

DY (1)
H35b   2   Ther ys a do in yonder wode; in faith, she woll
                not dy

DYAMOND (1)
R13.2   2   Sharper than thorn, dyamond or steyll,

DYD (9)
R18.1   3   That dyd complayne in suo pectore,
F13   2   For my complayntes it dyd me nevir good;
H25.8   2   I dyd her kysse;
H41.8   1   Thus how thay dyd we cannot say -
H50.1   2   Six coursys at the ryng dyd make,
H50.1   3   Of which four tymes he dyd it take;
H66.2   2   How well dyd ye your yough carry?
H66.3   4   I love trew wher I dyd mary:
H82.1   6   How thay dyd in ther most lust.

DYE (18)
R12.1   2   I love and shall unto I dye;
R13.1   6   And so shall contynew tyll I dye,
F7.1   5   Thoo that ye wolde untill ye dye
F11   6   Wherfor I am and shal be tyll I dye
F24.3   8   Willyng to dye.
F25.2   7   Tylle I dye;
F36b   2   Methought a maydynys childe causless shulde dye.
F37.3   2   My slepis be so feerfull, I thynk then sure to dye;
F37.4   3   'Remembir the, my creature, thou must nedis dye,
                I the ensure.

78

DYE (cont.)
  F37.4   4   Alas, to dye thou makyst me sure; yet then, good
                        Lord, do thou thi cure
  F41.4   5   Wed me or els I dye for thought!
  F49b   4   And aske forgeveness or evyr thou dye.'
  H16   4   Untyl I dye, alas, alas!
  H27.2   4   Alas, for wo I dye, I dye.
  H67.1   8   Untyll I dye.
  H106.1   4   My lyffe as one that dye would fayne;
  H107.3   8   Willyng to dye.

DYGEST (1)
  R12.2   4   All thoftes and fantyses to dygest.

DYGNITE (1)
  F47.1   4   Of marshiall power and also hye dygnite,

DYSCORAGES (1)
  H34.2   2   And dysdayne dyscorages all gentyl mynd.

DYSCORD (1)
  H64.1   1   Withowt dyscord

DYSCUSSE (1)
  H66.4   1   Then sone dyscusse that hens we must;

DYSDAYN (3)
  R10.5   3   Hade yn dysdayn;
  H18   5   Trustyng that dysdayn
  H106.2   6   In dysdayn I shall my lyfe endure,

DYSDAYNARES (1)
  H92.3   2   But all dysdaynares for to refuse?

DYSDAYNARS (1)
  H92.4   2   Though that dysdaynars wold therin put error,

DYSDAYNE (10)
  H34.1   2   In love he must be withowt dysdayne,
  H34.2   2   And dysdayne dyscorages all gentyl mynd.
  H34.4   2   Dysdayne abattyth and makith hym colde.
  H34.6   1   But dysdayne ys vice and shuld be refused;
  H34.7   2   With dysdayne bothe falce and subtell.
  H44.3   1   Butt envy reynyth with such dysdayne,
  H79.2   2   They wold that other shuld yt dysdayne;
  H82.1   3   Thow that age with gret dysdayne
  H92.2   2   And all mery company for to dysdayne;
  H106.2   5   Refrayne I must yet in dysdayne,

DYSDAYNYTH (1)
  H51.7   2   Who love dysdaynyth ys all of the village.

DYSMAYD (1)
  H31.8   5   Be not dysmayd,

DYSMAYE (1)
H47.2   2   Let no thought yow dysmaye!

DYSPLESANCE (1)
H107.3   1   With dysplesance

DYSPORTTYS (1)
H23.6   2   In goode dysporttys whych it dothe fend.

DYSPRAYSED (1)
H25.6   3   I dyspraysed her beawte;

DYSTRES (3)
R15.1   4   In grete dystres,
F5   3   Full lyk to drowne in wavis of dystres,
H106.1   3   My joyes, dystres; my sorows dowble;

DYVERS (1)
F46.2   3   Consideryng dyvers fayrer and fetter,

DYVERSITE (1)
F19   2   Houghevyr such dyversite in on person may be,

EASE (1)
F40b   1   Jhoone is sike and ill at ease;

EE (2)
H51.4   1   Wyth ee and mynd doth both agre;
H51.5   1   The ee doth loke and represent;

EFT (1)
F48.2   4   Yet wold Y eft be all to-torne.]

EGALL (1)
F31.1   2   Egall to the Fathir in deite,

EIGHTH (1)
H66.4   4   Thus sayth the kyng, the eighth Harry:

ELLES (2)
H51.3   1   Or elles from her which is her hayre;
H109.3   4   Or elles I shall for you be ded.

ELS (3)
R13.3   3   Or els yn feyth unkyndly she doth dele,
F41.4   5   Wed me or els I dye for thought!
H79.1   4   Els it war pyte that he shuld spede;

ELSE (2)
F2   6   Or else I thynke to be content
H79.2   1   Or else because they may not opteyne,

EMPRISE (1)
F44.3   7   Emprise infernall,

ENCHESON (1)
 F33.1   2 And be not hard-hartid, and for this encheson

ENCORAGITH (1)
 H34.4   1 Love encoragith and makyth on bold;

ENCRESE (1)
 F6.1   4 Encrese of payne

ENCRESSITH (1)
 H103.1   2 Which dayly encressith more and more;

END (3)
 H35.7   1 Here I leve and mak an end,
 H66.4   3 That all amend; and here an end,
 H92.7   4 An blysse opteyne at ower last end. Amen.

ENDAR (1)
 H106.3   3 For death ys endar principall

ENDE (3)
 R1.2   3 I shall bygge me a boure atte the wodes ende,
 F1   2 The more behynde, the nere my wayes ende;
 H25.11   1 Thus here an ende;

ENDEWID (1)
 F26   2 Endewid with vertu and goodly plesaunce,

ENDLES (1)
 F36.1   11 So ripe and endles was her payne.

ENDUR (1)
 H67.2   7 Whyls lyf endur,

ENDURE (12)
 R13.1   2 Thus under sylens I do endure,
 F6.2   6 Endure this
 F25.2   4 While I endure,
 F26   4 With welth and wordly joy long to endure,
 H28   2 Thus ever to endure;
 H47.5   3 Thus longe to endure,
 H67.2   5 But to endure
 H75   9 And thus I wyll endure;
 H103.2   2 To se the paynes that I endure
 H106.2   6 In dysdayn I shall my lyfe endure,
 H106.2   7 Endure, alas, withowt hope of recure.
 H108   6 But leve in payne whyls I endure

ENDURS (2)
 F29.1   1 As I me walkyd this endurs day
 F30.1   1 This endurs nyght

ENDYGHT (1)
 H29.1   1 Iff I had wytt for to endyght

ENDYNG (1)
F48.1   3   Hevyn bliss thyn eritage withoute endyng

ENERYTAUNCE (1)
F44.2   4   With joy to rejose his dew enerytaunce,

ENFORCE (1)
F47b   1   Enforce yourselfe as Goddis knyght

ENFORCYNG (1)
F47.1   6   Enforcyng yourselfe with all your myght

ENFORCYTH (1)
H34.2   1   For love enforcyth all nobyle kynd,

ENFORSED (1)
R2.1   2   Enforsed me this complaynte for to make,

ENGLAND (1)
H101.1   3   For all the golde in England

ENGLISSH (1)
F43.2   1   Rutterkyn can speke no Englissh;

ENGLOND (1)
H96b   1   Englond, be glad! Pluk up thy lusty hart!

ENMYS (1)
F34.1   7   Gayne gostly enmys thynk on my passion;

ENOUGH (1)
H65.1   4   And shot well enough:

ENRYCHYD (1)
F11   5   Thus hath now grace enrychyd my plesaunce,

ENSERCH (1)
H44.2   1   Nobyll men then wold suer enserch

ENSEW (1)
H92.6   2   As well vices as vertuus to ensew;

ENSUE (1)
H92.1   1   Lusti yough shuld us ensue,

ENSURE (5)
F25.2   8   I you ensure.
F37.4   3   'Remembir the, my creature, thou must nedis dye,
                 I the ensure.
F46.1   4   As fortune fallyth, I yow ensure;
F49.1   3   What paynys I sofferd, I the ensure,
H75   6   So my hart to her I ensure;

82

ENTENT (8)
```
R2.2      2   To myn entent, and so sayeth mo then I,
F22       6   To gett mystrust is his entent
F24.4     8   For myn entent.
F24.5     2   To an entent;
F25.3     2   With good entent,
H79.1     2   Hys entent must nedys be trew,
H107.4    8   Fro myn entent.
H107.5    2   To an entent;
```

ENTERLY (1)
```
F27.3     1   'On that I love most enterly.'
```

ENTRETID (2)
```
F33.1     5   Unkyndly entretid,
F33.2     8   Entretid, thus in most cruell wise
```

ENTRETYNG (1)
```
F31.3     1   A Jhesu, whi suffyrd thou such entretyng,
```

ENVIRED (1)
```
R7        1   Thow man, envired with temptacion,
```

ENVY (2)
```
F34.4     3   Gayne fals envy thynk on my charyte,
H44.3     1   Butt envy reynyth with such dysdayne,
```

EQUITE (1)
```
H92.5     1   With goode order, councell and equite,
```

ERITAGE (1)
```
F48.1     3   Hevyn bliss thyn eritage withoute endyng
```

ERLY (1)
```
R6        5   Both erly, late, by day and by nyghth.
```

ERROR (1)
```
H92.4     2   Though that dysdaynars wold therin put error,
```

ERTH (2)
```
F36.4     4   The erth quakyd, the son was dark, whos lyght was
                  past
F47.1     1   Soverayn lorde, in erth most excellent,
```

ERTHE (1)
```
F48.3     1   Witness, the erthe that did quake,
```

ERTHLY (1)
```
F5        6   That I am bownde above all erthly thyng
```

ESCHEW (2)
```
R12.3     6   The worst eschew,
R13.3     6   And all othyr for hyr sake to eschew,
```

ESE (1)
R4   7   That myght my herte in more ese bryng.

ESPECYALL (1)
H25.11   4   And in especyall

ESSHEWE (1)
F25.3   8   All other to esshewe.

ESTRIGE (1)
F44b   2   Good Lord, preserve the Estrige Fether!

EVER (17)
R6   4   Ever to plese hym with all myghth,
R10.5   8   Thus ever fynd I;
R10.6   1   Thus ever y fynd
F38.1   4   That helpis the ever at thi most nede.
F45.1   7   And ever she sang:
F46.2   4   Plesaunt, buxum, and ever obedient,
H28   2   Thus ever to endure;
H29.6   1   My hart she hath and ever shall
H31.4   4   So ever and ay
H33.1   3   So I am, ever hath bene,
H33.4   4   Be suere, and ever shall.
H40   4   My hart with her ever shall be.
H50.4   4   Next God but he and ever prest
H50.6   3   He hath my hart and ever shall.
H63.2   3   My hart ys yours where ever that I go;
H65.3   4   As well as any that ever I see:
H106.2   2   Exilide for ever which is my payne;

EVERMORE (2)
H24   4   To serve you evermore.
H27.1   4   Farewell, my joy, for evermore.

EVERY (19)
R11.3   2   Dame Petyles yn every place over all;
R12.3   4   But every man hath hys frewyll.
F10   3   In every place ryght hath residens
F10   5   Ther is trewly in every case consolacion
F10   8   Now raynyth trewly in every mannys syght.
F19   4   And so sodenly will chaunge in every degre;
F25.1   3   In every vayne
F32.2   5   To joy of every wordlis wight,
F36.1   2   And theruppon straynyd he was in every vayne;
F37.1   2   My mode is changid in every wise,
F40.1   1   Hit is so praty in every degre;
F44.2   3   In every case be his preservacion,
F46.1   1   Love is naturall to every wyght,
F46.1   2   Indyfferent to every creature,
H20   4   The byrdys sang on every syde
H31.2   4   'In every place
H50.3   1   My soverayne lorde in every thyng
H62.3   1   Every bowe for me ys to bygge;

EVERY (cont.)
  H74   1   Deme the best of every dowt

EVERYBODY (1)
  R3.1   5   'Wene ye that everybody lest to play?'

EVERYCHONE (1)
  F6.4   6   But everychone

EVYDENT (1)
  F47.1   3   With gyfftes grete and evydent

EVYLL (2)
  R10.4   7   Thus evyll Y fare,
  F32b   4   Or otherwise evyll apaide?

EVYR (4)
  F21   7   Hough that evyr it will happ I wote nere I.
  F41.4   3   The best chepe flessh that evyr I bought.'
  F45.2   7   And evyr she sang:
  F49b   4   And aske forgeveness or evyr thou dye.'

EXCELLENT (1)
  F47.1   1   Soverayn lorde, in erth most excellent,

EXCHO (1)
  H79.2   6   Wherfor, then, shuld we yt excho?

EXCUSE (1)
  R9   7   Besechyng yeure excuse, ther Y supprise;

EXILD (1)
  H18   2   Now am I exild my lady fro

EXILED (1)
  H106.2   1   My hope frome me is clene exiled,

EXILIDE (1)
  H106.2   2   Exilide for ever which is my payne;

EXPRESS (2)
  F20   3   Which that passyth my mynde for to express
  F31.4   3   And why, good Lord? Express thi mynd!

EXPRESSE (1)
  H47.1   1   Wherto shuld I expresse

EY (1)
  H51.6   2   Myne ey with hart doth me so juge.

EYLYTH (2)
  F7.1   1   O my desyre, what eylyth the,
  F7.1   8   O my desyre, what eylyth the?

EYRE (3)
```
F44.1    9   Ryght eyre for to be;
F44.2    7   This eyre of Brytayne,
F44.2    9   Ryght eyre for to be;
```

FACE (5)
```
F27.4    1   'I chese a floure fresshist of face.'
F31.3    2   As betyng, bobbyng, ye, spettyng on thi face?
F37.2    4   My face disfygurid, myn yes full daslyng;
H27.2    1   Oft to me her godely swet face
H50.5    3   Beholde his favor and his face,
```

FACION (1)
```
F40.1    3   In favoure and in facion (lo, will ye se?)
```

FADER (1)
```
F48.2    6   In the awter I am offerd my Fader beforne;
```

FADIR'S (1)
```
F30.2    6   My Fadir's will.
```

FAITH (2)
```
H35b     2   Ther ys a do in yonder wode; in faith, she woll
                     not dy
H49.3    3   In faith my lady lovith me well;
```

FAITHFULL (1)
```
F46.3    3   To put in one my faithfull trust,
```

FALCE (1)
```
H34.7    2   With dysdayne bothe falce and subtell.
```

FALL (4)
```
F21      5   Lest that mysaventure myght fall be chaunce;
F34b     3   'I, a synner that offt doth fall.'
H29.6    3   Happe what wyll happ, fall what shall,
H92.5    4   Yough shuld fall in grett myschaunce;
```

FALLYNG (1)
```
F37.3    4   Grete mowntens fallyng over me, thus slepe doth I
                     yn feere
```

FALLYTH (1)
```
F46.1    4   As fortune fallyth, I yow ensure;
```

FALS (4)
```
R10.2    4   Apon fals love!
F14      6   Other by colour or by fals semblaunce;
F33.1    4   Begylde and betraide by Judas' fals treson;
F34.4    3   Gayne fals envy thynk on my charyte,
```

FANTASY (1)
```
F7.2     6   And all be folissh fantasy
```

86

FANTYSES (1)
R12.2   4   All thoftes and fantyses to dygest.

FAR (1)
F37.2   3   My tast disordyrd all reson far passyng,

FARE (1)
R10.4   7   Thus evyll Y fare,

FAREWELL (6)
H27.1   4   Farewell, my joy, for evermore.
H27.3   4   Farewell, my joe, and welcom payne.
H31.7   1   Adew, farewell,
H63.1   1   Farewell, my joy, and my swete hart!
H63.1   2   Farewell myne owne hart rote -
H109.4 4   Adew, farewell and kysse me now!

FARTHER (1)
F1   1   The farther I go, the more behynde;

FAST (6)
F30.1   8   Full fast abowte
F36.4   8   Wepyng and wrang her handes fast.
F49.1   6   Fast I was naylyd for thyne offence;
H25.8   5   Ful fast unlast
H35.4   2   But he ran fast afore;
H47.5   1   I make you fast and sure;

FATHIR (1)
F31.1   2   Egall to the Fathir in deite,

FAUT (1)
H44.5   1   The faut in whome I cannot sett;

FAUTTES (1)
H92.7   3   And that we may ower fauttes amend,

FAVOR (1)
H50.5   3   Beholde his favor and his face,

FAVOURE (1)
F40.1   3   In favoure and in facion (lo, will ye se?)

FAY (1)
F41.1   1   Ay, besherewe yow! Be my fay

FAYER (2)
H109b   5   To gather the flowres both fayer and swete.
H109.1 1   Now yn this medow fayer and grene

FAYLL (1)
H25.10 1   I schall not fayll,

FAYN (2)
R10.5   5   Wher Y wold fayn,
H47.1   3   No myrth can make me fayn

FAYNE (5)
R20.2   2   Withowt cause, Gode knowyth; Y do not fayne.
F9   1   Love fayne wolde I;
F23.2   1   Nor nought cowde have, wolde I nevyr so fayne!
F25.1   5   I wolde full fayne
H106.1   4   My lyffe as one that dye would fayne;

FAYNEST (1)
F16   3   And sone to sende where they faynest wolde be,

FAYNTE (1)
H35.5   4   For faynte she myght nott bray.

FAYNYNG (1)
F18.1   5   For ye with your faynyng

FAYRE (10)
R3.1   2   Now thyngke ye this ys a fayre ray?
R9   1   Fayre and discrete, fresche wommanly figure,
F23.1   7   That hath byn your fayre lady and mastress.
F23.2   7   Have but yourselfe, fayre lady and mastres.
F27.6b   2   This fayre fressh floure full of beaute;
F29.2   2   I sawe a maide fayre inow;
F42.1   1   Who shall have my fayre lady?
H29.1   2   Of my lady, both fayre and fre,
H35.1   3   She lay so fayre, I cowde nott mys;
H51.3   2   And she to hym most seme most fayre.

FAYRER (1)
F46.2   3   Consideryng dyvers fayrer and fetter,

FAYREST (1)
F42.2   1   The fayrest man that best love can,

FAYTH (1)
F21   2   In stedfast fayth and trouth with assuraunce;

FAYTHFULLY (1)
F21   3   Then bownden were I such on faythfully

FEATTES (1)
H34.1   1   Whoso that wyll all feattes optayne,

FEATYS (1)
H23.4   1   As featys of armys, and suche other

FEE (1)
F48.1   10   That am the cheffe lorde of the fee.

FEELD (1)
F39.3   3   In feeld ne strete;

FEELE (1)
F37.3   1   My voice is so trobled, my seknes then feele I;

FEER (1)
F36.2   4   That with dispaire for feer and dred I was nere
                 forlore

FEERE (3)
F11   3   That was my feere is nowe my sykyrness;
F36.3   1   Saynt Jhon than said, 'Feere not, Mary; his
                 paynys al
F37.3   4   Grete mowntens fallyng over me, thus slepe doth I
                 yn feere

FEERFULL (2)
F36b   1   My feerfull dreme nevyr forgete can I:
F37.3   2   My slepis be so feerfull, I thynk then sure to dye;

FEETE (1)
F36.4   1   Unto the cross, handes and feete, nailid he was;

FEITHEFULL (1)
R7   3   Remembre how feithefull, how treu, how kynde

FELD (1)
H96.1   1   Ageynst the Frenchmen in the feld to fyght

FELDES (1)
H109.1b 4   That now in the feldes we may us sportt?

FELE (2)
R13.2   4   That wondyd soere myself Y fele,
R18.1   4   Sayng, 'Y fele puerum movere;

FELL (1)
F36.2   10   Wherewith she fell downe with paynys so smert;

FEND (1)
H23.6   2   In goode dysporttys whych it dothe fend.

FENDE (1)
F32.2   4   Thi son was doughti, the fende was adradde;

FER (2)
F4   1   So fer I trow from remedy,
F4   2   And from all hope so fer banysshid

FERE (5)
R13.1   1   So put yn fere I dare not speke;
R19.1   7   She stode yn fere
F21   4   To love, thowe I do fere to trace that dawnce,

FERE (cont.)
F24.2   1   I fere doutless
H107.2   1   I fere doutles

FERRE (1)
R15.5   4   In ferre cuntre

FERTHER (1)
F1   5   The trewer I serve, the ferther out of mynde;

FERVENT (1)
H108   3   But love my fo, that fervent creature

FEST (1)
F37.1   4   So shortly am I bydyn to a grevus fest,

FETE (2)
F33.3   5   My fete and handis sore
F48b   7   In hed, in fete, in handis, in hart;

FETHER (1)
F44b   2   Good Lord, preserve the Estrige Fether!

FETT (2)
H23.5   2   For therby corage is suerly owt fett:
H51.2   2   Frome Venus sure he must it fett;

FETTER (1)
F46.2   3   Consideryng dyvers fayrer and fetter,

FETY (1)
F39.2   8   Of hir fety:

FEYNYNG (1)
H40   1   I love trewly withowt feynyng;

FEYTH (5)
R13.3   3   Or els yn feyth unkyndly she doth dele,
H109.1b 1   Nay, in good feyth, I wyll not melle with you;
H109.2b 1   Nay, in good feyth, [etc.]
H109.3b 1   Nay, in good feyth, [etc.]
H109.4b 1   Nay, in good feyth, [etc.]

FIFTEEN (1)
H101.3   2   The age of fifteen yere,

FIGURE (1)
R9   1   Fayre and discrete, fresche wommanly figure,

FIRST (1)
F40.2   3   That God hath ordent in his first formacion,

FLAVOUR (1)
F27.1   3   Columbyne goldis of swete flavour?'

FLE (2)
H35.7   4   Hys bolt may fle no more.
H65.2   3   I have strengh to mak it fle

FLEE (2)
R12.3   2   Ys vertu, and vyce to flee;
R19.3   7   That away woll flee,

FLESSH (1)
F41.4   3   The best chepe flessh that evyr I bought.'

FLO (1)
R19.2   7   And flo her way;

FLORE (2)
R3.3   6   'Now have ye leyde me un the flore,
F37.2   2   To lusty plesure? Now lyyng in the flore,

FLOUR (1)
F27.1   1   'I love a flour of swete odour'

FLOURE (8)
F20   5   The bryghtest myrrour and floure of goodlyhed
F27b   2   'I love a floure of fressh beaute;'
F27.2   1   'Ther is a floure where so he be,
F27.4   1   'I chese a floure fresshist of face.'
F27.4b   2   'I love a floure of fressh beaute.'
F27.5   1   'The rose it is a ryall floure.'
F27.6b   2   This fayre fressh floure full of beaute;
F45.1   4   She gaderd a floure and set betwene;

FLOURE-DE-LUCE (1)
F45.2   3   The floure-de-luce she did on rewe,

FLOURIS (2)
F45.1   3   Among the flouris that fressh byn.
F45.2   1   In that garden be flouris of hewe:

FLOURS (1)
H20   2   To geder the flours down

FLOWERYS (1)
H33.2   3   When flowerys cannot be sene,

FLOWRES (1)
H109b   5   To gather the flowres both fayer and swete.

FLYGHT (1)
H96.1   4   Bowys and arows to put them all to flyght:

FO (3)
R10.1   8   Fortune ys my fo.
F38.2   6   Fo all my lyff-daies I have myspend:
H108   3   But love my fo, that fervent creature

91

FODE (2)
F13   4 To her only which is myn yes fode,
F41.2   3 Strawe, Jamys foder, ye play the fode;

FODER (1)
F41.2   3 Strawe, Jamys foder, ye play the fode;

FOLE (1)
F40.4   2 Be lost so sone? I am a fole:

FOLISSH (1)
F7.2   6 And all be folissh fantasy

FOLLOW (1)
H92.2   4 But follow hys mynd in all that we may.

FOLY (3)
R10.2   6 Hyt ys foly
F7.1   4 Syn that it is playnly foly;
F18.2   3 Hade so grete foly

FONE (1)
H104.4   3 Crist kepe you from your fone;

FOO (2)
H31.7   3 Adew, bothe frend and foo!
H62.4   4 That beawtye ys my foo;

FOR (170)
R2.1   2 Enforsed me this complaynte for to make,
R2.1   7 For yet Y am all drowned in the lake
R2.2   1 For sche weche ys of all godely the best
R2.2   7 For till she amende Y shall have noght truly
R3.1   3 'Let go Y say, straw for yeur tale!'
R3.1   7 Y trow for all youre gret afray
R3.2   7 Y wolde not yette for furty pence
R4   2 For of my hert ye have the governaunce;
R4   4 For yeu, dere hert, thoff Y suffere penaunce
R4   5 All for yeure sake, til God me so avaunce
R5   1 The hye desire that Y have for to se
R10.1   3 And all for one;
R10.1   6 For on alone
R10.4   2 For Y am bare
R12.1   5 For my pastaunce
R12.2   5 For idelnes
R13.3   4 For she hath that I hadde in store,
R13.3   6 And all othyr for hyr sake to eschew,
R13.3   7 And never to chaunge hyr for no new.
R15.7   3 And all for oone;
R18.2   3 But for my mysse _michi_ _deridere_;
F1   4 The lyghter leefe, the lother for to wende;
F2   2 Ye thynk for to discomfort me.
F3   3 For when nature wold oft that I shulde wynk,
F4   5 Cannot be well for to be wisht:

F6.1	6	For with twayne
F6.4	4	For that to mone,
F7.1	3	In willfullness so for to be,
F7.1	7	Butt yff hit be to wissh for one:
F7.2	5	So for to se ye betrayd,
F8	3	Renewde of God for owre consolacion
F13	2	For my complayntes it dyd me nevir good;
F13	7	Syth for my trouth she nedith no wittness.
F14	2	For why I stond as he that is abusyd;
F17	6	For where I shulde, they be mery,
F18.1	5	For ye with your faynyng
F20	3	Which that passyth my mynde for to express
F22	1	Alas, for lak of her presens,
F23.2	6	Wolde in no wise for joy nor hevyness
F24.2	5	For unkyndness
F24.4	8	For myn entent.
F25.2	5	For to applye
F27.2	2	And shall not yet be namyd for me;
F29.1	2	To the grenewode for to play
F29.4	2	That men sekyth for to spill,
F29.4	3	For them to save, it is my will;
F29.5	2	For mannys gilt is not withstone,
F29.5	3	For thou art he that hath all wrought,
F30.2	4	Thus for to ly,
F31b	2	That God hymselfe for sole mankynd
F31.2	4	With wepyng, wayling, ye, sownyng for wo.
F31.3	3	Drawne like a theffe, and for payne swetyng
F31.4	1	'Lo, man, for the that ware onkynd,
F32.2	3	They bet him for oure gilt, though he no syn hadd;
F33b	3	For the ran,
F33.1	2	And be not hard-hartid, and for this encheson
F33.1	3	Sith I for thi sowle sake was slayne in good seson,
F33.2	1	Thus nakyd am I nailid, O man, for thy sake;
F33.2	3	Remembir my tendir hart-rote for the brake,
F33.3	3	Thus bobbid, thus robbid, thus for thi love ded;
F33.3	4	Onfaynyd, not deynyd, my blode for to shede:
F33.3	8	Than I have done, O man, for the?
F34.1	1	Uppon the cross nailid I was for the,
F34.1	3	Forsake thi syn, man, for the love of me;
F34.1	6	Be not dispayryd, for I am not vengeable;
F34.2	5	My hert ryven for thi redempcion.
F34.2	7	Love for love be just convencion;
F34.3	7	My blode best triacle for thi transgression;
F34.5	7	Now for thi moders meke mediacion,
F36.1	7	Alas, all for my gilt,
F36.2	4	That with dispaire for feer and dred I was nere
		forlore
F36.2	5	For myne offence, she said,
F36.2	8	Me unto grace for to restore:
F36.3	2	He willfully doth suffir for love speciall
F37.1	6	Thus trobled am I yet I trust it shalbe for the
		best

F37.2	6	Thus trobled am I [yet I trust it shalbe for the best
F37.3	6	Thus trobled am I [yet I trust it shalbe for the best
F37.4	6	Thus trobled am I [yet I trust it shalbe for the best
F38.1	5	Alas, for sorow myne hart doth blede
F40b	2	I am full sory for Jhoon's disease.
F41.2	4	I am no hakney for your rode;
F41.4	4	Yet for his love that all hath wrought
F41.4	5	Wed me or els I dye for thought!
F44.1	9	Ryght eyre for to be;
F44.2	9	Ryght eyre for to be;
F44.3	3	For this yong prince, which is and daily shal
F48b	5	For thi love, man, have suffyrd deth
F48b	8	And for I wolde have thyne heritage agayne,
F48.1	5	Not covetyng more for all my smert
F48.2	2	That I suffird not for the this payne,
F48.3	7	And, man, for the more sykyrnesse,
F49.1	6	Fast I was naylyd for thyne offence;
H12	1	Alas, what shall I do for love?
H12	2	For love, alasse, what shall I do,
H14	2	And sore I sygh for one.
H23.5	2	For therby corage is suerly owt fett:
H23.6	1	Vertue it is then youth for to spend
H25.1	2	For me, for me,
H25.1	3	My love sche morneth for me.
H25.1	6	Morne ye no more for me.
H25.2	6	And morne no more for me.
H25.3	6	And morne no more for me.
H25.4	6	But styll to morne for me.
H25.6	1	Her for to say
H25.6	4	Yet for all that
H25.8	6	And sayd sche morned for me.
H25.9	6	And morne no more for me.
H25.10	6	With her that morneth for me.
H25.11	6	My love that mornyth for me.
H27.1	4	Farewell, my joy, for evermore.
H27.2	4	Alas, for wo I dye, I dye.
H29.1	1	Iff I had wytt for to endyght
H29.1	4	Shall no man know her name for me.
H29.2	4	Shall no mane know her name for me.
H29.3	2	Nor for no new me chaunge doth she,
H29.3	4	Shall no man know her name for me.
H29.4	3	For she to me ys allway kynd;
H29.4	4	Shall no man [know her name for me].
H29.5	1	Lernyng it war for women all
H29.5	2	Unto ther lovers trew for to be;
H29.5	4	Whill I leve her name for me.
H29.6	4	Shall no man [know her name for me].
H30	2	For care is cast into my hart,
H31.2	6	Forsake me for a new.
H34.2	1	For love enforcyth all nobyle kynd,

FOR (cont.)

H34.7	1	Grett pyte it ware, love for to compell
H35.4	4	For I myght shott no mere.
H35.5	2	For I fownd wher she lay;
H35.5	4	For faynte she myght nott bray.
H49.3	2	For I fynd women trew;
H49.3	4	She will change for no new.
H50.1	1	My soverayne lorde for my poure sake
H50.1	5	And of all other for to love best
H50.6	4	Of God I ask for hym request,
H51.9	1	For often tymes wher they do sewe
H51.10	1	For whoso lovith shuld love butt oone;
H62.2	3	For I cannott shote in playne
H62.3	1	Every bowe for me ys to bygge;
H62.6	2	For and my santes booke,
H62.6	3	And pray I wyll for them that may,
H62.6	4	For I may nowght but loke;
H63.2	4	For yow do I mone.
H64.1	7	For when one sole
H64.2	5	For to procure
H65b	4	For shote ryght well I may.
H79.1	1	Whoso that wyll for grace sew,
H82.2	1	For yf thay war in lyk case
H82.2	6	It ys for yough the metest play.
H92.1	3	For whatsoever they do hym tell,
H92.1	4	It ys not for hym we know yt well.
H92.2	1	For they wold have hym hys libertye refrayne
H92.2	2	And all mery company for to dysdayne;
H92.3	2	But all dysdaynares for to refuse?
H92.4	1	For in them consisteth gret honor,
H92.4	3	For they do sew to get them grace
H92.5	3	For withowt ther goode gydaunce
H92.6	1	For yough ys frayle and prompt to doo,
H97	2	That for our kyng so to provid,
H101.1	3	For all the golde in England
H103.3	3	For which my hart is lyk to brest,
H104.4	6	For you have myne alone.
H106.1	5	Myn yes for sorow salt ters doth rayne:
H106.2	2	Exilide for ever which is my payne;
H106.3	1	Oftyme for death forsoth I call
H106.3	3	For death ys endar principall
H106.4	6	Nay, nay, for why? Ther ys no space.
H107.2	5	For unkyndnes
H109.3	4	Or elles I shall for you be ded.
H109.4	1	Then for this onse I shal you spare,

FOR-THI (1)

F34.3	2	For-thi contrite of thy contricion;

FORBEDE (2)

H109b	6	Nay, God forbede! That may not be -
H109.1b	5	Nay, God forbede! That may not be;

FORCE (1)
F12   3 The son, the moone, had lost ther force and light;

FOREST (1)
R19.2   4 To a forest wyde

FOREVER (1)
F46.3   4 Forever yff she will trew be,

FORFENT (1)
H23.1   2 But vice in it shuld be forfent.

FORFOUGHT (1)
R10.3   7 Full low forfought

FORGETE (1)
F36b   1 My feerfull dreme nevyr forgete can I:

FORGEVENESS (1)
F49b   4 And aske forgeveness or evyr thou dye.'

FORGOTEN (1)
F12   7 Thi lady hath forgoten to be kynd.'

FORLORE (2)
F36.2   4 That with dispaire for feer and dred I was nere
                  forlore
H103.1   3 Thus withowt comfort I am forlore;

FORLORNE (2)
F29.3   2 To save mankynd that was forlorne;
F48.2   3 [Rather then manne sholde be forlorne

FORMACION (1)
F40.2   3 That God hath ordent in his first formacion,

FORMYD (1)
F44.1   2 Which formyd hast of thi most speciall grace

FORSAKE (3)
F6.3   6 Plesure forsake
F34.1   3 Forsake thi syn, man, for the love of me;
H31.2   6 Forsake me for a new.

FORSAKYN (5)
R11.1   4 My lady hath forsakyn me.
R11.2   4 My lady hath forsakyn me.
R11.3   4 My lady hath forsakyn me.]
R11.4   4 [My lady hath forsakyn me.]
F37.4   2 Nature hath forsakyn me, and lefft me thus alone.

FORSOTH (1)
H106.3   1 Oftyme for death forsoth I call

FORTHE (1)
F41.4   1   'Walke forthe your way, ye cost me nought;

FORTUNE (13)
R8   1   Now helpe, Fortune, of thy godenesse,
R10.1   8   Fortune ys my fo.
F1   7   Is it fortune or infortune this I fynde?
F21   6   Yet will I me trust to fortune applye;
F24.4   6   Fortune doth wry
F24.5   4   Wellcum, fortune.
F46.1   4   As fortune fallyth, I yow ensure;
H103b   2   Such is fortune! What remedy?
H103.1   5   Such is fortune! What remedy?
H103.2   5   Such is fortune! What remedy?
H103.3   5   Such is fortune! What remedy?
H107.4   6   Fortune doth wry
H107.5   4   Welcum, fortune.

FORTUNES (1)
H50.6   5   Off all gode fortunes to send hym best;

FORTUNEYS (1)
R2.1   6   Y most obey fortuneys ordynaunce,

FORTUNYD (1)
F37.1   1   A blessid Jhesu, hough fortunyd this?

FORTUNYS (1)
R13.2   5   And no help but Fortunys whele,

FOSTER (16)
R1.1   1   Y have ben a foster long and meney day;
R1.1   4   Foster woll Y be no more.
H62.1   1   I have bene a foster
H62.1   3   Foster wyl I be no more
H62.1   5   Yet have I bene a foster.
H62.2   5   Yet have I [bene a foster.]
H62.3   5   Yet have [I bene a foster.]
H62.4   5   Yet have I bene [a foster.]
H62.5   5   Yet have [I bene a foster.]
H62.6   5   Yet have [I bene a foster.]
H65b   1   I am a joly foster
H65b   3   And foster will I be styll
H65.1   5   I am a joly foster.
H65.2   5   I am [a joly foster.]
H65.3   5   I am [a joly foster.]
H65.4   5   I am [a joly foster.]

FOTE (1)
F34.2   4   Percide hand and fote of indignacion,

FOUND (1)
R18.1   2   And found a maydyn sub quadam arbore,

97

FOUNDE (1)
R15.1   2   Ther founde I Besse

FOUR (1)
H50.1   3   Of which four tymes he dyd it take;

FOWND (3)
F28   7   Lest cause in me be fownd of offens.
F41.4   2   Now have I fownd that I have sought,
H35.5   2   For I fownd wher she lay;

FOWNDE (1)
F30.2   10   As it is fownde,

FRAUNCE (1)
F44.1   8   Of Ynglond and Fraunce

FRAYLE (1)
H92.6   1   For yough ys frayle and prompt to doo,

FRE (7)
F9   5   A lady fre,
F27.4   5   In hart so fre, that best lykyth me.'
F32.1   2   That the Son of God shulde make us fre,
F36.3   3   He hath to man, to make hym fre that now is
                  thrall.
F44.3   4   Be thi servaunt with all his hart so fre.
H29.1   2   Of my lady, both fayre and fre,
H101.3   3   In all this lond, nowther fre nor bond,

FREE (1)
F49.1   4   Where thou were thrall, to make the free.

FRENCHMEN (1)
H96.1   1   Ageynst the Frenchmen in the feld to fyght

FREND (2)
F36.3   4   'O frend,' she said, 'I am sure he is inmortall.'
H31.7   3   Adew, bothe frend and foo!

FRESCHE (2)
R9   1   Fayre and discrete, fresche wommanly figure,
R9   2   That with yeure beute and fresche plesaunce pure

FRESSH (6)
F8   6   A rose most riall with levis fressh of hew,
F27b   2   'I love a floure of fressh beaute;'
F27.2   3   Prymeros, violet, or fressh daysy,
F27.4b   2   'I love a floure of fressh beaute.'
F27.6b   2   This fayre fressh floure full of beaute;
F45.1   3   Among the flouris that fressh byn.

FRESSHIST (1)
F27.4   1   'I chese a floure fresshist of face.'

```
FRETID (1)
F33.1    6  With sharpe corde sore fretid,

FREWYLL (1)
R12.3    4  But every man hath hys frewyll.

FRO (7)
R4       6  That Y fro yew may hyre sume gode tydyng,
R15.7    4  So fro my hert
F33.2    5  Thus toggid to and fro,
H18      2  Now am I exild my lady fro
H47.2    3  Thow ye now parte me fro,
H63.2    1  Thowgh you depart now thus me fro,
H107.4   8  Fro myn entent.

FROM (27)
R8       3  From thy servaund, the weche hathe plente
R14.2    2  Takyn away from me bycause of hevynes;
F3       5  That be won thought my rest from me doth go.
F4       1  So fer I trow from remedy,
F4       2  And from all hope so fer banysshid
F22      3  Tyll deth my lyff departe from hens!
F30.1    9  Her Son from colde;
F34.4    5  Whi did I this? To save the from prison.
F34.5    6  May washe us all from surfettes reprovable.
F36.3   11  From deth to lyff he aryse shall.'
F43.4    1  When rutterkyn from borde will ryse
F44b     1  From stormy wyndis and grevous wethir,
F46.1    5  So rennyth the chaunce from one to one:
F48.2   10  Witness, the bodies that rose from deth to lyve.
H15      3  Sens I must nedys from my love depart
H25.10   3  From all other that be,
H25.11   5  From jebardyse all
H27.1    1  A the syghes that cum from my hart
H27.1    3  Sen ye must nedes from me depart,
H51.3    1  Or elles from her which is her hayre;
H67.1    3  From dole dolours
H104.1   3  From care and from all mone;
H104.4   3  Crist kepe you from your fone;
H106.4   2  My chance contrarious from all plesure,
H106.4   3  From all plesure to gret penance;
H108     5  From her love nothinge can me revert

FROME (8)
H31.5    6  Cryst kepe yow frome all care.
H33.3    3  Frome all other only
H51.2    2  Frome Venus sure he must it fett;
H62.3    3  The glew is slypt frome the nyk;
H63.1    3  Frome yow a whyle must I depart;
H66.1    4  Frome them shall I never vary:
H82.1    2  Frome Venus' ways banysht to be;
H106.2   1  My hope frome me is clene exiled,
```

FROMPILL (1)
F41.3   2   What, wolde ye frompill me now? fy, fy!

FROWARD (3)
F34.1   8   Whi art thou froward, syth I am mercyable?
F34.2   8   Why art thou froward sith I am merciable?
F34.3   8   Be thou not froward syth I am merciable.

FRYND (1)
R15.5   2   Withoute a frynd

FUCHESAFFE (1)
R5   5   That ye wilde fuchesaffe to have mercy on me

FUL (1)
H25.8   5   Ful fast unlast

FULFYLL (1)
H109.3   2   Wherfore ye muste my mynde fulfyll,

FULL (25)
R2.1   4   Full oghfte or this, Y shall undertake.
R2.2   3   Ys full but late oute of hur kyndely rest
R10.3   7   Full low forfought
R18.2   2   Full oft with you solebam ludere;
F5   3   Full lyk to drowne in wavis of dystres,
F10   2   Full sylde covetise hath dominacion
F25.1   5   I wolde full fayne
F27.5   3   'Both be full swete and of lyke savoure;
F27.6b   2   This fayre fressh floure full of beaute;
F30.1   8   Full fast abowte
F30.2   17   Naylid full sore,
F32.3   1   Well I remember his wowndis were full smert,
F36.4   2   Full boistusly in the mortess he was downe cast;
F37.2   4   My face disfygurid, myn yes full daslyng;
F40b   2   I am full sory for Jhoon's disease.
F43.4   2   He will piss a galon-pot full at twise
H31.1   6   Her hart was full of payne.
H31.6   1   Adew, full swete,
H31.8   3   Her dere hart was full nere
H51.5   2   But mynd afformyth with full consent.
H105.1   1   The moder full manerly and mekly as a mayd,
H105.1   4   Full softly and full soberly unto her swet son
              she saide
H105.2   2   Full lovely lookyng on our Lord, the lanterne of
              lyght
H105.2   4   This reson that I rede you now, I rede it full
              ryght

FURST (1)
F46.3   1   But I will do as I saide furst,·

FURTY (1)
R3.2   7   Y wolde not yette for furty pence

FUSION (1)
F34.5   4 That thi fyve wellis plentuus of fusion,

FY (4)
R10.2   3 And now, fy, fy,
F41.3   2 What, wolde ye frompill me now? fy, fy!

FYGHT (1)
H96.1   1 Ageynst the Frenchmen in the feld to fyght

FYLDE (1)
F10   4 Nethir in towne ne fylde simulacion

FYND (9)
R10.5   8 Thus ever fynd I;
R10.6   1 Thus ever y fynd
F10   7 Men may fynd day ne nyght adulacion
F19   7 Wherfore I hope to fynd a speciall remedy
F31b   4 My witt nor reson may hit well fynd:
F37.2   5 Thou, Nature, hast lefft me; by the fynd I no rest:
F37.3   5 So wakyng ne sleping fynd I no rest:
H29.3   3 But allway trew I do her fynd;
H49.3   2 For I fynd women trew;

FYNDE (6)
R16.1   3 So propyr I can none fynde as she;
R20.3   1 When Y fynde you stedfast and certayne,
F1   3 The more I sech, the wers can I fynde;
F1   7 Is it fortune or infortune this I fynde?
H12   4 I do yow fynde
H38   3 I fynde you not trew;

FYSSH (1)
F43.2   2 His tong rennyth all on buttyrd fyssh,

FYVE (2)
F34.5   4 That thi fyve wellis plentuus of fusion,
F34.5   5 Callid thi fyve wondes by computacion,

FYXED (1)
H51.6   1 Thus am I fyxed withowt gruge,

GAD (1)
F41.2   1 'Be Gad, ye be a prety pode,

GADERD (1)
F45.1   4 She gaderd a floure and set betwene;

GALON-POT (1)
F43.4   2 He will piss a galon-pot full at twise

GAME (2)
H35.6   1 I was wery of the game,

GAME (cont.)
H105.3   4   Now, gracious God and goode swete babe, yet ons
                 this game agayne

GARDEN (3)
F45.1   1   In a glorius garden grene
F45.2   1   In that garden be flouris of hewe:
F45.2   5   This garden to rule be ryghtwis lawe.'

GATE (1)
H41.1   1   The knyght knokett at the castell gate;

GATHER (1)
H109b   5   To gather the flowres both fayer and swete.

GAYNE (3)
F34.1   7   Gayne gostly enmys thynk on my passion;
F34.4   3   Gayne fals envy thynk on my charyte,
F34.4   7   Swetter than bawme gayne gostly poyson:

GAYNESAY (1)
H82.2   3   Thay may not now than gaynesay

GEDER (1)
H20   2   To geder the flours down

GELOFIR (1)
F45.2   2   The gelofir gent, that she well knewe;

GELOFYR (1)
F27.3   2   'Gelofyr gentyll or rosemary,

GENT (2)
F45.2   2   The gelofir gent, that she well knewe;
H31.9   2   That lady gent;

GENTERY (1)
R3.3   4   Ys this the gentery that ye can?'

GENTILL (4)
F19   3   So goodly, so curtesly, so gentill in behavyng;
F34b   1   'A, gentill Jhesu!'
F45b   2   This gentill day day dawes,
F45b   3   This gentill day dawes,

GENTYL (2)
H34.2   2   And dysdayne dyscorages all gentyl mynd.
H49.1   1   A Robyn, gentyl Robyn,

GENTYLL (4)
F27.1   2   'Magerome, gentyll or lavendour,
F27.3   2   'Gelofyr gentyll or rosemary,
F34b   10 'A, I will, I will, gentyll Jhesu'.
H47.3   2   Of your most gentyll mynde,

GENTYLNES (1)
  H25.4   2 O her gentylnes!

GEORGE (1)
  H97   6 Sent George, graunt hym the victory!

GESS (1)
  F24.1   8 What may I gess?

GESSE (1)
  H107.1   8 What may I gesse?

GEST (1)
  F37.1   3 Nature of aquayntance ys turned to a gest,

GET (2)
  H44.6   2 Which of ther loves doth get them grace?
  H92.4   3 For they do sew to get them grace

GETE (1)
  H51.2   1 And whosoever may love gete,

GETT (3)
  F7.1   6 Yet other grace can ye gett non
  F22   6 To gett mystrust is his entent
  H44.5   2 But let them tell which love doth gett.

GEV (1)
  R3.3   5 Take to gev all, and be stille than!

GEVE (2)
  R13.3   2 And geve me salfe unto my sore?
  H109.1b 3 Why, wyll ye nott geve me no comfortt,

GEVYN (5)
  F14   4 And no cause gevyn to be so refusyd;
  H18   3 And no cause gevyn therto:
  H34.5   1 Love ys gevyn to God and man;
  H50.5   1 So many vertuse gevyn of grace
  H79.2   3 But love us a thyng gevyn by God;

GILT (3)
  F29.5   2 For mannys gilt is not withstone,
  F32.2   3 They bet him for oure gilt, though he no syn hadd;
  F36.1   7 Alas, all for my gilt,

GLAD (5)
  R20.3   2 Y am right glad, tristyng hit woll remanyne;
  H35.1   4 Lord, I was glad of it!
  H75   8 Glad to do her plesure
  H96b   1 Englond, be glad! Pluk up thy lusty hart!
  H104b   5 To make me glad

GLADD (1)
F32.2 1 Methynkyth in my reson thou owfte to be gladd

GLADLY (1)
F31.4 2 Gladly suffyrd I all this.'

GLADNESS (1)
F11   1 That was my woo is nowe my most gladness;

GLADNESSE (1)
R2.1 1 My wofull hert of all gladnesse baryeyne

GLEW (1)
H62.3 3 The glew is slypt frome the nyk;

GLORIUS (2)
F32.4 1 Glorius Lady, of hevyn hie quene,
F45.1 1 In a glorius garden grene

GO (20)
R3.1   3 'Let go Y say, straw for yeur tale!'
R3.2   4 A, kan ye that? Nou, gode, go hens!
R15.6 3 "Go wach a byrde!
F1   1 The farther I go, the more behynde;
F1   6 Thoo I go lose, yet am I teyd with a lyne:
F3   5 That be won thought my rest from me doth go.
F28   1 Complayne I may wherevyr I go,
F39.1 5 I go or stond;
F41.2 5 Go watch a bole, your bak is brode.
F49.1 7 Therfore remembir the or thou go hence.'
H25.10 5 My hart to go
H35.4 1 He to go and I to go,
H39   4 Now after wyll I go;
H41b   3 To the grenewode must we go, alas!
H62.4 2 Owt of her courte to go;
H63.2 3 My hart ys yours where ever that I go;
H109b 2 Mayde, whether go you?
H109b 3 I go to the medowe to mylke my cow.
H109.1b 2 I pray you, sir, lett me go mylke my cow!

GOD (32)
R2.2   5 Now Y pray God and that righth hertily
R3.3   1 Cum kys me! 'Nay!' Be God, ye shall!
R4   5 All for yeure sake, til God me so avaunce
R12.1 4 So God be plecyd, this lyve woll I;
R18.4 4 I shall lose God et vitam eternam.'
F8   3 Renewde of God for owre consolacion
F26   5 I pray God hartely, withoutyn mysaventure.
F31b   2 That God hymselfe for sole mankynd
F32.1 2 That t_e Son of God shulde make us fre,
F38.1 7 I crye God mercy, I will amend.
F38.2 2 To God above I call and crye;
F38.2 7 I crye God mercy, I will amend.
F40.2 3 That God hath ordent in his first formacion,

GOD (cont.)

F47.1	2	Whom God hath chose oure gyde to be,
F47.2	1	God hath gyff you of his goodness
H23.3	1	And they be plesant to God and man,
H27.4	2	As wol to God I cowld,
H31.5	5	To god perteynyng,
H34.5	1	Love ys gevyn to God and man;
H50.4	4	Next God but he and ever prest
H50.6	4	Of God I ask for hym request,
H62.5	1	My berd ys so hard, God wote,
H64.2	12	God yt amen.
H66.1	3	God and my ryght and my dewtye,
H66.4	2	Pray we to God and Seynt Mary
H79.2	3	But love us a thyng gevyn by God;
H92.7	1	Now unto God thys prayer we make,
H97	1	Pray we to God that all may gyde
H104.4	4	And God above
H105.3	4	Now, gracious God and goode swete babe, yet ons this game agayne
H109b	6	Nay, God forbede! That may not be -
H109.1b	5	Nay, God forbede! That may not be;

GODDIS (1)

| F47b | 1 | Enforce yourselfe as Goddis knyght |

GODE (8)

R2.1	5	Till gode tydinges com my sorwe to slake
R3.2	4	A, kan ye that? Nou, gode, go hens!
R4	6	That Y fro yew may hyre sume gode tydyng,
R12.3	3	Cumpany ys gode or yll,
R15.4	3	With gode devyse,
R20.2	2	Withowt cause, Gode knowyth; Y do not fayne.
H25.4	4	The Gode above
H50.6	5	Off all gode fortunes to send hym best;

GODELY (4)

R2.2	1	For sche weche ys of all godely the best
R5	2	The godely and wommanly bewte
R12.1	8	All godely sport
H27.2	1	Oft to me her godely swet face

GODENESSE (1)

| R8 | 1 | Now helpe, Fortune, of thy godenesse, |

GODLYEST (1)

| H50.5 | 4 | His personage most godlyest! |

GODNES (1)

| H29.1 | 3 | Of her godnes than wold I wryght; |

GOED (1)

| R18.2 | 4 | With right goed cause incipeo flere. |

GOLDE (1)
H101.1 3 For all the golde in England

GOLDIS (1)
F27.1 3 Columbyne goldis of swete flavour?'

GON (2)
R10.1 5 My myrth ys gon
R15.7 6 Thof he be gon.

GONE (10)
R14.2   1 My blossum bright ys gone,
R15.3   6 And now ys gone.
R19.3   1 Whan she was gone
F40.3   2 What shulde I say? My mynde is gone.
F45b   4 And I must home gone.
F46.3   5 And love her only whereever she gone:
H33.2   4 And grenewode levys be gone.
H39   3 My love is to the grenewode gone,
H104b   3 And where be ye gone?
H104.2   3 My myrth and joy is gone;

GOO (1)
R15.4 4 And let hym goo,

GOOD (27)
R12.1   1 Passetyme with good cumpanye
R12.2   2 Of good or yll some pastaunce;
F13   2 For my complayntes it dyd me nevir good;
F15   4 To be put owte of your good governaunce . . .
F25.3   2 With good entent,
F31.4   3 And why, good Lord? Express thi mynd!
F33.1   3 Sith I for thi sowle sake was slayne in good seson,
F37.4   4 Alas, to dye thou makyst me sure; yet then, good
                 Lord, do thou thi cure
F37.4   5 With all good sowlis to cause me lyve in rest.
F40b   3 Alak, good Jhoane, what may you please?
F40.1   2 Good Lord, who may a goodlyer be
F40.1   5 Alak, good Jhoone, [what may you please?
F40.2   5 Alak, good [Jhoone, what may you please?
F40.3   5 Alak, good Jhoan, [what may you please?
F40.4   1 Alas, good Jhoan, shall all my mone
F40.4   5 Alak, good Jhoan, [what may you please?
F43.3   1 Rutterkyn shall bryng you all good luk;
F44b   2 Good Lord, preserve the Estrige Fether!
F44.2   1 Wherfore, good Lord, syth of thi creacion
F44.3   1 Now, good Lady among thi sayntes all,
F46.2   1 One is good, but mo were bettyr
H106.4   4 Right suere to have no good aventure,
H106.4   5 Good aventure in me to have place:
H109.1b   1 Nay, in good feyth, I wyll not melle with you;
H109.2b   1 Nay, in good feyth, [etc.]
H109.3b   1 Nay, in good feyth, [etc.]
H109.4b   1 Nay, in good feyth, [etc.]

GOODE (8)
F32.4   5   His deth was swete, hit did us goode;
H23.6   2   In goode dysporttys whych it dothe fend.
H25.11   2   Goode Lorde, deffend
H31.8   4   And saide, 'Goode mayde,
H92.5   1   With goode order, councell and equite,
H92.5   2   Goode Lord, graunt us our mancyon to be!
H92.5   3   For withowt ther goode gydaunce
H105.3   4   Now, gracious God and goode swete babe, yet ons
                   this game agayne

GOODLY (4)
F19   3   So goodly, so curtesly, so gentill in behavyng;
F26   2   Endewid with vertu and goodly plesaunce,
F39.1   1   That goodly las,
H96.1   3   With spers and sheldys on goodly horsys lyght,

GOODLYER (1)
F40.1   2   Good Lord, who may a goodlyer be

GOODLYHED (1)
F20   5   The bryghtest myrrour and floure of goodlyhed,

GOODNESS (1)
F47.2   1   God hath gyff you of his goodness

GOSTLY (2)
F34.1   7   Gayne gostly enmys thynk on my passion;
F34.4   7   Swetter than bawme gayne gostly poyson:

GOTEN (2)
R15.3   5   Goten with child
H82.2   2   And wold then have goten grace,

GOTHE (2)
H35.3   1   There she gothe! Se ye nott,
H35.3   2   How she gothe over the playne?

GOVERNAUNCE (2)
R4   2   For of my hert ye have the governaunce;
F15   4   To be put owte of your good governaunce . . .

GOWNE (1)
F43.1   2   In a cloke withoute cote or gowne,

GRACE (17)
R9   6   Unly to yeure swete grace a thousande sithe
R13.1   7   Abydyng your grace yn hope of mercy.
F2   5   Sum other grace may cum, perde;
F5   4   Saffe helpe and grace of my lord and soverayne,
F7.1   6   Yet other grace can ye gett non
F8   4   By dropys of grace that on them down doth rayn;
F11   5   Thus hath now grace enrychyd my plesaunce,
F36.2   8   Me unto grace for to restore:

GRACE (cont.)

F38.2	3	I will axe grace while I am able,
F44.1	2	Which formyd hast of thi most speciall grace
H25.5	4	Now of sum grace
H44.6	2	Which of ther loves doth get them grace?
H50.5	1	So many vertuse gevyn of grace
H79.1	1	Whoso that wyll for grace sew,
H82.2	2	And wold then have goten grace,
H92.4	3	For they do sew to get them grace
H102.1	1	My lady hath me in that grace

GRACIOUS (1)

| H105.3 | 4 | Now, gracious God and goode swete babe, yet ons |
| | | this game agayne |

GRACIUS (1)

| R5 | 4 | Prayng to yeure gracius pyte |

GRAUNT (5)

F34.5	3	O Jhesu, graunt of thi benignite
F44.1	4	In honor to rayne, Lord, graunt hym tyme and space,
F48.1	1	A, man, I have yevyn and made a graunt
H92.5	2	Goode Lord, graunt us our mancyon to be!
H97	6	Sent George, graunt hym the victory!

GRAUNTE (1)

| H109.3 | 3 | And graunte me here your maydynhed, |

GRAVE (1)

| F34.3 | 5 | Role up this mater; grave it in thi reson: |

GRECE (1)

| F43.2 | 3 | Besmerde with grece abowte his disshe, |

GREFE (1)

| F11 | 4 | That was my grefe is now my alegeaunce. |

GREFFE (1)

| F23.2 | 3 | Wherfore of ryght ye shuld my greffe complayne, |

GRENE (9)

F42.1	3	Undir the levys grene?
F42.2	3	Undir the holy grene.
F45.1	1	In a glorius garden grene
H20	3	By the medows grene;
H33b	1	Grene growith the holy,
H33b	4	Grene growth the holy.
H33.1	1	As the holy grouth grene
H33.2	1	As the holy grouth grene
H109.1	1	Now yn this medow fayer and grene

GRENEWOD (1)

| H62.2 | 2 | Upon the grenewod bough, |

GRENEWODE (7)
```
R1.1     3   Y shall hong up my horne by the grenewode spray;
F29.1    2   To the grenewode for to play
F29.2    1   As I walkyd undir the grenewode bowe
F46b     1   Smale pathis to the grenewode,
H33.2    4   And grenewode levys be gone.
H39      3   My love is to the grenewode gone,
H41b     3   To the grenewode must we go, alas!
```

GRENWOD (3)
```
H65.1    2   Upon the grenwod bough?
H65.3    2   Upon the grenwod tre?
H65.4    2   Unto the grenwod spray?
```

GRENWODE (1)
```
H65.2    2   Opon the grenwode lynde?
```

GRET (12)
```
R2.2     4   Into gret sekenesse weche holdith hur grevowsly;
R3.1     7   Y trow for all youre gret afray
F23.2    2   My hart is yours with gret assuraunce.
F28      4   And she me takyth in gret disdayne:
F30.2    8   Gret passion
H47.5    2   It ys to me gret payne
H82.1    3   Thow that age with gret dysdayne
H92.4    1   For in them consisteth gret honor,
H97      4   He may acheffe this gret viage:
H106.1   6   Thus do I lyve in gret hevenes
H106.3   2   In releasse off my gret smert,
H106.4   3   From all plesure to gret penance;
```

GRETE (9)
```
R2.2     6   That she be voyded owte of the grete grevaunce;
R11.1    1   My herte ys yn grete mournyng,
R15.1    4   In grete dystres,
R19.1    10  Hyt ys grete wrong.'
F18.2    1   Hit were to grete pite
F18.2    3   Hade so grete foly
F37.3    4   Grete mowntens fallyng over me, thus slepe doth I
                 yn feere
F47.1    3   With gyfftes grete and evydent
F48.3    10  The grete daye of mannys mercy.
```

GRETLY (7)
```
R11.1    2   My mynd also gretly waylyng;
F19      1   Thus musyng in my mynd, gretly mervelyng
F24.4    3   And that gretly
F25.2    3   To you gretly
F38.1    2   Howgh gretly thou art bownd indede;
H107.4   3   And that gretly
H109.2   2   That ye gretly move my corage.
```

GRETT (2)
```
H34.7    1   Grett pyte it ware, love for to compell
```

GRETT (cont.)
H92.5   4 Yough shuld fall in grett myschaunce;

GRETTER (1)
F17   4 Yet moreovyr a gretter payne,

GREVANCE (1)
H107.3 2 To my grevance

GREVANS (1)
R20.1   1 Your light grevans shall not me constrayne

GREVAUNCE (3)
R2.2   6 That she be voyded owte of the grete grevaunce;
F23.1   4 That was my wele is now my most grevaunce.
F24.3   2 To my grevaunce

GREVE (2)
H24   2 They greve me passyng sore,
H27.1   2 They greve me passyng sore;

GREVES (1)
R19.1   5 The greves among.

GREVID (1)
F36.2   1 His grevous deth and her morenyng grevid me sore;

GREVITH (1)
F3   6 And yet mythynkyth hit grevith me moche more

GREVOS (1)
H28   1 With sorowfull syghs and grevos payne

GREVOUS (3)
F36.2   1 His grevous deth and her morenyng grevid me sore;
F44b   1 From stormy wyndis and grevous wethir,
H44.4   2 Inwardly most grevous and sore:

GREVOWSLY (1)
R2.2   4 Into gret sekenesse weche holdith hur grevowsly;

GREVUS (2)
F37.1   4 So shortly am I bydyn to a grevus fest,
H106.3 6 Yet my lyfe is to me so grevus

GREVUSLY (2)
F38.1   6 To thynk how grevusly I have offend:
F38.2   4 I have offendid so grevusly;

GREVYTH (1)
H31.7   6 My hart it grevyth me so.'

GRONE (2)
R19.3   4 With sorowfull grone,

110

GRONE (cont.)
F46.2   5   Tyll sum of them begyn to grone:

GROUTH (2)
H33.1   1   As the holy grouth grene
H33.2   1   As the holy grouth grene

GROWITH (1)
H33b   1   Grene growith the holy,

GROWTH (1)
H33b   4   Grene growth the holy.

GRUGE (1)
H51.6   1   Thus am I fyxed withowt gruge,

GRUGGE (1)
R12.1   3   Grugge so woll, but noon denye;

GRYNNED (1)
F33.1   8   They mowid, they grynned, they scornyd me,

GUERDONLESS (1)
F13   6   And lett me not allway be guerdonless,

GUP (9)
F41.1   6   Gup, Cristian Clowte, gup, Jak of the Vale,
F41.2   6   Gup, Cristian Clowte, gup, Jak of the Vale,
F41.3   6   Gup, Cristian Clowte, gup, Jak of the Vale,
F41.4   6   Gup, Cristian Clowte, your breth is stale,
F41.4   8   Gup, Cristian Clowte, gup, Jak of the Vale,

GY (1)
H67.1   4   Ower Lord yow gy;

GYDAUNCE (1)
H92.5   3   For withowt ther goode gydaunce

GYDE (3)
R19.2   3   I shull her gyde
F47.1   2   Whom God hath chose oure gyde to be,
H97   1   Pray we to God that all may gyde

GYDYD (1)
H92.6   3   Wherfor be thes he must be gydyd

GYFF (1)
F47.2   1   God hath gyff you of his goodness

GYFFTES (1)
F47.1   3   With gyfftes grete and evydent

GYSE (1)
F43.4   3   And the overplus undir the table of the newe gyse;

GYVE (1)
F40.3   4   I-wis, she will not gyve me a bone:

HACE (1)
H31.2   5   I wot he hace

HAD (6)
R19.2   10   That she had lovyd so long.
F12   3   The son, the moone, had lost ther force and light;
F19   6   As I of aquayntance had never byn afore;
H29.1   1   Iff I had wytt for to endyght
H31.8   1   She had nott said
H101.3   4   Methought I had no pere.

HADD (1)
F32.2   3   They bet him for oure gilt, though he no syn hadd;

HADDE (2)
R3.3   7   But hadde Y wyste when ye bygan,
R13.3   4   For she hath that I hadde in store,

HADE (3)
R10.5   3   Hade yn dysdayn;
F18.2   3   Hade so grete foly
F34.3   1   I hade on Petur and Mawdlen pyte

HAKNEY (1)
F41.2   4   I am no hakney for your rode;

HALFF (1)
H25.7   5   Halff in a swone,

HANCH (1)
H35.5   3   And arrow in her hanch she hent;

HAND (1)
F34.2   4   Percide hand and fote of indignacion,

HANDES (3)
F34.3   4   He put his handes depe in my syde adowne.
F36.4   1   Unto the cross, handes and feete, nailid he was;
F36.4   8   Wepyng and wrang her handes fast.

HANDIS (2)
F33.3   5   My fete and handis sore
F48b   7   In hed, in fete, in handis, in hart;

HANG (4)
F34.4   6   Afore thi hart hang this litell table,
H65.1   1   Wherfore shuld I hang up my bow
H65.2   1   Wherfor shuld I hang up myne arrow
H65.3   1   Wherfor shuld I hang up my horne

HANGE (1)
H62.2   1   Hange I wyl my nobyl bow

HAPP (2)
F21   7   Hough that evyr it will happ I wote nere I.
H29.6   3   Happe what wyll happ, fall what shall,

HAPPE (1)
H29.6   3   Happe what wyll happ, fall what shall,

HARD (4)
F12   5   Yett more mervell how that I hard the sownde
H31.1   2   I hard a may
H62.5   1   My berd ys so hard, God wote,
H105.3   3   Yet softly to her swete sonne methought I hard
              her sayn

HARD-HARTID (1)
F33.1   2   And be not hard-hartid, and for this encheson

HARDE (1)
F49b   2   I harde a voice lowde call and crye

HARDELY (2)
F18.1   8   Nay, nay, hardely!
F41.3   4   Be Crist, ye shal not! No, no, hardely!

HARDY (1)
H50.2   4   As hardy with the hardyest,

HARDYEST (1)
H50.2   4   As hardy with the hardyest,

HARE (1)
R10.4   6   As carles doth ane hare,

HARRY (1)
H66.4   4   Thus sayth the kyng, the eighth Harry:

HART (65)
F2   8   Wherefor, my hart, lett be, lett be!
F5   1   My wofull hart in paynfull weryness,
F7.2   4   Thynkyth my hart can be well payd
F11   7   Your trewe servant with thought, hart and body.
F23.2   2   My hart is yours with gret assuraunce.
F25.2   6   With hart, body,
F25.3   3   My hart is ment,
F27.4   3   The rose, I suppose? Thyn hart unbrace!'
F27.4   5   In hart so fre, that best lykyth me.'
F32.3   2   The crowne on his hed, the spere at his hart,
F34.4   6   Afore thi hart hang this litell table,
F36.1   5   Myn hart can yerne and mylt
F36.1   10   Hough it thirlyd her thoroughoute the hart,
F36.3   10   And yet verely I know in myn hart

F38.1	1	A myn hart, remembir the well
F38.1	5	Alas, for sorow myne hart doth blede
F44.3	4	Be thi servaunt with all his hart so fre.
F48b	7	In hed, in fete, in handis, in hart;
F48.1	6	But a lovyng and a contrite hart,
H15	1	O my hart and O my hart!
H15	2	My hart it is so sore,
H20	5	So meryly, it joyed my hart
H25.1	4	Alas, pour hart,
H25.3	2	To me hart roote
H25.3	4	Wherfore, swete hart,
H25.7	6	It rewyd my hart to se.
H25.10	5	My hart to go
H27.1	1	A the syghes that cum from my hart
H27.4	4	Unto my hart as now she shuld.
H28	3	Alas, pour hart, tyl that we mete agayne,
H29.2	1	I love her well with hart and mynd;
H29.2	3	My hart to have she doth me bynd;
H29.6	1	My hart she hath and ever shall
H30	2	For care is cast into my hart,
H31.1	6	Her hart was full of payne.
H31.2	3	Her dere hart was untrew;
H31.3	6	Wherfore my hart will brest.
H31.4	6	Myne owne swet hart, adew.
H31.7	6	My hart it grevyth me so.'
H31.8	3	Her dere hart was full nere
H33.4	3	Who hath my hart trewly,
H40	4	My hart with her ever shall be.
H47.2	1	Do way, dere hart, not so.
H50.1	4	Wherfor my hart I hym beqwest,
H50.4	3	My hart with joe that I be hete
H50.4	5	With hart and body to love best
H50.6	3	He hath my hart and ever shall.
H51.6	2	Myne ey with hart doth me so juge.
H63.1	1	Farewell, my joy, and my swete hart!
H63.1	2	Farewell myne owne hart rote -
H63.2	3	My hart ys yours where ever that I go;
H64.2	8	Ther no hart rewith
H65.2	4	And kyll bothe hart and hynd:
H75	3	That hath my hart in cure;
H75	6	So my hart to her I ensure;
H79.1	3	And love her in hart and dede,
H92.1	2	Hys mery hart shall sure all rew;
H96b	1	Englond, be glad! Pluk up thy lusty hart!
H103.1	1	A thorne hath percyd my hart ryght sore
H103.3	1	O my swet hart, whome I love best,
H103.3	3	For which my hart is lyk to brest,
H106.1	2	My body languisshyng, my hart in payn;
H106.3	4	Of all the sorowes within my hart;
H108	4	Whose unkyndnes hath kyld myn hart;

HART-ROTE (1)

| F33.2 | 3 | Remembir my tendir hart-rote for the brake, |

HARTE (1)
F48.3   8   The wounde in my harte the seale it is,

HARTELY (1)
F26   5   I pray God hartely, withoutyn mysaventure.

HARTES (2)
F34.1   5   To contryte hartes I do remission;
H64.1   4   Bothe hartes alone

HARTIS (1)
H16   1   Adew, adew, my hartis lust!

HAS (3)
R15.8   2   Has thus lefte me
F27.4   2   'What is his name that thou chosen has?
H92.3   3   Yough has as chef assurans

HAST (2)
F37.2   5   Thou, Nature, hast lefft me; by the fynd I no rest:
F44.1   2   Which formyd hast of thi most speciall grace

HASTE (1)
R3.1   6   Abyde awhile! What have ye haste?

HASTY (1)
R20.4   1   An olde seyde saw: hasty men sone slayne;

HATH (38)
R11.1   4   My lady hath forsakyn me.
R11.2   4   My lady hath forsakyn me.
R11.3   4   My lady hath forsakyn me.]
R11.4   4   [My lady hath forsakyn me.]
R12.3   4   But every man hath hys frewyll.
R13.2   3   So depe hath thrylled my hert ynwardly
R13.3   1   She hath me hurt; why shold she not hele,
R13.3   4   For she hath that I hadde in store,
F5   2   Which hath byn long plongyng with thought unseyne,
F10   2   Full sylde covetise hath dominacion
F10   3   In every place ryght hath residens
F10   6   The pore pepull no tyme hath but ryght
F11   5   Thus hath now grace enrychyd my plesaunce,
F12   7   Thi lady hath forgoten to be kynd.'
F15   1   I am he that hath you dayly servyd,
F18.1   6   Hath such a demyng
F23.1   7   That hath byn your fayre lady and mastress.
F29.5   3   For thou art he that hath all wrought,
F36.3   3   He hath to man, to make hym fre that now is
                           thrall.
F37.4   2   Nature hath forsakyn me, and lefft me thus alone.
F40.2   3   That God hath ordent in his first formacion,
F41.4   4   Yet for his love that all hath wrought
F47.1   2   Whom God hath chose oure gyde to be,
F47.2   1   God hath gyff you of his goodness

115

HATH (cont.)

H29.6	1	My hart she hath and ever shall
H31.3	2	Hath chosen a new
H33.1	3	So I am, ever hath bene,
H33.4	3	Who hath my hart trewly,
H44.1	1	If love now reynyd as it hath bene
H44.1	2	And war rewardit as it hath sene,
H50.6	3	He hath my hart and ever shall.
H62.4	1	Lady Venus hath commaundyd me
H75	3	That hath my hart in cure;
H102.1	1	My lady hath me in that grace
H103.1	1	A thorne hath percyd my hart ryght sore
H103.3	2	Whos unkyndnes hath me opprest,
H106.2	3	My payne with hope hath me begyled;
H108	4	Whose unkyndnes hath kyld myn hart;

HATHE (2)

| R8 | 3 | From thy servaund, the weche hathe plente |
| R9 | 3 | Arested hathe my herte in sodeyn wise, |

HAUKE (1)

| H75 | 5 | As the hauke to the lure, |

HAVE (55)

R1.1	1	Y have ben a foster long and meney day;
R2.1	3	Weche Y have songe with wepyng yen tweyne
R2.2	7	For till she amende Y shall have noght truly
R3.1	6	Abyde awhile! What have ye haste?
R3.3	6	'Now have ye leyde me un the flore,
R3.3	8	Be Criste, Y wolde have schytte the dore!'
R4	2	For of my hert ye have the governaunce;
R5	1	The hye desire that Y have for to se
R5	5	That ye wilde fuchesaffe to have mercy on me
R6	3	And yet Y have do my besynesse
R12.2	1	Yowth woll have nedes dalyaunce,
F15	3	And mervell I have syth I not deservid
F23.2	1	Nor nought cowde have, wolde I nevyr so fayne!
F23.2	4	And with pite have me in remembraunce
F23.2	7	Have but yourselfe, fayre lady and mastres.
F25.3	1	I have yow lent
F27.4b	1	'Now have I lovyd, and whom love ye?'
F27.6b	1	'Nowe have we lovyd, and love will we
F28	2	Syth I have done my besy payne
F29.3	1	'Son,' she sayd, 'I have the borne
F33.3	1	Off sharpe thorne I have worne a crowne on my hede,
F33.3	8	Than I have done, O man, for the?
F34b	4	What woldist thou have?
F34.2	2	Loke on them well, and have compassion;
F38.1	6	To thynk how grevusly I have offend:
F38.2	4	I have offendid so grevusly;
F38.2	6	Fo all my lyff-daies I have myspend:
F41.4	2	Now have I fownd that I have sought,
F42.1	1	Who shall have my fayre lady?
F47.2	7	To have recover of ther unryght.

HAVE (cont.)

F48b	5	For thi love, man, have suffyrd deth
F48b	8	And for I wolde have thyne heritage agayne,
F48.1	1	A, man, I have yevyn and made a graunt
H29.2	3	My hart to have she doth me bynd;
H35.3	3	And yf ye lust to have a shott,
H50.3	5	To have the prayse of all the best;
H50.5	2	Ther is none one-lyve that have;
H62.1	1	I have bene a foster
H62.1	5	Yet have I bene a foster.
H62.2	5	Yet have I [bene a foster.]
H62.3	5	Yet have [I bene a foster.]
H62.4	5	Yet have I bene [a foster.]
H62.5	5	Yet have [I bene a foster.]
H62.6	5	Yet have [I bene a foster.]
H64.1	10	Then helpe must have
H65b	2	And have ben many a day,
H65.2	3	I have strengh to mak it fle
H82.1	4	Wold have yough love to refrayn,
H82.2	2	And wold then have goten grace,
H92.2	1	For they wold have hym hys libertye refrayne
H104.4	6	For you have myne alone.
H106.4	4	Right suere to have no good aventure,
H106.4	5	Good aventure in me to have place:
H109.3	1	Ye have my hert; sey what ye wyll.

HAY (2)

| R19.1 | 1 | Hay how the mavys on a brere! |
| F30.1 | 18 | Lyth in hay.' |

HAYRE (1)

| H51.3 | 1 | Or elles from her which is her hayre; |

HE (48)

R15.7	5	Shall he not stert,
R15.7	6	Thof he be gon.
R15.8	1	Alas, that he
F14	2	For why I stond as he that is abusyd;
F15	1	I am he that hath you dayly servyd,
F27.2	1	'Ther is a floure where so he be,
F27.2	4	He pass them all in his degre;
F27.3	5	Here is not he that plesyth me.'
F27.4	4	'That same is he,
F29.5	3	For thou art he that hath all wrought,
F31.2	1	He that wrought this wordle of nought,
F32.2	3	They bet him for oure gilt, though he no syn hadd;
F32.3	6	That he suffird that sharpe shoure!
F32.4	6	He bought us with his precious blode:
F34.3	4	He put his handes depe in my syde adowne.
F36.1	1	To Calvery he bare his cross with doulfull payne,
F36.1	2	And theruppon straynyd he was in every vayne;
F36.3	2	He willfully doth suffir for love speciall
F36.3	3	He hath to man, to make hym fre that now is thrall.

HE (cont.)
```
F36.3    4   'O frend,' she said, 'I am sure he is inmortall.'
F36.3   11   From deth to lyff he aryse shall.'
F36.4    1   Unto the cross, handes and feete, nailid he was;
F36.4    2   Full boistusly in the mortess he was downe cast;
F36.4    5   When he lamentable
F36.4    9   Uppon her he cast his dedly loke,
F43.4    2   He will piss a galon-pot full at twise
F49.1    1   'Beholde', he saide, 'my creature,
H31.2    5   I wot he hace
H31.3    1   Seth he untrew
H31.9    1   In armys he hent
H34.1    2   In love he must be withowt dysdayne,
H35.4    1   He to go and I to go,
H35.4    2   But he ran fast afore;
H41.2    1   To call the porter he wold not blyn;
H41.2    2   The lady said he shuld not com in.
H41.4    2   He said, 'Desyre, your man, madame.'
H41.5    2   He said, 'Madame, as your prisoner.'
H41.6    1   He was cownselled to breffe a byll
H50.1    3   Of which four tymes he dyd it take;
H50.2    5   He provith hymselfe that I sey best,
H50.3    3   In that he doth no camparyng
H50.3    4   But of a trewth he worthyest
H50.4    4   Next God but he and ever prest
H50.6    3   He hath my hart and ever shall.
H51.2    2   Frome Venus sure he must it fett;
H79.1    4   Els it war pyte that he shuld spede;
H92.6    3   Wherfor be thes he must be gydyd
H97      4   He may acheffe this gret viage:
```

HED (2)
```
F32.3    2   The crowne on his hed, the spere at his hart,
F48b     7   In hed, in fete, in handis, in hart;
```

HEDE (1)
```
F33.3    1   Off sharpe thorne I have worne a crowne on my hede,
```

HELE (1)
```
R13.3    1   She hath me hurt; why shold she not hele,
```

HELL (1)
```
F38b     2   And thynk on the paynys that byn in hell.
```

HELP (3)
```
R13.2    5   And no help but Fortunys whele,
H96b     2   Help now thi kyng, thi kyng, and take his part!
H96.1    5   Help now thi king [and take his part!]
```

HELPE (4)
```
R8       1   Now helpe, Fortune, of thy godenesse,
F5       4   Saffe helpe and grace of my lord and soverayne,
H25.5    6   To helpe my love and me.
H64.1   10   Then helpe must have
```

HELPIS (1)
F38.1   4   That helpis the ever at thi most nede.

HENCE (1)
F49.1   7   Therfore remembir the or thou go hence.'

HENS (5)
R3.2   4   A, kan ye that? Nou, gode, go hens!
F22   3   Tyll deth my lyff departe from hens!
H66.4   1   Then sone dyscusse that hens we must;
H104.2   1   When ye be hens,
H106.3   5   A payne it is, hens to depart,

HENT (2)
H31.9   1   In armys he hent
H35.5   3   And arrow in her hanch she hent;

HER (86)
R13.1   4   To her which ys my yoyus plesure;
R13.2   1   The sterre of Venus which I call her ye,
R15.1   6   Makyng her moone.
R19.1   4   To se her chere
R19.2   1   I bade her abyde
R19.2   3   I shull her gyde
R19.2   7   And flo her way;
R19.2   9   To take her pray
F9   7   Her man to be
F13   4   To her only which is myn yes fode,
F13   5   Trustyng sumtyme that she will chaunge her mode
F20   2   With vertu connyng her maner is lede,
F20   4   Of her bounte, beaute and womanhode;
F20   7   Thes vertues byn pryntyd in her doutless.
F22   1   Alas, for lak of her presens,
F22   7   To send to her to make me shent.
F24.5   8   Such is her wone.
F28   3   To love her best and no mo
F28   6   Tyll that I cum tyll her presens,
F30.1   9   Her Son from colde;
F36.1   10 Hough it thirlyd her thoroughoute the hart,
F36.1   11 So ripe and endles was her payne.
F36.2   1   His grevous deth and her morenyng grevid me sore;
F36.2   2   With pale visage tremlyng she stode her child
                    before
F36.2   6   Her Son was so betraide,
F36.4   8   Wepyng and wrang her handes fast.
F36.4   9   Uppon her he cast his dedly loke,
F39.1   8   To comfort her:
F39.2   1   Her lusty chere,
F39.2   2   Her yes most clere,
F39.2   4   In her beaute;
F40.2   1   Her contynaunce with her lynyacion,
F46.3   5   And love her only whereever she gone:
H18   4   Wherfor to her I me complayn, hey now!
H25.4   1   O her kyndnesse,

119

H25.4	2	O her gentylnes!
H25.4	5	Her schuld not move
H25.6	1	Her for to say
H25.6	3	I dyspraysed her beawte;
H25.7	2	I to her lept
H25.7	3	And sett her on my knee:
H25.8	2	I dyd her kysse;
H25.8	4	And her smalle waste
H25.9	3	And prayd her to be ble,
H25.10	6	With her that morneth for me.
H27.2	1	Oft to me her godely swet face
H27.3	1	I was wont her to behold,
H27.4	1	And I thynk I se her yet,
H29.1	3	Of her godnes than wold I wryght;
H29.1	4	Shall no man know her name for me.
H29.2	1	I love her well with hart and mynd;
H29.2	4	Shall no mane know her name for me.
H29.3	3	But allway trew I do her fynd;
H29.3	4	Shall no man know her name for me.
H29.4	1	Yf I to her than war unkynd,
H29.4	4	Shall no man [know her name for me].
H29.5	4	Whill I leve her name for me.
H29.6	4	Shall no man [know her name for me].
H31.1	6	Her hart was full of payne.
H31.2	3	Her dere hart was untrew;
H31.3	3	And thynkes with her to rest,
H31.8	3	Her dere hart was full nere
H33.3	2	Promyse to her I make,
H33.3	4	To her I me betake.
H35.2	3	I stroke her so that downe she sanke,
H35.3	4	I warrant her barrayne.
H35.5	3	And arrow in her hanch she hent;
H40	3	To love her sure whill I am levyng,
H40	4	My hart with her ever shall be.
H51.3	1	Or elles from her which is her hayre;
H62.4	2	Owt of her courte to go;
H75	6	So my hart to her I ensure;
H75	8	Glad to do her plesure
H79.1	3	And love her in hart and dede,
H102.1	2	She takes me as her howne;
H102.1	3	Her mynd is in non other place:
H102.2	4	Her to remember mest
H105.1	2	Lokyng on her lytill son, so laughyng in lap layd,
H105.1	4	Full softly and full soberly unto her swet son she saide
H105.3	1	Musyng on her manners, so ny mard was my mayne,
H105.3	3	Yet softly to her swete sonne methought I hard her sayn
H107.5	8	Such ys her wone!
H108	5	From her love nothinge can me revert

HERE (20)

| R3.2 | 5 | What do ye here within oure spence? |

HERE (cont.)
R14.1	2	Here Y am mysylf alone;
R14.1	3	With a dulfull chere here I make my mone,
R14.2	3	With a dulfull chere [here I make my mone,
R19.1	9	What doyst thou here?
F27b	4	'Than shal be provid here anon
F27.3	5	Here is not he that plesyth me.'
F27.4b	4	'Than shall be provid here anon
F27.6	3	'To here talke of them is my delite.
F27.6b	4	Than may be provid here anon
F29b	2	Here I sytt alone, alas, alone!
F34.5	1	Lord, on all synfull here knelyng on kne,
F44.1	3	Arthur oure prynce to us here terrestriall,
F48b	1	Be hit knowyn to all that byn here
F48.2	1	If any man will say here agayne
H25.11	1	Thus here an ende;
H35.7	1	Here I leve and mak an end,
H41.5	1	She said, 'Desyre, what do ye here?'
H66.4	3	That all amend; and here an end,
H109.3	3	And graunte me here your maydynhed,

HERE-AFFTIR (1)
| F48b | 2 | And to all that here-afftir |

HERITAGE (1)
| F48b | 8 | And for I wolde have thyne heritage agayne, |

HERK (1)
| F39.3 | 8 | Herk, my lady!' |

HERT (16)
R2.1	1	My wofull hert of all gladnesse baryeyne
R4	2	For of my hert ye have the governaunce;
R4	4	For yeu, dere hert, thoff Y suffere penaunce
R10.3	6	My hert ys braught
R12.1	7	My hert ys sett
R13.1	3	Unwetyng how myn hert to-breke
R13.1	5	Of my pore hert she may be sure,
R13.2	3	So depe hath thrylled my hert ynwardly
R13.3	5	Myn hert and love; what wyll she more?
R15.5	3	With hert onfayn;
R15.7	4	So fro my hert
R20.2	3	With hert Y wyll you plece and your love attayne:
F34.2	5	My hert ryven for thi redempcion.
F36.2	9	'Yet thou are unkynd, which sleith myn hert,'
F38b	1	A, myn hert, remembir the well,
H109.3	1	Ye have my hert; sey what ye wyll.

HERTE (5)
R3.3	3	Ye herte my legge agenste the walle;
R4	7	That myght my herte in more ese bryng.
R9	3	Arested hathe my herte in sodeyn wise,
R11.1	1	My herte ys yn grete mournyng,
F2	1	A, a, my herte, I knowe yow well;

HERTILY (1)
R2.2   5   Now Y pray God and that righth hertily

HERTIS (1)
R9   5   My lyves ladi and my hertis cure,

HETE (1)
H50.4   3   My hart with joe that I be hete

HEVENES (1)
H106.1 6   Thus do I lyve in gret hevenes

HEVENESSE (1)
R8   4   Of sorwe and all hevenesse.

HEVINESS (1)
R6   2   That Y am thus in heviness?

HEVY (3)
F31.3   4   Both water and blode, ye, crucified an hevy case?
F32b   3   Whi shuld she hevy be?
F46.1   3   Chaungyng his course, now hevy, now lyght,

HEVYN (3)
F32.4   1   Glorius Lady, of hevyn hie quene,
F44.1   1   O blessed Lord of hevyn celestiall,
F48.1   3   Hevyn bliss thyn eritage withoute endyng

HEVYNES (2)
R14.2   2   Takyn away from me bycause of hevynes;
H47.1   2   My inward hevynes?

HEVYNESS (2)
F23.2   6   Wolde in no wise for joy nor hevyness
F29.1   3   And all hevyness to put away,

HEW (2)
F8   6   A rose most riall with levis fressh of hew,
H33.1   2   And never chaungyth hew,

HEWE (1)
F45.2   1   In that garden be flouris of hewe:

HEY (8)
H18   4   Wherfor to her I me complayn, hey now!
H31b   1   Hey nony nony nony nony no,
H31b   2   Hey nony nony nony nony no!
H75   1   Hey troly loly loly!
H75   4   Hey troly loly loly loly!
H75   7   Hey troly loly loly!
H75   10   Hey troly loly lo!
H109b   1   Hey troly loly lo!

HIE (3)
F8   1 Lett serch your myndis ye of hie consideracion!
F32.4   1 Glorius Lady, of hevyn hie quene,
H20   7 The nyghtyngale sang on hie

HIM (1)
F32.2   3 They bet him for oure gilt, though he no syn hadd;

HIR (2)
F34.5   8 At hir request be to us merciable.
F39.2   8 Of hir fety:

HIS (44)
F22   5 And thus is the tyme of his song;
F22   6 To gett mystrust is his entent
F27.2   4 He pass them all in his degre;
F27.4   2 'What is his name that thou chosen has?
F27.5   2 'The red or the white? Shewe his colour!'
F32.3   1 Well I remember his wowndis were full smert,
F32.3   2 The crowne on his hed, the spere at his hart,
F32.4   4 Thi dere sone is past his trobill and his tene;
F32.4   5 His deth was swete, hit did us goode,
F32.4   6 He bought us with his precious blode:
F34.3   4 He put his handes depe in my syde adowne.
F36.1   1 To Calvery he bare his cross with doulfull payne,
F36.1   3 A crowne of thorne as nedill sharpe shyfft in his
                brayne
F36.1   4 His modir dere tendirly wept and cowde not
                refrayne
F36.2   1 His grevous deth and her morenyng grevid me sore;
F36.2   3 Beholdyng ther his lymmys all to-rent and tore,
F36.3   1 Saynt Jhon than said, 'Feere not, Mary; his
                paynys al
F36.4   3 His vaynys all and synowis to-raff and brast;
F36.4   7 His moder rufully
F36.4   9 Uppon her he cast his dedly loke,
F40.2   3 That God hath ordent in his first formacion,
F41.4   4 Yet for his love that all hath wrought
F43.1   3 Save a raggid hode to kover his crowne,
F43.2   2 His tong rennyth all on buttyrd fyssh,
F43.2   3 Besmerde with grece abowte his disshe,
F43.3   3 Till his brayne be as wise as a duk;
F44.2   3 In every case be his preservacion,
F44.2   4 With joy to rejose his dew enerytaunce,
F44.2   5 His ryght to optayne,
F44.3   4 Be thi servaunt with all his hart so fre.
F44.3   9 His savegard to be;
F46.1   3 Chaungyng his course, now hevy, now lyght,
F47.2   1 God hath gyff you of his goodness
F48.2   8 Witness, the son that lost his lyghth,
H35.7   3 I thynk his bow ys well unbent,
H41.4   1 She asked hym what was his name;
H50.4   2 His cherfull contenance doth replete
H50.5   3 Beholde his favor and his face,

HIS (cont.)
H50.5	4	His personage most godlyest!
H96b	2	Help now thi kyng, thi kyng, and take his part!
H96.1	5	Help now thi king [and take his part!]

HIT (9)
R15.4	1	Now hit ys so,
R20.3	2	Y am right glad, tristyng hit woll remanyne;
F3	6	And yet mythynkyth hit grevith me moche more
F7.1	7	Butt yff hit be to wissh for one:
F18.2	1	Hit were to grete pite
F31b	4	My witt nor reson may hit well fynd:
F32.4	5	His deth was swete, hit did us goode;
F40.1	1	Hit is so praty in every degre;
F48b	1	Be hit knowyn to all that byn here

HODE (1)
| F43.1 | 3 | Save a raggid hode to kover his crowne, |

HOLDE (1)
| R20.4 | 3 | Speke or ye smyte, barke or ye byte; holde yowre |
| | | hondes twane |

HOLDITH (1)
| R2.2 | 4 | Into gret sekenesse weche holdith hur grevowsly; |

HOLE (2)
| F33.1 | 1 | Beholde me, I pray the, with all thi hole reson, |
| F41.2 | 2 | And I love you an hole cart-lode.' |

HOLY (5)
F42.2	3	Undir the holy grene.
H33b	1	Grene growith the holy,
H33b	4	Grene growth the holy.
H33.1	1	As the holy grouth grene
H33.2	1	As the holy grouth grene

HOME (1)
| F45b | 4 | And I must home gone. |

HONDES (1)
| R20.4 | 3 | Speke or ye smyte, barke or ye byte; holde yowre |
| | | hondes twane |

HONEST (1)
| H92.3 | 4 | Honest myrth with vertus pastance. |

HONESTE (1)
| R12.3 | 1 | Cumpany with honeste |

HONG (1)
| R1.1 | 3 | Y shall hong up my horne by the grenewode spray; |

HONOR (3)
```
F44.1    4    In honor to rayne, Lord, graunt hym tyme and space,
F44.2    6    In honor to rayne,
H92.4    1    For in them consisteth gret honor,
```

HOPE (9)
```
R13.1    7    Abydyng your grace yn hope of mercy.
F4       2    And from all hope so fer banysshid
F19      7    Wherfore I hope to fynd a speciall remedy
F47.2    6    In your person all ther hope is pyght
H38      2    Hope and trust,
H106.1   7    Withowte hope or comfort off redresse.
H106.2   1    My hope frome me is clene exiled,
H106.2   3    My payne with hope hath me begyled;
H106.2   7    Endure, alas, withowt hope of recure.
```

HOPPID (1)
```
F29.2    3    A childe she hoppid; she song, she lough;
```

HORE (1)
```
R1.1     2    My lockes ben hore.
```

HORNE (6)
```
R1.1     3    Y shall hong up my horne by the grenewode spray;
H35b     1    Blow thi horne, hunter, and blow thi horne on hye!
H35b     3    Now blow thi horne, hunter, and blow thi horne,
                   joly hunter
H65.3    1    Wherfor shuld I hang up my horne
```

HORSYS (1)
```
H96.1    3    With spers and sheldys on goodly horsys lyght,
```

HOT (1)
```
R20.4    2    Love me lytell and longe; hot love doth not reyne;
```

HOUGH (3)
```
F21      7    Hough that evyr it will happ I wote nere I.
F36.1    10   Hough it thirlyd her thoroughoute the hart,
F37.1    1    A blessid Jhesu, hough fortunyd this?
```

HOUGHEVYR (1)
```
F19      2    Houghevyr such dyversite in on person may be,
```

HOW (27)
```
R6       1    O blessed lord, how may this be
R7       3    Remembre how feithefull, how treu, how kynde
R13.1    3    Unwetyng how myn hert to-breke
R19.1    1    Hay how the mavys on a brere!
R20b     1    How shall Y plece a creature uncerteyne?
R20.1    4    How sholde Y [plece a creature uncerteyne?]
R20.2    4    How sholde Y plece a creature oncertayne?
R20.3    4    How sholde Y plece a creature oncerteyne?
R20.4    4    How sholde Y plece a creature oncertayne?
F12      5    Yett more mervell how that I hard the sownde
```

HOW (cont.)
F31b	1	Jhesu, mercy, how may this be,
F31b	5	Jhesu, mercy, how may this be?
F31.1	5	Jhesu, mercy, [how may this be?]
F31.2	5	Jhesu, mercy, [how may this be?]
F31.3	5	Jhesu, mercy, [how may this be?]
F31.4	5	[Jhesu, mercy, how may this be?]
F38.1	6	To thynk how grevusly I have offend:
H35.3	2	How she gothe over the playne?
H41.8	1	Thus how thay dyd we cannot say -
H49.1	2	Tel me how thy lemman doth,
H66.2	2	How well dyd ye your yough carry?
H82.1	6	How thay dyd in ther most lust.
H92.3	1	How shuld yough hymselfe best use
H109.1	4	How sey ye, mayde? Be ye content?
H109.4	3	How in the medow ye mylke your cow.

HOWGH (1)
| F38.1 | 2 | Howgh gretly thou art bownd indede; |

HOWND (1)
| H65.4 | 1 | Wherfor shuld I tye up my hownd |

HOWNE (1)
| H102.1 | 2 | She takes me as her howne; |

HOWSE (1)
| F30.1 | 14 | Is in this howse |

HOYDA (3)
| F43b | 1 | Hoyda, hoyda, joly rutterkin! |
| F43b | 2 | Like a rutterkin, hoyda! |

HUGE (1)
| R3.1 | 8 | Ye will not make to huge a waste. |

HUMANITE (1)
| F31b | 3 | Wolde take on Hym humanite? |

HUMBLE (1)
| F34.5 | 2 | Thy deth remembryng of humble afeccion, |

HUMILITE (1)
| F34.4 | 1 | Thynk agayne, pride, on my humilite; |

HUNTE (1)
| R12.1 | 6 | Hunte, syng and daunce; |

HUNTER (3)
H35b	1	Blow thi horne, hunter, and blow thi horne on hye!
H35b	3	Now blow thi horne, hunter, and blow thi horne,
		joly hunter

HUNTER'S (1)
 H35.7   2 Now of this hunter's lore;

HUR (2)
 R2.2   3 Ys full but late oute of hur kyndely rest
 R2.2   4 Into gret sekenesse weche holdith hur grevowsly;

HURT (2)
 R13.3   1 She hath me hurt; why shold she not hele,
 H66.3   3 I hurt no man, I do no wrong;

HURTIS (1)
 F47.2   4 And specially hurtis of thi commynalte,

HYD (1)
 R15.6   6 The smocke ys hyd."

HYE (6)
 R5   1 The hye desire that Y have for to se
 F30.2   14 That is so hye,
 F38.2   5 Me to amend I will me hye
 F47.1   4 Of marshiall power and also hye dygnite,
 H33b   3 Thow wynter blastys blow never so hye,
 H35b   1 Blow thi horne, hunter, and blow thi horne on hye!

HYGHT (1)
 H41.3   2 Strangenes that lady hyght.

HYM (23)
 R6   4 Ever to plese hym with all myghth,
 R15.4   4 And let hym goo,
 F5   5 Is nowe be hym so comfortide agayne
 F5   7 To love and dred hym as my lord and kyng.
 F31b   3 Wolde take on Hym humanite?
 F36.1   6 When I sawe hym so spilt,
 F36.3   3 He hath to man, to make hym fre that now is
                thrall.
 F38.1   3 Thou thynkyst on hym nevir a dele
 F40.2   2 To hym that wolde of such recreacion
 F44.1   4 In honor to rayne, Lord, graunt hym tyme and space,
 H22   3 Avaunce hym to the companye
 H34.4   2 Dysdayne abattyth and makith hym colde.
 H35.4   3 I bad hym shott and strik the do,
 H41.4   1 She asked hym what was his name;
 H50.1   4 Wherfor my hart I hym beqwest,
 H50.6   4 Of God I ask for hym request,
 H50.6   5 Off all gode fortunes to send hym best;
 H51.3   2 And she to hym most seme most fayre.
 H92.1   3 For whatsoever they do hym tell,
 H92.1   4 It ys not for hym we know yt well.
 H92.2   1 For they wold have hym hys libertye refrayne
 H97   3 To send hym power to hys corage
 H97   6 Sent George, graunt hym the victory!

127

HYMSELFE (4)
F31b   2   That God hymselfe for sole mankynd
H50.2 5   He provith hymselfe that I sey best,
H64.1 11 Hymselfe to save
H92.3 1   How shuld yough hymselfe best use

HYMSELFF (1)
H22   1   Whoso that wyll hymselff applye

HYND (1)
H65.2 4   And kyll bothe hart and hynd:

HYNDER (1)
H51.9 2   Thay hynder lovers that wolde be trew.

HYNG (1)
F48.3 6   Myn owne seale therto I hyng;

HYR (3)
R13.2 7   Ther of right I apeyle hyr to be my surgyon.
R13.3 6   And all othyr for hyr sake to eschew,
R13.3 7   And never to chaunge hyr for no new.

HYRE (1)
R4   6   That Y fro yew may hyre sume gode tydyng,

HYS (8)
R12.3 4   But every man hath hys frewyll.
H35.7 4   Hys bolt may fle no more.
H41.6 2   And shew my lady hys oune wyll.
H79.1 2   Hys entent must nedys be trew,
H92.1 2   Hys mery hart shall sure all rew;
H92.2 1   For they wold have hym hys libertye refrayne
H92.2 4   But follow hys mynd in all that we may.
H97   3   To send hym power to hys corage

HYT (4)
R10.2 6   Hyt ys foly
R18.4 2   Shall Y hyt kepe vel interficiam?
R18.4 3   Yf Y sley hyt, quo loco fugiam?
R19.1 10 Hyt ys grete wrong.'

HYTHER (1)
F29.4 4   Therfor I cum hyther alone.'

I (429)
R1.2   3   I shall bygge me a boure atte the wodes ende,
R2.2   2   To myn entent, and so sayeth mo then I,
R10.2 1   Sumtyme was I
R10.2 5   Love I deny;
R10.2 8   This do I prove.
R10.3 1   Wheras I sought,
R10.5 8   Thus ever fynd I;
R10.6 5   I am put behynd,

128

I (cont.)

R11.3	1	Such a mastras I may calle
R11.4	1	I trow on me she wold rewe
R12.1	2	I love and shall unto I dye;
R12.1	4	So God be plecyd, this lyve woll I;
R13.1	1	So put yn fere I dare not speke;
R13.1	2	Thus under sylens I do endure,
R13.1	6	And so shall contynew tyll I dye,
R13.2	1	The sterre of Venus which I call her ye,
R13.2	7	Ther of right I apeyle hyr to be my surgyon,
R13.3	4	For she hath that I hadde in store,
R14.1	3	With a dulfull chere here I make my mone,
R14.2	3	With a dulfull chere [here I make my mone,
R15.1	2	Ther founde I besse
R15.5	1	Now may I wynd
R15.5	5	Men wene I be
R15.7	1	I cannot kepe
R16.1	3	So propyr I can none fynde as she;
R18.4	4	I shall lose God et vitam eternam.'
R19.1	3	I drew me nere
R19.2	1	I bade her abyde
R19.2	3	I shull her gyde
F1	1	The farther I go, the more behynde;
F1	3	The more I sech, the wers can I fynde;
F1	5	The trewer I serve, the ferther out of mynde;
F1	6	Thoo I go lose, yet am I teyd with a lyne:
F1	7	Is it fortune or infortune this I fynde?
F2	1	A, a, my herte, I knowe yow well;
F2	3	Nay, nay, nay, nay, I warne the well,
F2	6	Or else I thynke to be content
F2	7	With my desyre tyll I be spent:
F3	3	For when nature wold oft that I shulde wynk,
F4	1	So fer I trow from remedy,
F4	3	Was nevir man saff only I;
F4	6	To thynk my sorows, well may I complayne;
F5	6	That I am bownde above all erthly thyng
F6.2	3	Assuryd am I;
F6.2	5	That I wis
F6.3	4	I undyrtake
F6.4	3	That I must sett by;
F9	1	Love fayne wolde I;
F9	2	Yff I coude spye
F9	6	I wolde bynde me
F11	6	Wherfor I am and shal be tyll I dye
F12	1	Benedicite! Whate dremyd I this nyght?
F12	5	Yett more mervell how that I hard the sownde
F13	1	To complayne me, alas, why shulde I so?
F13	3	But be constraynt, now must I shew my woo
F14	1	Alas, it is I that wote nott what to say,
F14	2	For why I stond as he that is abusyd;
F14	3	Ther as I trusted I was late cast away,
F15	1	I am he that hath you dayly servyd,
F15	2	Thow I be lytyll in your remembraunce;
F15	3	And mervell I have syth I not deservid

F16	2	I pray daily ther paynys to asswage
F17	1	But why am I so abusyd?
F17	5	I wote nott where I may complayn;
F17	6	For where I shulde, they be mery,
F17	7	When that they knowe I am sory.
F19	6	As I of aquayntance had never byn afore;
F19	7	Wherfore I hope to fynd a speciall remedy
F21	1	I love, loved, and loved wolde I be
F21	3	Then bownden were I such on faythfully
F21	4	To love, thowe I do fere to trace that dawnce,
F21	6	Yet will I me trust to fortune applye;
F21	7	Hough that evyr it will happ I wote nere I.
F22	2	Whom I serve and shall as long,
F23.2	1	Nor nought cowde have, wolde I nevyr so fayne!
F24.1	8	What may I gess?
F24.2	1	I fere doutless
F24.4	2	Bounden am I
F24.5	5	Yet I ne went
F25.1	5	I wolde full fayne
F25.2	1	I thynk suerly
F25.2	2	Bounden were I
F25.2	4	While I endure,
F25.2	7	Tylle I dye;
F25.2	8	I you ensure.
F25.3	1	I have yow lent
F25.3	5	I am content
F25.3	7	Thowe I be shent,
F26	5	I pray God hartely, withoutyn mysaventure.
F27b	1	'I love, I love, and whom love ye?'
F27b	2	'I love a floure of fressh beaute;'
F27b	3	'I love another as well as ye.'
F27.1	1	'I love a flour of swete odour'
F27.3	1	'On that I love most enterly.'
F27.4	1	'I chese a floure fresshist of face.'
F27.4	3	The rose, I suppose? Thyn hart unbrace!'
F27.4b	1	'Now have I lovyd, and whom love ye?'
F27.4b	2	'I love a floure of fressh beaute.'
F27.4b	3	'I love anothyr as well as ye.'
F27.6	1	'I love the rose, both red and white.'
F28	1	Complayne I may wherevyr I go,
F28	2	Syth I have done my besy payne
F28	5	I-wiss yet will I not me complayne
F28	6	Tyll that I cum tyll her presens,
F29b	2	Here I sytt alone, alas, alone!
F29.1	1	As I me walkyd this endurs day
F29.2	1	As I walkyd undir the grenewode bowe
F29.2	2	I sawe a maide fayre inow;
F29.3	1	'Son,' she sayd, 'I have the borne
F29.3	3	Therfor I pray the, son, no more,
F29.4	4	Therfor I cum hyther alone.'
F29.5	4	And I, thy modir, alone.'
F30.1	2	I sawe a syght
F30.2	12	Suffyr shall I.

I (cont.)

F30.2	15	Ther shall I be,
F31.4	2	Gladly suffyrd I all this.'
F32.3	1	Well I remember his wowndis were full smert,
F33.1	1	Beholde me, I pray the, with all thi hole reson,
F33.1	3	Sith I for thi sowle sake was slayne in good seson,
F33.2	1	Thus nakyd am I nailid, O man, for thy sake;
F33.2	2	I love the, then love me; why slepist thou? Awake!
F33.3	1	Off sharpe thorne I have worne a crowne on my hede,
F33.3	7	What myght I suffir more
F33.3	8	Than I have done, O man, for the?
F34b	3	'I, a synner that offt doth fall.'
F34b	5	'Mercy, Lord, of the I crave.'
F34b	7	'Ye, my maker I call the.'
F34b	8	Than leve thi syn, or I nyll the,
F34b	9	And thynk on this lesson that now I teche the.
F34b	10	'A, I will, I will, gentyll Jhesu'.
F34.1	1	Uppon the cross nailid I was for the,
F34.1	5	To contryte hartes I do remission;
F34.1	6	Be not dispayryd, for I am not vengeable;
F34.1	8	Whi art thou froward, syth I am mercyable?
F34.2	8	Why art thou froward sith I am merciable?
F34.3	1	I hade on Petur and Mawdlen pyte
F34.3	6	Syth I am kynd, why are thou unstable?
F34.3	8	Be thou not froward syth I am merciable.
F34.4	5	Whi did I this? To save the from prison.
F34.4	8	Be thou not affraide sith I am merciable.
F36b	1	My feerfull dreme nevyr forgete can I:
F36.1	6	When I sawe hym so spilt,
F36.1	8	Tho I wept and sore did complayne
F36.2	4	That with dispaire for feer and dred I was nere forlore
F36.3	4	'O frend,' she said, 'I am sure he is inmortall.'
F36.3	7	I must nedis wofull be,
F36.3	10	And yet verely I know in myn hart
F36.4	10	Wherwith sodenly anon I awoke,
F37.1	4	So shortly am I bydyn to a grevus fest,
F37.1	5	Whereas I am ybid with bodily rest;
F37.1	6	Thus trobled am I yet I trust it shalbe for the best
F37.2	5	Thou, Nature, hast lefft me; by the fynd I no rest:
F37.2	6	Thus trobled am I [yet I trust it shalbe for the best
F37.3	1	My voice is so trobled, my seknes then feele I;
F37.3	2	My slepis be so feerfull, I thynk then sure to dye;
F37.3	4	Grete mowntens fallyng over me, thus slepe doth I yn feere
F37.3	5	So wakyng ne sleping fynd I no rest:
F37.3	6	Thus trobled am I [yet I trust it shalbe for the best
F37.4	1	Now, mercyfull Jhesu, to the make I my mone;
F37.4	3	'Remembir the, my creature, thou must nedis dye, I the ensure.

I (cont.)

F37.4	6	Thus trobled am I [yet I trust it shalbe for the best
F38.1	6	To thynk how grevusly I have offend:
F38.1	7	I crye God mercy, I will amend.
F38.2	2	To God above I call and crye;
F38.2	3	I will axe grace while I am able,
F38.2	4	I have offendid so grevusly;
F38.2	5	Me to amend I will me hye
F38.2	6	Fo all my lyff-daies I have myspend:
F38.2	7	I crye God mercy, I will amend.
F39b	2	Whom I now seke
F39b	4	I dare well say,
F39.1	4	I wote not where
F39.1	5	I go or stond;
F39.1	6	I thynk me bond,
F39.1	7	I se, in lond,
F39.2	3	I know no pere
F39.3	2	I cannot mete
F39.3	4	Woffull am I.
F40b	2	I am full sory for Jhoon's disease.
F40b	4	I shal bere the cost, be swete Sent Denys!
F40.1	6	I shal bere the cost, be swete Sent Denys!]
F40.2	6	I shal bere the cost, be swete Sent Denys!]
F40.3	2	What shulde I say? My mynde is gone.
F40.3	3	Yff she and I were together alone,
F40.3	6	I shal bere the cost, be swete Sent Denys!]
F40.4	2	Be lost so sone? I am a fole:
F40.4	6	I shal bere the cost, be swete Sent Denys!]
F41.1	5	Tully, valy, strawe, let be I say!
F41.2	2	And I love yow an hole cart-lode.'
F41.2	4	I am no hakney for your rode;
F41.3	5	I will not be japed bodely.
F41.4	2	Now have I fownd that I have sought,
F41.4	3	The best chepe flessh that evyr I bought.'
F41.4	5	Wed me or els I dye for thought!
F42.1	2	Who but I, who but I, who but I,
F45b	4	And I must home gone.
F45.1	2	Sawe I syttyng a comly quene
F45.1	5	The lyly-whighte rose methought I sawe,
F45.1	6	The lyly-whighte rose methought I sawe,
F45.2	6	The lyly-whighte rose methought I sawe,
F46b	2	Will I love and shall I love,
F46b	3	Will I love and shall I love
F46.1	4	As fortune fallyth, I yow ensure;
F46.3	1	But I will do as I saide furst,
F48b	4	That I Jhesus off Nazareth
F48b	8	And for I wolde have thyne heritage agayne,
F48b	9	Therefore I suffird all this payne.
F48.1	1	A, man, I have yevyn and made a graunt
F48.1	4	As long as I am Lord and Kyng,
F48.1	8	Love thi neyboure as I love the!
F48.1	9	This is that I axe of the,
F48.2	2	That I suffird not for the this payne,

I (cont.)

F48.2	6	In the awter I am offerd my Fader beforne;
F48.3	6	Myn owne seale therto I hyng;
F49b	1	In a slumbir late as I was,
F49b	2	I harde a voice lowde call and crye
F49.1	2	Whome I did make so lyke unto me,
F49.1	3	What paynys I sofferd, I the ensure,
F49.1	6	Fast I was naylyd for thyne offence;
H12	1	Alas, what shall I do for love?
H12	2	For love, alasse, what shall I do,
H12	4	I do yow fynde
H14	1	Alone I leffe, alone,
H14	2	And sore I sygh for one.
H15	3	Sens I must nedys from my love depart
H16	3	Wyth dowbyl sorow complayn I must
H16	4	Untyl I dye, alas, alas!
H18	2	Now am I exild my lady fro
H18	4	Wherfor to her I me complayn, hey now!
H23.2	1	Pastymes ther be I nought treulye
H24	3	That I cannot be prest
H25.2	4	My love, I say,
H25.5	1	Alas, thought I,
H25.6	2	I tooke this way,
H25.6	3	I dyspraysed her beawte;
H25.7	2	I to her lept
H25.8	1	When I sawe this
H25.8	2	I dyd her kysse;
H25.9	1	Then as I ought
H25.9	2	I me bethought
H25.10	1	I schall not fayll,
H27.2	4	Alas, for wo I dye, I dye.
H27.3	1	I was wont her to behold,
H27.4	1	And I thynk I se her yet,
H27.4	2	As wol to God I cowld,
H28	4	Joy shall I never ye may be sure.
H29.1	1	Iff I had wytt for to endyght
H29.1	3	Of her godnes than wold I wryght;
H29.2	1	I love her well with hart and mynd;
H29.2	2	She ys right trew, I do it se.
H29.3	3	But allway trew I do her fynd;
H29.4	1	Yf I to her than war unkynd,
H29.4	2	Pytte it war that I shuld be,
H29.5	3	Promyse I mak that know non shall
H29.5	4	Whill I leve her name for me.
H30	1	Alac, alac, what shall I do,
H31.1	2	I hard a may
H31.2	5	I wot he hace
H31.3	5	And I so trew,
H31.4	1	And now I may
H31.4	3	Optayne that I do sew,
H31.7	4	I cannott tell
H31.7	5	Wher I shall dwell,
H33.1	3	So I am, ever hath bene,
H33.3	2	Promyse to her I make,

133

I (cont.)

H33.3	4	To her I me betake.
H34.5	2	To woman also, I thynk, the same.
H35.1	3	She lay so fayre, I cowde nott mys;
H35.1	4	Lord, I was glad of it!
H35.2	1	As I stod under a bank
H35.2	3	I stroke her so that downe she sanke,
H35.3	4	I warrant her barrayne.
H35.4	1	He to go and I to go,
H35.4	3	I bad hym shott and strik the do,
H35.4	4	For I myght shott no mere.
H35.5	2	For I fownd wher she lay;
H35.6	1	I was wery of the game,
H35.6	2	I went to tavern to drynk;
H35.7	1	Here I leve and mak an end,
H35.7	3	I thynk his bow ys well unbent,
H38	3	I fynde you not trew;
H39	4	Now after wyll I go;
H40	1	I love trewly withowt feynyng;
H40	3	To love her sure whill I am levyng,
H41b	1	Yow and I and Amyas,
H41b	2	Amyas and yow and I,
H41b	4	Yow and I, my lyff, and Amyas.
H44.5	1	The faut in whome I cannot sett;
H44.6	1	To lovers I put now suer this cace -
H44.7	2	Better than do I, I thynk it so.
H47.1	1	Wherto shuld I expresse
H47.3	1	When I remembyr me
H47.3	4	That I shuld be unkynde.
H47.4	4	I love you and no mo.
H47.5	1	I make you fast and sure;
H49.2	1	My lady is unkynde I wis.
H49.3	1	I cannot thynk such doubylnes
H49.3	2	For I fynd women trew;
H50b	2	My soverayne lord I shall love best.
H50.1	4	Wherfor my hart I hym beqwest,
H50.2	5	He provith hymselfe that I sey best,
H50.4	1	My soverayne lorde when that I mete,
H50.4	3	My hart with joe that I be hete
H50.6	4	Of God I ask for hym request,
H51.6	1	Thus am I fyxed withowt gruge,
H51.10	2	Chaunge who so wyll, I wyll be none.
H56	2	I trust ryght wel of retorn agane.
H62.1	1	I have bene a foster
H62.1	3	Foster wyl I be no more
H62.1	4	No lenger shote I may;
H62.1	5	Yet have I bene a foster.
H62.2	1	Hange I wyl my nobyl bow
H62.2	3	For I cannott shote in playne
H62.2	5	Yet have I [bene a foster.]
H62.3	4	When I shuld shoote I myse;
H62.3	5	Yet have [I bene a foster.]
H62.4	5	Yet have I bene [a foster.]
H62.5	2	When I shulde maydyns kysse,

I (cont.)

H62.5	5	Yet have [I bene a foster.]
H62.6	1	Now will I take to me my bedes
H62.6	3	And pray I wyll for them that may,
H62.6	4	For I may nowght but loke;
H62.6	5	Yet have [I bene a foster.]
H63.1	3	Frome yow a whyle must I depart;
H63.2	3	My hart ys yours where ever that I go;
H63.2	4	For yow do I mone.
H65b	1	I am a joly foster
H65b	3	And foster will I be styll
H65b	4	For shote ryght well I may.
H65.1	1	Wherfore shuld I hang up my bow
H65.1	3	I cane bend and draw a bow
H65.1	5	I am a joly foster.
H65.2	1	Wherfor shuld I hang up myne arrow
H65.2	3	I have strengh to mak it fle
H65.2	5	I am [a joly foster.]
H65.3	1	Wherfor shuld I hang up my horne
H65.3	3	I can blow the deth of a dere
H65.3	4	As well as any that ever I see:
H65.3	5	I am [a joly foster.]
H65.4	1	Wherfor shuld I tye up my hownd
H65.4	3	I can luge and make a sute
H65.4	5	I am [a joly foster.]
H66.1	2	I trust in age to tarry;
H66.1	4	Frome them shall I never vary:
H66.2	1	I pray you all that aged be,
H66.2	3	I thynk sum wars of yche degre;
H66.2	4	Therin a wager lay dar I:
H66.3	3	I hurt no man, I do no wrong;
H66.3	4	I love trew wher I dyd mary:
H67.1	8	Untyll I dye.
H68	2	I trust we shall mete oftener.
H75	6	So my hart to her I ensure;
H75	9	And thus I wyll endure;
H92.2	3	But I wyll not so whatsoever thay say,
H101.1	1	And I war a maydyn,
H101.1	4	I wold not do amysse.
H101.2	1	When I was a wanton wench
H101.3	1	When I was come to
H101.3	4	Methought I had no pere.
H102b	1	Why shall not I?
H102b	2	Why shall not I to my lady
H102b	3	Why shall not I be trew?
H102b	4	Why shall not I?
H102.1	5	Why shall not I?
H102.2	5	Why shall not I?
H103.1	3	Thus withowt comfort I am forlore;
H103.2	1	Bewayll I may myn adventure
H103.2	2	To se the paynes that I endure
H103.3	1	O my swet hart, whome I love best,
H104b	4	I am so sad;
H105.2	1	I mene this by Mary, our Maker's moder of myght,

I (cont.)
H105.2	3	Thus saying to our Saviour; this saw I in my syght;
H105.2	4	This reson that I rede you now, I rede it full ryght
H105.3	3	Yet softly to her swete sonne methought I hard her sayn
H106.1	6	Thus do I lyve in gret hevenes
H106.2	4	Begyled am I, and cannot refrayne;
H106.2	5	Refrayne I must yet in dysdayne,
H106.2	6	In dysdayn I shall my lyfe endure,
H106.3	1	Oftyme for death forsoth I call
H107.1	8	What may I gesse?
H107.2	1	I fere doutles
H107.4	2	Bowndon am I
H107.5	5	Yet I ne went
H108	1	I love unloved; suche is myn aventure,
H108	2	And cannot cesse tyl I sore smart,
H108	6	But leve in payne whyls I endure
H109b	3	I go to the medowe to mylke my cow.
H109b	4	Than at the medow I wyll you mete
H109b	7	I wysse my mother then shall us se!
H109.1	3	And yf ye wyll, I shall consent;
H109.1b	1	Nay, in good feyth, I wyll not melle with you;
H109.1b	2	I pray you, sir, lett me go mylke my cow!
H109.1b	6	I wysse my mothyr than shall us se!
H109.2	3	Syth I love you, love me agayne;
H109.3	4	Or elles I shall for you be ded.
H109.4	1	Then for this onse I shal you spare,

I-WIS (1)
| F40.3 | 4 | I-wis, she will not gyve me a bone: |

I-WISS (2)
| F28 | 5 | I-wiss yet will I not me complayne |
| F41.3 | 1 | I-wiss, ye dele uncurtesly; |

IDELNES (1)
| R12.2 | 5 | For idelnes |

IF (2)
| F48.2 | 1 | If any man will say here agayne |
| H44.1 | 1 | If love now reynyd as it hath bene |

IFF (2)
| R11.4 | 2 | Iff my sorow and woe she knew: |
| H29.1 | 1 | Iff I had wytt for to endyght |

ILL (2)
| F29.4 | 1 | 'Modyr, methynkyth it is ryght ill, |
| F40b | 1 | Jhoone is sike and ill at ease; |

IN (166)
| R2.1 | 7 | For yet Y am all drowned in the lake |
| R3.2 | 8 | My moder cam in, or that ye wende.' |

R4	7	That myght my herte in more ese bryng.
R5	3	Till that Y may in yeure presaunce
R6	2	That Y am thus in heviness?
R9	3	Arested hathe my herte in sodeyn wise,
R13.3	4	For she hath that I hadde in store,
R15.1	1	In wyldernes
R15.1	4	In grete dystres,
R15.5	4	In ferre cuntre
R15.8	4	In wyldernes,
F2	4	Thoo that all this yet in vayne be,
F5	1	My wofull hart in paynfull weryness,
F5	3	Full lyk to drowne in wavis of dystres,
F6.1	2	In absent,
F6.3	2	In your mynd
F7.1	3	In willfullness so for to be,
F7.2	3	Sum tyme is lost and all in vayne
F7.2	7	In whom ther is no remedy;
F9	4	In Venus' trace
F10	3	In every place ryght hath residens
F10	4	Nethir in towne ne fylde simulacion
F10	5	Ther is trewly in every case consolacion
F10	8	Now raynyth trewly in every mannys syght.
F12	6	Of onys voice sayyng, 'Bere in thy mynd,
F15	2	Thow I be lytyll in your remembraunce;
F17	2	Syth worde and dede is take in vayne,
F19	1	Thus musyng in my mynd, gretly mervelyng
F19	2	Houghevyr such dyversite in on person may be,
F19	3	So goodly, so curtesly, so gentill in behavyng;
F19	4	And so sodenly will chaunge in every degre;
F20	7	Thes vertues byn pryntyd in her doutless.
F21	2	In stedfast fayth and trouth with assuraunce;
F23.2	4	And with pite have me in remembraunce
F23.2	6	Wolde in no wise for joy nor hevyness
F24.1	3	In remembryng
F24.3	5	Lo, in this traunce,
F24.3	6	Now in substaunce
F25.1	3	In every vayne
F26	3	In whom all vertu is knytt withouten varyaunce,
F27b	5	Yff we three can agre in on.'
F27.2	4	He pass them all in his degre;
F27.4	5	In hart so fre, that best lykyth me.'
F27.4b	5	Yff we three can agre in oon.'
F27.6b	5	That we three be agrede in oon.'
F28	4	And she me takyth in gret disdayne:
F28	7	Lest cause in me be fownd of offens.
F29.5	1	'Sone', she sayd, 'let it be in thy thought,
F30.1	3	All in my slepe:
F30.1	14	Is in this howse
F30.1	18	Lyth in hay.'
F31.1	2	Egall to the Fathir in deite,
F32.1	1	Sith it concludid was in the Trinite
F32.2	1	Methynkyth in my reson thou owfte to be gladd
F33.1	3	Sith I for thi sowle sake was slayne in good seson,

F33.2	6	Thus wrappid all in woo,
F33.2	8	Entretid, thus in most cruell wise
F33.2	9	Was like a lombe offerd in sacrifice:
F34.2	6	Lett now us twayne in this thyng be tretable:
F34.3	3	Saynt Tomas of Indes, in crudelite
F34.3	4	He put his handes depe in my syde adowne.
F34.3	5	Role up this mater; grave it in thi reson:
F36.1	2	And theruppon straynyd he was in every vayne;
F36.1	3	A crowne of thorne as nedill sharpe shyfft in his brayne
F36.3	10	And yet verely I know in myn hart
F36.4	2	Full boistusly in the mortess he was downe cast;
F37.1	2	My mode is changid in every wise,
F37.2	2	To lusty plesure? Now lyyng in the flore,
F37.4	5	With all good sowlis to cause me lyve in rest.
F38b	2	And thynk on the paynys that byn in hell.
F39.1	7	I se, in lond,
F39.2	4	In her beaute;
F39.3	3	In feeld ne strete;
F40.1	1	Hit is so praty in every degre;
F40.1	3	In favoure and in facion (lo, will ye se?)
F40.2	3	That God hath ordent in his first formacion,
F43.1	2	In a cloke withoute cote or gowne,
F44.1	4	In honor to rayne, Lord, graunt hym tyme and space,
F44.2	3	In every case be his preservacion,
F44.2	6	In honor to rayne,
F44.3	2	Pray to thi Son, the secund in Trinite,
F45.1	1	In a glorius garden grene
F45.2	1	In that garden be flouris of hewe:
F46.3	3	To put in one my faithfull trust,
F47b	2	To strenkyth your comyns in ther ryght.
F47.1	1	Soverayn lorde, in erth most excellent,
F47.1	7	To strenkyth your comyns in ther ryght.
F47.2	6	In your person all ther hope is pyght
F48b	7	In hed, in fete, in handis, in hart;
F48.1	7	And that thou be in charite;
F48.2	6	In the awter I am offerd my Fader beforne;
F48.3	8	The wounde in my harte the seale it is,
F49b	1	In a slumbir late as I was,
H20	1	In May, that lusty sesoun
H23.1	2	But vice in it shuld be forfent.
H23.5	1	Comparysons in them may lawfully be sett,
H23.6	2	In goode dysporttys whych it dothe fend.
H25.2	1	In lovys daunce
H25.7	5	Halff in a swone,
H25.10	4	In well and wo
H25.11	4	And in especyall
H27.2	3	And now absence to be in place
H27.3	2	And take in armys twayne;
H31.2	4	'In every place
H31.4	2	In no maner a way
H31.9	1	In armys he hent
H31.9	3	In voydyng care and mone

H31.9	6	In wyldernes alone.
H34.1	2	In love he must be withowt dysdayne,
H35b	2	Ther ys a do in yonder wode; in faith, she woll not dy
H35.5	3	And arrow in her hanch she hent;
H41.2	2	The lady said he shuld not com in.
H44.5	1	The faut in whome I cannot sett;
H47.3	3	It may in no wyse agre
H49.3	3	In faith my lady lovith me well;
H50b	1	Whilles lyve or breth is in my brest
H50.3	1	My soverayne lorde in every thyng
H50.3	3	In that he doth no camparyng
H62.2	3	For I cannott shote in playne
H62.2	4	Nor yett in rough;
H64.1	5	To set in one
H64.1	8	Ys in the dole
H65.4	4	As well as any in May:
H66.1	2	I trust in age to tarry;
H67.1	5	In all socours
H75	3	That hath my hart in cure;
H79.1	3	And love her in hart and dede,
H79.2	4	In that therfor can be non odde,
H79.2	5	But perfite in dede and betwene two.
H82.1	5	In ther myndes consyder thei must
H82.1	6	How thay dyd in ther most lust.
H82.2	1	For yf thay war in lyk case
H92.2	4	But follow hys mynd in all that we may.
H92.4	1	For in them consisteth gret honor,
H92.5	4	Yough shuld fall in grett myschaunce;
H96.1	1	Ageynst the Frenchmen in the feld to fyght
H96.1	2	In the quarell of the church and in the ryght,
H101.1	3	For all the golde in England
H101.3	3	In all this lond, nowther fre nor bond,
H102.1	1	My lady hath me in that grace
H102.1	3	Her mynd is in non other place:
H105.1	2	Lokyng on her lytill son, so laughyng in lap layd,
H105.2	3	Thus saying to our Saviour; this saw I in my syght;
H106.1	1	My thought oppressed, my mynd in trouble,
H106.1	2	My body languisshyng, my hart in payn;
H106.1	6	Thus do I lyve in gret hevenes
H106.2	5	Refrayne I must yet in dysdayne,
H106.2	6	In dysdayn I shall my lyfe endure,
H106.3	2	In releasse off my gret smert,
H106.4	5	Good aventure in me to have place:
H107.1	3	In remembryng
H107.3	5	Lo, in this trance,
H107.3	6	Now in substance
H108	6	But leve in payne whyls I endure
H109.1b	1	Nay, in good feyth, I wyll not melle with you;
H109.1b	4	That now in the feldes we may us sportt?
H109.2b	1	Nay, in good feyth, [etc.]
H109.3b	1	Nay, in good feyth, [etc.]
H109.4	3	How in the medow ye mylke your cow.

139

IN (cont.)
H109.4b 1   Nay, in good feyth, [etc.]

INDEDE (2)
F38.1   2   Howgh gretly thou art bownd indede;
H82.2   5   Wherfor indede the trouth to say

INDES (1)
F34.3   3   Saynt Tomas of Indes, in crudelite

INDIGNACION (1)
F34.2   4   Percide hand and fote of indignacion,

INDYFFERENT (1)
F46.1   2   Indyfferent to every creature,

INERYTAUNCE (1)
F44.1   7   Be inerytaunce

INFANT (1)
H68   4   Vive le prince, le infant rosary!

INFERNALL (1)
F44.3   7   Emprise infernall,

INFORTUNE (1)
F1   7   Is it fortune or infortune this I fynde?

INFYNYT (1)
F31.1   1   Crist, that was of infynyt myght,

INFYNYTLY (1)
F30.2   9   Infynytly,

INMORTAL (1)
F31.1   3   Inmortal, inpassible, the wordlis lyght,

INMORTALL (1)
F36.3   4   'O frend,' she said, 'I am sure he is inmortall.'

INOW (1)
F29.2   2   I sawe a maide fayre inow;

INPASSIBLE (1)
F31.1   3   Inmortal, inpassible, the wordlis lyght,

INSACIENTLY (1)
H103.2 3   Insaciently withowt recure;

INSEW (1)
R12.3   5   The best insew,

INTENT (1)
H31.9   5   To ther intent

140

INTO (3)
```
R2.2    4   Into gret sekenesse weche holdith hur grevowsly;
F48.3   5   Into witness of which thyng
H30     2   For care is cast into my hart,
```

INWARD (1)
```
H47.1   2   My inward hevynes?
```

INWARDLY (1)
```
H44.4   2   Inwardly most grevous and sore:
```

IS (118)
```
F1      7   Is it fortune or infortune this I fynde?
F5      5   Is nowe be hym so comfortide agayne
F6.2    4   Yet reson is
F7.1    4   Syn that it is playnly foly;
F7.2    3   Sum tyme is lost and all in vayne
F7.2    7   In whom ther is no remedy;
F8      5   Through whose swete showris now sprong ther is ayen
F10     1   Nowe the lawe is led be clere conciens
F10     5   Ther is trewly in every case consolacion
F11     1   That was my woo is nowe my most gladness;
F11     2   That was my payne is nowe my joyus chaunce;
F11     3   That was my feere is nowe my sykyrness;
F11     4   That was my grefe is now my alegeaunce.
F13     4   To her only which is myn yes fode,
F14     1   Alas, it is I that wote nott what to say,
F14     2   For why I stond as he that is abusyd;
F14     5   But pite it is that trust shulde be mysusyd
F14     7   Wher that is usyd can be no surance.
F17     2   Syth worde and dede is take in vayne,
F20     2   With vertu connyng her maner is lede,
F22     4   Absens it is that wolde me wrong;
F22     5   And thus is the tyme of his song;
F22     6   To gett mystrust is his entent
F23.1   1   That was my joy is now my woo and payne;
F23.1   2   That was my bliss is now my displesaunce;
F23.1   3   That was my trust is now my wanhope playne;
F23.1   4   That was my wele is now my most grevaunce.
F23.2   2   My hart is yours with gret assuraunce.
F24.2   3   Is now to cess
F24.3   7   Such is my daunce
F24.5   3   It is ny spent;
F24.5   8   Such is her wone.
F25.3   3   My hart is ment,
F26     3   In whom all vertu is knytt withouten varyaunce,
F27.1   5   Is non of them that lykyth me.'
F27.2   1   'Ther is a floure where so he be,
F27.3   5   Here is not he that plesyth me.'
F27.4   2   'What is his name that thou chosen has?
F27.4   4   'That same is he,
F27.5   1   'The rose it is a ryall floure.'
F27.6   2   'Is that your pure perfytt appetite?'
F27.6   3   'To here talke of them is my delite.
```

141

IS (cont.)

F27.6b	3	Most worthy it is, as thynkyth me.
F29.4	1	'Modyr, methynkyth it is ryght ill,
F29.4	3	For them to save, it is my will;
F29.5	2	For mannys gilt is not withstone,
F30.1	14	Is in this howse
F30.2	5	It is sothely
F30.2	10	As it is fownde,
F30.2	14	That is so hye,
F32.2	6	So nowe is knowen thi sonnys myght:
F32.4	4	Thi dere sone is past his trobill and his tene;
F34b	2	Who is that that dothe me call?
F36.3	3	He hath to man, to make hym fre that now is thrall.
F36.3	4	'O frend,' she said, 'I am sure he is inmortall.'
F36.3	9	Is by nature constraynyd to smert,
F37.1	2	My mode is changid in every wise,
F37.3	1	My voice is so trobled, my seknes then feele I;
F37.3	3	My dreme is so mervelous, serpentis semyth me to tere
F39b	3	Ther is non lyke
F39.2	7	Sis is witness
F40b	1	Jhoone is sike and ill at ease;
F40.1	1	Hit is so praty in every degre;
F40.3	1	She is my lytell praty on;
F40.3	2	What shulde I say? My mynde is gone.
F41.2	5	Go watch a bole, your bak is brode.
F41.4	6	Gup, Cristian Clowte, your breth is stale,
F43.1	1	Rutterkyn is com unto oure towne
F44.2	2	Is this noble prince of riall lynage,
F44.3	3	For this yong prince, which is and daily shal
F45.2	4	And said, 'The white rose is most trewe
F46.1	1	Love is naturall to every wyght,
F46.2	1	One is good, but mo were bettyr
F46.3	2	So it is best, as thynkyth me,
F47.1	5	Sith it is so, now let your labour be
F47.2	6	In your person all ther hope is pyght
F48.1	9	This is that I axe of the,
F48.3	8	The wounde in my harte the seale it is,
H15	2	My hart it is so sore,
H17	5	A bud is spryngynge
H23.1	1	The tyme of youthe is to be spent;
H23.5	2	For therby corage is suerly owt fett:
H23.6	1	Vertue it is then youth for to spend
H25.3	1	It is no boote
H30	2	For care is cast into my hart,
H34.3	2	Is wors then deth? Let it be proved!
H39	3	My love is to the grenewode gone,
H40	2	My love, she is so trew to me.
H49.2	1	My lady is unkynde I wis.
H49.2	2	Alac, why is she so?
H50b	1	Whilles lyve or breth is in my brest
H50.5	2	Ther is none one-lyve that have;
H50.6	1	The soverayne lorde that is of all,

IS (cont.)

H51.3	1	Or elles from her which is her hayre;
H51.4	2	There is no bote; ther must it be.
H56	1	Departure is my chef payne;
H62.3	3	The glew is slypt frome the nyk;
H75	2	My love is lusty, plesant and demure
H102.1	3	Her mynd is in non other place:
H103b	2	Such is fortune! What remedy?
H103.1	5	Such is fortune! What remedy?
H103.2	5	Such is fortune! What remedy?
H103.3	3	For which my hart is lyk to brest,
H103.3	5	Such is fortune! What remedy?
H104b	6	Yt is but you, my love, alone.
H104.1	5	No joy it is
H104.2	3	My myrth and joy is gone;
H104.2	5	Is no resort
H104.3	4	Is nothing,
H106.2	1	My hope frome me is clene exiled,
H106.2	2	Exilide for ever which is my payne;
H106.3	5	A payne it is, hens to depart,
H106.3	6	Yet my lyfe is to me so grevus
H106.3	7	That deth is plesur and nothyng noyus.
H107.2	3	Is now to cese
H107.3	7	Such is my chance
H107.5	3	It is ny spent;
H108	1	I love unloved; suche is myn aventure,

IT (73)

F1	7	Is it fortune or infortune this I fynde?
F3	4	Then be it they that doth me trobill so
F6.3	5	It wolde me make
F7.1	4	Syn that it is playnly foly;
F7.2	2	Cannot avayle, it shal be sayd;
F13	2	For my complayntes it dyd me nevir good;
F14	1	Alas, it is I that wote nott what to say,
F14	5	But pite it is that trust shulde be mysusyd
F21	7	Hough that evyr it will happ I wote nere I.
F22	4	Absens it is that wolde me wrong;
F24.5	3	It is ny spent;
F24.5	7	But she it ment,
F27.5	1	'The rose it is a ryall floure.'
F27.5	5	That day to se it lykyth well me.'
F27.6b	3	Most worthy it is, as thynkyth me.
F29.4	1	'Modyr, methynkyth it is ryght ill,
F29.4	3	For them to save, it is my will;
F29.5	1	'Sone', she sayd, 'let it be in thy thought,
F30.2	5	It is sothely
F30.2	10	As it is fownde,
F32.1	1	Sith it concludid was in the Trinite
F33b	4	It may not be naid;
F34.3	5	Role up this mater; grave it in thi reson:
F36.1	10	Hough it thirlyd her thoroughoute the hart,
F37.1	6	Thus trobled am I yet I trust it shalbe for the best

F37.2	6	Thus trobled am I [yet I trust it shalbe for the best
F37.3	6	Thus trobled am I [yet I trust it shalbe for the best
F37.4	6	Thus trobled am I [yet I trust it shalbe for the best
F40.1	4	But it were an angell of the Trinite?
F46.3	2	So it is best, as thynkyth me,
F47.1	5	Sith it is so, now let your labour be
F48.3	8	The wounde in my harte the seale it is,
H15	2	My hart it is so sore,
H20	5	So meryly, it joyed my hart
H23.1	2	But vice in it shuld be forfent.
H23.6	1	Vertue it is then youth for to spend
H23.6	2	In goode dysporttys whych it dothe fend.
H25.3	1	It is no boote
H25.7	6	It rewyd my hart to se.
H27.4	3	Ther myght no joys compare with it
H29.2	2	She ys right trew, I do it se.
H29.4	2	Pytte it war that I shuld be,
H29.5	1	Lernyng it war for women all
H31.7	6	My hart it grevyth me so.'
H34.3	2	Is wors then deth? Let it be proved!
H34.6	2	Yet never the lesse it ys to moch used.
H34.7	1	Grett pyte it ware, love for to compell
H35.1	4	Lord, I was glad of it!
H44.1	1	If love now reynyd as it hath bene
H44.1	2	And war rewardit as it hath sene,
H44.2	2	All ways wherby thay myght it rech;
H44.7	1	And unto them which doth it know
H44.7	2	Better than do I, I thynk it so.
H47.3	3	It may in no wyse agre
H47.5	2	It ys to me gret payne
H50.1	3	Of which four tymes he dyd it take;
H51.1	1	Thow that men do call it dotage,
H51.2	2	Frome Venus sure he must it fett;
H51.4	2	There is no bote; ther must it be.
H51.8	2	It were pete thay shuld optayne;
H62.1	3	Thay stand abak and make it strange;
H65.2	3	I have strengh to mak it fle
H79.1	4	Els it war pyte that he shuld spede;
H82.2	6	It ys for yough the metest play.
H92.1	4	It ys not for hym we know yt well.
H102.1	4	Now sith it ys thus known,
H102.2	1	My lady sayth of trouth it ys
H104.1	5	No joy it is
H105.2	4	This reson that I rede you now, I rede it full ryght
H105.3	2	Save it plesyd me so passyngly that past was my payn
H106.3	5	A payne it is, hens to depart,
H107.5	3	It is ny spent;
H107.5	7	But she it ment,

ITT (1)
F19   8   To lett itt over pass, and thynk theron no more.

IVE (2)
H33b   2   So doth the ive,
H33.2   2   With ive all alone

IYEVYN (1)
F48.3   9   Iyevyn upon the mownt of Calvary,

JAK (4)
F41.1   6   Gup, Cristian Clowte, gup, Jak of the Vale,
F41.2   6   Gup, Cristian Clowte, gup, Jak of the Vale,
F41.3   6   Gup, Cristian Clowte, gup, Jak of the Vale,
F41.4   8   Gup, Cristian Clowte, gup, Jak of the Vale,

JAMYS (1)
F41.2   3   Strawe, Jamys foder, ye play the fode;

JAPED (1)
F41.3   5   I will not be japed bodely.

JEBARDYSE (1)
H25.11   5   From jebardyse all

JEWIS (2)
F32.2   2   When Jewis with treson to deth thi son ladde;
F33.1   7   The Jewis me thretid,

JHESU (13)
F30b   3   Kys thi moder, Jhesu,
F31b   1   Jhesu, mercy, how may this be,
F31b   5   Jhesu, mercy, how may this be?
F31.1   5   Jhesu, mercy, [how may this be?]
F31.2   5   Jhesu, mercy, [how may this be?]
F31.3   1   A Jhesu, whi suffyrd thou such entretyng,
F31.3   5   Jhesu, mercy, [how may this be?]
F31.4   5   [Jhesu, mercy, how may this be?]
F34b   1   'A, gentill Jhesu!'
F34b   10   'A, I will, I will, gentyll Jhesu'.
F34.5   3   O Jhesu, graunt of thi benignite
F37.1   1   A blessid Jhesu, hough fortunyd this?
F37.4   1   Now, mercyfull Jhesu, to the make I my mone;

JHESUS (1)
F48b   4   That I Jhesus off Nazareth

JHOAN (3)
F40.3   5   Alak, good Jhoan, [what may you please?
F40.4   1   Alas, good Jhoan, shall all my mone
F40.4   5   Alak, good Jhoan, [what may you please?

JHOANE (1)
F40b   3   Alak, good Jhoane, what may you please?

JHON (2)
F36.3   1   Saynt Jhon than said, 'Feere not, Mary; his
                paynys al
F48.3   3   Witness, Mari, wittness, Seynt Jhon,

JHOON'S (1)
F40b   2   I am full sory for Jhoon's disease.

JHOONE (3)
F40b   1   Jhoone is sike and ill at ease;
F40.1   5   Alak, good Jhoone, [what may you please?
F40.2   5   Alak, good [Jhoone, what may you please?

JOE (2)
H27.3   4   Farewell, my joe, and welcom payne.
H50.4   3   My hart with joe that I be hete

JOLY (8)
F43b   1   Hoyda, hoyda, joly rutterkin!
H22   2   To passe the tyme of youth joly,
H35b   3   Now blow thi horne, hunter, and blow thi horne,
                joly hunter
H65b   1   I am a joly foster
H65.1   5   I am a joly foster.
H65.2   5   I am [a joly foster.]
H65.3   5   I am [a joly foster.]
H65.4   5   I am [a joly foster.]

JOSEPH (1)
F30.1 10   Joseph seyd, 'Wiff,

JOY (16)
R2.2   8   But sorfull joy and paynefull plesaunce.
F23.1   1   That was my joy is now my woo and payne;
F23.2   6   Wolde in no wise for joy nor hevyness
F26   4   With welth and wordly joy long to endure,
F30.1 11   My joy, my leff,
F31.2   2   That made both paynys and joy also,
F31.4   4   'The to purchace both joy and bliss.'
F32.2   5   To joy of every wordlis wight,
F44.2   4   With joy to rejose his dew enerytaunce,
H16   2   Adew, my joy and my solace!
H27.1   4   Farewell, my joy, for evermore.
H28   4   Joy shall I never ye may be sure.
H63.1   1   Farewell, my joy, and my swete hart!
H82.2   4   That which then was most ther joy;
H104.1 5   No joy it is
H104.2 3   My myrth and joy is gone;

JOYE (1)
R2.1   8   Of sorfull joye and paynefull plesaunce.

JOYED (2)
F27.6   4   Joyed may we be

146

JOYED (cont.)
  H20   5 So meryly, it joyed my hart

JOYES (1)
  H106.1 3 My joyes, dystres; my sorows dowble;

JOYFULL (1)
  F32.4   3 Remembir thi joys that joyfull aye byn!

JOYFULLY (1)
  H20   8 Joyfully, so merely,

JOYS (2)
  F32.4   3 Remembir thi joys that joyfull aye byn!
  H27.4   3 Ther myght no joys compare with it

JOYUS (1)
  F11   2 That was my payne is nowe my joyus chaunce;

JUDAS' (1)
  F33.1   4 Begylde and betraide by Judas' fals treson;

JUGE (1)
  H51.6   2 Myne ey with hart doth me so juge.

JUGEMENT (1)
  F46.2   2 Affter my reason and jugement,

JUST (1)
  F34.2   7 Love for love be just convencion;

KAN (1)
  R3.2   4 A, kan ye that? Nou, gode, go hens!

KENE (1)
  H20   9 Among the thornys kene.

KEPE (7)
  R15.7   1 I cannot kepe
  R18.4   2 Shall Y hyt kepe _vel interficiam?_
  F30.1   7 To kepe she sought
  H12   5 To kepe yow me unto?
  H31.5   6 Cryst kepe yow frome all care.
  H104.4 3 Crist kepe you from your fone;
  H104.4 5 Kepe your love

KING (1)
  H96.1   5 Help now thi king [and take his part!]

KNE (1)
  F34.5   1 Lord, on all synfull here knelyng on kne,

KNEE (1)
  H25.7   3 And sett her on my knee:

147

KNELYNG (1)
F34.5   1   Lord, on all synfull here knelyng on kne,

KNEW (1)
R11.4   2   Iff my sorow and woe she knew:

KNEWE (1)
F45.2   2   The gelofir gent, that she well knewe;

KNOKETT (1)
H41.1   1   The knyght knokett at the castell gate;

KNOW (12)
F36.3   10   And yet verely I know in myn hart
F39.2   3   I know no pere
H15   4   And know no cause wherefore.
H29.1   4   Shall no man know her name for me.
H29.2   4   Shall no mane know her name for me.
H29.3   4   Shall no man know her name for me.
H29.4   4   Shall no man [know her name for me].
H29.5   3   Promyse I mak that know non shall
H29.6   4   Shall no man [know her name for me].
H44.7   1   And unto them which doth it know
H49.1   3   And thow shal know of myne.
H92.1   4   It ys not for hym we know yt well.

KNOWE (3)
F2   1   A, a, my herte, I knowe yow well;
F17   7   When that they knowe I am sory.
F18.2   8   Thus knowe we well.

KNOWEN (1)
F32.2   6   So nowe is knowen thi sonnys myght:

KNOWITH (1)
F20   6   Which that all men knowith, both more and less;

KNOWN (1)
H102.1   4   Now sith it ys thus known,

KNOWYN (1)
F48b   1   Be hit knowyn to all that byn here

KNOWYTH (1)
R20.2   2   Withowt cause, Gode knowyth; Y do not fayne.

KNYGHT (2)
F47b   1   Enforce yourselfe as Goddis knyght
H41.1   1   The knyght knokett at the castell gate;

KNYTT (1)
F26   3   In whom all vertu is knytt withouten varyaunce,

KOUDE (1)
R4   3   And thogh Y wolde, Y koude me noght refrayne

KOVER (1)
F43.1   3   Save a raggid hode to kover his crowne,

KYLD (1)
H108   4   Whose unkyndnes hath kyld myn hart;

KYLL (1)
H65.2   4   And kyll bothe hart and hynd:

KYND (5)
F12   7   Thi lady hath forgoten to be kynd.'
F34.3   6   Syth I am kynd, why are thou unstable?
H12   3   Syth now so kynd
H29.4   3   For she to me ys allway kynd;
H34.2   1   For love enforcyth all nobyle kynd,

KYNDE (1)
R7   3   Remembre how feithefull, how treu, how kynde

KYNDELY (1)
R2.2   3   Ys full but late oute of hur kyndely rest

KYNDNES (1)
H41.7   1   Kyndnes said she wold yt bere,

KYNDNESSE (1)
H25.4   1   O her kyndnesse,

KYNDYLD (1)
H101.2 4   They kyndyld my corage.

KYNG (8)
F5   7   To love and dred hym as my lord and kyng.
F30.1   16 My Sone, a Kyng
F48.1   4   As long as I am Lord and Kyng,
H50.3   2   Above all other as a kyng,
H66.4   4   Thus sayth the kyng, the eighth Harry:
H96b   2   Help now thi kyng, thi kyng, and take his part!
H97   2   That for our kyng so to provid,

KYS (2)
R3.3   1   Cum kys me! 'Nay!' Be God, ye shall!
F30b   3   Kys thi moder, Jhesu,

KYSSE (3)
H25.8   2   I dyd her kysse;
H62.5   2   When I shulde maydyns kysse,
H109.4 4   Adew, farewell and kysse me now!

LABOUR (1)
F47.1   5   Sith it is so, now let your labour be

LADDE (1)
‣F32.2   2   When Jewis with treson to deth thi son ladde;

LADI (1)
R9   5   My lyves ladi and my hertis cure,

LADY (33)
R11.1   4   My lady hath forsakyn me.
R11.2   4   My lady hath forsakyn me.
R11.3   4   My lady hath forsakyn me.]
R11.4   4   [My lady hath forsakyn me.]
F9   5   A lady fre,
F12   7   Thi lady hath forgoten to be kynd.'
F23.1   7   That hath byn your fayre lady and mastress.
F23.2   7   Have but yourselfe, fayre lady and mastres.
F32.1   7   Now blessid Lady, wepe no more:
F32.2   8   Now, blessid Lady, wepe [no more:
F32.3   8   Now, blessid Lady, wepe no more:
F32.4   1   Glorius Lady, of hevyn hie quene,
F32.4   8   Now blessid Lady, wepe no more:
F39.3   8   Herk, my lady!'
F42.1   1   Who shall have my fayre lady?
F44.3   1   Now, good Lady among thi sayntes all,
H18   2   Now am I exild my lady fro
H29.1   2   Of my lady, both fayre and fre,
H31.9   2   That lady gent;
H33.1   4   Unto my lady trew.
H33.3   1   Now unto my lady
H33.4   1   Adew, myne owne lady,
H41.1   2   The lady mervelyd who was therat.
H41.2   2   The lady said he shuld not com in.
H41.3   1   The portres was a lady bryght;
H41.3   2   Strangenes that lady hyght.
H41.6   2   And shew my lady hys oune wyll.
H49.2   1   My lady is unkynde I wis.
H49.3   3   In faith my lady lovith me well;
H62.4   1   Lady Venus hath commaundyd me
H102b   2   Why shall not I to my lady
H102.1 1   My lady hath me in that grace
H102.2 1   My lady sayth of trouth it ys

LADY'S (1)
H31.6   3   To be a lady's pere!'

LAIDIS (1)
F32.1   4   Yet when oure Laidis Son was slayne

LAK (1)
F22   1   Alas, for lak of her presens,

LAKE (1)
R2.1   7   For yet Y am all drowned in the lake

150

LAKKYTH (1)
  F7.1   2 Whan that desert lakkyth remedy,

LAMBE (1)
  R7   4 This lyon and lambe was, causyng pyte;

LAMENTABLE (2)
  F36.4   5 When he lamentable
  F38.2   1 With wepyng teris most lamentable

LANGUISSHYNG (1)
  H106.1 2 My body languisshyng, my hart in payn;

LANTERNE (1)
  H105.2 2 Full lovely lookyng on our Lord, the lanterne of
               lyght

LAP (1)
  H105.1 2 Lokyng on her lytill son, so laughyng in lap layd,

LAS (1)
  F39.1   1 That goodly las,

LAST (2)
  H25.7   1 At last sche wept;
  H92.7   4 An blysse opteyne at ower last end. Amen.

LATE (4)
  R2.2   3 Ys full but late oute of hur kyndely rest
  R6   5 Both erly, late, by day and by nyghth.
  F14   3 Ther as I trusted I was late cast away,
  F49b   1 In a slumbir late as I was,

LAUGHYNG (1)
  H105.1 2 Lokyng on her lytill son, so laughyng in lap layd,

LAVENDOUR (1)
  F27.1   2 'Magerome, gentyll or lavendour,

LAWE (2)
  F10   1 Nowe the lawe is led be clere conciens
  F45.2   5 This garden to rule be ryghtwis lawe.'

LAWFULLY (1)
  H23.5   1 Comparysons in them may lawfully be sett,

LAWGHYNG (1)
  F30b   4 With a lawghyng chere.'

LAY (5)
  R18.3   2 Bycause Y lay with quidam clericus?
  F32.4   2 Lay downe all thi wepyng, let no more be sene!
  H35.1   3 She lay so fayre, I cowde nott mys;
  H35.5   2 For I fownd wher she lay;

151

LAY (cont.)
H66.2   4 Therin a wager lay dar I:

LAYD (1)
H105.1   2 Lokyng on her lytill son, so laughyng in lap layd,

LED (1)
F10   1 Nowe the lawe is led be clere conciens

LEDE (3)
R1.2   4 Ther to lede my lyffe.
R10.4   4 To lede my lyf;
F20   2 With vertu connyng her maner is lede,

LEEFE (1)
F1   4 The lyghter leefe, the lother for to wende;

LEFE (1)
R15.4   2 Lefe of my woe

LEFF (2)
R3.1   4 Leff werke a twenty-a-devell away!
F30.1   11 My joy, my leff,

LEFFE (2)
F48b   3 To me shal be leffe and dere,
H14   1 Alone I leffe, alone,

LEFFT (2)
F37.2   5 Thou, Nature, hast lefft me; by the fynd I no rest:
F37.4   2 Nature hath forsakyn me, and lefft me thus alone.

LEFT (1)
H41.8   2 We left them ther and went ower way.

LEFTE (1)
R15.8   2 Has thus lefte me

LEGGE (1)
R3.3   3 Ye herte my legge agenste the walle;

LEMMAN (1)
H49.1   2 Tel me how thy lemman doth,

LENGER (1)
H62.1   4 No lenger shote I may;

LENT (3)
F24.5   1 My lyff was lent
F25.3   1 I have yow lent
H107.5   1 My lyf was lent

LEPT (1)
H25.7   2 I to her lept

152

LEPYS (1)
R16.1   4   She daunces and she lepys,

LERNYNG (1)
H29.5   1   Lernyng it war for women all

LES (1)
H107.2   6   Withowtyn les

LESS (2)
F20   6   Which that all men knowith, both more and less;
F24.2   6   Withouten less

LESSE (1)
H34.6   2   Yet never the lesse it ys to moch used.

LESSON (2)
F34b   9   And thynk on this lesson that now I teche the.
F34.4   2   Cum to scole; record well this lesson:

LEST (3)
R3.1   5   'Wene ye that everybody lest to play?'
F21   5   Lest that mysaventure myght fall be chaunce;
F28   7   Lest cause in me be fownd of offens.

LET (17)
R3.1   3   'Let go Y say, straw for yeur tale!'
R15.4   4   And let hym goo,
F27.1   4   'Nay, nay, let be;
F29.5   1   'Sone', she sayd, 'let it be in thy thought,
F32.4   2   Lay downe all thi wepyng, let no more be sene!
F39.3   7   And let us daunce
F41.1   5   Tully, valy, strawe, let be I say!
F47.1   5   Sith it is so, now let your labour be
H25.5   5   Let se purchase
H34.3   2   Is wors then deth? Let it be proved!
H44.5   2   But let them tell which love doth gett.
H47.2   2   Let no thought yow dysmaye!
H64.1   3   Now let us be;
H64.2   3   Let us now pray
H82.1   1   Let not us that yong men be
H97   5   Now let us syng this rownd all thre;
H109.2   4   Let us make one, though we be twayne!

LETE (1)
H17   2   Now lete us synge

LETT (8)
R12.1   10   Who shall me lett?
F2   8   Wherefor, my hart, lett be, lett be!
F8   1   Lett serch your myndis ye of hie consideracion!
F13   6   And lett me not allway be guerdonless,
F19   8   To lett itt over pass, and thynk theron no more.
F34.2   6   Lett now us twayne in this thyng be tretable:

153

LETT (cont.)
H109.1b 2 I pray you, sir, lett me go mylke my cow!

LEVE (7)
F34b   8 Than leve thi syn, or I nyll the,
F39.3   5 'Leve, love, this chance,
F40.4   3 Leve this array! Anothir day
H29.5   4 Whill I leve her name for me.
H35.7   1 Here I leve and mak an end,
H63.2   2 And leve me all alone,
H108   6 But leve in payne whyls I endure

LEVIS (1)
F8   6 A rose most riall with levis fressh of hew,

LEVYNG (1)
H40   3 To love her sure whill I am levyng,

LEVYS (2)
F42.1   3 Undir the levys grene?
H33.2   4 And grenewode levys be gone.

LEYDE (1)
R3.3   6 'Now have ye leyde me un the flore,

LIBERTYE (1)
H92.2   1 For they wold have hym hys libertye refrayne

LIFF (1)
F32.3   3 They betyng they broysyng, or liff did depart;

LIGHT (3)
R20.1   1 Your light grevans shall not me constrayne
R20.3   3 But light credens turnyth your love agayne:
F12   3 The son, the moone, had lost ther force and light;

LIKE (7)
F31.3   3 Drawne like a theffe, and for payne swetyng
F33.2   9 Was like a lombe offerd in sacrifice:
F43b   2 Like a rutterkin, hoyda!
F43.1   4 Like a rutter:
F43.2   4 Like a rutter:
F43.3   4 Like a rutter:
F43.4   4 Like a rutter:

LITELL (1)
F34.4   6 Afore thi hart hang this litell table,

LO (11)
F24.3   5 Lo, in this traunce,
F31.4   1 'Lo, man, for the that ware onkynd,
F40.1   3 In favoure and in facion (lo, will ye se?)
H39   1 Trolly lolly loly lo,
H39   2 Syng troly loly lo!

LO (cont.)
  H39   5   Syng trolly loly lo loly lo!
  H62.5   4   Lo, age ys cause of this;
  H75   10   Hey troly loly lo!
  H107.3 5   Lo, in this trance,
  H109b   1   Hey troly loly lo!

LOCKES (1)
  R1.1   2   My lockes ben hore.

LOKE (4)
  F34.2   2   Loke on them well, and have compassion;
  F36.4   9   Uppon her he cast his dedly loke,
  H51.5   1   The ee doth loke and represent;
  H62.6   4   For I may nowght but loke;

LOKKED (1)
  H30   3   And trew love lokked therto?

LOKYNG (1)
  H105.1 2   Lokyng on her lytill son, so laughyng in lap layd,

LOLLY (1)
  H39   1   Trolly lolly loly lo,

LOLY (13)
  H39   1   Trolly lolly loly lo,
  H39   2   Syng troly loly lo!
  H39   5   Syng trolly loly lo loly lo!
  H75   1   Hey troly loly loly!
  H75   4   Hey troly loly loly loly!
  H75   7   Hey troly loly loly!
  H75   10   Hey troly loly lo!
  H109b   1   Hey troly loly lo!

LOMBE (1)
  F33.2   9   Was like a lombe offerd in sacrifice:

LOND (2)
  F39.1   7   I se, in lond,
  H101.3 3   In all this lond, nowther fre nor bond,

LONG (8)
  R1.1   1   Y have ben a foster long and meney day;
  R19.2 10   That she had lovyd so long.
  F5   2   Which hath byn long plongyng with thought unseyne,
  F9   8   So long a space.
  F22   2   Whom I serve and shall as long,
  F26   4   With welth and wordly joy long to endure,
  F48.1   4   As long as I am Lord and Kyng,
  H62.1   2   Long and many a day;

LONGE (2)
  R20.4   2   Love me lytell and longe; hot love doth not reyne;

155

LONGE (cont.)
H47.5   3   Thus longe to endure,

LOOKYNG (1)
H105.2   2   Full lovely lookyng on our Lord, the lanterne of
                 lyght

LORD (19)
R6   1   O blessed lord, how may this be
F5   4   Saffe helpe and grace of my lord and soverayne,
F5   7   To love and dred hym as my lord and kyng.
F31.4   3   And why, good Lord? Express thi mynd!
F34b   5   'Mercy, Lord, of the I crave.'
F34.5   1   Lord, on all synfull here knelyng on kne,
F37.4   4   Alas, to dye thou makyst me sure; yet then, good
                 Lord, do thou thi cure
F40.1   2   Good Lord, who may a goodlyer be
F44b   2   Good Lord, preserve the Estrige Fether!
F44.1   1   O blessed Lord of hevyn celestiall,
F44.1   4   In honor to rayne, Lord, graunt hym tyme and space,
F44.2   1   Wherfore, good Lord, syth of thi creacion
F48.1   4   As long as I am Lord and Kyng,
H35.1   4   Lord, I was glad of it!
H50b   2   My soverayne lord I shall love best.
H50.2   1   My soverayne lord of pusant pure
H67.1   4   Ower Lord yow gy;
H92.5   2   Goode Lord, graunt us our mancyon to be!
H105.2   2   Full lovely lookyng on our Lord, the lanterne of
                 lyght

LORDE (14)
F47.1   1   Soverayn lorde, in erth most excellent,
F48.1   10   That am the cheffe lorde of the fee.
H25.11   2   Goode Lorde, deffend
H50.1   1   My soverayne lorde for my poure sake
H50.1   6   My soverayne lorde.
H50.2   6   My soverayne lorde.
H50.3   1   My soverayne lorde in every thyng
H50.3   6   My soverayne lorde.
H50.4   1   My soverayne lorde when that I mete,
H50.4   6   My soverayne lorde.
H50.5   6   My soverayne lorde.
H50.6   1   The soverayne lorde that is of all,
H50.6   2   My soverayne lorde save principall!
H50.6   6   My soverayne lorde.

LORE (1)
H35.7   2   Now of this hunter's lore;

LORNE (1)
F48.2   5   Yet, man, that thou sholdest not be lorne,

LOSE (2)
R18.4   4   I shall lose God *et vitam eternam*.'

LOSE (cont.)
F1   6   Thoo I go lose, yet am I teyd with a lyne:

LOST (5)
F7.2   3   Sum tyme is lost and all in vayne
F12   3   The son, the moone, had lost ther force and light;
F40.4   2   Be lost so sone? I am a fole:
F48.2   8   Witness, the son that lost his lyghth,
H102.2 2   No love that can be lost;

LOTH (1)
R20.1   3   That ye loth Y love -- wrappe that yn your trayne!

LOTHER (1)
F1   4   The lyghter leefe, the lother for to wende;

LOUGH (1)
F29.2   3   A childe she hoppid; she song, she lough;

LOVE (108)
R9   8   Sum love comaundes me this aventure,
R9   9   Thorffe with yeur beute that Y most love and prise.
R10.2   4   Apon fals love!
R10.2   5   Love I deny;
R10.2   7   To love vaynly;
R10.3   2   And love dere bought
R10.5   6   Love doth refrayn,
R12.1   2   I love and shall unto I dye;
R13.3   5   Myn hert and love; what wyll she more?
R20.1   3   That ye loth Y love -- wrappe that yn your trayne!
R20.2   3   With hert Y wyll you plece and your love attayne:
R20.3   3   But light credens turnyth your love agayne:
R20.4   2   Love me lytell and longe; hot love doth not reyne;
F5   7   To love and dred hym as my lord and kyng.
F9   1   Love fayne wolde I;
F21   1   I love, loved, and loved wolde I be
F21   4   To love, thowe I do fere to trace that dawnce,
F27b   1   'I love, I love, and whom love ye?'
F27b   2   'I love a floure of fressh beaute;'
F27b   3   'I love another as well as ye.'
F27.1   1   'I love a flour of swete odour'
F27.3   1   'On that I love most enterly.'
F27.4b 1   'Now have I lovyd, and whom love ye?'
F27.4b 2   'I love a floure of fressh beaute.'
F27.4b 3   'I love anothyr as well as ye.'
F27.6   1   'I love the rose, both red and white.'
F27.6b 1   'Nowe have we lovyd, and love will we
F28   3   To love her best and no mo
F33.2   2   I love the, then love me; why slepist thou? Awake!
F33.3   3   Thus bobbid, thus robbid, thus for thi love ded;
F34.1   3   Forsake thi syn, man, for the love of me;
F34.2   7   Love for love be just convencion;
F36.3   2   He willfully doth suffir for love speciall
F39.3   5   'Leve, love, this chance,

LOVE (cont.)

F41.2	2	And I love you an hole cart-lode.'
F41.4	4	Yet for his love that all hath wrought
F42.2	1	The fayrest man that best love can,
F46b	2	Will I love and shall I love,
F46b	3	Will I love and shall I love
F46.1	1	Love is naturall to every wyght,
F46.3	5	And love her only whereever she gone:
F48b	5	For thi love, man, have suffyrd deth
F48.1	8	Love thi neyboure as I love the!
H12	1	Alas, what shall I do for love?
H12	2	For love, alasse, what shall I do,
H15	3	Sens I must nedys from my love depart
H25.1	1	My love sche morneth
H25.1	3	My love sche morneth for me.
H25.2	4	My love, I say,
H25.2	5	Your love do way
H25.5	6	To helpe my love and me.
H25.6	6	So trew of love was sche.
H25.11	6	My love that mornyth for me.
H29.2	1	I love her well with hart and mynd;
H30	3	And trew love lokked therto?
H31.8	6	My love, my derlyng dere.'
H34.1	2	In love he must be withowt dysdayne,
H34.2	1	For love enforcyth all nobyle kynd,
H34.3	1	Wherfor to love and be not loved
H34.4	1	Love encoragith and makyth on bold;
H34.5	1	Love ys gevyn to God and man;
H34.7	1	Grett pyte it ware, love for to compell
H39	3	My love is to the grenewode gone,
H40	1	I love trewly withowt feynyng;
H40	2	My love, she is so trew to me.
H40	3	To love her sure whill I am levyng,
H44.1	1	If love now reynyd as it hath bene
H44.5	2	But let them tell which love doth gett.
H47.4	4	I love you and no mo.
H50b	2	My soverayne lord I shall love best.
H50.1	5	And of all other for to love best
H50.4	5	With hart and body to love best
H51.2	1	And whosoever may love gete,
H51.7	1	Love maynteynyth all noble courage;
H51.7	2	Who love dysdaynyth ys all of the village.
H51.10	1	For whoso lovith shuld love butt oone;
H64.1	12	And love to optayne.
H64.2	4	Onys love sure
H64.2	7	Wher love so sewith,
H66.3	4	I love trew wher I dyd mary:
H75	2	My love is lusty, plesant and demure
H79.1	3	And love her in hart and dede,
H79.1	5	Many oone sayth that love ys yll,
H79.2	3	But love us a thyng gevyn by God;
H82.1	4	Wold have yough love to refrayn,
H102.2	2	No love that can be lost;
H103.3	1	O my swet hart, whome I love best,

LOVE (cont.)
H104b	2	My love, my love?
H104b	6	Yt is but you, my love, alone.
H104.1	6	But you, my love, alone.
H104.2	6	But you, my love, alone.
H104.3	6	But yow, my love, alone.
H104.4	5	Kepe your love
H108	1	I love unloved; suche is myn aventure,
H108	3	But love my fo, that fervent creature
H108	5	From her love nothinge can me revert
H108	7	And love unloved; such ys myne adventure.
H109.2	3	Syth I love you, love me agayne;

LOVED (3)
| F21 | 1 | I love, loved, and loved wolde I be |
| H34.3 | 1 | Wherfor to love and be not loved |

LOVELY (1)
| H105.2 | 2 | Full lovely lookyng on our Lord, the lanterne of lyght |

LOVER (2)
| R10.2 | 2 | A lover trewly, |
| R10.6 | 2 | My lover unkynd, |

LOVERS (8)
R10.4	1	All lovers beware,
H25.11	3	All lovers that trew be,
H29.5	2	Unto ther lovers trew for to be;
H44.3	2	And causith lovers owtwardly to refrayne,
H44.6	1	To lovers I put now suer this cace -
H51.8	1	Soch lovers though thay take payne
H51.9	2	Thay hynder lovers that wolde be trew.
H64.2	2	That lovers be

LOVES (1)
| H44.6 | 2 | Which of ther loves doth get them grace? |

LOVETH (1)
| H50.5 | 5 | A vengeance on them that lovith nott best |

LOVITH (2)
| H49.3 | 3 | In faith my lady lovith me well; |
| H51.10 | 1 | For whoso lovith shuld love butt oone; |

LOVYD (4)
R10.5	7	Not lovyd agayn,
R19.2	10	That she had lovyd so long.
F27.4b	1	'Now have I lovyd, and whom love ye?'
F27.6b	1	Nowe have we lovyd, and love will we

LOVYNG (2)
| R10.5 | 2 | Lovyng yn vayne, |
| F48.1 | 6 | But a lovyng and a contrite hart, |

LOVYS (3)
R10.3   8   Yn lovys daunce.
H25.2   1   In lovys daunce
H64.1   9   Of lovys payne,

LOVYST (1)
F34b   6   Why, lovyst thou me?

LOVYTH (2)
H49.2   3   She lovyth another better than me
H51.1   2   Who lovyth not wantith corage.

LOW (1)
R10.3   7   Full low forfought

LOWDE (1)
F49b   2   I harde a voice lowde call and crye

LOYALL (1)
H67.2   8   Loyall and playne.

LUGE (1)
H65.4   3   I can luge and make a sute

LUK (1)
F43.3   1   Rutterkyn shall bryng you all good luk;

LULLAY (1)
F30.1   5   She sang lullay

LURE (1)
H75   5   As the hauke to the lure,

LUST (3)
H16   1   Adew, adew, my hartis lust!
H35.3   3   And yf ye lust to have a shott,
H82.1   6   How thay dyd in ther most lust.

LUSTI (1)
H92.1   1   Lusti yough shuld us ensue,

LUSTY (6)
F37.2   2   To lusty plesure? Now lyyng in the flore,
F39.2   1   Her lusty chere,
H20   1   In may, that lusty sesoun
H22   4   Of lusty bloddys and chevalry.
H75   2   My love is lusty, plesant and demure
H96b   1   Englond, be glad! Pluk up thy lusty hart!

LY (1)
F30.2   4   Thus for to ly,

LYE (1)
F18.2   5   When that ye do lye,

LYF (3)
 R10.4   4   To lede my lyf;
 H67.2   7   Whyls lyf endur,
 H107.5   1   My lyf was lent

LYFE (2)
 H106.2   6   In dysdayn I shall my lyfe endure,
 H106.3   6   Yet my lyfe is to me so grevus

LYFF (4)
 F22   3   Tyll deth my lyff departe from hens!
 F24.5   1   My lyff was lent
 F36.3   11   From deth to lyff he aryse shall.'
 H41b   4   Yow and I, my lyff, and Amyas.

LYFF-DAIES (1)
 F38.2   6   Fo all my lyff-daies I have myspend:

LYFFE (3)
 R1.2   4   Ther to lede my lyffe.
 F25.3   6   My lyffe to spente,
 H106.1   4   My lyffe as one that dye would fayne;

LYGHT (5)
 F31.1   3   Inmortal, inpassible, the wordlis lyght,
 F36.4   4   The erth quakyd, the son was dark, whos lyght was
                  past
 F46.1   3   Chaungyng his course, now hevy, now lyght,
 H96.1   3   With spers and sheldys on goodly horsys lyght,
 H105.2   2   Full lovely lookyng on our Lord, the lanterne of
                  lyght

LYGHTER (1)
 F1   4   The lyghter leefe, the lother for to wende;

LYGHTH (1)
 F48.2   8   Witness, the son that lost his lyghth,

LYK (3)
 F5   3   Full lyk to drowne in wavis of dystres,
 H82.2   1   For yf thay war in lyk case
 H103.3   3   For which my hart is lyk to brest,

LYKE (3)
 F27.5   3   'Both be full swete and of lyke savoure;
 F39b   3   Ther is non lyke
 F49.1   2   Whome I did make so lyke unto me,

LYKYTH (4)
 F27.1   5   Is non of them that lykyth me.'
 F27.2   5   That best lykyth me.'
 F27.4   5   In hart so fre, that best lykyth me.'
 F27.5   5   That day to se it lykyth well me.'

LYLY-WHIGHTE (3)
F45.1   5   The lyly-whighte rose methought I sawe,
F45.1   6   The lyly-whighte rose methought I sawe,
F45.2   6   The lyly-whighte rose methought I sawe,

LYMMYS (1)
F36.2   3   Beholdyng ther his lymmys all to-rent and tore,

LYNAGE (1)
F44.2   2   Is this noble prince of riall lynage,

LYNDE (1)
H65.2   2   Opon the grenwode lynde?

LYNE (1)
F1   6   Thoo I go lose, yet am I teyd with a lyne:

LYNYACION (1)
F40.2   1   Her contynaunce with her lynyacion,

LYON (1)
R7   4   This lyon and lambe was, causyng pyte;

LYST (1)
F33.3   9   Cum when thou lyst, welcum to me!

LYTELL (2)
R20.4   2   Love me lytell and longe; hot love doth not reyne;
F40.3   1   She is my lytell praty on;

LYTH (1)
F30.1 18   Lyth in hay.'

LYTILL (1)
H105.1 2   Lokyng on her lytill son, so laughyng in lap layd,

LYTYLL (3)
R16b   2   Thou lytyll, pretty Besse,
F4   4   So mekyll dred, so lytyll trust
F15   2   Thow I be lytyll in your remembraunce;

LYVE (5)
R12.1   4   So God be plecyd, this lyve woll I;
F37.4   5   With all good sowlis to cause me lyve in rest.
F48.2 10   Witness, the bodies that rose from deth to lyve.
H50b   1   Whilles lyve or breth is in my brest
H106.1 6   Thus do I lyve in gret hevenes

LYVES (1)
R9   5   My lyves ladi and my hertis cure,

LYVING (2)
R10.4   8   Lyving yn stryf;
R10.5   1   Lyving yn payn,

LYYNG (1)
F37.2   2   To lusty plesure? Now lyyng in the flore,

MADAM (1)
F25.1   1   Madam, defrayne!

MADAME (2)
H41.4   2   He said, 'Desyre, your man, madame.'
H41.5   2   He said, 'Madame, as your prisoner.'

MADE (3)
F30.1   17   That made all thyng
F31.2   2   That made both paynys and joy also,
F48.1   1   A, man, I have yevyn and made a graunt

MAGEROME (1)
F27.1   2   'Magerome, gentyll or lavendour,

MAIDE (1)
F29.2   2   I sawe a maide fayre inow;

MAIST (1)
F33.1   9   Condemp to deth, as thou maist se;

MAJESTE (1)
F47.2   5   Which crye and call unto your Majeste.

MAK (3)
H29.5   3   Promyse I mak that know non shall
H35.7   1   Here I leve and mak an end,
H65.2   3   I have strengh to mak it fle

MAKE (25)
R2.1   2   Enforsed me this complaynte for to make,
R3.1   1   'Be pes, ye make me spille my ale!'
R3.1   8   Ye will not make to huge a waste.
R3.2   6   Recke ye not to make us shende?
R14.1   3   With a dulfull chere here I make my mone,
R14.2   3   With a dulfull chere [here I make my mone,
F6.3   5   It wolde me make
F18.1   7   To make a belevyng:
F22   7   To send her to make me shent.
F32.1   2   That the Son of God shulde make us fre,
F34.1   4   Be repentant; make playne confession.
F36.3   3   He hath to man, to make hym fre that now is
                    thrall.
F37.4   1   Now, mercyfull Jhesu, to the make I my mone;
F49.1   2   Whome I did make so lyke unto me,
F49.1   4   Where thou were thrall, to make the free.
H33.3   2   Promyse to her I make,
H47.1   3   No myrth can make me fayn
H47.5   1   I make you fast and sure;
H50.1   2   Six coursys at the ryng dyd make,
H62.5   3   Thay stand abak and make it strange;

163

MAKE (cont.)
H65.4   3   I can luge and make a sute
H67.2   1   And make you sure
H92.7   1   Now unto God thys prayer we make,
H104b   5   To make me glad
H109.2   4   Let us make one, though we be twayne!

MAKER (1)
F34b   7   'Ye, my maker I call the.'

MAKER'S (1)
H105.2   1   I mene this by Mary, our Maker's moder of myght,

MAKES (1)
H104.1   2   Makes me so mery

MAKITH (1)
H34.4   2   Dysdayne abattyth and makith hym colde.

MAKYNG (3)
R15.1   6   Makyng her moone.
R15.8   6   Makyng my moon.'
R19.3   3   Makyng my mone

MAKYST (1)
F37.4   4   Alas, to dye thou makyst me sure; yet then, good
                  Lord, do thou thi cure

MAKYTH (1)
H34.4   1   Love encoragith and makyth on bold;

MAN (29)
R3.3   2   'Be Criste, Y nelle, what ses the man?
R7   1   Thow man, envired with temptacion,
R10.6   6   As man that ys blynd,
R12.3   4   But every man hath hys frewyll.
F4   3   Was nevir man saff only I;
F9   7   Her man to be
F30.2   16   Man to restore,
F31.4   1   'Lo, man, for the that ware onkynd,
F33b   2   My blode, man,
F33.2   1   Thus nakyd am I nailid, O man, for thy sake;
F33.2   7   Whereas never man was so
F33.3   8   Than I have done, O man, for the?
F34.1   3   Forsake thi syn, man, for the love of me;
F36.3   3   He hath to man, to make hym fre that now is
                  thrall.
F42.2   1   The fayrest man that best love can,
F48b   5   For thi love, man, have suffyrd deth
F48.1   1   A, man, I have yevyn and made a graunt
F48.2   1   If any man will say here agayne
F48.2   5   Yet, man, that thou sholdest not be lorne,
F48.3   7   And, man, for the more sykyrnesse,
F49b   3   'Amende the, man, of thi trespace,

MAN (cont.)
H23.3	1	And they be plesant to God and man,
H29.1	4	Shall no man know her name for me.
H29.3	4	Shall no man know her name for me.
H29.4	4	Shall no man [know her name for me].
H29.6	4	Shall no man [know her name for me].
H34.5	1	Love ys gevyn to God and man;
H41.4	2	He said, 'Desyre, your man, madame.'
H66.3	3	I hurt no man, I do no wrong;

MANCYON (1)
| H92.5 | 2 | Goode Lord, graunt us our mancyon to be! |

MANE (1)
| H29.2 | 4 | Shall no mane know her name for me. |

MANER (2)
| F20 | 2 | With vertu connyng her maner is lede, |
| H31.4 | 2 | In no maner a way |

MANERLY (10)
F39b	5	So manerly
F39.1	9	So manerly
F39.2	9	So manerly
F39.3	9	So manerly
F41.1	7	With manerly Margery, milk and ale.
F41.2	7	With manerly [Margery, milk and ale.]
F41.3	7	With manerly Margery, [milke and ale.]
F41.4	7	With manerly Margery, milke and ale;
F41.4	9	With manerly Margery, [milke and ale.]
H105.1	1	The moder full manerly and mekly as a mayd,

MANKYND (2)
| F29.3 | 2 | To save mankynd that was forlorne; |
| F31b | 2 | That God hymselfe for sole mankynd |

MANKYNDE (1)
| R16.1 | 2 | And Besse ys mankynde; |

MANNE (1)
| F48.2 | 3 | [Rather then manne sholde be forlorne |

MANNERS (1)
| H105.3 | 1 | Musyng on her manners, so ny mard was my mayne, |

MANNYS (3)
F10	8	Now raynyth trewly in every mannys syght.
F29.5	2	For mannys gilt is not withstone,
F48.3	10	The grete daye of mannys mercy.

MANY (7)
F30.2	11	Many a wownd
F48.3	4	And othir wittness, many one;
H50.5	1	So many vertuse gevyn of grace

MANY (cont.)
H62.1   2 Long and many a day;
H65b   2 And have ben many a day,
H79.1   5 Many oone sayth that love ys yll,
H101.1   2 As many one ys,

MANYFOLD (1)
H27.3   3 And now with syghs manyfold,

MARD (1)
H105.3   1 Musyng on her manners, so ny mard was my mayne,

MARGARET (1)
F39b   1 Margaret meke

MARGARIT (1)
F39.3   1 My Margarit

MARGERY (5)
F41.1   7 With manerly Margery, milk and ale.
F41.2   7 With manerly [Margery, milk and ale.]
F41.3   7 With manerly Margery, [milke and ale.]
F41.4   7 With manerly Margery, milke and ale;
F41.4   9 With manerly Margery, [milke and ale.]

MARI (1)
F48.3   3 Witness, Mari, wittness, Seynt Jhon,

MARSHIALL (1)
F47.1   4 Of marshiall power and also hye dygnite,

MARY (6)
F30b   2 Seyd Mary, 'A, my dere;
F30.1   4 Mary, that may,
F36.3   1 Saynt Jhon than said, 'Feere not, Mary; his
                    paynys al
H66.3   4 I love trew wher I dyd mary:
H66.4   2 Pray we to God and Seynt Mary
H105.2   1 I mene this by Mary, our Maker's moder of myght,

MASTRAS (1)
R11.3   1 Such a mastras I may calle

MASTRES (2)
R12.2   6 Ys cheff mastres
F23.2   7 Have but yourselfe, fayre lady and mastres.

MASTRESS (1)
F23.1   7 That hath byn your fayre lady and mastress.

MATER (1)
F34.3   5 Role up this mater; grave it in thi reson:

166

MATERNALL (1)
 F44.3   6   Modir maternall,

MAVYS (1)
 R19.1   1   Hay how the mavys on a brere!

MAWDE (1)
 F39.2   6   Mawde and Anes,

MAWDLEN (1)
 F34.3   1   I hade on Petur and Mawdlen pyte

MAY (64)
 R1.2   1   All the whiles that Y may my bowe bende
 R3.2   1   After asay then may ye wette;
 R4   6   That Y fro yew may hyre sume gode tydyng,
 R5   3   Till that Y may in yeure presaunce
 R6   1   O blessed lord, how may this be
 R11.3   1   Such a mastras I may calle
 R13.1   5   Of my pore hert she may be sure,
 R15.5   1   Now may I wynd
 F2   5   Sum other grace may cum, perde;
 F4   6   To thynk my sorows, well may I complayne;
 F10   7   Men may fynd day ne nyght adulacion
 F17   5   I wote nott where I may complayn;
 F19   2   Houghevyr such dyversite in on person may be,
 F24.1   8   What may I gess?
 F27.6   4   Joyed may we be
 F27.6b 4   Than may be provid here anon
 F28   1   Complayne I may wherevyr I go,
 F30.1   4   Mary, that may,
 F31b   1   Jhesu, mercy, how may this be,
 F31b   4   My witt nor reson may hit well fynd:
 F31b   5   Jhesu, mercy, how may this be?
 F31.1   5   Jhesu, mercy, [how may this be?]
 F31.2   5   Jhesu, mercy, [how may this be?]
 F31.3   5   Jhesu, mercy, [how may this be?]
 F31.4   5   [Jhesu, mercy, how may this be?]
 F33b   4   It may not be naid;
 F34.5   6   May washe us all from surfettes reprovable.
 F40b   3   Alak, good Jhoane, what may you please?
 F40.1   2   Good Lord, who may a goodlyer be
 F40.1   5   Alak, good Jhoone, [what may you please?
 F40.2   5   Alak, good [Jhoone, what may you please?
 F40.3   5   Alak, good Jhoan, [what may you please?
 F40.4   5   Alak, good Jhoan, [what may you please?
 H20   1   In May, that lusty sesoun
 H23.2   2   Whych one may use, and vice denye;
 H23.4   2   Wherby actyvenesse oon may utter.
 H23.5   1   Comparysons in them may lawfully be sett,
 H28   4   Joy shall I never ye may be sure.
 H31.1   2   I hard a may
 H31.4   1   And now I may
 H35.7   4   Hys bolt may fle no more.

167

MAY (cont.)

H47.2	4	We shall mete when we may.
H47.3	3	It may in no wyse agre
H51.2	1	And whosoever may love gete,
H62.1	4	No lenger shote I may;
H62.6	3	And pray I wyll for them that may,
H62.6	4	For I may nowght but loke;
H65b	4	For shote ryght well I may.
H65.4	4	As well as any in May:
H67.2	6	Ye may be sure,
H79.2	1	Or else because they may not opteyne,
H82.2	3	Thay may not now than gaynesay
H92.2	4	But follow hys mynd in all that we may.
H92.7	2	That this rude play may well be take,
H92.7	3	And that we may ower fauttes amend,
H97	1	Pray we to God that all may gyde
H97	4	He may acheffe this gret viage:
H103.2	1	Bewayll I may myn adventure
H106.4	1	Thus may ye se my wofull chance,
H107.1	8	What may I gesse?
H109b	6	Nay, God forbede! That may not be -
H109.1	2	We may us sport and not be sene;
H109.1b	4	That now in the feldes we may us sportt?
H109.1b	5	Nay, God forbede! That may not be;

MAYD (1)

H105.1	1	The moder full manerly and mekly as a mayd,

MAYDE (5)

R15.2	2	'Y was a mayde
R15.5	6	A mayde agayn.
H31.8	4	And saide, 'Goode mayde,
H109b	2	Mayde, whether go you?
H109.1	4	How sey ye, mayde? Be ye content?

MAYDYN (2)

R18.1	2	And found a maydyn sub quadam arbore,
H101.1	1	And I war a maydyn,

MAYDYNHED (1)

H109.3	3	And graunte me here your maydynhed,

MAYDYNS (2)

F46b	4	No mo maydyns but one.
H62.5	2	When I shulde maydyns kysse,

MAYDYNYS (1)

F36b	2	Methought a maydynys childe causless shulde dye.

MAYNE (1)

H105.3	1	Musyng on her manners, so ny mard was my mayne,

MAYNTEN (1)

F8	7	All myrthis to maynten, all sorous to subdewe.

MAYNTEYNYTH (1)
H51.7   1   Love maynteynyth all noble courage;

ME (169)
R1.2   3   I shall bygge me a boure atte the wodes ende,
R2.1   2   Enforsed me this complaynte for to make,
R3.1   1   'Be pes, ye make me spille my ale!'
R3.2   2   Why blame ye me withoute offence?
R3.3   1   Cum kys me! 'Nay!' Be God, ye shall!
R3.3   6   'Now have ye leyde me un the flore,
R4   1   Absens of you causeth me to sygh and complayne
R4   3   And thogh Y wolde, Y koude me noght refrayne
R4   5   All for yeure sake, til God me so avaunce
R5   5   That ye wilde fuchesaffe to have mercy on me
R7   5   And say after me, and be noght unkynde:
R9   8   Sum love comaundes me this aventure,
R10.3   3   Settyth me at nought,
R11.1   4   My lady hath forsakyn me.
R11.2   4   My lady hath forsakyn me.
R11.3   4   My lady hath forsakyn me.]
R11.4   1   I trow on me she wold rewe
R11.4   4   [My lady hath forsakyn me.]
R12.1   10   Who shall me lett?
R12.2   3   Company me thynckyth then best
R12.3   10   Y shall use me.
R13.3   1   She hath me hurt; why shold she not hele,
R13.3   2   And geve me salfe unto my sore?
R14.2   2   Takyn away from me bycause of hevynes;
R15.3   3   To me alone,
R15.3   4   And me begylyd,
R15.8   2   Has thus lefte me
R16b   3   Come over the burne, Besse, to me!
R16.1   6   Cum over the burne, Besse, to me!
R18.3   3   They wyll me bete cum virgis ac fustibus
R18.3   4   And me sore chast coram omnibus.
R19.1   3   I drew me nere
R19.2   6   She seyd me nay
R20.1   1   Your light grevans shall not me constrayne
R20.2   1   Your on-syttyng speche puttyth me to payne
R20.4   2   Love me lytell and longe; hot love doth not reyne;
F2   2   Ye thynk for to discomfort me.
F3   1   What causyth me wofull thoughtis to thynk
F3   4   Then be it they that doth me trobill so
F3   5   That be won thought my rest from me doth go.
F3   6   And yet mythynkyth hit grevith me moche more
F3   7   That no thought can reless me of my sore.
F6.3   5   It wolde me make
F9   6   I wolde bynde me
F13   1   To complayne me, alas, why shulde I so?
F13   2   For my complayntes it dyd me nevir good;
F13   6   And lett me not allway be guerdonless,
F19   5   As solen, as stately, as strange toward me,
F21   6   Yet will I me trust to fortune applye;
F22   4   Absens it is that wolde me wrong;

ME (cont.)

F22	7	To send to her to make me shent.
F23.1	6	Onryghtfully shewyng me unkyndness,
F23.2	4	And with pite have me in remembraunce
F24.1	7	Me contraryyng;
F24.2	8	Me doth avaunce
F25.1	2	Ye me retayne
F27.1	5	Is non of them that lykyth me.'
F27.2	2	And shall not yet be namyd for me;
F27.2	5	That best lykyth me.'
F27.3	5	Here is not he that plesyth me.'
F27.4	5	In hart so fre, that best lykyth me.'
F27.5	5	That day to se it lykyth well me.'
F27.6b	3	Most worthy it is, as thynkyth me.
F28	4	And she me takyth in gret disdayne:
F28	5	I-wiss yet will I not me complayne
F28	7	Lest cause in me be fownd of offens.
F29.1	1	As I me walkyd this endurs day
F33.1	1	Beholde me, I pray the, with all thi hole reson,
F33.1	7	The Jewis me thretid,
F33.1	8	They mowid, they grynned, they scornyd me,
F33.2	2	I love the, then love me; why slepist thou? Awake!
F33.3	9	Cum when thou lyst, welcum to me!
F34b	2	Who is that that dothe me call?
F34b	6	Why, lovyst thou me?
F34.1	3	Forsake thi syn, man, for the love of me;
F36.2	1	His grevous deth and her morenyng grevid me sore;
F36.2	8	Me unto grace for to restore:
F37.2	1	Where art thou, Nature, that wont were me to store
F37.2	5	Thou, Nature, hast lefft me; by the fynd I no rest:
F37.3	3	My dreme is so mervelous, serpentis semyth me to tere
F37.3	4	Grete mowntens fallyng over me, thus slepe doth I yn feere
F37.4	2	Nature hath forsakyn me, and lefft me thus alone.
F37.4	4	Alas, to dye thou makyst me sure; yet then, good Lord, do thou thi cure
F37.4	5	With all good sowlis to cause me lyve in rest.
F38.2	5	Me to amend I will me hye
F39.1	2	When she me bas,
F39.1	6	I thynk me bond,
F40.3	4	I-wis, she will not gyve me a bone:
F41.3	2	What, wolde ye frompill me now? fy, fy!
F41.4	1	'Walke forthe your way, ye cost me nought;
F41.4	5	Wed me or els I dye for thought!
F46.3	2	So it is best, as thynkyth me,
F48b	3	To me shal be leffe and dere,
F49.1	2	Whome I did make so lyke unto me,
H12	5	To kepe yow me unto?
H18	4	Wherfor to her I me complayn, hey now!
H24	2	They greve me passyng sore,
H25.1	2	For me, for me,
H25.1	3	My love sche morneth for me.
H25.1	6	Morne ye no more for me.

ME (cont.)

H25.2	6	And morne no more for me.
H25.3	2	To me hart roote
H25.3	6	And morne no more for me.
H25.4	3	What sayd sche then to me?
H25.4	6	But styll to morne for me.
H25.5	6	To helpe my love and me.
H25.8	6	And sayd sche morned for me.
H25.9	2	I me bethought
H25.9	6	And morne no more for me.
H25.10	6	With her that morneth for me.
H25.11	6	My love that mornyth for me.
H27.1	2	They greve me passyng sore;
H27.1	3	Sen ye must nedes from me depart,
H27.2	1	Oft to me her godely swet face
H29.1	4	Shall no man know her name for me.
H29.2	3	My hart to have she doth me bynd;
H29.2	4	Shall no mane know her name for me.
H29.3	2	Nor for no new me chaunge doth she,
H29.3	4	Shall no man know her name for me.
H29.4	3	For she to me ys allway kynd;
H29.4	4	Shall no man [know her name for me].
H29.5	4	Whill I leve her name for me.
H29.6	4	Shall no man [know her name for me].
H31.2	6	Forsake me for a new.
H31.7	6	My hart it grevyth me so.'
H33.3	4	To her I me betake.
H40	2	My love, she is so trew to me.
H47.1	3	No myrth can make me fayn
H47.2	3	Thow ye now parte me fro,
H47.3	1	When I remembyr me
H47.5	2	It ys to me gret payne
H49.1	2	Tel me how thy lemman doth,
H49.2	3	She lovyth another better than me
H49.3	3	In faith my lady lovith me well;
H51.6	2	Myne ey with hart doth me so juge.
H62.3	1	Every bowe for me ys to bygge;
H62.4	1	Lady Venus hath commaundyd me
H62.4	3	Ryght playnly she shewith me
H62.6	1	Now will I take to me my bedes
H63.2	1	Thowgh you depart now thus me fro,
H63.2	2	And leve me all alone,
H64.1	6	Best semyth me.
H66.1	1	Though sum saith that yough rulyth me,
H66.1	5	Though sum say that yough rulyth me.
H66.2	5	Though sum sayth [that yough rulyth me.]
H66.3	5	Thow sum saith [that yough rulyth me.]
H66.4	5	Though sum [saith that yough rulyth me.]
H67.2	3	Shall me solur
H102.1	1	My lady hath me in that grace
H102.1	2	She takes me as her howne;
H103.3	2	Whos unkyndnes hath me opprest,
H104b	5	To make me glad
H104.1	2	Makes me so mery

ME (cont.)
H104.2 4 Me to comfort
H105.3 2 Save it plesyd me so passyngly that past was my
           payn
H106.2 1 My hope frome me is clene exiled,
H106.2 3 My payne with hope hath me begyled;
H106.3 6 Yet my lyfe is to me so grevus
H106.4 5 Good aventure in me to have place:
H107.2 8 Me doth avance
H108   5 From her love nothinge can me revert
H109.1b 2 I pray you, sir, lett me go mylke my cow!
H109.1b 3 Why, wyll ye nott geve me no comfortt,
H109.2 3 Syth I love you, love me agayne;
H109.3 3 And graunte me here your maydynhed,
H109.4 4 Adew, farewell and kysse me now!

MEANE (1)
H35.6   4 What do yow meane or thynk?

MEDE (1)
H35.2   2 The dere shoffe on the mede;

MEDIACION (1)
F34.5   7 Now for thi moders meke mediacion,

MEDOW (3)
H109b   4 Than at the medow I wyll you mete
H109.1 1 Now yn this medow fayer and grene
H109.4 3 How in the medow ye mylke your cow.

MEDOWE (1)
H109b   3 I go to the medowe to mylke my cow.

MEDOWS (1)
H20   3 By the medows grene;

MEKE (2)
F34.5   7 Now for thi moders meke mediacion,
F39b   1 Margaret meke

MEKLY (1)
H105.1 1 The moder full manerly and mekly as a mayd,

MEKYLL (1)
F4   4 So mekyll dred, so lytyll trust

MELLE (1)
H109.1b 1 Nay, in good feyth, I wyll not melle with you;

MEN (10)
R15.5   5 Men wene I be
R15.6   1 This young men say
R15.6   4 Men tellyth yn town
R20.4   1 An olde seyde saw: hasty men sone slayne;

MEN (cont.)
F10   7   Men may fynd day ne nyght adulacion
F20   6   Which that all men knowith, both more and less;
F29.4   2   That men sekyth for to spill,
H44.2   1   Nobyll men then wold suer enserch
H51.1   1   Thow that men do call it dotage,
H82.1   1   Let not us that yong men be

MENE (1)
H105.2   1   I mene this by Mary, our Maker's moder of myght,

MENEY (1)
R1.1   1   Y have ben a foster long and meney day;

MENT (3)
F24.5   7   But she it ment,
F25.3   3   My hart is ment,
H107.5   7   But she it ment,

MERCIABLE (4)
F34.2   8   Why art thou froward sith I am merciable?
F34.3   8   Be thou not froward syth I am merciable.
F34.4   8   Be thou not affraide sith I am merciable.
F34.5   8   At hir request be to us merciable.

MERCY (12)
R5   5   That ye wilde fuchesaffe to have mercy on me
R13.1   7   Abydyng your grace yn hope of mercy.
F31b   1   Jhesu, mercy, how may this be,
F31b   5   Jhesu, mercy, how may this be?
F31.1   5   Jhesu, mercy, [how may this be?]
F31.2   5   Jhesu, mercy, [how may this be?]
F31.3   5   Jhesu, mercy, [how may this be?]
F31.4   5   [Jhesu, mercy, how may this be?]
F34b   5   'Mercy, Lord, of the I crave.'
F38.1   7   I crye God mercy, I will amend.
F38.2   7   I crye God mercy, I will amend.
F48.3   10   The grete daye of mannys mercy.

MERCYABLE (1)
F34.1   8   Whi art thou froward, syth I am mercyable?

MERCYFULL (1)
F37.4   1   Now, mercyfull Jhesu, to the make I my mone;

MERE (1)
H35.4   4   For I myght shott no mere.

MERELY (1)
H20   8   Joyfully, so merely,

MERVELL (2)
F12   5   Yett more mervell how that I hard the sownde
F15   3   And mervell I have syth I not deservid

173

MERVELOUS (1)
F37.3   3 My dreme is so mervelous, serpentis semyth me to
               tere

MERVELYD (1)
H41.1   2 The lady mervelyd who was therat.

MERVELYNG (1)
F19   1 Thus musyng in my mynd, gretly mervelyng

MERY (4)
F17   6 For where I shulde, they be mery,
H92.1   2 Hys mery hart shall sure all rew;
H92.2   2 And all mery company for to dysdayne;
H104.1   2 Makes me so mery

MERYLY (1)
H20   5 So meryly, it joyed my hart

MEST (1)
H102.2   4 Her to remember mest

METE (10)
F39.3   2 I cannot mete
H28   3 Alas, pour hart, tyl that we mete agayne,
H31.6   2 Adew, ryght mete
H47.1   4 Tyl that we mete agayne.
H47.2   4 We shall mete when we may.
H47.5   4 Tyll that we mete agayne.
H50.4   1 My soverayne lorde when that I mete,
H68   2 I trust we shall mete oftener.
H109b   4 Than at the medow I wyll you mete
H109.2   1 Ye be so nyce and so mete of age

METEST (1)
H82.2   6 It ys for yough the metest play.

METHOUGHT (7)
F12   2 Methought the worlde was turnyd up so downe,
F36b   2 Methought a maydynys childe causless shulde dye.
F45.1   5 The lyly-whighte rose methought I sawe,
F45.1   6 The lyly-whighte rose methought I sawe,
F45.2   6 The lyly-whighte rose methought I sawe,
H101.3   4 Methought I had no pere.
H105.3   3 Yet softly to her swete sonne methought I hard
               her sayn

METHYNK (1)
H107.4   1 Methynk trewly

METHYNKYTH (3)
F24.4   1 Methynkyth truly
F29.4   1 'Modyr, methynkyth it is ryght ill,
F32.2   1 Methynkyth in my reson thou owfte to be gladd

174

MILK (2)
```
F41.1    7    With manerly Margery, milk and ale.
F41.2    7    With manerly [Margery, milk and ale.]
```

MILKE (3)
```
F41.3    7    With manerly Margery, [milke and ale.]
F41.4    7    With manerly Margery, milke and ale;
F41.4    9    With manerly Margery, [milke and ale.]
```

MO (5)
```
R2.2     2    To myn entent, and so sayeth mo then I,
F28      3    To love her best and no mo
F46b     4    No mo maydyns but one.
F46.2    1    One is good, but mo were bettyr
H47.4    4    I love you and no mo.
```

MOCH (1)
```
H34.6    2    Yet never the lesse it ys to moch used.
```

MOCHE (1)
```
F3       6    And yet mythynkyth hit grevith me moche more
```

MODE (2)
```
F13      5    Trustyng sumtyme that she will chaunge her mode
F37.1    2    My mode is changid in every wise,
```

MODER (6)
```
R3.2     8    My moder cam in, or that ye wende.'
F30b     3    Kys thi moder, Jhesu,
F30.2    1    'My moder dere,
F36.4    7    His moder rufully
H105.1   1    The moder full manerly and mekly as a mayd,
H105.2   1    I mene this by Mary, our Maker's moder of myght,
```

MODERLY (1)
```
F36.3    6    'Of moderly pete
```

MODERS (1)
```
F34.5    7    Now for thi moders meke mediacion,
```

MODIR (3)
```
F29.5    4    And I, thy modir, alone.'
F36.1    4    His modir dere tendirly wept and cowde not
                       refrayne
F44.3    6    Modir maternall,
```

MODYR (1)
```
F29.4    1    'Modyr, methynkyth it is ryght ill,
```

MONE (11)
```
R10.1    7    Whych causyth my mone;
R14.1    3    With a dulfull chere here I make my mone,
R14.2    3    With a dulfull chere [here I make my mone,
R19.3    3    Makyng my mone
```

MONE (cont.)

F6.4	4	For that to mone,
F37.4	1	Now, mercyfull Jhesu, to the make I my mone;
F40.4	1	Alas, good Jhoan, shall all my mone
H31.9	3	In voydyng care and mone
H63.2	4	For yow do I mone.
H104.1	3	From care and from all mone;
H104.3	3	To swage sumwhat my mone;

MOON (1)

R15.8	6	Makyng my moon.'

MOONE (2)

R15.1	6	Makyng her moone.
F12	3	The son, the moone, had lost ther force and light;

MORE (34)

R1.1	4	Foster woll Y be no more.
R4	7	That myght my herte in more ese bryng.
R11.2	1	The more sorow ys my payn
R13.3	5	Myn hert and love; what wyll she more?
F1	1	The farther I go, the more behynde;
F1	2	The more behynde, the nere my wayes ende;
F1	3	The more I sech, the wers can I fynde;
F3	6	And yet mythynkyth hit grevith me moche more
F12	5	Yett more mervell how that I hard the sownde
F19	8	To lett itt over pass, and thynk theron no more.
F20	6	Which that all men knowith, both more and less;
F24.1	2	And more morenyng
F29.3	3	Therfor I pray the, son, no more,
F32.1	7	Now blessid Lady, wepe no more:
F32.2	8	Now, blessid Lady, wepe [no more:
F32.3	8	Now, blessid Lady, wepe no more:
F32.4	2	Lay downe all thi wepyng, let no more be sene!
F32.4	8	Now blessid Lady, wepe no more:
F33.3	7	What myght I suffir more
F36.2	11	Unneth on worde cowde she speke more.
F48.1	5	Not covetyng more for all my smert
F48.3	7	And, man, for the more sykyrnesse,
H18	7	And never more to remayne.
H25.1	6	Morne ye no more for me.
H25.2	6	And morne no more for me.
H25.3	6	And morne no more for me.
H25.9	6	And morne no more for me.
H35.7	4	Hys bolt may fle no more.
H44.4	1	Which puttes them to more and more
H62.1	3	Foster wyl I be no more
H103.1	2	Which dayly encressith more and more;
H107.1	2	And more mornyng

MORENYNG (2)

F24.1	2	And more morenyng
F36.2	1	His grevous deth and her morenyng grevid me sore;

MOREOVYR (1)
F17   4   Yet moreovyr a gretter payne,

MORNE (6)
F36.3   5   'Why than so depe morne ye?'
H25.1   6   Morne ye no more for me.
H25.2   6   And morne no more for me.
H25.3   6   And morne no more for me.
H25.4   6   But styll to morne for me.
H25.9   6 · And morne no more for me.

MORNED (1)
H25.8   6   And sayd sche morned for me.

MORNETH (3)
H25.1   1   My love sche morneth
H25.1   3   My love sche morneth for me.
H25.10   6   With her that morneth for me.

MORNYNG (3)
R10.1   2   Mornyng alone,
H17   4   Adew mornyng,
H107.1   2   And more mornyng

MORNYTH (1)
H25.11   6   My love that mornyth for me.

MORTALITE (1)
F31.1   4   And wolde so take mortalite!

MORTESS (1)
F36.4   2   Full boistusly in the mortess he was downe cast;

MOST (22)
R2.1   6   Y most obey fortuneys ordynaunce,
R9   9   Thorffe with yeur beute that Y most love and prise.
F8   6   A rose most riall with levis fressh of hew,
F11   1   That was my woo is nowe my most gladness;
F20   1   Most clere of colour and rote of stedfastness,
F23.1   4   That was my wele is now my most grevaunce.
F27.3   1   'On that I love most enterly.'
F27.6b   3   Most worthy it is, as thynkyth me.
F33.2   8   Entretid, thus in most cruell wise
F38.1   4   That helpis the ever at thi most nede.
F38.2   1   With wepyng teris most lamentable
F39.2   2   Her yes most clere,
F44.1   2   Which formyd hast of thi most speciall grace
F45.2   4   And said, 'The white rose is most trewe
F47.1   1   Soverayn lorde, in erth most excellent,
H44.4   2   Inwardly most grevous and sore:
H47.3   2   Of your most gentyll mynde,
H50.5   4   His personage most godlyest!
H51.3   2   And she to hym most seme most fayre.
H82.1   6   How thay dyd in ther most lust.

MOST (cont.)
H82.2   4   That which then was most ther joy;

MOTHER (1)
H109b   7   I wysse my mother then shall us se!

MOTHYR (1)
H109.1b 6   I wysse my mothyr than shall us se!

MOURNYNG (1)
R11.1   1   My herte ys yn grete mournyng,

MOVE (2)
H25.4   5   Her schuld not move
H109.2   2   That ye gretly move my corage.

MOWID (1)
F33.1   8   They mowid, they grynned, they scornyd me,

MOWNT (1)
F48.3   9   Iyevyn upon the mownt of Calvary,

MOWNTENS (1)
F37.3   4   Grete mowntens fallyng over me, thus slepe doth I
                 yn feere

MUCH (1)
F23.2   5   Much the rathir sith my suryd constaunce

MUST (23)
R19.3   8   Yll must she the,
F6.4   3   That I must sett by;
F13   3   But be constraynt, now must I shew my woo
F36.3   7   I must nedis wofull be,
F37.4   3   'Remembir the, my creature, thou must nedis dye,
                 I the ensure.
F45b   4   And I must home gone.
H15   3   Sens I must nedys from my love depart
H16   3   Wyth dowbyl sorow complayn I must
H25.2   3   Of absence nedes must be,
H27.1   3   Sen ye must nedes from me depart,
H34.1   2   In love he must be withowt dysdayne,
H41b   3   To the grenewode must we go, alas!
H51.2   2   Frome Venus sure he must it fett;
H51.4   2   There is no bote; ther must it be.
H63.1   3   Frome yow a whyle must I depart;
H64.1   10   Then helpe must have
H66.4   1   Then sone dyscusse that hens we must;
H79.1   2   Hys entent must nedys be trew,
H82.1   5   In ther myndes consyder thei must
H92.6   3   Wherfor be thes he must be gydyd
H92.6   4   And vertuus pastaunce must be theryn usyd.
H106.2   5   Refrayne I must yet in dysdayne,
H109.4   2   But the nexte tyme ye must beware

MUSTE (1)
  H109.3 2 Wherfore ye muste my mynde fulfyll,

MUSYNG (4)
  F19   1 Thus musyng in my mynd, gretly mervelyng
  F24.1   1 Sumwhat musyng
  H105.3   1 Musyng on her manners, so ny mard was my mayne,
  H107.1   1 Sumwhat musyng

MY (290)
  R1.1   2 My lockes ben hore.
  R1.1   3 Y shall hong up my horne by the grenewode spray;
  R1.2   1 All the whiles that Y may my bowe bende
  R1.2   4 Ther to lede my lyffe.
  R2.1   1 My wofull hert of all gladnesse baryeyne
  R2.1   5 Till gode tydinges com my sorwe to slake
  R3.1   1 'Be pes, ye make me spille my ale!'
  R3.2   8 My moder cam in, or that ye wende.'
  R3.3   3 Ye herte my legge agenste the walle;
  R4   2 For of my hert ye have the governaunce;
  R4   7 That myght my herte in more ese bryng.
  R6   3 And yet Y have do my besynesse
  R9   3 Arested hathe my herte in sodeyn wise,
  R9   4 Y recommaunde my symple service sure,
  R9   5 My lyves ladi and my hertis cure,
  R10.1   5 My myrth ys gon
  R10.1   7 Whych causyth my mone;
  R10.1   8 Fortune ys my fo.
  R10.3   4 This ys my chaunce;
  R10.3   6 My hert ys braught
  R10.4   4 To lede my lyf;
  R10.6   2 My lover unkynd,
  R11.1   1 My herte ys yn grete mournyng,
  R11.1   2 My mynd also gretly waylyng;
  R11.1   4 My lady hath forsakyn me.
  R11.2   1 The more sorow ys my payn
  R11.2   4 My lady hath forsakyn me.
  R11.3   4 My lady hath forsakyn me.]
  R11.4   2 Iff my sorow and woe she knew:
  R11.4   4 [My lady hath forsakyn me.]
  R12.1   5 For my pastaunce
  R12.1   7 My hert ys sett
  R12.1   9 To my cumfort:
  R12.3   7 My mynde shall be;
  R13.1   4 To her which ys my yoyus plesure;
  R13.1   5 Of my pore hert she may be sure,
  R13.2   3 Sò depe hath thrylled my hert ynwardly
  R13.2   6 And only she which my wound begunne;
  R13.2   7 Ther of right I apeyle hyr to be my surgyon.
  R13.3   2 And geve me salfe unto my sore?
  R14.1   3 With a dulfull chere here I make my mone,
  R14.1   4 Pyteusly, my own sylf alone.
  R14.2   1 My blossum bright ys gone,
  R14.2   3 With a dulfull chere [here I make my mone,

179

R14.2	4	Pyteusly, my own sylf alone.]
R15.4	2	Lefe of my woe
R15.7	4	So fro my hert
R15.8	6	Makyng my moon.'
R18.2	3	But for my mysse _michi_ _deridere_;
R19.3	3	Makyng my mone
R19.3	5	This ys my song:
F1	2	The more behynde, the nere my wayes ende;
F2	1	A, a, my herte, I knowe yow well;
F2	7	With my desyre tyll I be spent:
F2	8	Wherefor, my hart, lett be, lett be!
F3	2	Syn thoughtis byn cheff causers of my woo;
F3	5	That be won thought my rest from me doth go.
F3	7	That no thought can reless me of my sore.
F4	6	To thynk my sorows, well may I complayne;
F5	1	My wofull hart in paynfull weryness,
F5	4	Saffe helpe and grace of my lord and soverayne,
F5	7	To love and dred hym as my lord and kyng.
F7.1	1	O my desyre, what eylyth the,
F7.1	8	O my desyre, what eylyth the?
F7.2	4	Thynkyth my hart can be well payd
F7.2	8	O my desyre, what aylyth the?
F11	1	That was my woo is nowe my most gladness;
F11	2	That was my payne is nowe my joyus chaunce;
F11	3	That was my feere is nowe my sykyrness;
F11	4	That was my grefe is now my alegeaunce.
F11	5	Thus hath now grace enrychyd my plesaunce,
F13	2	For my complayntes it dyd me nevir good;
F13	3	But be constraynt, now must I shew my woo
F13	7	Syth for my trouth she nedith no wittness.
F17	3	And my service allway refusyd,
F19	1	Thus musyng in my mynd, gretly mervelyng
F20	3	Which that passyth my mynde for to express
F22	3	Tyll deth my lyff departe from hens!
F23.1	1	That was my joy is now my woo and payne;
F23.1	2	That was my bliss is now my displesaunce;
F23.1	3	That was my trust is now my wanhope playne;
F23.1	4	That was my wele is now my most grevaunce.
F23.2	2	My hart is yours with gret assuraunce.
F23.2	3	Wherfore of ryght ye shuld my greffe complayne,
F23.2	5	Much the rathir sith my suryd constaunce
F24.2	4	My wofull chaunce;
F24.3	2	To my grevaunce
F24.3	7	Such is my daunce
F24.5	1	My lyff was lent
F25.1	7	That of my payne
F25.3	3	My hart is ment,
F25.3	6	My lyffe to spente,
F26	1	O rote of trouth, o princess to my pay,
F27.6	3	'To here talke of them is my delite.
F28	2	Syth I have done my besy payne
F29.4	3	For them to save, it is my will;
F30b	1	'A, my dere, a, my dere Son,'

F30b	2	Seyd Mary, 'A, my dere;
F30.1	3	All in my slepe:
F30.1	11	My joy, my leff,
F30.1	13	'Nothyng, my spouse,
F30.1	15	Unto my pay;
F30.1	16	My Sone, a Kyng
F30.2	1	'My moder dere,
F30.2	6	My Fadir's will.
F31b	4	My witt nor reson may hit well fynd:
F32.2	1	Methynkyth in my reson thou owfte to be gladd
F33b	2	My blode, man,
F33b	5	My body bloo and wan,
F33.2	3	Remembir my tendir hart-rote for the brake,
F33.2	4	With paynys my vaynys constraynyd to crake;
F33.3	1	Off sharpe thorne I have worne a crowne on my hede,
F33.3	4	Onfaynyd, not deynyd, my blode for to shede:
F33.3	5	My fete and handis sore
F34b	7	'Ye, my maker I call the.'
F34.1	7	Gayne gostly enmys thynk on my passion;
F34.2	1	My blody wowndes downe railyng be this tre,
F34.2	5	My hert ryven for thi redempcion.
F34.3	4	He put his handes depe in my syde adowne.
F34.3	7	My blode best triacle for thi transgression;
F34.4	1	Thynk agayne, pride, on my humilite;
F34.4	3	Gayne fals envy thynk on my charyte,
F34.4	4	My blode all spent by distillacion.
F36b	1	My feerfull dreme nevyr forgete can I:
F36.1	7	Alas, all for my gilt,
F36.4	11	And of my dreme was sore agast.
F37.1	2	My mode is changid in every wise,
F37.2	3	My tast disordyrd all reson far passyng,
F37.2	4	My face disfygurid, myn yes full daslyng;
F37.3	1	My voice is so trobled, my seknes then feele I;
F37.3	2	My slepis be so feerfull, I thynk then sure to dye;
F37.3	3	My dreme is so mervelous, serpentis semyth me to tere
F37.4	1	Now, mercyfull Jhesu, to the make I my mone;
F37.4	3	'Remembir the, my creature, thou must nedis dye, I the ensure.
F38.2	6	Fo all my lyff-daies I have myspend:
F39.3	1	My Margarit
F39.3	8	Herk, <u>my lady</u>!'
F40.3	1	She is my lytell praty on;
F40.3	2	What shulde I say? My mynde is gone.
F40.4	1	Alas, good Jhoan, shall all my mone
F41.1	1	Ay, besherewe yow! Be my fay
F41.1	3	Avent, avent, my popagay!
F41.3	3	'What, and ye shal be my piggesnye?'
F42.1	1	Who shall have my fayre lady?
F46.2	2	Affter my reason and jugement,
F46.3	3	To put in one my faithfull trust,
F48.1	5	Not covetyng more for all my smert
F48.2	6	In the awter I am offerd my Fader beforne;

F48.3	8	The wounde in my harte the seale it is,
F49.1	1	'Beholde', he saide, 'my creature,
H15	1	O my hart and O my hart!
H15	2	My hart it is so sore,
H15	3	Sens I must nedys from my love depart
H16	1	Adew, adew, my hartis lust!
H16	2	Adew, my joy and my solace!
H18	2	Now am I exild my lady fro
H20	5	So meryly, it joyed my hart
H24	1	The thowghtes within my brest,
H25.1	1	My love sche morneth
H25.1	3	My love sche morneth for me.
H25.2	4	My love, I say,
H25.5	6	To helpe my love and me.
H25.7	3	And sett her on my knee:
H25.7	6	It rewyd my hart to se.
H25.9	5	Of my report
H25.10	5	My hart to go
H25.11	6	My love that mornyth for me.
H27.1	1	A the syghes that cum from my hart
H27.1	4	Farewell, my joy, for evermore.
H27.3	4	Farewell, my joe, and welcom payne.
H27.4	4	Unto my hart as now she shuld.
H29.1	2	Of my lady, both fayre and fre,
H29.2	3	My hart to have she doth me bynd;
H29.6	1	My hart she hath and ever shall
H30	2	For care is cast into my hart,
H31.3	6	Wherfore my hart will brest.
H31.5	3	Adew, all my welfare!
H31.6	6	She said, 'Adew my dere!'
H31.7	6	My hart it grevyth me so.'
H31.8	6	My love, my derlyng dere.'
H33.1	4	Unto my lady trew.
H33.3	1	Now unto my lady
H33.4	2	Adew, my specyall,
H33.4	3	Who hath my hart trewly,
H39	3	My love is to the grenewode gone,
H40	2	My love, she is so trew to me.
H40	4	My hart with her ever shall be.
H41b	4	Yow and I, my lyff, and Amyas.
H41.6	2	And shew my lady hys oune wyll.
H47.1	2	My inward hevynes?
H49.2	1	My lady is unkynde I wis.
H49.3	3	In faith my lady lovith me well;
H50b	1	Whilles lyve or breth is in my brest
H50b	2	My soverayne lord I shall love best.
H50.1	1	My soverayne lorde for my poure sake
H50.1	4	Wherfor my hart I hym beqwest,
H50.1	6	My soverayne lorde.
H50.2	1	My soverayne lord of pusant pure
H50.2	6	My soverayne lorde.
H50.3	1	My soverayne lorde in every thyng
H50.3	6	My soverayne lorde.

MY (cont.)

H50.4	1	My soverayne lorde when that I mete,
H50.4	3	My hart with joe that I be hete
H50.4	6	My soverayne lorde.
H50.5	6	My soverayne lorde.
H50.6	2	My soverayne lorde save principall!
H50.6	3	He hath my hart and ever shall.
H50.6	6	My soverayne lorde.
H56	1	Departure is my chef payne;
H62.2	1	Hange I wyl my nobyl bow
H62.4	4	That beawtye ys my foo;
H62.5	1	My berd ys so hard, God wote,
H62.6	1	Now will I take to me my bedes
H62.6	2	For and my santes booke,
H63.1	1	Farewell, my joy, and my swete hart!
H63.2	3	My hart ys yours where ever that I go;
H65.1	1	Wherfore shuld I hang up my bow
H65.3	1	Wherfor shuld I hang up my horne
H65.4	1	Wherfor shuld I tye up my hownd
H66.1	3	God and my ryght and my dewtye,
H67.1	6	Unto my pours
H75	2	My love is lusty, plesant and demure
H75	3	That hath my hart in cure;
H75	6	So my hart to her I ensure;
H101.2	4	They kyndyld my corage.
H102b	2	Why shall not I to my lady
H102.1	1	My lady hath me in that grace
H102.2	1	My lady sayth of trouth it ys
H103.1	1	A thorne hath percyd my hart ryght sore
H103.3	1	O my swet hart, whome I love best,
H103.3	3	For which my hart is lyk to brest,
H104b	2	My love, my love?
H104b	6	Yt is but you, my love, alone.
H104.1	6	But you, my love, alone.
H104.2	3	My myrth and joy is gone;
H104.2	6	But you, my love, alone.
H104.3	3	To swage sumwhat my mone;
H104.3	6	But yow, my love, alone.
H104.4	1	Thus with my care
H105.2	3	Thus saying to our Saviour; this saw I in my syght;
H105.3	1	Musyng on her manners, so ny mard was my mayne,
H105.3	2	Save it plesyd me so passyngly that past was my payn
H106.1	1	My thought oppressed, my mynd in trouble,
H106.1	2	My body languisshyng, my hart in payn;
H106.1	3	My joyes, dystres; my sorows dowble;
H106.1	4	My lyffe as one that dye would fayne;
H106.2	1	My hope frome me is clene exiled,
H106.2	2	Exilide for ever which is my payne;
H106.2	3	My payne with hope hath me begyled;
H106.2	6	In dysdayn I shall my lyfe endure,
H106.3	2	In releasse off my gret smert,
H106.3	4	Of all the sorowes within my hart;
H106.3	6	Yet my lyfe is to me so grevus

MY (cont.)

H106.4	1	Thus may ye se my wofull chance,
H106.4	2	My chance contrarious from all plesure,
H107.1	7	My contraryng,
H107.2	4	My wofull chance;
H107.3	2	To my grevance
H107.3	7	Such is my chance
H107.5	1	My lyf was lent
H108	3	But love my fo, that fervent creature
H109b	3	I go to the medowe to mylke my cow.
H109b	7	I wysse my mother then shall us se!
H109.1b	2	I pray you, sir, lett me go mylke my cow!
H109.1b	6	I wysse my mothyr than shall us se!
H109.2	2	That ye gretly move my corage.
H109.3	1	Ye have my hert; sey what ye wyll.
H109.3	2	Wherfore ye muste my mynde fulfyll,

MYGHT (13)

R4	7	That myght my herte in more ese bryng.
F21	5	Lest that mysaventure myght fall be chaunce;
F25.1	8	Ye myght redress.
F31.1	1	Crist, that was of infynyt myght,
F32.2	6	So nowe is knowen thi sonnys myght:
F33.3	7	What myght I suffir more
F40.2	4	Myght wel be calde an conjuracion.
F47.1	6	Enforcyng yourselfe with all your myght
H27.4	3	Ther myght no joys compare with it
H35.4	4	For I myght shott no mere.
H35.5	4	For faynte she myght nott bray.
H44.2	2	All ways wherby thay myght it rech;
H105.2	1	I mene this by Mary, our Maker's moder of myght,

MYGHTH (1)

| R6 | 4 | Ever to plese hym with all myghth, |

MYLD (1)

| R15.3 | 2 | Spake wordes myld |

MYLKE (3)

H109b	3	I go to the medowe to mylke my cow.
H109.1b	2	I pray you, sir, lett me go mylke my cow!
H109.4	3	How in the medow ye mylke your cow.

MYLT (1)

| F36.1 | 5 | Myn hart can yerne and mylt |

MYN (17)

R2.2	2	To myn entent, and so sayeth mo then I,
R13.1	3	Unwetyng how myn hert to-breke
R13.3	5	Myn hert and love; what wyll she more?
F13	4	To her only which is myn yes fode,
F24.4	8	For myn entent.
F36.1	5	Myn hart can yerne and mylt
F36.2	9	'Yet thou are unkynd, which sleith myn hert,'

MYN (cont.)

F36.3	10	And yet verely I know in myn hart
F37.2	4	My face disfygurid, myn yes full daslyng;
F38b	1	A, myn hert, remembir the well,
F38.1	1	A myn hart, remembir the well
F48.3	6	Myn owne seale therto I hyng;
H103.2	1	Bewayll I may myn adventure
H106.1	5	Myn yes for sorow salt ters doth rayne:
H107.4	8	Fro myn entent.
H108	1	I love unloved; suche is myn aventure,
H108	4	Whose unkyndnes hath kyld myn hart;

MYND (12)

R11.1	2	My mynd also gretly waylyng;
F6.3	2	In your mynd
F12	6	Of onys voice sayyng, 'Bere in thy mynd,
F19	1	Thus musyng in my mynd, gretly mervelyng
F31.4	3	And why, good Lord? Express thi mynd!
H29.2	1	I love her well with hart and mynd;
H34.2	2	And dysdayne dyscorages all gentyl mynd.
H51.4	1	Wyth ee and mynd doth both agre;
H51.5	2	But mynd afformyth with full consent.
H92.2	4	But follow hys mynd in all that we may.
H102.1	3	Her mynd is in non other place:
H106.1	1	My thought oppressed, my mynd in trouble,

MYNDE (9)

R7	2	Unto Calvery caste thy mynde.
R10.6	7	Allmost owt of mynde;
R12.3	7	My mynde shall be;
F1	5	The trewer I serve, the ferther out of mynde;
F20	3	Which that passyth my mynde for to express
F40.3	2	What shulde I say? My mynde is gone.
H25.3	5	Your mynde revert
H47.3	2	Of your most gentyll mynde,
H109.3	2	Wherfore ye muste my mynde fulfyll,

MYNDES (1)

H82.1	5	In ther myndes consyder thei must

MYNDIS (1)

F8	1	Lett serch your myndis ye of hie consideracion!

MYNE (11)

F36.2	5	For myne offence, she said,
F38.1	5	Alas, for sorow myne hart doth blede
H31.4	6	Myne owne swet hart, adew.
H33.4	1	Adew, myne owne lady,
H49.1	3	And thow shal know of myne.
H51.6	2	Myne ey with hart doth me so juge.
H62.3	2	Myne arow ny worne ys;
H63.1	2	Farewell myne owne hart rote -
H65.2	1	Wherfor shuld I hang up myne arrow
H104.4	6	For you have myne alone.

MYNE (cont.)
H108   7   And love unloved; such ys myne adventure.

MYRROUR (1)
F20   5   The bryghtest myrrour and floure of goodlyhed,

MYRTH (4)
R10.1   5   My myrth ys gon
H47.1   3   No myrth can make me fayn
H92.3   4   Honest myrth with vertus pastance.
H104.2   3   My myrth and joy is gone;

MYRTHIS (1)
F8   7   All myrthis to maynten, all sorous to subdewe.

MYS (1)
H35.1   3   She lay so fayre, I cowde nott mys;

MYSAVENTURE (2)
F21   5   Lest that mysaventure myght fall be chaunce:
F26   5   I pray God hartely, withoutyn mysaventure.

MYSCHAUNCE (1)
H92.5   4   Yough shuld fall in grett myschaunce;

MYSDONE (1)
F47.2   3   All mysdone thynges to redress,

MYSE (1)
H62.3   4   When I shuld shoote I myse;

MYSELF (2)
R13.2   4   That wondyd soere myself Y fele,
F29.1   4   Myself alone;

MYSPEND (1)
F38.2   6   Fo all my lyff-daies I have myspend:

MYSSE (2)
R18.2   3   But for my mysse michi deridere;
H104.1   4   But when ye mysse,

MYSTRUST (1)
F22   6   To gett mystrust is his entent

MYSUSYD (1)
F14   5   But pite it is that trust shulde be mysusyd

MYSYLF (2)
R14.1   2   Here Y am mysylf alone;
R15.8   3   Mysylf alone,

MYTHYNKYTH (1)
F3   6   And yet mythynkyth hit grevith me moche more

NAID (1)
F33b   4   It may not be naid;

NAILID (3)
F33.2   1   Thus nakyd am I nailid, O man, for thy sake;
F34.1   1   Uppon the cross nailid I was for the,
F36.4   1   Unto the cross, handes and feete, nailid he was;

NAILIS (2)
F33.3   6   The sturdy nailis bore;
F34.2   3   The crowne of thorne, the spere, the nailis thre,

NAKYD (1)
F33.2   1   Thus nakyd am I nailid, O man, for thy sake;

NAME (8)
F27.4   2   'What is his name that thou chosen has?
H29.1   4   Shall no man know her name for me.
H29.2   4   Shall no mane know her name for me.
H29.3   4   Shall no man know her name for me.
H29.4   4   Shall no man [know her name for me].
H29.5   4   Whill I leve her name for me.
H29.6   4   Shall no man [know her name for me].
H41.4   1   She asked hym what was his name;

NAMYD (1)
F27.2   2   And shall not yet be namyd for me;

NATURALL (1)
F46.1   1   Love is naturall to every wyght,

NATURE (6)
F3   3   For when nature wold oft that I shulde wynk,
F36.3   9   Is by nature constraynyd to smert,
F37.1   3   Nature of aquayntance ys turned to a gest,
F37.2   1   Where art thou, Nature, that wont were me to store
F37.2   5   Thou, Nature, hast lefft me; by the fynd I no rest:
F37.4   2   Nature hath forsakyn me, and lefft me thus alone.

NAY (19)
R3.3   1   Cum kys me! 'Nay!' Be God, ye shall!
R19.2   6   She seyd me nay
F2   3   Nay, nay, nay, nay, I warne the well,
F18.1   8   Nay, nay, hardely!
F27.1   4   'Nay, nay, let be;
F27.3   4   'Nay certenly;
H106.4 6   Nay, nay, for why? Ther ys no space.
H109b   6   Nay, God forbede! That may not be -
H109.1b 1   Nay, in good feyth, I wyll not melle with you;
H109.1b 5   Nay, God forbede! That may not be;
H109.2b 1   Nay, in good feyth, [etc.]
H109.3b 1   Nay, in good feyth, [etc.]
H109.4b 1   Nay, in good feyth, [etc.]

NAYLID (1)
F30.2   17   Naylid full sore,

NAYLIS (1)
F49.1   5   Upon the cross with naylis thre

NAYLYD (1)
F49.1   6   Fast I was naylyd for thyne offence;

NAZARETH (1)
F48b   4   That I Jhesus off Nazareth

NE (6)
F10   4   Nethir in towne ne fylde simulacion
F10   7   Men may fynd day ne nyght adulacion
F24.5   5   Yet I ne went
F37.3   5   So wakyng ne sleping fynd I no rest:
F39.3   3   In feeld ne strete;
H107.5   5   Yet I ne went

NECESSARY (1)
H66.3   2   None can sey but necessary;

NEDE (1)
F38.1   4   That helpis the ever at thi most nede.

NEDES (3)
R12.2   1   Yowth woll have nedes dalyaunce,
H25.2   3   Of absence nedes must be,
H27.1   3   Sen ye must nedes from me depart,

NEDILL (1)
F36.1   3   A crowne of thorne as nedill sharpe shyfft in his
             brayne

NEDIS (2)
F36.3   7   I must nedis wofull be,
F37.4   3   'Remembir the, my creature, thou must nedis dye,
             I the ensure.

NEDITH (1)
F13   7   Syth for my trouth she nedith no wittness.

NEDYS (2)
H15   3   Sens I must nedys from my love depart
H79.1   2   Hys entent must nedys be trew,

NELLE (1)
R3.3   2   'Be Criste, Y nelle, what ses the man?

NERE (6)
R19.1   3   I drew me nere
R19.1   8   And seyd, 'No nere!
F1   2   The more behynde, the nere my wayes ende;

NERE (cont.)
F21   7   Hough that evyr it will happ I wote nere I.
F36.2   4   That with dispaire for feer and dred I was nere
                   forlore
H31.8   3   Her dere hart was full nere

NETHIR (1)
F10   4   Nethir in towne ne fylde simulacion

NEVER (11)
R13.3   7   And never to chaunge hyr for no new.
F19   6   As I of aquayntance had never byn afore;
F32.2   7   Therfor, thowe deth be never so sore,
F32.3   7   Therfore though deth be never so sore,
F33.2   7   Whereas never man was so
H18   7   And never more to remayne.
H28   4   Joy shall I never ye may be sure.
H33b   3   Thow wynter blastys blow never so hye,
H33.1   2   And never chaungyth hew,
H34.6   2   Yet never the lesse it ys to moch used.
H66.1   4   Frome them shall I never vary:

NEVIR (5)
F4   3   Was nevir man saff only I;
F7.2   1   Treuth nor service nevir so playne
F13   2   For my complayntes it dyd me nevir good;
F32.4   7   Therefore, though deth be nevir so sore,
F38.1   3   Thou thynkyst on hym nevir a dele

NEVYR (3)
F23.2   1   Nor nought cowde have, wolde I nevyr so fayne!
F32.1   6   Therfore, though deth be nevyr so sore,
F36b   1   My feerfull dreme nevyr forgete can I:

NEW (5)
R13.3   7   And never to chaunge hyr for no new.
H29.3   2   Nor for no new me chaunge doth she,
H31.2   6   Forsake me for a new.
H31.3   2   Hath chosen a new
H49.3   4   She will change for no new.

NEWE (1)
F43.4   3   And the overplus undir the table of the newe gyse;

NEXT (1)
H50.4   4   Next God but he and ever prest

NEXTE (1)
H109.4   2   But the nexte tyme ye must beware

NEYBOURE (1)
F48.1   8   Love thi neyboure as I love the!

R1.1	4	Foster woll Y be no more.
R1.2	2	Shall Y wedde no wiffe;
R10.6	4	No place to resorte.
R10.6	8	Alone ys no cumfort.
R13.2	5	And no help but Fortunys whele,
R13.3	7	And never to chaunge hyr for no new.
R19.1	8	And seyd, 'No nere!
F3	7	That no thought can reless me of my sore.
F7.2	7	In whom ther is no remedy;
F10	6	The pore pepull no tyme hath but ryght
F13	7	Syth for my trouth she nedith no wittness.
F14	4	And no cause gevyn to be so refusyd;
F14	7	Wher that is usyd can be no surance.
F19	8	To lett itt over pass, and thynk theron no more.
F23.2	6	Wolde in no wise for joy nor hevyness
F24.2	7	And no redress
F24.3	3	And no suraunce
F28	3	To love her best and no mo
F29.3	3	Therfor I pray the, son, no more,
F32.1	7	Now blessid Lady, wepe no more:
F32.2	3	They bet him for oure gilt, though he no syn hadd;
F32.2	8	Now, blessid Lady, wepe [no more:
F32.3	8	Now, blessid Lady, wepe no more:
F32.4	2	Lay downe all thi wepyng, let no more be sene!
F32.4	8	Now blessid Lady, wepe no more:
F37.2	5	Thou, Nature, hast lefft me; by the fynd I no rest:
F37.3	5	So wakyng ne sleping fynd I no rest:
F39.2	3	I know no pere
F41.2	4	I am no hakney for your rode;
F41.3	4	Be Crist, ye shal not! No, no, hardely!
F43.2	1	Rutterkyn can speke no Englissh;
F46b	4	No mo maydyns but one.
H15	4	And know no cause wherefore.
H18	3	And no cause gevyn therto:
H25.1	6	Morne ye no more for me.
H25.2	6	And morne no more for me.
H25.3	1	It is no boote
H25.3	6	And morne no more for me.
H25.9	6	And morne no more for me.
H27.4	3	Ther myght no joys compare with it
H29.1	4	Shall no man know her name for me.
H29.2	4	Shall no mane know her name for me.
H29.3	2	Nor for no new me chaunge doth she,
H29.3	4	Shall no man know her name for me.
H29.4	4	Shall no man [know her name for me].
H29.6	4	Shall no man [know her name for me].
H31b	1	Hey nony nony nony nony no,
H31b	2	Hey nony nony nony nony no!
H31.4	2	In no maner a way
H35.1	2	And yet she bledes no whytt;
H35.4	4	For I myght shott no mere.
H35.7	4	Hys bolt may fle no more.
H47.1	3	No myrth can make me fayn

190

NO (cont.)
H47.2	2	Let no thought yow dysmaye!
H47.3	3	It may in no wyse agre
H47.4	4	I love you and no mo.
H49.2	4	And yet she will say no.
H49.3	4	She will change for no new.
H50.3	3	In that he doth no camparyng
H51.4	2	There is no bote; ther must it be.
H62.1	3	Foster wyl I be no more
H62.1	4	No lenger shote I may;
H64.2	8	Ther no hart rewith
H66.3	3'	I hurt no man, I do no wrong;
H67.2	2	No creatur
H79.1	6	But those be thay which can no skyll:
H101.3	4	Methought I had no pere.
H102.2	2	No love that can be lost;
H104.1	5	No joy it is
H104.2	5	Is no resort
H104.3	5	No comforting
H106.4	4	Right suere to have no good aventure,
H106.4	6	Nay, nay, for why? Ther ys no space.
H107.2	7	And no redresse
H107.3	3	And no surance
H109.1b	3	Why, wyll ye nott geve me no comfortt,

NOBLE (2)
F44.2	2	Is this noble prince of riall lynage,
H51.7	1	Love maynteynyth all noble courage;

NOBYL (1)
H62.2	1	Hange I wyl my nobyl bow

NOBYLE (1)
H34.2	1	For love enforcyth all nobyle kynd,

NOBYLL (1)
H44.2	1	Nobyll men then wold suer enserch

NOGHT (3)
R2.2	7	For till she amende Y shall have noght truly
R4	3	And thogh Y wolde, Y koude me noght refrayne
R7	5	And say after me, and be noght unkynde:

NON (7)
F6.4	5	Remedy non
F7.1	6	Yet other grace can ye gett non
F27.1	5	Is non of them that lykyth me.'
F39b	3	Ther is non lyke
H29.5	3	Promyse I mak that know non shall
H79.2	4	In that therfor can be non odde,
H102.1	3	Her mynd is in non other place:

NONE (5)
R16.1	3	So propyr I can none fynde as she;

NONE (cont.)

H50.5	2	Ther is none one-lyve that have;
H51.10	2	Chaunge who so wyll, I wyll be none.
H63.1	4	Ther ys none other bote.
H66.3	2	None can sey but necessary;

NONY (8)

H31b	1	Hey nony nony nony nony no,
H31b	2	Hey nony nony nony nony no!

NOON (1)

R12.1	3	Grugge so woll, but noon denye;

NOR (8)

F7.2	1	Treuth nor service nevir so playne
F23.2	1	Nor nought cowde have, wolde I nevyr so fayne!
F23.2	6	Wolde in no wise for joy nor hevyness
F31b	4	My witt nor reson may hit well fynd:
H29.3	2	Nor for no new me chaunge doth she,
H62.2	4	Nor yett in rough;
H67.2	4	Nor yet retayne;
H101.3	3	In all this lond, nowther fre nor bond,

NOT (65)

R3.1	8	Ye will not make to huge a waste.
R3.2	3	'Ywisse, wanton, ye shull not yette!
R3.2	6	Recke ye not to make us shende?
R3.2	7	Y wolde not yette for furty pence
R10.5	7	Not lovyd agayn,
R13.1	1	So put yn fere I dare not speke;
R13.1	1	She hath me hurt; why shold she not hele,
R15.7	5	Shall he not stert,
R20.1	1	Your light grevans shall not me constrayne
R20.2	2	Withowt cause, Gode knowyth; Y do not fayne.
R20.4	2	Love me lytell and longe; hot love doth not reyne;
F6.1	3	And wote not why
F13	6	And lett me not allway be guerdonless,
F15	3	And mervell I have syth I not deservid
F27.2	2	And shall not yet be namyd for me;
F27.3	5	Here is not he that plesyth me.'
F28	5	I-wiss yet will I not me complayne
F29.5	2	For mannys gilt is not withstone,
F33b	4	It may not be naid;
F33.1	2	And be not hard-hartid, and for this encheson
F33.3	4	Onfaynyd, not deynyd, my blode for to shede:
F34.1	6	Be not dispayryd, for I am not vengeable;
F34.3	8	Be thou not froward syth I am merciable.
F34.4	8	Be thou not affraide sith I am merciable.
F36.1	4	His modir dere tendirly wept and cowde not refrayne
F36.3	1	Saynt Jhon than said, 'Feere not, Mary; his paynys al
F39.1	4	I wote not where
F40.3	4	I-wis, she will not gyve me a bone:

NOT (cont.)
```
F41.3    4   Be Crist, ye shal not! No, no, hardely!
F41.3    5   I will not be japed bodely.
F48.1    5   Not covetyng more for all my smert
F48.2    2   That I suffird not for the this payne,
F48.2    5   Yet, man, that thou sholdest not be lorne,
H25.4    5   Her schuld not move
H25.6    5   Stynt wold sche not,
H25.10   1   I schall not fayll,
H29.3    1   She doth not waver as the wynde,
H31.3    4   And will not rew,
H31.8    5   Be not dysmayd,
H34.3    1   Wherfor to love and be not loved
H35b     2   Ther ys a do in yonder wode; in faith, she woll
                 not dy
H35.2    4   But yet she was not dede.
H38      3   I fynde you not trew;
H41.2    1   To call the porter he wold not blyn;
H41.2    2   The lady said he shuld not com in.
H47.2    1   Do way, dere hart, not so.
H47.4    3   Ye ar not varyable;
H51.1    2   Who lovyth not wantith corage.
H79.2    1   Or else because they may not opteyne,
H82.1    1   Let not us that yong men be
H82.2    3   Thay may not now than gaynesay
H92.1    4   It ys not for hym we know yt well.
H92.2    3   But I wyll not so whatsoever thay say,
H101.1   4   I wold not do amysse.
H102b    1   Why shall not I?
H102b    2   Why shall not I to my lady
H102b    3   Why shall not I be trew?
H102b    4   Why shall not I?
H102.1   5   Why shall not I?
H102.2   5   Why shall not I?
H109b    6   Nay, God forbede! That may not be -
H109.1   2   We may us sport and not be sene;
H109.1b  1   Nay, in good feyth, I wyll not melle with you;
H109.1b  5   Nay, God forbede! That may not be;
```

NOTES (1)
```
R19.1    2   She satt and sang with notes clere;
```

NOTHING (2)
```
F41.1    4   What, will ye do nothing but play?
H104.3   4   Is nothing,
```

NOTHINGE (1)
```
H108     5   From her love nothinge can me revert
```

NOTHYNG (3)
```
F18.1    3   Avaylyth nothyng;
F30.1   13   'Nothyng, my spouse,
H106.3   7   That deth is plesur and nothyng noyus.
```

NOTT (9)
F14	1	Alas, it is 1 that wote nott what to say,
F17	5	I wote nott where I may complayn;
F18.2	4	That cowde nott tell,
H31.8	1	She had nott said
H35.1	3	She lay so fayre, I cowde nott mys;
H35.3	1	There she gothe! Se ye nott,
H35.5	4	For faynte she myght nott bray.
H50.5	5	A vengeance on them that loveth nott best
H109.1b	3	Why, wyll ye nott geve me no comfortt,

NOU (1)
| R3.2 | 4 | A, kan ye that? Nou, gode, go hens! |

NOUGHT (5)
R10.3	3	Settyth me at nought,
F23.2	1	Nor nought cowde have, wolde I nevyr so fayne!
F31.2	1	He that wrought this wordle of nought,
F41.4	1	'Walke forthe your way, ye cost me nought:
H23.2	1	Pastymes ther be I nought treulye

NOW (77)
R2.2	5	Now Y pray God and that righth hertily
R3.1	2	Now thyngke ye this ys a fayre ray?
R3.3	6	'Now have ye leyde me un the flore,
R8	1	Now helpe, Fortune, of thy godenesse,
R10.3	3	And now, fy, fy,
R15.3	6	And now ys gone.
R15.4	1	Now hit ys so,
R15.5	1	Now may I wynd
R18.3	1	Now what shall Y say meis parentibus
F8	5	Through whose swete showris now sprong ther is ayen
F10	8	Now raynyth trewly in every mannys syght.
F11	4	That was my grefe is now my alegeaunce.
F11	5	Thus hath now grace enrychyd my plesaunce,
F13	3	But be constraynt, now must I shew my woo
F23.1	1	That was my joy is now my woo and payne;
F23.1	2	That was my bliss is now my displesaunce;
F23.1	3	That was my trust is now my wanhope playne;
F23.1	4	That was my wele is now my most grevaunce.
F24.2	3	Is now to cess
F24.3	6	Now in substaunce
F27.4b	1	'Now have I lovyd, and whom love ye?'
F30.2	3	And now be styll;
F32.1	7	Now blessid Lady, wepe no more:
F32.2	8	Now, blessid Lady, wepe [no more:
F32.3	8	Now, blessid Lady, wepe no more:
F32.4	8	Now blessid Lady, wepe no more:
F34b	9	And thynk on this lesson that now I teche the.
F34.2	6	Lett now us twayne in this thyng be tretable:
F34.5	7	Now for thi moders meke mediacion,
F36.3	3	He hath to man, to make hym fre that now is thrall.
F37.2	2	To lusty plesure? Now lyyng in the flore,

NOW (cont.)

F37.4	1	Now, mercyfull Jhesu, to the make I my mone;
F39b	2	Whom I now seke
F41.3	2	What, wolde ye frompill me now? fy, fy!
F41.4	2	Now have I fownd that I have sought,
F44.1	10	Wherfore now syng we:
F44.2	10	Wherefore now syng we:
F44.3	1	Now, good Lady among thi sayntes all,
F44.3	10	Wherefore now syng we:
F46.1	3	Chaungyng his course, now hevy, now lyght,
F47.1	5	Sith it is so, now let your labour be
H12	3	Syth now so kynd
H17	2	Now lete us synge
H18	2	Now am I exild my lady fro
H18	4	Wherfor to her I me complayn, hey now!
H25.5	4	Now of sum grace
H27.2	3	And now absence to be in place
H27.3	3	And now with syghs manyfold,
H27.4	4	Unto my hart as now she shuld.
H31.4	1	And now I may
H33.3	1	Now unto my lady
H35b	3	Now blow thi horne, hunter, and blow thi horne, joly hunter
H35.6	3	Now the construccyon of the same -
H35.7	2	Now of this hunter's lore;
H39	4	Now after wyll I go;
H44.1	1	If love now reynyd as it hath bene
H44.6	1	To lovers I put now suer this cace -
H47.2	3	Thow ye now parte me fro,
H62.6	1	Now will I take to me my bedes
H63.2	1	Thowgh you depart now thus me fro,
H64.1	3	Now let us be;
H64.2	1	Wherfor now we
H64.2	3	Let us now pray
H82.2	3	Thay may not now than gaynesay
H92.7	1	Now unto God thys prayer we make,
H96b	2	Help now thi kyng, thi kyng, and take his part!
H96.1	5	Help now thi king [and take his part!]
H97	5	Now let us syng this rownd all thre;
H102.1	4	Now sith it ys thus known,
H105.2	4	This reson that I rede you now, I rede it full ryght
H105.3	4	Now, gracious God and goode swete babe, yet ons this game agayne
H107.2	3	Is now to cese
H107.3	6	Now in substance
H109.1	1	Now yn this medow fayer and grene
H109.1b	4	That now in the feldes we may us sportt?
H109.4	4	Adew, farewell and kysse me now!

NOWE (7)

F5	5	Is nowe be hym so comfortide agayne
F10	1	Nowe the lawe is led be clere conciens
F11	1	That was my woo is nowe my most gladness;

NOWE (cont.)
F11   2 That was my payne is nowe my joyus chaunce;
F11   3 That was my feere is nowe my sykyrness;
F27.6b 1 'Nowe have we lovyd, and love will we
F32.2 6 So nowe is knowen thi sonnys myght:

NOWGHT (1)
H62.6 4 For I may nowght but loke;

NOWTHER (1)
H101.3 3 In all this lond, nowther fre nor bond,

NOYUS (1)
H106.3 7 That deth is plesur and nothyng noyus.

NY (4)
F24.5 3 It is ny spent;
H62.3 2 Myne arow ny worne ys;
H105.3 1 Musyng on her manners, so ny mard was my mayne,
H107.5 3 It is ny spent;

NYCE (1)
H109.2 1 Ye be so nyce and so mete of age

NYE (1)
H27.2 2 Was wont to cast an nye;

NYGHT (4)
F10   7 Men may fynd day ne nyght adulacion
F12   1 Benedicite! Whate dremyd I this nyght?
F30.1 1 This endurs nyght
H17   3 Both day and nyght,

NYGHTH (2)
R6   5 Both erly, late, by day and by nyghth.
F48.2 7 Witness, the daye turnyd to nyghth,

NYGHTYNGALE (1)
H20   7 The nyghtyngale sang on hie

NYK (1)
H62.3 3 The glew is slypt frome the nyk;

NYLL (1)
F34b   8 Than leve thi syn, or I nyll the,

NYSE (1)
F41.1 2 This wanton clarkis be nyse allway.

O (17)
R6   1 O blessed lord, how may this be
F7.1   1 O my desyre, what eylyth the,
F7.1   8 O my desyre, what eylyth the?
F7.2   8 O my desyre, what aylyth the?

O (cont.)

F26	1	O rote of trouth, o princess to my pay,
F33.2	1	Thus nakyd am I nailid, O man, for thy sake;
F33.3	8	Than I have done, O man, for the?
F34.5	3	O Jhesu, graunt of thi benignite
F36.3	4	'O frend,' she said, 'I am sure he is inmortall.'
F44.1	1	O blessed Lord of hevyn celestiall,
F44.3	5	O celestiall
H15	1	O my hart and O my hart!
H25.4	1	O her kyndnesse,
H25.4	2	O her gentylnes!
H103.3	1	O my swet hart, whome I love best,

OBEDIENT (1)
| F46.2 | 4 | Plesaunt, buxum, and ever obedient, |

OBEY (1)
| R2.1 | 6 | Y most obey fortuneys ordynaunce, |

ODDE (1)
| H79.2 | 4 | In that therfor can be non odde, |

ODOUR (1)
| F27.1 | 1 | 'I love a flour of swete odour' |

OF (155)
R2.1	1	My wofull hert of all gladnesse baryeyne
R2.1	8	Of sorfull joye and paynefull plesaunce.
R2.2	1	For sche weche ys of all godely the best
R2.2	3	Ys full but late oute of hur kyndely rest
R2.2	6	That she be voyded owte of the grete grevaunce;
R4	1	Absens of you causeth me to sygh and complayne
R4	2	For of my hert ye have the governaunce;
R8	1	Now helpe, Fortune, of thy godenesse,
R8	4	Of sorwe and all hevenesse.
R10.4	3	Of yoy, yn care
R10.6	7	Allmost owt of mynde;
R12.2	2	Of good or yll some pastaunce;
R12.2	7	Of vices all;
R12.2	10	Ys best of all?
R13.1	5	Of my pore hert she may be sure,
R13.1	7	Abydyng your grace yn hope of mercy.
R13.2	1	The sterre of Venus which I call her ye,
R13.2	7	Ther of right I apeyle hyr to be my surgyon.
R14.2	2	Takyn away from me bycause of hevynes;
R15.4	2	Lefe of my woe
F1	5	The trewer I serve, the ferther out of mynde;
F3	2	Syn thoughtis byn cheff causers of my woo;
F3	7	That no thought can reless me of my sore.
F5	3	Full lyk to drowne in wavis of dystres,
F5	4	Saffe helpe and grace of my lord and soverayne,
F6.1	4	Encrese of payne
F6.4	2	Of one alone
F8	1	Lett serch your myndis ye of hie consideracion!

F8	2	Beholde the soveren sede of this rosis twayn,
F8	3	Renewde of God for owre consolacion
F8	4	By dropys of grace that on them down doth rayn;
F8	6	A rose most riall with levis fressh of hew,
F12	6	Of onys voice sayyng, 'Bere in thy mynd,
F15	4	To be put owte of your good governaunce . . .
F19	6	As I of aquayntance had never byn afore;
F20	1	Most clere of colour and rote of stedfastness,
F20	4	Of her bounte, beaute and womanhode;
F20	5	The bryghtest myrrour and floure of goodlyhed,
F22	1	Alas, for lak of her presens,
F22	5	And thus is the tyme of his song;
F23.2	3	Wherfore of ryght ye shuld my greffe complayne,
F24.1	6	Of such welyng
F24.3	4	Of remedy;
F25.1	7	That of my payne
F26	1	O rote of trouth, o princess to my pay,
F27b	2	'I love a floure of fressh beaute;'
F27.1	1	'I love a flour of swete odour'
F27.1	3	Columbyne goldis of swete flavour?'
F27.1	5	Is non of them that lykyth me.'
F27.4	1	'I chese a floure fresshist of face.'
F27.4b	2	'I love a floure of fressh beaute.'
F27.5	3	'Both be full swete and of lyke savoure;
F27.6	3	'To here talke of them is my delite.
F27.6b	2	This fayre fressh floure full of beaute;
F28	7	Lest cause in me be fownd of offens.
F31.1	1	Crist, that was of infynyt myght,
F31.2	1	He that wrought this wordle of nought,
F32.1	2	That the Son of God shulde make us fre,
F32.1	3	Though deth be bewaylid by waies of pite,
F32.2	5	To joy of every wordlis wight,
F32.4	1	Glorius Lady, of hevyn hie quene,
F34b	5	'Mercy, Lord, of the I crave.'
F34.1	3	Forsake thi syn, man, for the love of me;
F34.2	3	The crowne of thorne, the spere, the nailis thre,
F34.2	4	Percide hand and fote of indignacion,
F34.3	2	For-thi contrite of thy contricion;
F34.3	3	Saynt Tomas of Indes, in crudelite
F34.5	2	Thy deth remembryng of humble afeccion,
F34.5	3	O Jhesu, graunt of thi benignite
F34.5	4	That thi fyve wellis plentuus of fusion,
F36.1	3	A crowne of thorne as nedill sharpe shyfft in his brayne
F36.1	9	To se the sharpe swerde of sorow smert,
F36.3	6	'Of moderly pete
F36.4	11	And of my dreme was sore agast.
F37.1	3	Nature of aquayntance ys turned to a gest,
F39.2	8	Of hir fety:
F40.1	4	But it were an angell of the Trinite?
F40.2	2	To hym that wolde of such recreacion
F41.1	6	Gup, Cristian Clowte, gup, Jak of the Vale,
F41.2	6	Gup, Cristian Clowte, gup, Jak of the Vale,

OF (cont.)

F41.3	6	Gup, Cristian Clowte, gup, Jak of the Vale,
F41.4	8	Gup, Cristian Clowte, gup, Jak of the Vale,
F43.3	2	A stoupe of bere up at a pluk,
F43.4	3	And the overplus undir the table of the newe gyse;
F44.1	1	O blessed Lord of hevyn celestiall,
F44.1	2	Which formyd hast of thi most speciall grace
F44.1	5	Which of aliaunce
F44.1	6	Oure prince of plesaunce
F44.1	8	Of Ynglond and Fraunce
F44.2	1	Wherfore, good Lord, syth of thi creacion
F44.2	2	Is this noble prince of riall lynage,
F44.2	7	This eyre of Brytayne,
F44.2	8	Of Castell and Spayne,
F45.2	1	In that garden be flouris of hewe:
F46.2	5	Tyll sum of them begyn to grone:
F47.1	4	Of marshiall power and also hye dygnite,
F47.2	1	God hath gyff you of his goodness
F47.2	4	And specially hurtis of thi commynalte,
F47.2	7	To have recover of ther unryght.
F48.1	9	This is that I axe of the,
F48.1	10	That am the cheffe lorde of the fee.
F48.3	5	Into witness of which thyng
F48.3	9	Iyevyn upon the mownt of Calvary,
F48.3	10	The grete daye of mannys mercy.
F49b	3	'Amende the, man, of thi trespace,
H17	6	Of the red rose and the whyght.
H22	2	To passe the tyme of youth joly,
H22	4	Of lusty bloddys and chevalry.
H23.1	1	The tyme of youthe is to be spent;
H23.4	1	As featys of armys, and suche other
H25.2	3	Of absence nedes must be,
H25.5	4	Now of sum grace
H25.6	6	So trew of love was sche.
H25.9	5	Of my report
H29.1	2	Of my lady, both fayre and fre,
H29.1	3	Of her godnes than wold I wryght;
H31.1	6	Her hart was full of payne.
H35.1	4	Lord, I was glad of it!
H35.6	1	I was wery of the game,
H35.6	3	Now the construccyon of the same -
H35.7	2	Now of this hunter's lore;
H44.6	2	Which of ther loves doth get them grace?
H47.3	2	Of your most gentyll mynde,
H49.1	3	And thow shal know of myne.
H50.1	3	Of which four tymes he dyd it take;
H50.1	5	And of all other for to love best
H50.2	1	My soverayne lord of pusant pure
H50.2	2	As the chefteyne of a waryowere,
H50.3	4	But of a trewth he worthyest
H50.3	5	To have the prayse of all the best;
H50.5	1	So many vertuse gevyn of grace
H50.6	1	The soverayne lorde that is of all,
H50.6	4	Of God I ask for hym request,

OF (cont.)

H51.7	2	Who love dysdaynyth ys all of the village.
H56	2	I trust ryght wel of retorn agane.
H62.4	2	Owt of her courte to go;
H62.5	4	Lo, age ys cause of this;
H64.1	9	Of lovys payne,
H65.3	3	I can blow the deth of a dere
H66.2	3	I thynk sum wars of yche degre;
H66.3	1	Pastymes of yough sumtyme among,
H74	1	Deme the best of every dowt
H96.1	2	In the quarell of the church and in the ryght,
H101.2	2	Of twelve yere of age,
H101.3	2	The age of fifteen yere,
H102.2	1	My lady sayth of trouth it ys
H105.2	1	I mene this by Mary, our Maker's moder of myght,
H105.2	2	Full lovely lookyng on our Lord, the lanterne of lyght
H106.2	7	Endure, alas, withowt hope of recure.
H106.3	4	Of all the sorowes within my hart;
H107.1	6	Of such walyng
H107.3	4	Of remedy;
H109.2	1	Ye be so nyce and so mete of age

OFF (5)

F33.3	1	Off sharpe thorne I have worne a crowne on my hede,
F48b	4	That I Jhesus off Nazareth
H50.6	5	Off all gode fortunes to send hym best;
H106.1	7	Withowte hope or comfort off redresse.
H106.3	2	In releasse off my gret smert,

OFFENCE (3)

R3.2	2	Why blame ye me withoute offence?
F36.2	5	For myne offence, she said,
F49.1	6	Fast I was naylyd for thyne offence;

OFFEND (1)

| F38.1 | 6 | To thynk how grevusly I have offend: |

OFFENDID (1)

| F38.2 | 4 | I have offendid so grevusly; |

OFFENS (2)

| F6.2 | 2 | Withoute offens, |
| F28 | 7 | Lest cause in me be fownd of offens. |

OFFERD (2)

| F33.2 | 9 | Was like a lombe offerd in sacrifice: |
| F48.2 | 6 | In the awter I am offerd my Fader beforne; |

OFFT (1)

| F34b | 3 | 'I, a synner that offt doth fall.' |

OFT (3)

| R18.2 | 2 | Full oft with you _solebam_ _ludere_; |

OFT (cont.)
 F3   3   For when nature wold oft that I shulde wynk,
 H27.2   1   Oft to me her godely swet face

OFTEN (1)
 H51.9   1   For often tymes wher they do sewe

OFTENER (1)
 H68   2   I trust we shall mete oftener.

OFTYME (1)
 H106.3   1   Oftyme for death forsoth I call

OGHFTE (1)
 R2.1   4   Full oghfte or this, Y shall undertake.

OLDE (1)
 R20.4   1   An olde seyde saw: hasty men sone slayne;

ON (42)
 R5   5   That ye wilde fuchesaffe to have mercy on me
 R10.1   6   For on alone
 R11.4   1   I trow on me she wold rewe
 R19.1   1   Hay how the mavys on a brere!
 R19.3   6   'Such on as she,
 F8   4   By dropys of grace that on them down doth rayn;
 F19   2   Houghevyr such dyversite in on person may be,
 F21   3   Then bownden were I such on faythfully
 F27b   5   Yff we three can agre in on.'
 F27.3   1   'On that I love most enterly.'
 F27.5   4   All on they be;
 F30.2   13   On Calvery,
 F31b   3   Wolde take on Hym humanite?
 F31.3   2   As betyng, bobbyng, ye, spettyng on thi face?
 F32.3   2   The crowne on his hed, the spere at his hart,
 F32.3   4   All was on red blod withoute any shirt;
 F33.3   1   Off sharpe thorne I have worne a crowne on my hede,
 F34b   9   And thynk on this lesson that now I teche the.
 F34.1   7   Gayne gostly enmys thynk on my passion;
 F34.2   2   Loke on them well, and have compassion;
 F34.3   1   I hade on Petur and Mawdlen pyte
 F34.4   1   Thynk agayne, pride, on my humilite;
 F34.4   3   Gayne fals envy thynk on my charyte,
 F34.5   1   Lord, on all synfull here knelyng on kne,
 F36.2   11   Unneth on worde cowde she speke more.
 F38b   2   And thynk on the paynys that byn in hell.
 F38.1   3   Thou thynkyst on hym nevir a dele
 F40.3   1   She is my lytell praty on;
 F43.2   2   His tong rennyth all on buttyrd fyssh,
 F45.2   3   The floure-de-luce she did on rewe,
 H20   4   The byrdys sang on every syde
 H20   7   The nyghtyngale sang on hie
 H25.7   3   And sett her on my knee:
 H34.4   1   Love encoragith and makyth on bold;

ON (cont.)
```
H35b      1   Blow thi horne, hunter, and blow thi horne on hye!
H35.2     2   The dere shoffe on the mede;
H50.5     5   A vengeance on them that loveth nott best
H96.1     3   With spers and sheldys on goodly horsys lyght,
H105.1    2   Lokyng on her lytill son, so laughyng in lap layd,
H105.2    2   Full lovely lookyng on our Lord, the lanterne of
                lyght
H105.3    1   Musyng on her manners, so ny mard was my mayne,
```

ON-SYTTYNG (1)
```
R20.2     1   Your on-syttyng speche puttyth me to payne
```

ONCERTAYNE (2)
```
R20.2     4   How sholde Y plece a creature oncertayne?
R20.4     4   How sholde Y plece a creature oncertayne?
```

ONCERTEYNE (1)
```
R20.3     4   How sholde Y plece a creature oncerteyne?
```

ONE (16)
```
R10.1     3   And all for one;
F6.4      2   Of one alone
F7.1      7   Butt yff hit be to wissh for one:
F46b      4   No mo maydyns but one.
F46.1     5   So rennyth the chaunce from one to one:
F46.2     1   One is good, but mo were bettyr
F46.3     3   To put in one my faithfull trust,
F48.3     4   And othir wittness, many one;
H14       2   And sore I sygh for one.
H23.2     2   Whych one may use, and vice denye;
H64.1     5   To set in one
H64.1     7   For when one sole
H101.1    2   As many one ys,
H106.1    4   My lyffe as one that dye would fayne;
H109.2    4   Let us make one, though we be twayne!
```

ONE-LYVE (1)
```
H50.5     2   Ther is none one-lyve that have;
```

ONFAYN (1)
```
R15.5     3   With hert onfayn;
```

ONFAYNYD (1)
```
F33.3     4   Onfaynyd, not deynyd, my blode for to shede:
```

ONKYND (1)
```
F31.4     1   'Lo, man, for the that ware onkynd,
```

ONKYNDLY (1)
```
R11.2     2   So onkyndly thus to be slayn;
```

ONLY (8)
```
R5        6   And only to be putte to yeure rememoraunce.
```

ONLY (cont.)
R13.2   6   And only she which my wound begunne;
F4   3   Was nevir man saff only I;
F13   4   To her only which is myn yes fode,
F23.1   5   What causyth this but only yowre plesaunce
F46.3   5   And love her only whereever she gone:
H33.3   3   Frome all other only
H92.4   4   All only reches to purchase.

ONRYGHTFULLY (1)
F23.1   6   Onryghtfully shewyng me unkyndness,

ONS (1)
H105.3 4   Now, gracious God and goode swete babe, yet ons
                this game agayne

ONSE (2)
R8   2   And onse withdrawe thy adversite
H109.4 1   Then for this onse I shal you spare,

ONYS (2)
F12   6   Of onys voice sayyng, 'Bere in thy mynd,
H64.2   4   Onys love sure

OON (3)
F27.4b 5   Yff we three can agre in oon.'
F27.6b 5   That we three be agrede in oon.'
H23.4   2   Wherby actyvenesse oon may utter.

OONE (3)
R15.7   3   And all for oone;
H51.10 1   For whoso lovith shuld love butt oone;
H79.1   5   Many oone sayth that love ys yll,

OPON (1)
H65.2   2   Opon the grenwode lynde?

OPPRESSED (1)
H106.1 1   My thought oppressed, my mynd in trouble,

OPPREST (1)
H103.3 2   Whos unkyndnes hath me opprest,

OPTAYNE (5)
F44.2   5   His ryght to optayne,
H31.4   3   Optayne that I do sew,
H34.1   1   Whoso that wyll all feattes optayne,
H51.8   2   It were pete thay shuld optayne;
H64.1   12 And love to optayne.

OPTEYNE (2)
H79.2   1   Or else because they may not opteyne,
H92.7   4   An blysse opteyne at ower last end. Amen.

OR (33)

R2.1	4	Full oghfte or this, Y shall undertake.
R3.2	8	My moder cam in, or that ye wende.'
R12.2	2	Of good or yll some pastaunce;
R12.3	3	Cumpany ys gode or yll,
R13.2	2	Sharper than thorn, dyamond or steyll,
R13.3	3	Or els yn feyth unkyndly she doth dele,
R20.4	3	Speke or ye smyte, barke or ye byte; holde yowre hondes twane
F1	7	Is it fortune or infortune this I fynde?
F2	6	Or else I thynke to be content
F14	6	Other by colour or by fals semblaunce;
F16	4	Withoute disease or adversyte.
F27.1	2	'Magerome, gentyll or lavendour,
F27.2	3	Prymeros, violet, or fressh daysy,
F27.3	2	'Gelofyr gentyll or rosemary,
F27.3	3	Camamyll, borage, or savery?'
F27.5	2	'The red or the white? Shewe his colour!'
F32b	4	Or otherwise evyll apaide?
F32.3	3	They betyng they broysyng, or liff did depart;
F34b	8	Than leve thi syn, or I nyll the,
F39.1	5	I go or stond;
F41.4	5	Wed me or els I dye for thought!
F43.1	2	In a cloke withoute cote or gowne,
F49b	4	And aske forgeveness or evyr thou dye.'
F49.1	7	Therfore remembir the or thou go hence.'
H35.6	4	What do yow meane or thynk?
H50b	1	Whilles lyve or breth is in my brest
H51.3	1	Or elles from her which is her hayre;
H67.1	2	All tymes or ours
H79.2	1	Or else because they may not opteyne,
H104.3	2	To daunce or syng,
H106.1	7	Withowte hope or comfort off redresse.
H109.3	4	Or elles I shall for you be ded.

ORDENT (1)

F40.2	3	That God hath ordent in his first formacion,

ORDER (1)

H92.5	1	With goode order, councell and equite,

ORDYNAUNCE (1)

R2.1	6	Y most obey fortuneys ordynaunce,

OTHER (13)

F2	5	Sum other grace may cum, perde;
F7.1	6	Yet other grace can ye gett non
F14	6	Other by colour or by fals semblaunce;
F25.3	8	All other to esshewe.
H23.4	1	As featys of armys, and suche other
H25.10	3	From all other that be,
H31.1	1	This other day
H33.3	3	Frome all other only
H50.1	5	And of all other for to love best

OTHER (cont.)
```
 H50.3    2   Above all other as a kyng,
 H63.1    4   Ther ys none other bote.
 H79.2    2   They wold that other shuld yt dysdayne;
 H102.1   3   Her mynd is in non other place:
```

OTHERS (1)
```
 R15.2    3   As others be,
```

OTHERWISE (1)
```
 F32b     4   Or otherwise evyll apaide?
```

OTHIR (1)
```
 F48.3    4   And othir wittness, many one;
```

OTHYR (1)
```
 R13.3    6   And all othyr for hyr sake to eschew,
```

OUGHT (1)
```
 H25.9    1   Then as I ought
```

OUNE (1)
```
 H41.6    2   And shew my lady hys oune wyll.
```

OUR (5)
```
 H92.5    2   Goode Lord, graunt us our mancyon to be!
 H97      2   That for our kyng so to provid,
 H105.2   1   I mene this by Mary, our Maker's moder of myght,
 H105.2   2   Full lovely lookyng on our Lord, the lanterne of
                  lyght
 H105.2   3   Thus saying to our Saviour; this saw I in my syght;
```

OURE (11)
```
 R3.2     5   What do ye here within oure spence?
 F27.6    5   Oure prince to se, and rosys thre.'
 F32.1    4   Yet when oure Laidis Son was slayne
 F32.1    5   Oure sowlis comfort cam agayne;
 F32.2    3   They bet him for oure gilt, though he no syn hadd;
 F32.3    5   But blessid be that oure,
 F43.1    1   Rutterkyn is com unto oure towne
 F44.1    3   Arthur oure prynce to us here terrestriall,
 F44.1    6   Oure prince of plesaunce
 F47.1    2   Whom God hath chose oure gyde to be,
 H25.2    2   Syth that oure chaunce
```

OURS (1)
```
 H67.1    2   All tymes or ours
```

OUT (1)
```
 F1       5   The trewer I serve, the ferther out of mynde;
```

OUTE (1)
```
 R2.2     3   Ys full but late oute of hur kyndely rest
```

205

OVER (7)
R11.3   2   Dame Petyles yn every place over all;
R16b   1   Come over the burne, Besse,
R16b   3   Come over the burne, Besse, to me!
R16.1   6   Cum over the burne, Besse, to me!
F19   8   To lett itt over pass, and thynk theron no more.
F37.3   4   Grete mowntens fallyng over me, thus slepe doth I
                    yn feere
H35.3   2   How she gothe over the playne?

OVERPLUS (1)
F43.4   3   And the overplus undir the table of the newe gyse;

OWER (4)
H41.8   2   We left them ther and went ower way.
H67.1   4   Ower Lord yow gy;
H92.7   3   And that we may ower fauttes amend,
H92.7   4   An blysse opteyne at ower last end. Amen.

OWFTE (1)
F32.2   1   Methynkyth in my reson thou owfte to be gladd

OWN (2)
R14.1   4   Pyteusly, my own sylf alone.
R14.2   4   Pyteusly, my own sylf alone.]

OWNE (4)
F48.3   6   Myn owne seale therto I hyng;
H31.4   6   Myne owne swet hart, adew.
H33.4   1   Adew, myne owne lady,
H63.1   2   Farewell myne owne hart rote -

OWRE (1)
F8   3   Renewde of God for owre consolacion

OWT (4)
R10.6   7   Allmost owt of mynde;
H23.5   2   For therby corage is suerly owt fett:
H62.4   2   Owt of her courte to go;
H74   2   Tyll the trowth be tryed owt.

OWTE (2)
R2.2   6   That she be voyded owte of the grete grevaunce;
F15   4   To be put owte of your good governaunce . . .

OWTWARDLY (1)
H44.3   2   And causith lovers owtwardly to refrayne,

PALE (1)
F36.2   2   With pale visage tremlyng she stode her child
                    before

PART (2)
H96b   2   Help now thi kyng, thi kyng, and take his part!

PART (cont.)
H96.1   5   Help now thi king [and take his part!]

PARTE (1)
H47.2   3   Thow ye now parte me fro.

PASS (2)
F19   8   To lett itt over pass, and thynk theron no more.
F27.2   4   He pass them all in his degre;

PASSE (1)
H22   2   To passe the tyme of youth joly,

PASSE-THE-DAY (1)
R12.2   9   But passe-the-day

PASSETYME (1)
R12.1   1   Passetyme with good cumpanye

PASSINGLY (1)
H105.1   3   So pretyly, so pertly, so passingly well apayd,

PASSION (2)
F30.2   8   Gret passion
F34.1   7   Gayne gostly enmys thynk on my passion;

PASSYNG (4)
F37.2   3   My tast disordyrd all reson far passyng,
H24   2   They greve me passyng sore,
H27.1   2   They greve me passyng sore;
H104.3   1   The tyme passyng

PASSYNGLY (1)
H105.3   2   Save it plesyd me so passyngly that past was my
                     payn

PASSYTH (1)
F20   3   Which that passyth my mynde for to express

PAST (3)
F32.4   4   Thi dere sone is past his trobill and his tene;
F36.4   4   The erth quakyd, the·son was dark, whos lyght was
                     past
H105.3   2   Save it plesyd me so passyngly that past was my
                     payn

PASTANCE (1)
H92.3   4   Honest myrth with vertus pastance.

PASTAUNCE (3)
R12.1   5   For my pastaunce
R12.2   2   Of good or yll some pastaunce;
H92.6   4   And vertuus pastaunce must be theryn usyd.

PASTYMES (2)
H23.2   1   Pastymes ther be I nought treulye
H66.3   1   Pastymes of yough sumtyme among,

PATHIS (1)
F46b   1   Smale pathis to the grenewode,

PAY (3)
F26   1   O rote of trouth, o princess to my pay,
F30.1   15 Unto my pay;
F34.1   2   Suffyrd deth to pay thi rawnsum;

PAYD (1)
F7.2   4   Thynkyth my hart can be well payd

PAYN (4)
R10.5   1   Lyving yn payn,
R11.2   1   The more sorow ys my payn
H105.3 2   Save it plesyd me so passyngly that past was my
            payn
H106.1 2   My body languisshyng, my hart in payn;

PAYNE (24)
R20.2   1   Your on-syttyng speche puttyth me to payne
F6.1   4   Encrese of payne
F11   2   That was my payne is nowe my joyus chaunce;
F17   4   Yet moreovyr a gretter payne,
F23.1   1   That was my joy is now my woo and payne;
F25.1   7   That of my payne
F28   2   Syth I have done my besy payne
F31.2   3   And suffyr wolde payne as sorowfull thought,
F31.3   3   Drawne like a theffe, and for payne swetyng
F36.1   1   To Calvery he bare his cross with doulfull payne,
F36.1   11 So ripe and endles was her payne.
F48b   9   Therefore I suffird all this payne.
F48.2   2   That I suffird not for the this payne,
H27.3   4   Farewell, my joe, and welcom payne.
H28   1   With sorowfull syghs and grevos payne
H31.1   6   Her hart was full of payne.
H47.5   2   It ys to me gret payne
H51.8   1   Soch lovers though thay take payne
H56   1   Departure is my chef payne;
H64.1   9   Of lovys payne,
H106.2 2   Exilide for ever which is my payne;
H106.2 3   My payne with hope hath me begyled;
H106.3 5   A payne it is, hens to depart,
H108   6   But leve in payne whyls I endure

PAYNEFULL (2)
R2.1   8   Of sorfull joye and paynefull plesaunce.
R2.2   8   But sorfull joy and paynefull plesaunce.

PAYNES (1)
H103.2 2   To se the paynes that I endure

PAYNFULL (1)
 F5   1   My wofull hart in paynfull weryness,

PAYNYD (1)
 F33.3   2   So paynyd, so straynyd, so rufull, so red;

PAYNYS (7)
 F16   2   I pray daily ther paynys to asswage
 F31.2   2   That made both paynys and joy also,
 F33.2   4   With paynys my vaynys constraynyd to crake;
 F36.2 10   Wherewith she fell downe with paynys so smert;
 F36.3   1   Saynt Jhon than said, 'Feere not, Mary; his
                  paynys al
 F38b   2   And thynk on the paynys that byn in hell.
 F49.1   3   What paynys I sofferd, I the ensure,

PENANCE (1)
 H106.4 3   From all plesure to gret penance;

PENAUNCE (1)
 R4   4   For yeu, dere hert, thoff Y suffere penaunce

PENCE (1)
 R3.2   7   Y wolde not yette for furty pence

PEPULL (1)
 F10   6   The pore pepull no tyme hath but ryght

PERCIDE (1)
 F34.2   4   Percide hand and fote of indignacion,

PERCYD (1)
 H103.1 1   A thorne hath percyd my hart ryght sore

PERDE (1)
 F2   5   Sum other grace may cum, perde;

PERE (3)
 F39.2   3   I know no pere
 H31.6   3   To be a lady's pere!'
 H101.3 4   Methought I had no pere.

PERFITE (1)
 H79.2   5   But perfite in dede and betwene two.

PERFYTT (1)
 F27.6   2   'Is that your pure perfytt appetite?'

PERSON (2)
 F19   2   Houghevyr such dyversite in on person may be,
 F47.2   6   In your person all ther hope is pyght

PERSONAGE (1)
 H50.5   4   His personage most godlyest!

209

PERTEYNYNG (1)
H31.5 5 To god perteynyng,

PERTLY (1)
H105.1 3 So pretyly, so pertly, so passingly well apayd,

PES (1)
R3.1 1 'Be pes, ye make me spille my ale!'

PETE (3)
F36.3 6 'Of moderly pete
H25.3 3 But anguysch and pete,
H51.8 2 It were pete thay shuld optayne;

PETEUSLY (1)
H31.1 3 Ryght peteusly complayne;

PETUR (1)
F34.3 1 I hade on Petur and Mawdlen pyte

PETYLES (1)
R11.3 2 Dame Petyles yn every place over all;

PIGGESNYE (1)
F41.3 3 'What, and ye shal be my piggesnye?'

PISS (1)
F43.4 2 He will piss a galon-pot full at twise

PITE (4)
F14 5 But pite it is that trust shulde be mysusyd
F18.2 1 Hit were to grete pite
F23.2 4 And with pite have me in remembraunce
F32.1 3 Though deth be bewaylid by waies of pite,

PLACE (7)
R10.6 4 No place to resorte.
R11.3 2 Dame Petyles yn every place over all;
F10 3 In every place ryght hath residens
H27.2 3 And now absence to be in place
H31.2 4 'In every place
H102.1 3 Her mynd is in non other place:
H106.4 5 Good aventure in me to have place:

PLANLY (1)
H107.4 5 Seyng planly

PLAY (9)
R3.1 5 'Wene ye that everybody lest to play?'
R15.4 6 And play the wyse.
R15.6 2 Yn sport and play,
F29.1 2 To the grenewode for to play
F40.4 4 We shall both play, when we ar sole:
F41.1 4 What, will ye do nothing but play?

210

PLAY (cont.)
F41.2	3	Strawe, Jamys foder, ye play the fode;
H82.2	6	It ys for yough the metest play.
H92.7	2	That this rude play may well be take,

PLAYNE (6)
F7.2	1	Treuth nor service nevir so playne
F23.1	3	That was my trust is now my wanhope playne;
F34.1	4	Be repentant; make playne confession.
H35.3	2	How she gothe over the playne?
H62.2	3	For I cannott shote in the playne
H67.2	8	Loyall and playne.

PLAYNLY (3)
F7.1	4	Syn that it is playnly foly;
F24.4	5	Sayng playnly,
H62.4	3	Ryght playnly she shewith me

PLEASE (5)
F40b	3	Alak, good Jhoane, what may you please?
F40.1	5	Alak, good Jhoone, [what may you please?
F40.2	5	Alak, good [Jhoone, what may you please?
F40.3	5	Alak, good Jhoan, [what may you please?
F40.4	5	Alak, good Jhoan, [what may you please?

PLECE (6)
R20b	1	How shall Y plece a creature uncerteyne?
R20.1	4	How sholde Y [plece a creature uncerteyne?]
R20.2	3	With hert Y wyll you plece and your love attayne:
R20.2	4	How sholde Y plece a creature oncertayne?
R20.3	4	How sholde Y plece a creature oncerteyne?
R20.4	4	How sholde Y plece a creature oncertayne?

PLECYD (1)
| R12.1 | 4 | So God be plecyd, this lyve woll I; |

PLENTE (1)
| R8 | 3 | From thy servaund, the weche hathe plente |

PLENTUUS (1)
| F34.5 | 4 | That thi fyve wellis plentuus of fusion, |

PLESANT (2)
| H23.3 | 1 | And they be plesant to God and man, |
| H75 | 2 | My love is lusty, plesant and demure |

PLESAUNCE (7) ·
R2.1	8	Of sorfull joye and paynefull plesaunce.
R2.2	8	But sorfull joy and paynefull plesaunce.
R9	2	That with yeure beute and fresche plesaunce pure
F11	5	Thus hath now grace enrychyd my plesaunce,
F23.1	5	What causyth this but only yowre plesaunce
F26	2	Endewid with vertu and goodly plesaunce,
F44.1	6	Oure prince of plesaunce

PLESAUNT (1)
F46.2   4   Plesaunt, buxum, and ever obedient,

PLESE (1)
R6   4   Ever to plese hym with all myghth,

PLESERS (1)
R18.2   1   Adew, plesers antiquo tempore!

PLESUR (1)
H106.3   7   That deth is plesur and nothyng noyus.

PLESURE (6)
R13.1   4   To her which ys my yoyus plesure;
F6.3   6   Plesure forsake
F37.2   2   To lusty plesure? Now lyyng in the flore,
H75   8   Glad to do her plesure
H106.4   2   My chance contrarious from all plesure,
H106.4   3   From all plesure to gret penance;

PLESYD (1)
H105.3   2   Save it plesyd me so passyngly that past was my
                  payn

PLESYTH (1)
F27.3   5   Here is not he that plesyth me.'

PLONGYNG (1)
F5   2   Which hath byn long plongyng with thought unseyne,

PLUK (2)
F43.3   2   A stoupe of bere up at a pluk,
H96b   1   Englond, be glad! Pluk up thy lusty hart!

PODE (1)
F41.2   1   'Be Gad, ye be a prety pode,

POPAGAY (1)
F41.1   3   Avent, avent, my popagay!

PORE (2)
R13.1   5   Of my pore hert she may be sure,
F10   6   The pore pepull no tyme hath but ryght

PORTER (1)
H41.2   1   To call the porter he wold not blyn;

PORTRES (1)
H41.3   1   The portres was a lady bryght;

POUR (2)
H25.1   4   Alas, pour hart,
H28   3   Alas, pour hart, tyl that we mete agayne,

POURE (1)
H50.1   1   My soverayne lorde for my poure sake

POURS (1)
H67.1   6   Unto my pours

POWER (2)
F47.1   4   Of marshiall power and also hye dygnite,
H97   3   To send hym power to hys corage

POYSON (1)
F34.4   7   Swetter than bawme gayne gostly poyson:

PRATELY (5)
F9   3   So prately
F39b   7   So prately
F39.1   11 So prately
F39.2   11 So prately
F39.3   11 So prately

PRATY (2)
F40.1   1   Hit is so praty in every degre;
F40.3   1   She is my lytell praty on;

PRAY (13)
R2.2   5   Now Y pray God and that righth hertily
R19.2   9   To take her pray
F16   2   I pray daily ther paynys to asswage
F26   5   I pray God hartely, withoutyn mysaventure.
F29.3   3   Therfor I pray the, son, no more,
F33.1   1   Beholde me, I pray the, with all thi hole reson,
F44.3   2   Pray to thi Son, the secund in Trinite,
H62.6   3   And pray I wyll for them that may,
H64.2   3   Let us now pray
H66.2   1   I pray you all that aged be,
H66.4   2   Pray we to God and Seynt Mary
H97   1   Pray we to God that all may gyde
H109.1b 2   I pray you, sir, lett me go mylke my cow!

PRAYD (1)
H25.9   3   And prayd her to be ble,

PRAYER (1)
H92.7   1   Now unto God thys prayer we make,

PRAYNG (1)
R5   4   Prayng to yeure gracius pyte

PRAYSE (1)
H50.3   5   To have the prayse of all the best;

PRECIOUS (1)
F32.4   6   He bought us with his precious blode:

PRESAUNCE (1)
R5   3   Till that Y may in yeure presaunce

PRESENS (2)
F22   1   Alas, for lak of her presens,
F28   6   Tyll that I cum tyll her presens,

PRESERVACION (1)
F44.2   3   In every case be his preservacion,

PRESERVE (1)
F44b   2   Good Lord, preserve the Estrige Fether!

PREST (2)
H24   3   That I cannot be prest
H50.4   4   Next God but he and ever prest

PRETY (2)
R16b   2   Thou lytyll, pretty Besse,
F41.2   1   'Be Gad, ye be a pretty pode,

PRETYLY (1)
H105.1 3   So pretyly, so pertly, so passingly well apayd,

PRIDE (1)
F34.4   1   Thynk agayne, pride, on my humilite;

PRINCE (4)
F27.6   5   Oure prince to se, and rosys thre.'
F44.1   6   Oure prince of plesaunce
F44.2   2   Is this noble prince of riall lynage,
F44.3   3   For this yong prince, which is and daily shal

PRINCESS (1)
F26   1   O rote of trouth, o princess to my pay,

PRINCIPALL (2)
H50.6   2   My soverayne lorde save principall!
H106.3 3   For death ys endar principall

PRISE (1)
R9   9   Thorffe with yeur beute that Y most love and prise.

PRISON (1)
F34.4   5   Whi did I this? To save the from prison.

PRISONER (1)
H41.5   2   He said, 'Madame, as your prisoner.'

PROCURE (1)
H64.2   5   For to procure

PROMPT (1)
H92.6   1   For yough ys frayle and prompt to doo,

PROMYSE (2)
H29.5   3   Promyse I mak that know non shall
H33.3   2   Promyse to her I make,

PROPYR (1)
R16.1   3   So propyr I can none fynde as she;

PROVE (1)
R10.2   8   This do I prove.

PROVED (1)
H34.3   2   Is wors then deth? Let it be proved!

PROVID (4)
F27b   4   'Than shal be provid here anon
F27.4b   4   'Than shall be provid here anon
F27.6b   4   Than may be provid here anon
H97   2   That for our kyng so to provid,

PROVITH (1)
H50.2   5   He provith hymselfe that I sey best,

PRYMEROS (1)
F27.2   3   Prymeros, violet, or fressh daysy,

PRYNCE (1)
F44.1   3   Arthur oure prynce to us here terrestriall,

PRYNTYD (1)
F20   7   Thes vertues byn pryntyd in her doutless.

PURCHACE (1)
F31.4   4   'The to purchace both joy and bliss.'

PURCHASE (2)
H25.5   5   Let se purchase
H92.4   4   All only reches to purchase.

PURE (3)
R9   2   That with yeure beute and fresche plesaunce pure
F27.6   2   'Is that your pure perfytt appetite?'
H50.2   1   My soverayne lord of pusant pure

PUSANT (1)
H50.2   1   My soverayne lord of pusant pure

PUT (9)
R10.6   5   I am put behynd,
R13.1   1   So put yn fere I dare not speke;
F15   4   To be put owte of your good governaunce . . .
F29.1   3   And all hevyness to put away,
F34.3   4   He put his handes depe in my syde adowne.
F46.3   3   To put in one my faithfull trust,
H44.6   1   To lovers I put now suer this cace -

PUT (cont.)
H92.4   2   Though that dysdaynars wold therin put error,
H96.1   4   Bowys and arows to put them all to flyght:

PUTTE (1)
R5   6   And only to be putte to yeure rememoraunce.

PUTTES (1)
H44.4   1   Which puttes them to more and more

PUTTYTH (1)
R20.2   1   Your on-syttyng speche puttyth me to payne

PYGHT (1)
F47.2   6   In your person all ther hope is pyght

PYTE (6)
R5   4   Prayng to yeure gracius pyte
R7   4   This lyon and lambe was, causyng pyte;
F34.3   1   I hade on Petur and Mawdlen pyte
H34.7   1   Grett pyte it ware, love for to compell
H41.7   2   And Pyte said she wold be ther.
H79.1   4   Els it war pyte that he shuld spede;

PYTEUSLY (3)
R14.1   4   Pyteusly, my own sylf alone.
R14.2   4   Pyteusly, my own sylf alone.]
R15.2   6   Right pyteusly;

PYTTE (1)
H29.4   2   Pytte it war that I shuld be,

QUAKE (1)
F48.3   1   Witness, the erthe that did quake,

QUAKYD (1)
F36.4   4   The erth quakyd, the son was dark, whos lyght was
            past

QUARELL (1)
H96.1   2   In the quarell of the church and in the ryght,

QUENE (2)
F32.4   1   Glorius Lady, of hevyn hie quene,
F45.1   2   Sawe I syttyng a comly quene

RAGGID (1)
F43.1   3   Save a raggid hode to kover his crowne,

RAILYNG (1)
F34.2   1   My blody wowndes downe railyng be this tre,

RAN (3)
F33b   3   For the ran,

RAN (cont.)
H25.7   4   The terys ran down
H35.4   2   But he ran fast afore;

RATHER (1)
F48.2   3   [Rather then manne sholde be forlorne

RATHIR (1)
F23.2   5   Much the rathir sith my suryd constaunce

RAWNSUM (1)
F34.1   2   Suffyrd deth to pay thi rawnsum;

RAY (1)
R3.1   2   Now thyngke ye this ys a fayre ray?

RAYN (1)
F8   4   By dropys of grace that on them down doth rayn;

RAYNE (3)
F44.1   4   In honor to rayne, Lord, graunt hym tyme and space,
F44.2   6   In honor to rayne,
H106.1   5   Myn yes for sorow salt ters doth rayne:

RAYNYTH (1)
F10   8   Now raynyth trewly in every mannys syght.

REASON (1)
F46.2   2   Affter my reason and jugement,

RECH (1)
H44.2   2   All ways wherby thay myght it rech;

RECHES (1)
H92.4   4   All only reches to purchase.

RECKE (1)
R3.2   6   Recke ye not to make us shende?

RECOMMAUNDE (1)
R9   4   Y recommaunde my symple service sure,

RECORD (1)
F34.4   2   Cum to scole; record well this lesson:

RECOVER (1)
F47.2   7   To have recover of ther unryght.

RECREACION (1)
F40.2   2   To hym that wolde of such recreacion

RECURE (2)
H103.2   3   Insaciently withowt recure;
H106.2   7   Endure, alas, withowt hope of recure.

RED (5)
F27.5   2   'The red or the white? Shewe his colour!'
F27.6   1   'I love the rose, both red and white.'
F32.3   4   All was on red blod withoute any shirt;
F33.3   2   So paynyd, so straynyd, so rufull, so red;
H17   6   Of the red rose and the whyght.

REDE (2)
H105.2 4   This reson that I rede you now, I rede it full
                ryght

REDEMPCION (1)
F34.2   5   My hert ryven for thi redempcion.

REDRESS (3)
F24.2   7   And no redress
F25.1   8   Ye myght redress.
F47.2   3   All mysdone thynges to redress,

REDRESSE (2)
H106.1 7   Withowte hope or comfort off redresse.
H107.2 7   And no redresse

REFFUSE (1)
R12.3   9   Vyce to reffuse,

REFRAYN (2)
R10.5   6   Love doth refrayn,
H82.1   4   Wold have yough love to refrayn,

REFRAYNE (6)
R4   3   And thogh Y wolde, Y koude me noght refrayne
F36.1   4   His modir dere tendirly wept and cowde not
                refrayne
H44.3   2   And causith lovers owtwardly to refrayne,
H92.2   1   For they wold have hym hys libertye refrayne
H106.2 4   Begyled am I, and cannot refrayne;
H106.2 5   Refrayne I must yet in dysdayne,

REFUSE (1)
H92.3   2   But all dysdaynares for to refuse?

REFUSED (1)
H34.6   1   But dysdayne ys vice and shuld be refused;

REFUSYD (2)
F14   4   And no cause gevyn to be so refusyd;
F17   3   And my service allway refusyd,

REJOSE (1)
F44.2   4   With joy to rejose his dew enerytaunce,

RELEASSE (1)
H106.3 2   In releasse off my gret smert,

218

RELESS (1)
F3   7   That no thought can reless me of my sore.

REMANYNE (1)
R20.3   2   Y am right glad, tristyng hit woll remanyne;

REMAYNE (1)
H18   7   And never more to remayne.

REMEDY (26)
R10.5   4   What remedy?
R11.1   3   Alas, alas, what remedy?
R11.2   3   Alas, alas, what remedy?
R11.3   3   Alas, alas, [what remedy?
R11.4   3   Alas, alas, what remedy?
F4   1   So fer I trow from remedy,
F6.4   5   Remedy non
F7.1   2   Whan that desert lakkyth remedy,
F7.2   7   In whom ther is no remedy;
F19   7   Wherfore I hope to fynd a speciall remedy
F24.3   4   Of remedy;
H25.5   2   What remedy?
H64.2   11 What remedy?
H103b   1   What remedy, what remedy?
H103b   2   Such is fortune! What remedy?
H103.1 4   What remedy, what remedy?
H103.1 5   Such is fortune! What remedy?
H103.2 4   What remedy, what remedy?
H103.2 5   Such is fortune! What remedy?
H103.3 4   What remedy, what remedy?
H103.3 5   Such is fortune! What remedy?
H107.3 4   Of remedy;

REMEDYLES (3)
R15.1   5   Remedyles,
R15.8   5   Remedyles,
H107.2 2   Remedyles

REMEDYLESS (1)
F24.2   2   Remedyless

REMEMBER (2)
F32.3   1   Well I remember his wowndis were full smert,
H102.2 4   Her to remember mest

REMEMBIR (6)
F32.4   3   Remembir thi joys that joyfull aye byn!
F33.2   3   Remembir my tendir hart-rote for the brake,
F37.4   3   'Remembir the, my creature, thou must nedis dye,
                  I the ensure.
F38b   1   A, myn hert, remembir the well,
F38.1   1   A myn hart, remembir the well
F49.1   7   Therfore remembir the or thou go hence.'

219

REMEMBRAUNCE (2)
F15   2   Thow I be lytyll in your remembraunce;
F23.2   4   And with pite have me in remembraunce

REMEMBRE (1)
R7   3   Remembre how feithefull, how treu, how kynde

REMEMBRYNG (3)
F24.1   3   In remembryng
F34.5   2   Thy deth remembryng of humble afeccion,
H107.1 3   In remembryng

REMEMBYR (1)
H47.3   1   When I remembyr me

REMEMORAUNCE (1)
R5   6   And only to be putte to yeure rememoraunce.

REMISSION (1)
F34.1   5   To contryte hartes I do remission;

RENEWDE (1)
F8   3   Renewde of God for owre consolacion

RENNYTH (2)
F43.2   2   His tong rennyth all on buttyrd fyssh,
F46.1   5   So rennyth the chaunce from one to one:

REPENTANT (2)
F34.1   4   Be repentant; make playne confession.
F48.1   2   To the, and thou wilt be repentant;

REPLETE (2)
H31.6   5   And yes replete
H50.4   2   His cherfull contenance doth replete

REPORT (1)
H25.9   5   Of my report

REPRESENT (1)
H51.5   1   The ee doth loke and represent;

REPROVABLE (1)
F34.5   6   May washe us all from surfettes reprovable.

REQUEST (2)
F34.5   8   At hir request be to us merciable.
H50.6   4   Of God I ask for hym request,

RESIDENS (1)
F10   3   In every place ryght hath residens

RESON (7)
F6.2   4   Yet reson is

RESON (cont.)
```
F31b     4  My witt nor reson may hit well fynd:
F32.2    1  Methynkyth in my reson thou owfte to be gladd
F33.1    1  Beholde me, I pray the, with all thi hole reson,
F34.3    5  Role up this mater; grave it in thi reson:
F37.2    3  My tast disordyrd all reson far passyng,
H105.2   4  This reson that I rede you now, I rede it full
                  ryght
```

RESORT (1)
```
H104.2   5  Is no resort
```

RESORTE (1)
```
R10.6    4  No place to resorte.
```

REST (7)
```
R2.2     3  Ys full but late oute of hur kyndely rest
F3       5  That be won thought my rest from me doth go.
F37.1    5  Whereas I am ybid with bodily rest;
F37.2    5  Thou, Nature, hast lefft me; by the fynd I no rest:
F37.3    5  So wakyng ne sleping fynd I no rest:
F37.4    5  With all good sowlis to cause me lyve in rest.
H31.3    3  And thynkes with her to rest,
```

RESTORE (2)
```
F30.2   16  Man to restore,
F36.2    8  Me unto grace for to restore:
```

RETAYLLE (1)
```
H25.10   2  But suere retaylle
```

RETAYNE (2)
```
F25.1    2  Ye me retayne
H67.2    4  Nor yet retayne;
```

RETORN (1)
```
H56      2  I trust ryght wel of retorn agane.
```

REVERT (2)
```
H25.3    5  Your mynde revert
H108     5  From her love nothinge can me revert
```

REVYVED (1)
```
H25.8    3  Therwyth revyved sche,
```

REW (2)
```
H31.3    4  And will not rew,
H92.1    2  Hys mery hart shall sure all rew;
```

REWARDIT (1)
```
H44.1    2  And war rewardit as it hath sene,
```

REWE (2)
```
R11.4    1  I trow on me she wold rewe
```

221

REWE (cont.)
F45.2   3   The floure-de-luce she did on rewe,

REWITH (1)
H64.2   8   Ther no hart rewith

REWYD (1)
H25.7   6   It rewyd my hart to se.

REYNE (1)
R20.4   2   Love me lytell and longe; hot love doth not reyne;

REYNYD (1)
H44.1   1   If love now reynyd as it hath bene

REYNYTH (1)
H44.3   1   Butt envy reynyth with such dysdayne,

RIALL (2)
F8   6   A rose most riall with levis fressh of hew,
F44.2   2   Is this noble prince of riall lynage,

RIGHT (6)
R13.2   7   Ther of right I apeyle hyr to be my surgyon.
R15.2   6   Right pyteusly;
R18.2   4   With right goed cause incipeo flere.
R20.3   2   Y am right glad, tristyng hit woll remanyne;
H29.2   2   She ys right trew, I do it se.
H106.4   4   Right suere to have no good aventure,

RIGHTH (1)
R2.2   5   Now Y pray God and that righth hertily

RIPE (1)
F36.1   11   So ripe and endles was her payne.

ROBBID (1)
F33.3   3   Thus bobbid, thus robbid, thus for thi love ded;

ROBYN (2)
H49.1   1   A Robyn, gentyl Robyn,

RODE (1)
F41.2   4   I am no hakney for your rode;

ROLE (1)
F34.3   5   Role up this mater; grave it in thi reson:

ROOTE (1)
H25.3   2   To me hart roote

ROSE (10)
F8   6   A rose most riall with levis fressh of hew,
F27.4   3   The rose, I suppose? Thyn hart unbrace!'

222

ROSE (cont.)
```
F27.5    1    'The rose it is a ryall floure.'
F27.6    1    'I love the rose, both red and white.'
F45.1    5    The lyly-whighte rose methought I sawe,
F45.1    6    The lyly-whighte rose methought I sawe,
F45.2    4    And said, 'The white rose is most trewe
F45.2    6    The lyly-whighte rose methought I sawe,
F48.2   10    Witness, the bodies that rose from deth to lyve.
H17      6    Of the red rose and the whyght.
```

ROSEMARY (1)
```
F27.3    2    'Gelofyr gentyll or rosemary,
```

ROSIS (1)
```
F8       2    Beholde the soveren sede of this rosis twayn,
```

ROSYS (1)
```
F27.6    5    Oure prince to se, and rosys thre.'
```

ROTE (3)
```
F20      1    Most clere of colour and rote of stedfastness,
F26      1    O rote of trouth, o princess to my pay,
H63.1    2    Farewell myne owne hart rote -
```

ROUGH (1)
```
H62.2    4    Nor yett in rough;
```

ROWND (1)
```
H97      5    Now let us syng this rownd all thre;
```

RUDE (1)
```
H92.7    2    That this rude play may well be take,
```

RUFULL (1)
```
F33.3    2    So paynyd, so straynyd, so rufull, so red;
```

RUFULLY (1)
```
F36.4    7    His moder rufully
```

RULE (1)
```
F45.2    5    This garden to rule be ryghtwis lawe.'
```

RULYTH (5)
```
H66.1    1    Though sum saith that yough rulyth me,
H66.1    5    Though sum say that yough rulyth me.
H66.2    5    Though sum sayth [that yough rulyth me.]
H66.3    5    Thow sum saith [that yough rulyth me.]
H66.4    5    Though sum [saith that yough rulyth me.]
```

RUTTER (4)
```
F43.1    4    Like a rutter:
F43.2    4    Like a rutter:
F43.3    4    Like a rutter:
F43.4    4    Like a rutter:
```

RUTTERKIN (2)
F43b   1   Hoyda, hoyda, joly rutterkin!
F43b   2   Like a rutterkin, hoyda!

RUTTERKYN (4)
F43.1   1   Rutterkyn is com unto oure towne
F43.2   1   Rutterkyn can speke no Englissh;
F43.3   1   Rutterkyn shall bryng you all good luk;
F43.4   1   When rutterkyn from borde will ryse

RYALL (1)
F27.5   1   'The rose it is a ryall floure.'

RYGHT (18)
F10   3   In every place ryght hath residens
F10   6   The pore pepull no tyme hath but ryght
F23.2   3   Wherfore of ryght ye shuld my greffe complayne,
F29.4   1   'Modyr, methynkyth it is ryght ill,
F44.1   9   Ryght eyre for to be;
F44.2   5   His ryght to optayne,
F44.2   9   Ryght eyre for to be;
F47b   2   To strenkyth your comyns in ther ryght.
F47.1   7   To strenkyth your comyns in ther ryght.
H31.1   3   Ryght peteusly complayne;
H31.6   2   Adew, ryght mete
H56   2   I trust ryght wel of retorn agane.
H62.4   3   Ryght playnly she shewith me
H65b   4   For shote ryght well I may.
H66.1   3   God and my ryght and my dewtye,
H96.1   2   In the quarell of the church and in the ryght,
H103.1 1   A thorne hath percyd my hart ryght sore
H105.2 4   This reson that I rede you now, I rede it full
                ryght

RYGHTWIS (1)
F45.2   5   This garden to rule be ryghtwis lawe.'

RYNG (1)
H50.1   2   Six coursys at the ryng dyd make,

RYSE (1)
F43.4   1   When rutterkyn from borde will ryse

RYVE (1)
F48.2   9   Witness, the vale that then did ryve,

RYVEN (1)
F34.2   5   My hert ryven for thi redempcion.

SACRIFICE (1)
F33.2   9   Was like a lombe offerd in sacrifice:

SAD (1)
H104b   4   I am so sad;

SAFF (1)
F4   3   Was nevir man saff only I;

SAFFE (1)
F5   4   Saffe helpe and grace of my lord and soverayne,

SAID (13)
F36.2   5   For myne offence, she said,
F36.3   1   Saynt Jhon than said, 'Feere not, Mary; his
                paynys al
F36.3   4   'O frend,' she said, 'I am sure he is inmortall.'
F45.2   4   And said, 'The white rose is most trewe
H31.2   1   Sshe said, alas,
H31.6   6   She said, 'Adew my dere!'
H31.8   1   She had nott said
H41.2   2   The lady said he shuld not com in.
H41.4   2   He said, 'Desyre, your man, madame.'
H41.5   1   She said, 'Desyre, what do ye here?'
H41.5   2   He said, 'Madame, as your prisoner.'
H41.7   1   Kyndnes said she wold yt bere,
H41.7   2   And Pyte said she wold be ther.

SAIDE (4)
F46.3   1   But I will do as I saide furst,
F49.1   1   'Beholde', he saide, 'my creature,
H31.8   4   And saide, 'Goode mayde,
H105.1 4   Full softly and full soberly unto her swet son
                she saide

SAITH (3)
H66.1   1   Though sum saith that yough rulyth me,
H66.3   5   Thow sum saith [that yough rulyth me.]
H66.4   5   Though sum [saith that yough rulyth me.]

SAKE (5)
R4   5   All for yeure sake, til God me so avaunce
R13.3   6   And all othyr for hyr sake to eschew,
F33.1   3   Sith I for thi sowle sake was slayne in good seson,
F33.2   1   Thus nakyd am I nailid, O man, for thy sake;
H50.1   1   My soverayne lorde for my poure sake

SALFE (1)
R13.3   2   And geve me salfe unto my sore?

SALT (1)
H106.1 5   Myn yes for sorow salt ters doth rayne:

SAME (3)
F27.4   4   'That same is he,
H34.5   2   To woman also, I thynk, the same.
H35.6   3   Now the construccyon of the same -

SANG (6)
R19.1   2   She satt and sang with notes clere;

225

SANG (cont.)
F30.1   5   She sang lullay
F45.1   7   And ever she sang:
F45.2   7   And evyr she sang:
H20   4   The byrdys sang on every syde
H20   7   The nyghtyngale sang on hie

SANKE (1)
H35.2   3   I stroke her so that downe she sanke,

SANTES (1)
H62.6   2   For and my santes booke,

SATT (1)
R19.1   2   She satt and sang with notes clere;

SAVE (7)
F29.3   2   To save mankynd that was forlorne;
F29.4   3   For them to save, it is my will;
F34.4   5   Whi did I this? To save the from prison.
F43.1   3   Save a raggid hode to kover his crowne,
H50.6   2   My soverayne lorde save principall!
H64.1   11   Hymselfe to save
H105.3   2   Save it plesyd me so passyngly that past was my
                  payn

SAVEGARD (1)
F44.3   9   His savegard to be;

SAVERY (1)
F27.3   3   Camamyll, borage, or savery?'

SAVIOUR (1)
H105.2   3   Thus saying to our Saviour; this saw I in my syght;

SAVOURE (1)
F27.5   3   'Both be full swete and of lyke savoure;

SAW (2)
R20.4   1   An olde seyde saw: hasty men sone slayne;
H105.2   3   Thus saying to our Saviour; this saw I in my syght;

SAWE (8)
F29.2   2   I sawe a maide fayre inow;
F30.1   2   I sawe a syght
F36.1   6   When I sawe hym so spilt,
F45.1   2   Sawe I syttyng a comly quene
F45.1   5   The lyly-whighte rose methought I sawe,
F45.1   6   The lyly-whighte rose methought I sawe,
F45.2   6   The lyly-whighte rose methought I sawe,
H25.8   1   When I sawe this

SAY (18)
R3.1   3   'Let go Y say, straw for yeur tale!''

SAY (cont.)
R7	5	And say after me, and be noght unkynde:
R12.2	8	Than who can say
R15.6	1	This young men say
R18.3	1	Now what shall Y say _meis_ _parentibus_
F14	1	Alas, it is I that wote nott what to say,
F30.1	12	Say what ye wolde.'
F39b	4	I dare well say,
F40.3	2	What shulde I say? My mynde is gone.
F41.1	5	Tully, valy, strawe, let be I say!
F48.2	1	If any man will say here agayne
H25.2	4	My love, I say,
H25.6	1	Her for to say
H41.8	1	Thus how thay dyd we cannot say -
H49.2	4	And yet she will say no.
H66.1	5	Though sum say that yough rulyth me.
H82.2	5	Wherfor indede the trouth to say
H92.2	3	But I wyll not so whatsoever thay say,

SAYD (6)
F7.2	2	Cannot avayle, it shal be sayd;
F29.3	1	'Son,' she sayd, 'I have the borne
F29.5	1	'Sone', she sayd, 'let it be in thy thought,
H25.4	3	What sayd sche then to me?
H25.8	6	And sayd sche morned for me.
H31.1	4	She sayd allway

SAYETH (1)
| R2.2 | 2 | To myn entent, and so sayeth mo then I, |

SAYING (1)
| H105.2 | 3 | Thus saying to our Saviour; this saw I in my syght; |

SAYN (1)
| H105.3 | 3 | Yet softly to her swete sonne methought I hard |
| | | her sayn |

SAYNG (2)
| R18.1 | 4 | Sayng, 'Y fele _puerum_ _movere_; |
| F24.4 | 5 | Sayng playnly, |

SAYNT (2)
F34.3	3	Saynt Tomas of Indes, in crudelite
F36.3	1	Saynt Jhon than said, 'Feere not, Mary; his
		paynys al

SAYNTES (1)
| F44.3 | 1 | Now, good Lady among thi sayntes all, |

SAYTH (4)
H66.2	5	Though sum sayth [that yough rulyth me.]
H66.4	4	Thus sayth the kyng, the eighth Harry:
H79.1	5	Many oone sayth that love ys yll,
H102.2	1	My lady sayth of trouth it ys

SAYYNG (1)
F12   6   Of onys voice sayyng, 'Bere in thy mynd,

SCHALL (1)
H25.10 1   I schall not fayll,

SCHE (9)
R2.2   1   For sche weche ys of all godely the best
H25.1   1   My love sche morneth
H25.1   3   My love sche morneth for me.
H25.4   3   What sayd sche then to me?
H25.6   5   Stynt wold sche not,
H25.6   6   So trew of love was sche.
H25.7   1   At last sche wept;
H25.8   3   Therwyth revyved sche,
H25.8   6   And sayd sche morned for me.

SCHULD (1)
H25.4   5   Her schuld not move

SCHYTTE (1)
R3.3   8   Be Criste, Y wolde have schytte the dore!'

SCOLE (1)
F34.4   2   Cum to scole; record well this lesson:

SCORNYD (1)
F33.1   8   They mowid, they grynned, they scornyd me,

SE (18)
R5   1   The hye desire that Y have for to se
R19.1   4   To se her chere
F7.2   5   So for to se ye betrayd,
F27.5   5   That day to se it lykyth well me.'
F27.6   5   Oure prince to se, and rosys thre.'
F33.1   9   Condemp to deth, as thou maist se;
F36.1   9   To se the sharpe swerde of sorow smert,
F39.1   7   I se, in lond,
F40.1   3   In favoure and in facion (lo, will ye se?)
H25.5   5   Let se purchase
H25.7   6   It rewyd my hart to se.
H27.4   1   And I thynk I se her yet,
H29.2   2   She ys right trew, I do it se.
H35.3   1   There she gothe! Se ye nott,
H103.2 2   To se the paynes that I endure
H106.4 1   Thus may ye se my wofull chance,
H109b   7   I wysse my mother then shall us se!
H109.1b 6   I wysse my mothyr than shall us se!

SEALE (2)
F48.3   6   Myn owne seale therto I hyng;
F48.3   8   The wounde in my harte the seale it is,

SECH (1)
F1   3   The more I sech, the wers can I fynde;

SECRET (1)
R15.1   3   Secret, alone,

SECUND (1)
F44.3   2   Pray to thi Son, the secund in Trinite,

SEDE (1)
F8   2   Beholde the soveren sede of this rosis twayn,

SEE (2)
F12   4   The see also drownyd both towre and towne:
H65.3   4   As well as any that ever I see:

SEID (1)
R18.4   1   With the seid child, quid faciam?

SEKE (1)
F39b   2   Whom I now seke

SEKENESSE (1)
R2.2   4   Into gret sekenesse weche holdith hur grevowsly;

SEKNES (1)
F37.3   1   My voice is so trobled, my seknes then feele I;

SEKYTH (1)
F29.4   2   That men sekyth for to spill,

SEMBLAUNCE (1)
F14   6   Other by colour or by fals semblaunce;

SEME (1)
H51.3   2   And she to hym most seme most fayre.

SEMYTH (2)
F37.3   3   My dreme is so mervelous, serpentis semyth me to
                tere
H64.1   6   Best semyth me.

SEN (2)
H25.1   5   Sen we depart
H27.1   3   Sen ye must nedes from me depart,

SEND (3)
F22   7   To send to her to make me shent.
H50.6   5   Off all gode fortunes to send hym best;
H97   3   To send hym power to hys corage

SENDE (1)
F16   3   And sone to sende where they faynest wolde be,

229

SENE (4)
F32.4   2   Lay downe all thi wepyng, let no more be sene!
H33.2   3   When flowerys cannot be sene,
H44.1   2   And war rewardit as it hath sene,
H109.1   2   We may us sport and not be sene;

SENS (1)
H15   3   Sens I must nedys from my love depart

SENT (6)
F40b   4   I shal bere the cost, be swete Sent Denys!
F40.1   6   I shal bere the cost, be swete Sent Denys!]
F40.2   6   I shal bere the cost, be swete Sent Denys!]
F40.3   6   I shal bere the cost, be swete Sent Denys!]
F40.4   6   I shal bere the cost, be swete Sent Denys!]
H97   6   Sent George, graunt hym the victory!

SERCH (1)
F8   1   Lett serch your myndis ye of hie consideracion!

SERPENTIS (1)
F37.3   3   My dreme is so mervelous, serpentis semyth me to
                   tere

SERVANT (1)
F11   7   Your trewe servant with thought, hart and body.

SERVAUND (1)
R8   3   From thy servaund, the weche hathe plente

SERVAUNT (1)
F44.3   4   Be thi servaunt with all his hart so fre.

SERVE (3)
F1   5   The trewer I serve, the ferther out of mynde;
F22   2   Whom I serve and shall as long,
H24   4   To serve you evermore.

SERVICE (3)
R9   4   Y recommaunde my symple service sure,
F7.2   1   Treuth nor service nevir so playne
F17   3   And my service allway refusyd,

SERVYD (1)
F15   1   I am he that hath you dayly servyd,

SES (1)
R3.3   2   'Be Criste, Y nelle, what ses the man?

SESON (1)
F33.1   3   Sith I for thi sowle sake was slayne in good seson,

SESOUN (1)
H20   1   In May, that lusty sesoun

SET (2)
F45.1   4   She gaderd a floure and set betwene;
H64.1   5   To set in one

SETH (1)
H31.3   1   Seth he untrew

SETT (5)
R12.1   7   My hert ys sett
F6.4   3   That I must sett by;
H23.5   1   Comparysons in them may lawfully be sett,
H25.7   3   And sett her on my knee:
H44.5   1   The faut in whome I cannot sett;

SETTYTH (1)
R10.3   3   Settyth me at nought,

SEW (3)
H31.4   3   Optayne that I do sew,
H79.1   1   Whoso that wyll for grace sew,
H92.4   3   For they do sew to get them grace

SEWE (1)
H51.9   1   For often tymes wher they do sewe

SEWITH (1)
H64.2   7   Wher love so sewith,

SEY (4)
H50.2   5   He provith hymselfe that I sey best,
H66.3   2   None can sey but necessary;
H109.1   4   How sey ye, mayde? Be ye content?
H109.3   1   Ye have my hert; sey what ye wyll.

SEYD (5)
R15.2   1   'Alas,' she seyd,
R19.1   8   And seyd, 'No nere!
R19.2   6   She seyd me nay
F30b   2   Seyd Mary, 'A, my dere;
F30.1   10   Joseph seyd, 'Wiff,

SEYDE (1)
R20.4   1   An olde seyde saw: hasty men sone slayne;

SEYNG (1)
H107.4   5   Seyng planly

SEYNT (2)
F48.3   3   Witness, Mari, wittness, Seynt Jhon,
H66.4   2   Pray we to God and Seynt Mary

SHAL (15)
F7.2   2   Cannot avayle, it shal be sayd;
F11   6   Wherfor I am and shal be tyll I dye

SHAL (cont.)

F27b	4	'Than shal be provid here anon
F40b	4	I shal bere the cost, be swete Sent Denys!
F40.1	6	I shal bere the cost, be swete Sent Denys!]
F40.2	6	I shal bere the cost, be swete Sent Denys!]
F40.3	6	I shal bere the cost, be swete Sent Denys!]
F40.4	6	I shal bere the cost, be swete Sent Denys!]
F41.3	3	'What, and ye shal be my piggesnye?'
F41.3	4	Be Crist, ye shal not! No, no, hardely!
F44.3	3	For this yong prince, which is and daily shal
F48b	3	To me shal be leffe and dere,
H18	6	Sone shal be slayne
H49.1	3	And thow shal know of myne.
H109.4	1	Then for this onse I shal you spare,

SHALBE (4)

F37.1	6	Thus trobled am I yet I trust it shalbe for the best
F37.2	6	Thus trobled am I [yet I trust it shalbe for the best
F37.3	6	Thus trobled am I [yet I trust it shalbe for the best
F37.4	6	Thus trobled am I [yet I trust it shalbe for the best

SHALL (62)

R1.1	3	Y shall hong up my horne by the grenewode spray;
R1.2	2	Shall Y wedde no wiffe;
R1.2	3	I shall bygge me a boure atte the wodes ende,
R2.1	4	Full oghfte or this, Y shall undertake.
R2.2	7	For'till she amende Y shall have noght truly
R3.3	1	Cum kys me! 'Nay!' Be God, ye shall!
R12.1	2	I love and shall unto I dye;
R12.1	10	Who shall me lett?
R12.3	7	My mynde shall be;
R12.3	10	Y shall use me.
R13.1	6	And so shall contynew tyll I dye,
R15.7	5	Shall he not stert,
R18.3	1	Now what shall Y say meis parentibus
R18.4	2	Shall Y hyt kepe vel interficiam?
R18.4	4	I shall lose God et vitam eternam.'
R20b	1	How shall Y plece a creature uncerteyne?
R20.1	1	Your light grevans shall not me constrayne
F22	2	Whom I serve and shall as long,
F27.2	2	And shall not yet be namyd for me;
F27.4b	4	'Than shall be provid here anon
F30.2	12	Suffyr shall I.
F30.2	15	Ther shall I be,
F36.3	11	From deth to lyff he aryse shall.'
F40.4	1	Alas, good Jhoan, shall all my mone
F40.4	4	We shall both play, when we ar sole:
F42.1	1	Who shall have my fayre lady?
F43.3	1	Rutterkyn shall bryng you all good luk;
F46b	2	Will I love and shall I love,

SHALL (cont.)

F46b	3	Will I love and shall I love
H12	1	Alas, what shall I do for love?
H12	2	For love, alasse, what shall I do,
H28	4	Joy shall I never ye may be sure.
H29.1	4	Shall no man know her name for me.
H29.2	4	Shall no mane know her name for me.
H29.3	4	Shall no man know her name for me.
H29.4	4	Shall no man [know her name for me].
H29.5	3	Promyse I mak that know non shall
H29.6	1	My hart she hath and ever shall
H29.6	3	Happe what wyll happ, fall what shall,
H29.6	4	Shall no man [know her name for me].
H30	1	Alac, alac, what shall I do,
H31.7	5	Wher I shall dwell,
H33.4	4	Be suere, and ever shall.
H40	4	My hart with her ever shall be.
H47.2	4	We shall mete when we may.
H50b	2	My soverayne lord I shall love best.
H50.6	3	He hath my hart and ever shall.
H66.1	4	Frome them shall I never vary:
H67.2	3	Shall me solur
H68	2	I trust we shall mete oftener.
H92.1	2	Hys mery hart shall sure all rew;
H102b	1	Why shall not I?
H102b	2	Why shall not I to my lady
H102b	3	Why shall not I be trew?
H102b	4	Why shall not I?
H102.1	5	Why shall not I?
H102.2	5	Why shall not I?
H106.2	6	In dysdayn I shall my lyfe endure,
H109b	7	I wysse my mother then shall us se!
H109.1	3	And yf ye wyll, I shall consent;
H109.1b	6	I wysse my mothyr than shall us se!
H109.3	4	Or elles I shall for you be ded.

SHARPE (5)

F32.3	6	That he suffird that sharpe shoure!
F33.1	6	With sharpe corde sore fretid,
F33.3	1	Off sharpe thorne I have worne a crowne on my hede,
F36.1	3	A crowne of thorne as nedill sharpe shyfft in his brayne
F36.1	9	To se the sharpe swerde of sorow smert,

SHARPER (1)

R13.2	2	Sharper than thorn, dyamond or steyll,

SHE (90)

R2.2	6	That she be voyded owte of the grete grevaunce;
R2.2	7	For till she amende Y shall have noght truly
R11.4	1	I trow on me she wold rewe
R11.4	2	Iff my sorow and woe she knew:
R13.1	5	Of my pore hert she may be sure,
R13.2	6	And only she which my wound begunne;

R13.3	1	She hath me hurt; why shold she not hele,
R13.3	3	Or els yn feyth unkyndly she doth dele,
R13.3	4	For she hath that I hadde in store,
R13.3	5	Myn hert and love; what wyll she more?
R15.2	1	'Alas,' she seyd,
R16.1	3	So propyr I can none fynde as she;
R16.1	4	She daunces and she lepys,
R19.1	2	She satt and sang with notes clere;
R19.1	7	She stode yn fere
R19.2	6	She seyd me nay
R19.2	8	She wolde assay
R19.2	10	That she had lovyd so long.
R19.3	1	Whan she was gone
R19.3	6	'Such on as she,
R19.3	8	Yll must she the,
R19.3	9	Wherever she be
F13	5	Trustyng sumtyme that she will chaunge her mode
F13	7	Syth for my trouth she nedith no wittness.
F24.5	7	But she it ment,
F28	4	And she me takyth in gret disdayne:
F29.2	3	A childe she hoppid; she song, she lough;
F29.3	1	'Son,' she sayd, 'I have the borne
F29.5	1	'Sone', she sayd, 'let it be in thy thought,
F30.1	5	She sang lullay
F30.1	7	To kepe she sought
F32b	3	Whi shuld she hevy be?
F36.2	2	With pale visage tremlyng she stode her child before
F36.2	5	For myne offence, she said,
F36.2	10	Wherewith she fell downe with paynys so smert;
F36.2	11	Unneth on worde cowde she speke more.
F36.3	4	'O frend,' she said, 'I am sure he is inmortall.'
F39b	8	She delis allway.
F39.1	2	When she me bas,
F39.1	12	She delis allway.]
F39.2	12	She delis allway.]
F39.3	12	She delis allway.]
F40.3	1	She is my lytell praty on;
F40.3	3	Yff she and I were together alone,
F40.3	4	I-wis, she will not gyve me. a bone:
F45.1	4	She gaderd a floure and set betwene;
F45.1	7	And ever she sang:
F45.2	2	The gelofir gent, that she well knewe;
F45.2	3	The floure-de-luce she did on rewe,
F45.2	7	And evyr she sang:
F46.3	4	Forever yff she will trew be,
F46.3	5	And love her only whereever she gone:
H27.4	4	Unto my hart as now she shuld.
H29.2	2	She ys right trew, I do it se.
H29.2	3	My hart to have she doth me bynd;
H29.3	1	She doth not waver as the wynde,
H29.3	2	Nor for no new me chaunge doth she,
H29.4	3	For she to me ys allway kynd;

SHE (cont.)
H29.6   1   My hart she hath and ever shall
H31.1   4   She sayd allway
H31.6   6   She said, 'Adew my dere!'
H31.8   1   She had nott said
H35b   2   Ther ys a do in yonder wode; in faith, she woll
                  not dy
H35.1   2   And yet she bledes no whytt;
H35.1   3   She lay so fayre, I cowde nott mys;
H35.2   3   I stroke her so that downe she sanke,
H35.2   4   But yet she was not dede.
H35.3   1   There she gothe! Se ye nott,
H35.3   2   How she gothe over the playne?
H35.5   2   For I fownd wher she lay;
H35.5   3   And arrow in her hanch she hent;
H35.5   4   For faynte she myght nott bray.
H40   2   My love, she is so trew to me.
H41.4   1   She asked hym what was his name;
H41.5   1   She said, 'Desyre, what do ye here?'
H41.7   1   Kyndnes said she wold yt bere,
H41.7   2   And Pyte said she wold be ther.
H49.2   2   Alac, why is she so?
H49.2   3   She lovyth another better than me
H49.2   4   And yet she will say no.
H49.3   4   She will change for no new.
H51.3   2   And she to hym most seme most fayre.
H62.4   3   Ryght playnly she shewith me
H102.1   2   She takes me as her howne;
H105.1   4   Full softly and full soberly unto her swet son
                  she saide
H107.5   7   But she it ment,

SHEDE (1)
F33.3   4   Onfaynyd, not deynyd, my blode for to shede:

SHELDYS (1)
H96.1   3   With spers and sheldys on goodly horsys lyght,

SHENDE (1)
R3.2   6   Recke ye not to make us shende?

SHENT (4)
F22   7   To send to her to make me shent.
F24.5   6   Thus to be shent;
F25.3   7   Thowe I be shent,
H107.5   6   Thus to be shent;

SHEW (2)
F13   3   But be constraynt, now must I shew my woo
H41.6   2   And shew my lady hys oune wyll.

SHEWE (1)
F27.5   2   'The red or the white? Shewe his colour!'

SHEWITH (1)
H62.4   3   Ryght playnly she shewith me

SHEWYNG (1)
F23.1   6   Onryghtfully shewyng me unkyndness,

SHIRT (1)
F32.3   4   All was on red blod withoute any shirt;

SHOFFE (1)
H35.2   2   The dere shoffe on the mede;

SHOLD (1)
R13.3   1   She hath me hurt; why shold she not hele,

SHOLDE (5)
R20.1   4   How sholde Y [plece a creature uncerteyne?]
R20.2   4   How sholde Y plece a creature oncertayne?
R20.3   4   How sholde Y plece a creature oncerteyne?
R20.4   4   How sholde Y plece a creature oncertayne?
F48.2   3   [Rather then manne sholde be forlorne

SHOLDEST (1)
F48.2   5   Yet, man, that thou sholdest not be lorne,

SHOOTE (1)
H62.3   4   When I shuld shoote I myse;

SHORTLY (1)
F37.1   4   So shortly am I bydyn to a grevus fest,

SHOT (1)
H65.1   4   And shot well enough:

SHOTE (3)
H62.1   4   No lenger shote I may;
H62.2   3   For I cannott shote in playne
H65b   4   For shote ryght well I may.

SHOTT (3)
H35.3   3   And yf ye lust to have a shott,
H35.4   3   I bad hym shott and strik the do,
H35.4   4   For I myght shott no mere.

SHOURE (1)
F32.3   6   That he suffird that sharpe shoure!

SHOWRIS (1)
F8   5   Through whose swete showris now sprong ther is ayen

SHULD (23)
F23.2   3   Wherfore of ryght ye shuld my greffe complayne,
F32b   3   Whi shuld she hevy be?
H23.1   2   But vice in it shuld be forfent.

236

SHULD (cont.)

H23.3	2	Those shuld we covit wyn who can;
H27.4	4	Unto my hart as now she shuld.
H29.4	2	Pytte it war that I shuld be,
H34.6	1	But dysdayne ys vice and shuld be refused;
H41.2	2	The lady said he shuld not com in.
H47.1	1	Wherto shuld I expresse
H47.3	4	That I shuld be unkynde.
H51.8	2	It were pete thay shuld optayne;
H51.10	1	For whoso lovith shuld love butt oone;
H62.3	4	When I shuld shoote I myse;
H65.1	1	Wherfore shuld I hang up my bow
H65.2	1	Wherfor shuld I hang up myne arrow
H65.3	1	Wherfor shuld I hang up my horne
H65.4	1	Wherfor shuld I tye up my hownd
H79.1	4	Els it war pyte that he shuld spede;
H79.2	2	They wold that other shuld yt dysdayne;
H79.2	6	Wherfor, then, shuld we yt excho?
H92.1	1	Lusti yough shuld us ensue,
H92.3	1	How shuld yough hymselfe best use
H92.5	4	Yough shuld fall in grett myschaunce;

SHULDE (8)

F3	3	For when nature wold oft that I shulde wynk,
F13	1	To complayne me, alas, why shulde I so?
F14	5	But pite it is that trust shulde be mysusyd
F17	6	For where I shulde, they be mery,
F32.1	2	That the Son of God shulde make us fre,
F36b	2	Methought a maydynys childe causless shulde dye.
F40.3	2	What shulde I say? My mynde is gone.
H62.5	2	When I shulde maydyns kysse,

SHULL (2)

R3.2	3	'Ywisse, wanton, ye shull not yette!
R19.2	3	I shull her gyde

SHYFFT (1)

F36.1	3	A crowne of thorne as nedill sharpe shyfft in his brayne

SIKE (1)

F40b	1	Jhoone is sike and ill at ease;

SIMULACION (1)

F10	4	Nethir in towne ne fylde simulacion

SIR (1)

H109.1b	2	I pray you, sir, lett me go mylke my cow!

SIS (1)

F39.2	7	Sis is witness

SITH (7)

F23.2	5	Much the rathir sith my suryd constaunce

SITH (cont.)
F32.1   1   Sith it concludid was in the Trinite
F33.1   3   Sith I for thi sowle sake was slayne in good seson,
F34.2   8   Why art thou froward sith I am merciable?
F34.4   8   Be thou not affraide sith I am merciable.
F47.1   5   Sith it is so, now let your labour be
H102.1 4   Now sith it ys thus known,

SITHE (1)
R9   6   Unly to yeure swete grace a thousande sithe

SIX (1)
H50.1   2   Six coursys at the ryng dyd make,

SKYLL (1)
H79.1   6   But those be thay which can no skyll:

SLAKE (1)
R2.1   5   Till gode tydinges com my sorwe to slake

SLAYN (1)
R11.2   2   So onkyndly thus to be slayn;

SLAYNE (4)
R20.4   1   An olde seyde saw: hasty men sone slayne;
F32.1   4   Yet when oure Laidis Son was slayne
F33.1   3   Sith I for thi sowle sake was slayne in good seson,
H18   6   Sone shal be slayne

SLEITH (1)
F36.2   9   'Yet thou are unkynd, which sleith myn hert,'

SLEPE (2)
F30.1   3   All in my slepe:
F37.3   4   Grete mowntens fallyng over me, thus slepe doth I
                yn feere

SLEPING (1)
F37.3   5   So wakyng ne sleping fynd I no rest:

SLEPIS (1)
F37.3   2   My slepis be so feerfull, I thynk then sure to dye;

SLEPIST (1)
F33.2   2   I love the, then love me; why slepist thou? Awake!

SLEY (1)
R18.4   3   Yf Y sley hyt, quo loco fugiam?

SLUMBIR (1)
F49b   1   In a slumbir late as I was,

SLYPT (1)
H62.3   3   The glew is slypt frome the nyk;

238

SMALE (1)
F46b   1   Smale pathis to the grenewode,

SMALLE (1)
H25.8   4   And her smalle waste

SMART (1)
H108   2   And cannot cesse tyl I sore smart,

SMERT (7)
F32.3   1   Well I remember his wowndis were full smert,
F36.1   9   To se the sharpe swerde of sorow smert,
F36.2 10   Wherewith she fell downe with paynys so smert;
F36.3   9   Is by nature constraynyd to smert,
F48b   6   Uppon the crosse with woundis smert
F48.1   5   Not covetyng more for all my smert
H106.3 2   In releasse off my gret smert,

SMOCKE (1)
R15.6   6   The smocke ys hyd."

SMYTE (1)
R20.4   3   Speke or ye smyte, barke or ye byte; holde yowre
                hondes twane

SNARE (1)
R10.4   5   Takyn yn a snare

SO (119)
R2.2   2   To myn entent, and so sayeth mo then I,
R4   5   All for yeure sake, til God me so avaunce
R10.1   4   Alas, why so?
R11.2   2   So onkyndly thus to be slayn;
R12.1   3   Grugge so woll, but noon denye;
R12.1   4   So God be plecyd, this lyve woll I;
R13.1   1   So put yn fere I dare not speke;
R13.1   6   And so shall contynew tyll I dye,
R13.2   3   So depe hath thrylled my hert ynwardly
R15.4   1   Now hit ys so,
R15.7   4   So fro my hert
R16.1   3   So propyr I can none fynde as she;
R19.2 10   That she had lovyd so long.
F3   4   Then be it they that doth me trobill so
F4   1   So fer I trow from remedy,
F4   2   And from all hope so fer banysshid
F4   4   So mekyll dred, so lytyll trust
F5   5   Is nowe be hym so comfortide agayne
F6.3   3   So unkyndly;
F7.1   3   In willfullness so for to be,
F7.2   1   Treuth nor service nevir so playne
F7.2   5   So for to se ye betrayd,
F9   3   So prately
F9   8   So long a space.
F12   2   Methought the worlde was turnyd up so downe,

239

SO (cont.)

F13	1	To complayne me, alas, why shulde I so?
F14	4	And no cause gevyn to be so refusyd;
F17	1	But why am I so abusyd?
F18.2	3	Hade so grete foly
F18.2	6	Then speke ye so swetely
F19	3	So goodly, so curtesly, so gentill in behavyng;
F19	4	And so sodenly will chaunge in every degre;
F23.2	1	Nor nought cowde have, wolde I nevyr so fayne!
F27.2	1	'Ther is a floure where so he be,
F27.4	5	In hart so fre, that best lykyth me.'
F30.2	14	That is so hye,
F31.1	4	And wolde so take mortalite!
F32b	1	Affraid, alas, and whi so sodenli?
F32b	2	Whi so dismaid?
F32.1	6	Therfore, though deth be nevyr so sore,
F32.2	6	So nowe is knowen thi sonnys myght:
F32.2	7	Therfor, thowe deth be never so sore,
F32.3	7	Therfore though deth be never so sore,
F32.4	7	Therefore, though deth be nevir so sore,
F33.2	7	Whereas never man was so
F33.3	2	So paynyd, so straynyd, so rufull, so red;
F36.1	6	When I sawe hym so spilt,
F36.1	11	So ripe and endles was her payne.
F36.2	6	Her Son was so betraide,
F36.2	10	Wherewith she fell downe with paynys so smert;
F36.3	5	'Why than so depe morne ye?'
F37.1	4	So shortly am I bydyn to a grevus fest,
F37.3	1	My voice is so trobled, my seknes then feele I;
F37.3	2	My slepis be so feerfull, I thynk then sure to dye;
F37.3	3	My dreme is so mervelous, serpentis semyth me to tere
F37.3	5	So wakyng ne sleping fynd I no rest:
F38.2	4	I have offendid so grevusly;
F39b	5	So manerly
F39b	6	So curtesly
F39b	7	So prately
F39.1	9	So manerly
F39.1	10	[So curtesly
F39.1	11	So prately
F39.2	9	So manerly
F39.2	10	[So curtesly
F39.2	11	So prately
F39.3	9	So manerly
F39.3	10	[So curtesly
F39.3	11	So prately
F40.1	1	Hit is so praty in every degre;
F40.4	2	Be lost so sone? I am a fole:
F44.3	4	Be thi servaunt with all his hart so fre.
F46.1	5	So rennyth the chaunce from one to one:
F46.3	2	So it is best, as thynkyth me,
F47.1	5	Sith it is so, now let your labour be
F49.1	2	Whome I did make so lyke unto me,
H12	3	Syth now so kynd

SO (cont.)

H15	2	My hart it is so sore,
H20	5	So meryly, it joyed my hart
H20	6	They toyned so clene;
H20	8	Joyfully, so merely,
H25.6	6	So trew of love was sche.
H31.3	5	And I so trew,
H31.4	4	So ever and ay
H31.7	6	My hart it grevyth me so.'
H33b	2	So doth the ive,
H33b	3	Thow wynter blastys blow never so hye,
H33.1	3	So I am, ever hath bene,
H35.1	3	She lay so fayre, I cowde nott mys;
H35.2	3	I stroke her so that downe she sanke,
H40	2	My love, she is so trew to me.
H44.7	2	Better than do I, I thynk it so.
H47.2	1	Do way, dere hart, not so.
H49.2	2	Alac, why is she so?
H50.5	1	So many vertuse gevyn of grace
H51.6	2	Myne ey with hart doth me so juge.
H51.10	2	Chaunge who so wyll, I wyll be none.
H62.5	1	My berd ys so hard, God wote,
H64.2	7	Wher love so sewith,
H75	6	So my hart to her I ensure;
H92.2	3	But I wyll not so whatsoever thay say,
H97	2	That for our kyng so to provid,
H104b	4	I am so sad;
H104.1	2	Makes me so mery
H105.1	2	Lokyng on her lytill son, so laughyng in lap layd,
H105.1	3	So pretyly, so pertly, so passingly well apayd,
H105.3	1	Musyng on her manners, so ny mard was my mayne,
H105.3	2	Save it plesyd me so passyngly that past was my payn
H106.3	6	Yet my lyfe is to me so grevus
H109.2	1	Ye be so nyce and so mete of age

SOBERLY (1)

| H105.1 | 4 | Full softly and full soberly unto her swet son she saide |

SOCH (1)

| H51.8 | 1 | Soch lovers though thay take payne |

SOCOURS (1)

| H67.1 | 5 | In all socours |

SODENLI (1)

| F32b | 1 | Affraid, alas, and whi so sodenli? |

SODENLY (2)

| F19 | 4 | And so sodenly will chaunge in every degre; |
| F36.4 | 10 | Wherwith sodenly anon I awoke, |

SODEYN (1)
R9   3   Arested hathe my herte in sodeyn wise,

SOERE (1)
R13.2   4   That wondyd soere myself Y fele,

SOFFERD (1)
F49.1   3   What paynys I sofferd, I the ensure,

SOFTLY (2)
H105.1 4   Full softly and full soberly unto her swet son
                she saide
H105.3 3   Yet softly to her swete sonne methought I hard
                her sayn

SOLACE (1)
H16   2   Adew, my joy and my solace!

SOLE (3)
F31b   2   That God hymselfe for sole mankynd
F40.4   4   We shall both play, when we ar sole:
H64.1   7   For when one sole

SOLEN (1)
F19   5   As solen, as stately, as strange toward me,

SOLUR (1)
H67.2   3   Shall me solur

SOME (1)
R12.2   2   Of good or yll some pastaunce;

SON (15)
F12   3   The son, the moone, had lost ther force and light;
F29.3   1   'Son,' she sayd, 'I have the borne
F29.3   3   Therfor I pray the, son, no more,
F30b   1   'A, my dere, a, my dere Son,'
F30.1   9   Her Son from colde;
F32.1   2   That the Son of God shulde make us fre,
F32.1   4   Yet when oure Laidis Son was slayne
F32.2   2   When Jewis with treson to deth thi son ladde;
F32.2   4   Thi son was doughti, the fende was adradde;
F36.2   6   Her Son was so betraide,
F36.4   4   The erth quakyd, the son was dark, whos lyght was
                past
F44.3   2   Pray to thi Son, the secund in Trinite,
F48.2   8   Witness, the son that lost his lyghth,
H105.1 2   Lokyng on her lytill son, so laughyng in lap layd,
H105.1 4   Full softly and full soberly unto her swet son
                she saide

SONE (8)
R20.4   1   An olde seyde saw: hasty men sone slayne;
F16   3   And sone to sende where they faynest wolde be,

SONE (cont.)
```
F29.5    1   'Sone', she sayd, 'let it be in thy thought,
F30.1   16   My Sone, a Kyng
F32.4    4   Thi dere sone is past his trobill and his tene;
F40.4    2   Be lost so sone? I am a fole:
H18      6   Sone shal be slayne
H66.4    1   Then sone dyscusse that hens we must;
```

SONG (3)
```
R19.3    5   This ys my song:
F22      5   And thus is the tyme of his song;
F29.2    3   A childe she hoppid; she song, she lough;
```

SONGE (1)
```
R2.1     3   Weche Y have songe with wepyng yen tweyne
```

SONNE (1)
```
H105.3   3   Yet softly to her swete sonne methought I hard
                 her sayn
```

SONNYS (1)
```
F32.2    6   So nowe is knowen thi sonnys myght:
```

SOORE (1)
```
R15.7    2   But soore Y wepe
```

SORE (23)
```
R13.3    2   And geve me salfe unto my sore?
R18.3    4   And me sore chast coram omnibus.
F3       7   That no thought can relesse me of my sore.
F30.1    6   And sore did wepe.
F30.2   17   Naylid full sore,
F32.1    6   Therfore, though deth be nevyr so sore,
F32.2    7   Therfor, thowe deth be never so sore,
F32.3    7   Therfore though deth be never so sore,
F32.4    7   Therefore, though deth be nevir so sore,
F33.1    6   With sharpe corde sore fretid,
F33.3    5   My fete and handis sore
F36.1    8   Tho I wept and sore did complayne
F36.2    1   His grevous deth and her morenyng grevid me sore;
F36.2    7   With wondis sore araid,
F36.4   11   And of my dreme was sore agast.
H14      2   And sore I sygh for one.
H15      2   My hart it is so sore,
H24      2   They greve me passyng sore,
H27.1    2   They greve me passyng sore;
H35.1    1   Sore this dere strykyn ys,
H44.4    2   Inwardly most grevous and sore:
H103.1   1   A thorne hath percyd my hart ryght sore
H108     2   And cannot cesse tyl I sore smart,
```

SORFULL (2)
```
R2.1     8   Of sorfull joye and paynefull plesaunce.
R2.2     8   But sorfull joy and paynefull plesaunce.
```

SOROUS (1)
F8   7   All myrthis to maynten, all sorous to subdewe.

SOROW (7)
R11.2   1   The more sorow ys my payn
R11.4   2   Iff my sorow and woe she knew:
R15.4   5   With sorow allso,
F36.1   9   To se the sharpe swerde of sorow smert,
F38.1   5   Alas, for sorow myne hart doth blede
H16   3   Wyth dowbyl sorow complayn I must
H106.1 5   Myn yes for sorow salt ters doth rayne:

SOROWES (1)
H106.3 4   Of all the sorowes within my hart;

SOROWFULL (3)
R19.3   4   With sorowfull grone,
F31.2   3   And suffyr wolde payne as sorowfull thought,
H28   1   With sorowfull syghs and grevos payne

SOROWS (2)
F4   6   To thynk my sorows, well may I complayne;
H106.1 3   My joyes, dystres; my sorows dowble;

SORWE (2)
R2.1   5   Till gode tydinges com my sorwe to slake
R8   4   Of sorwe and all hevenesse.

SORY (2)
F17   7   When that they knowe I am sory.
F40b   2   I am full sory for Jhoon's disease.

SOTHELY (1)
F30.2   5   It is sothely

SOUGHT (3)
R10.3   1   Wheras I sought,
F30.1   7   To kepe she sought
F41.4   2   Now have I fownd that I have sought,

SOVERAYN (1)
F47.1   1   Soverayn lorde, in erth most excellent,

SOVERAYNE (14)
F5   4   Saffe helpe and grace of my lord and soverayne,
H50b   2   My soverayne lord I shall love best.
H50.1   1   My soverayne lorde for my poure sake
H50.1   6   My soverayne lorde.
H50.2   1   My soverayne lord of pusant pure
H50.2   6   My soverayne lorde.
H50.3   1   My soverayne lorde in every thyng
H50.3   6   My soverayne lorde.
H50.4   1   My soverayne lorde when that I mete,
H50.4   6   My soverayne lorde.

SOVERAYNE (cont.)
H50.5   6   My soverayne lorde.
H50.6   1   The soverayne lorde that is of all,
H50.6   2   My soverayne lorde save principall!
H50.6   6   My soverayne lorde.

SOVERAYNTE (1)
F47.2   2   Wisdome with strenkyth and soveraynte

SOVEREN (1)
F8   2   Beholde the soveren sede of this rosis twayn,

SOWLE (1)
F33.1   3   Sith I for thi sowle sake was slayne in good seson,

SOWLIS (2)
F32.1   5   Oure sowlis comfort cam agayne;
F37.4   5   With all good sowlis to cause me lyve in rest.

SOWNDE (1)
F12   5   Yett more mervell how that I hard the sownde

SOWNYNG (1)
F31.2   4   With wepyng, wayling, ye, sownyng for wo.

SPACE (3)
F9   8   So long a space.
F44.1   4   In honor to rayne, Lord, graunt hym tyme and space,
H106.4   6   Nay, nay, for why? Ther ys no space.

SPAKE (1)
R15.3   2   Spake wordes myld

SPARE (1)
H109.4   1   Then for this onse I shal you spare,

SPAYNE (1)
F44.2   8   Of Castell and Spayne,

SPECHE (1)
R20.2   1   Your on-syttyng speche puttyth me to payne

SPECIALL (3)
F19   7   Wherfore I hope to fynd a speciall remedy
F36.3   2   He willfully doth suffir for love speciall
F44.1   2   Which formyd hast of thi most speciall grace

SPECIALLY (1)
F47.2   4   And specially hurtis of thi commynalte,

SPECYALL (1)
H33.4   2   Adew, my specyall,

245

SPEDE (1)
H79.1   4   Els it war pyte that he shuld spede;

SPEKE (5)
R13.1   1   So put yn fere I dare not speke;
R20.4   3   Speke or ye smyte, barke or ye byte; holde yowre
                hondes twane
F18.2   6   Then speke ye so swetely
F36.2 11   Unneth on worde cowde she speke more.
F43.2   1   Rutterkyn can speke no Englissh;

SPENCE (1)
R3.2   5   What do ye here within oure spence?

SPEND (1)
H23.6   1   Vertue it is then youth for to spend

SPENT (6)
F2   7   With my desyre tyll I be spent:
F24.5   3   It is ny spent;
F34.4   4   My blode all spent by distillacion.
H23.1   1   The tyme of youthe is to be spent;
H31.9   4   That day they spent
H107.5 3   It is ny spent;

SPENTE (1)
F25.3   6   My lyffe to spente,

SPERE (3)
F32.3   2   The crowne on his hed, the spere at his hart,
F34.2   3   The crowne of thorne, the spere, the nailis thre,
H50.2   3   With spere and swerd at the barryoure

SPERS (1)
H96.1   3   With spers and sheldys on goodly horsys lyght,

SPETTYNG (1)
F31.3   2   As betyng, bobbyng, ye, spettyng on thi face?

SPILL (1)
F29.4   2   That men sekyth for to spill,

SPILLE (1)
R3.1   1   'Be pes, ye make me spille my ale!'

SPILT (1)
F36.1   6   When I sawe hym so spilt,

SPORT (3)
R12.1   8   All godely sport
R15.6   2   Yn sport and play,
H109.1 2   We may us sport and not be sene;

SPORTT (1)
H109.1b 4 That now in the feldes we may us sportt?

SPOUSE (1)
F30.1 13 'Nothyng, my spouse,

SPRAY (2)
R1.1   3 Y shall hong up my horne by the grenewode spray;
H65.4 2 Unto the grenwod spray?

SPRONG (1)
F8   5 Through whose swete showris now sprong ther is ayen

SPRYNGYNGE (1)
H17   5 A bud is spryngynge

SPYE (1)
F9   2 Yff I coude spye

SSHE (1)
H31.2 1 Sshe said, alas,

STALE (1)
F41.4 6 Gup, Cristian Clowte, your breth is stale,

STAND (1)
H62.5 3 Thay stand abak and make it strange;

STATELY (1)
F19   5 As solen, as stately, as strange toward me,

STEDFAST (2)
R20.3 1 When Y fynde you stedfast and certayne,
F21   2 In stedfast fayth and trouth with assuraunce;

STEDFASTNESS (1)
F20   1 Most clere of colour and rote of stedfastness,

STERRE (1)
R13.2 1 The sterre of Venus which I call her ye,

STERT (1)
R15.7 5 Shall he not stert,

STEYLL (1)
R13.2 2 Sharper than thorn, dyamond or steyll,

STILL (1)
F29.3 4 But be still alone.'

STILLE (1)
R3.3   5 Take to gev all, and be stille than!

STOD (1)
H35.2   1 As I stod under a bank

STODE (2)
R19.1   7 She stode yn fere
F36.2   2 With pale visage tremlyng she stode her child
               before

STOND (2)
F14   2 For why I stond as he that is abusyd;
F39.1   5 I go or stond;

STONDES (1)
R16.1   5 And Crist stondes and clepys;

STONYS (1)
F48.3   2 Witness, stonys that all to-brake,

STOP (1)
R19.2   2 And stop a tyde;

STORE (2)
R13.3   4 For she hath that I hadde in store,
F37.2   1 Where art thou, Nature, that wont were me to store

STORMY (1)
F44b   1 From stormy wyndis and grevous wethir,

STOUPE (1)
F43.3   2 A stoupe of bere up at a pluk,

STRANGE (2)
F19   5 As solen, as stately, as strange toward me,
H62.5   3 Thay stand abak and make it strange;

STRANGENES (1)
H41.3   2 Strangenes that lady hyght.

STRAW (1)
R3.1   3 'Let go Y say, straw for yeur tale!'

STRAWE (2)
F41.1   5 Tully, valy, strawe, let be I say!
F41.2   3 Strawe, Jamys foder, ye play the fode;

STRAYNYD (2)
F33.3   2 So paynyd, so straynyd, so rufull, so red;
F36.1   2 And theruppon straynyd he was in every vayne;

STRENGH (1)
H65.2   3 I have strengh to mak it fle

STRENKYTH (3)
F47b   2 To strenkyth your comyns in ther ryght.

STRENKYTH (cont.)
F47.1   7   To strenkyth your comyns in ther ryght.
F47.2   2   Wisdome with strenkyth and soveraynte

STRETE (1)
F39.3   3   In feeld ne strete;

STRIK (1)
H35.4   3   I bad hym shott and strik the do,

STROKE (1)
H35.2   3   I stroke her so that downe she sanke,

STRONG (1)
R19.3   10   Yn castell strong.'

STRYF (1)
R10.4   8   Lyving yn stryf;

STRYKYN (1)
H35.1   1   Sore this dere strykyn ys,

STURDY (1)
F33.3   6   The sturdy nailis bore;

STYLL (3)
F30.2   3   And now be styll;
H25.4   6   But styll to morne for me.
H65b   3   And foster will I be styll

STYNT (1)
H25.6   5   Stynt wold sche not,

SUBDEWE (1)
F8   7   All myrthis to maynten, all sorous to subdewe.

SUBSTANCE (1)
H107.3   6   Now in substance

SUBSTAUNCE (1)
F24.3   6   Now in substaunce

SUBTELL (1)
H34.7   2   With dysdayne bothe falce and subtell.

SUCH (20)
R11.3   1   Such a mastras I may calle
R19.3   6   'Such on as she,
F18.1   6   Hath such a demyng
F19   2   Houghevyr such dyversite in on person may be,
F21   3   Then bownden were I such on faythfully
F24.1   6   Of such welyng
F24.3   7   Such is my daunce
F24.5   8   Such is her wone.

249

SUCH (cont.)
F31.3	1	A Jhesu, whi suffyrd thou such entretyng,
F40.2	2	To hym that wolde of such recreacion
H44.3	1	Butt envy reynyth with such dysdayne,
H49.3	1	I cannot thynk such doubylnes
H103b	2	Such is fortune! What remedy?
H103.1	5	Such is fortune! What remedy?
H103.2	5	Such is fortune! What remedy?
H103.3	5	Such is fortune! What remedy?
H107.1	6	Of such walyng
H107.3	7	Such is my chance
H107.5	8	Such ys her wone!
H108	7	And love unloved; such ys myne adventure.

SUCHE (2)
| H23.4 | 1 | As featys of armys, and suche other |
| H108 | 1 | I love unloved; suche is myn aventure, |

SUER (2)
| H44.2 | 1 | Nobyll men then wold suer enserch |
| H44.6 | 1 | To lovers I put now suer this cace - |

SUERE (3)
H25.10	2	But suere retaylle
H33.4	4	Be suere, and ever shall.
H106.4	4	Right suere to have no good aventure,

SUERLY (2)
| F25.2 | 1 | I thynk suerly |
| H23.5 | 2 | For therby corage is suerly owt fett: |

SUFFERE (1)
| R4 | 4 | For yeu, dere hert, thoff Y suffere penaunce |

SUFFIR (2)
| F33.3 | 7 | What myght I suffir more |
| F36.3 | 2 | He willfully doth suffir for love speciall |

SUFFIRD (3)
F32.3	6	That he suffird that sharpe shoure!
F48b	9	Therefore I suffird all this payne.
F48.2	2	That I suffird not for the this payne,

SUFFYR (2)
| F30.2 | 12 | Suffyr shall I. |
| F31.2 | 3 | And suffyr wolde payne as sorowfull thought, |

SUFFYRD (4)
F31.3	1	A Jhesu, whi suffyrd thou such entretyng,
F31.4	2	Gladly suffyrd I all this.'
F34.1	2	Suffyrd deth to pay thi rawnsum;
F48b	5	For thi love, man, have suffyrd deth

SUM (11)
```
R9       8   Sum love comaundes me this aventure,
F2       5   Sum other grace may cum, perde;
F7.2     3   Sum tyme is lost and all in vayne
F46.2    5   Tyll sum of them begyn to grone:
H25.5    4   Now of sum grace
H66.1    1   Though sum saith that yough rulyth me,
H66.1    5   Though sum say that yough rulyth me.
H66.2    3   I thynk sum wars of yche degre;
H66.2    5   Though sum sayth [that yough rulyth me.]
H66.3    5   Thow sum saith [that yough rulyth me.]
H66.4    5   Though sum [saith that yough rulyth me.]
```

SUME (1)
```
R4       6   That Y fro yew may hyre sume gode tydyng,
```

SUMTYME (3)
```
R10.2    1   Sumtyme was I
F13      5   Trustyng sumtyme that she will chaunge her mode
H66.3    1   Pastymes of yough sumtyme among,
```

SUMWHAT (3)
```
F24.1    1   Sumwhat musyng
H104.3   3   To swage sumwhat my mone;
H107.1   1   Sumwhat musyng
```

SUPPOSE (1)
```
F27.4    3   The rose, I suppose? Thyn hart unbrace!'
```

SUPPRISE (1)
```
R9       7   Besechyng yeure excuse, ther Y supprise;
```

SURANCE (2)
```
F14      7   Wher that is usyd can be no surance.
H107.3   3   And no surance
```

SURAUNCE (1)
```
F24.3    3   And no suraunce
```

SURE (13)
```
R9       4   Y recommaunde my symple service sure,
R13.1    5   Of my pore hert she may be sure,
F36.3    4   'O frend,' she said, 'I am sure he is inmortall.'
F37.3    2   My slepis be so feerfull, I thynk then sure to dye;
F37.4    4   Alas, to dye thou makyst me sure; yet then, good
                 Lord, do thou thi cure
H28      4   Joy shall I never ye may be sure.
H40      3   To love her sure whill I am levyng,
H47.5    1   I make you fast and sure;
H51.2    2   Frome Venus sure he must it fett;
H64.2    4   Onys love sure
H67.2    1   And make you sure
H67.2    6   Ye may be sure,
H92.1    2   Hys mery hart shall sure all rew;
```

SURFETTES (1)
F34.5   6   May washe us all from surfettes reprovable.

SURGYON (1)
R13.2   7   Ther of right I apeyle hyr to be my surgyon.

SURYD (1)
F23.2   5   Much the rathir sith my suryd constaunce

SUTE (1)
H65.4   3   I can luge and make a sute

SWAGE (1)
H104.3 3   To swage sumwhat my mone;

SWERD (1)
H50.2   3   With spere and swerd at the barryoure

SWERDE (1)
F36.1   9   To se the sharpe swerde of sorow smert,

SWET (4)
H27.2   1   Oft to me her godely swet face
H31.4   6   Myne owne swet hart, adew.
H103.3 1   O my swet hart, whome I love best,
H105.1 4   Full softly and full soberly unto her swet son
            she saide

SWETE (17)
R9   6   Unly to yeure swete grace a thousande sithe
F8   5   Through whose swete showris now sprong ther is ayen
F27.1   1   'I love a flour of swete odour'
F27.1   3   Columbyne goldis of swete flavour?'
F27.5   3   'Both be full swete and of lyke savoure;
F32.4   5   His deth was swete, hit did us goode;
F40b   4   I shal bere the cost, be swete Sent Denys!
F40.1   6   I shal bere the cost, be swete Sent Denys!]
F40.2   6   I shal bere the cost, be swete Sent Denys!]
F40.3   6   I shal bere the cost, be swete Sent Denys!]
F40.4   6   I shal bere the cost, be swete Sent Denys!]
H25.3   4   Wherfore, swete hart,
H31.6   1   Adew, full swete,
H63.1   1   Farewell, my joy, and my swete hart!
H105.3 3   Yet softly to her swete sonne methought I hard
            her sayn
H105.3 4   Now, gracious God and goode swete babe, yet ons
            this game agayne
H109b   5   To gather the flowres both fayer and swete.

SWETELY (1)
F18.2   6   Then speke ye so swetely

SWETTER (1)
F34.4   7   Swetter than bawme gayne gostly poyson:

252

SWETTYNG (1)
 H31.5   2 Adew, swettyng,

SWETYNG (1)
 F31.3   3 Drawne like a theffe, and for payne swetyng

SWONE (1)
 H25.7   5 Halff in a swone,

SYDE (2)
 F34.3   4 He put his handes depe in my syde adowne.
 H20   4 The byrdys sang on every syde

SYGH (2)
 R4   1 Absens of you causeth me to sygh and complayne
 H14   2 And sore I sygh for one.

SYGHES (1)
 H27.1   1 A the syghes that cum from my hart

SYGHS (2)
 H27.3   3 And now with syghs manyfold,
 H28   1 With sorowfull syghs and grevos payne

SYGHT (3)
 F10   8 Now raynyth trewly in every mannys syght.
 F30.1   2 I sawe a syght
 H105.2 3 Thus saying to our Saviour; this saw I in my syght;

SYKYRNESS (1)
 F11   3 That was my feere is nowe my sykyrness;

SYKYRNESSE (1)
 F48.3   7 And, man, for the more sykyrnesse,

SYLDE (1)
 F10   2 Full sylde covetise hath dominacion

SYLENS (1)
 R13.1   2 Thus under sylens I do endure,

SYLF (2)
 R14.1   4 Pyteusly, my own sylf alone.
 R14.2   4 Pyteusly, my own sylf alone.]

SYMPLE (1)
 R9   4 Y recommaunde my symple service sure,

SYN (5)
 F3   2 Syn thoughtis byn cheff causers of my woo;
 F7.1   4 Syn that it is playnly foly;
 F32.2   3 They bet him for oure gilt, though he no syn hadd;
 F34b   8 Than leve thi syn, or I nyll the,
 F34.1   3 Forsake thi syn, man, for the love of me;

SYNFULL (1)
F34.5   1   Lord, on all synfull here knelyng on kne,

SYNG (8)
R12.1   6   Hunte, syng and daunce;
F44.1   10   Wherfore now syng we:
F44.2   10   Wherefore now syng we:
F44.3   10   Wherefore now syng we:
H39   2   Syng troly loly lo!
H39   5   Syng trolly loly lo loly lo!
H97   5   Now let us syng this rownd all thre;
H104.3   2   To daunce or syng,

SYNGE (1)
H17   2   Now lete us synge

SYNNER (1)
F34b   3   'I, a synner that offt doth fall.'

SYNOWIS (1)
F36.4   3   His vaynys all and synowis to-raff and brast;

SYTH (11)
F13   7   Syth for my trouth she nedith no wittness.
F15   3   And mervell I have syth I not deservid
F17   2   Syth worde and dede is take in vayne,
F28   2   Syth I have done my besy payne
F34.1   8   Whi art thou froward, syth I am mercyable?
F34.3   6   Syth I am kynd, why are thou unstable?
F34.3   8   Be thou not froward syth I am merciable.
F44.2   1   Wherfore, good Lord, syth of thi creacion
H12   3   Syth now so kynd
H25.2   2   Syth that oure chaunce
H109.2   3   Syth I love you, love me agayne;

SYTT (1)
F29b   2   Here I sytt alone, alas, alone!

SYTTYNG (1)
F45.1   2   Sawe I syttyng a comly quene

TABLE (2)
F34.4   6   Afore thi hart hang this litell table,
F43.4   3   And the overplus undir the table of the newe gyse;

TAKE (13)
R3.3   5   Take to gev all, and be stille than!
R19.2   9   To take her pray
F17   2   Syth worde and dede is take in vayne,
F31b   3   Wolde take on Hym humanite?
F31.1   4   And wolde so take mortalite!
H25.9   4   To take comfort
H27.3   2   And take in armys twayne;
H50.1   3   Of which four tymes he dyd it take;

TAKE (cont.)
H51.8   1   Soch lovers though thay take payne
H62.6   1   Now will I take to me my bedes
H92.7   2   That this rude play may well be take,
H96b   2   Help now thi kyng, thi kyng, and take his part!
H96.1   5   Help now thi king [and take his part!]

TAKES (1)
H102.1 2   She takes me as her howne;

TAKYN (2)
R10.4   5   Takyn yn a snare
R14.2   2   Takyn away from me bycause of hevynes;

TAKYTH (1)
F28   4   And she me takyth in gret disdayne:

TALE (1)
R3.1   3   'Let go Y say, straw for yeur tale!'

TALKE (1)
F27.6   3   'To here talke of them is my delite.

TARRY (1)
H66.1   2   I trust in age to tarry;

TAST (1)
F37.2   3   My tast disordyrd all reson far passyng,

TAVERN (1)
H35.6   2   I went to tavern to drynk;

TECHE (1)
F34b   9   And thynk on this lesson that now I teche the.

TEL (1)
H49.1   2   Tel me how thy lemman doth,

TELL (5)
F4   7   But them to tell cannott availe.
F18.2   4   That cowde nott tell,
H31.7   4   I cannott tell
H44.5   2   But let them tell which love doth gett.
H92.1   3   For whatsoever they do hym tell,

TELLYTH (1)
R15.6   4   Men tellyth yn town

TEMPTACION (1)
R7   1   Thow man, envired with temptacion,

TENDIR (1)
F33.2   3   Remembir my tendir hart-rote for the brake,

TENDIRLY (1)
F36.1   4   His modir dere tendirly wept and cowde not
                  refrayne

TENE (1)
F32.4   4   Thi dere sone is past his trobill and his tene;

TERE (1)
F37.3   3   My dreme is so mervelous, serpentis semyth me to
                  tere

TERIS (1)
F38.2   1   With wepyng teris most lamentable

TERRESTRIALL (2)
F36.3   8   As a woman terrestriall
F44.1   3   Arthur oure prynce to us here terrestriall,

TERS (1)
H106.1   5   Myn yes for sorow salt ters doth rayne:

TERYS (2)
H25.7   4   The terys ran down
H31.6   4   With terys wete

TEYD (1)
F1   6   Thoo I go lose, yet am I teyd with a lyne:

TH' (1)
H107.1   4   Th' unstedfastnes;

THAN (18)
R3.3   5   Take to gev all, and be stille than!
R12.2   8   Than who can say
R13.2   2   Sharper than thorn, dyamond or steyll,
F27b   4   'Than shal be provid here anon
F27.4b   4   'Than shall be provid here anon
F27.6b   4   Than may be provid here anon
F33.3   8   Than I have done, O man, for the?
F34b   8   Than leve thi syn, or I nyll the,
F34.4   7   Swetter than bawme gayne gostly poyson:
F36.3   1   Saynt Jhon than said, 'Feere not, Mary; his
                  paynys al
F36.3   5   'Why than so depe morne ye?'
H29.1   3   Of her godnes than wold I wryght;
H29.4   1   Yf I to her than war unkynd,
H44.7   2   Better than do I, I thynk it so.
H49.2   3   She lovyth another better than me
H82.2   3   Thay may not now than gaynesay
H109b   4   Than at the medow I wyll you mete
H109.1b 6   I wysse my mothyr than shall us se!

THAT (199)
R1.2   1   All the whiles that Y may my bowe bende

256

R2.2	5	Now Y pray God and that righth hertily
R2.2	6	That she be voyded owte of the grete grevaunce;
R3.1	5	'Wene ye that everybody lest to play?'
R3.2	4	A, kan ye that? Nou, gode, go hens!
R3.2	8	My moder cam in, or that ye wende.'
R3.3	4	Ys this the gentery that ye can?'
R4	6	That Y fro yew may hyre sume gode tydyng,
R4	7	That myght my herte in more ese bryng.
R5	1	The hye desire that Y have for to se
R5	3	Till that Y may in yeure presaunce
R5	5	That ye wilde fuchesaffe to have mercy on me
R6	2	That Y am thus in heviness?
R9	2	That with yeure beute and fresche plesaunce pure
R9	9	Thorffe with yeur beute that Y most love and prise.
R10.6	6	As man that ys blynd,
R13.2	4	That wondyd soere myself Y fele,
R13.3	4	For she hath that I hadde in store,
R15.8	1	Alas, that he
R18.1	3	That dyd complayne in suo pectore,
R19.2	10	That she had lovyd so long.
R19.3	7	That away woll flee,
R20.1	3	That ye loth Y love -- wrappe that yn your trayne!
F2	4	Thoo that all this yet in vayne be,
F3	3	For when nature wold oft that I shulde wynk,
F3	4	Then be it they that doth me trobill so
F3	5	That be won thought my rest from me doth go.
F3	7	That no thought can relesse me of my sore.
F5	6	That I am bownde above all erthly thyng
F6.2	5	That I wis
F6.4	3	That I must sett by;
F6.4	4	For that to mone,
F7.1	2	Whan that desert lakkyth remedy,
F7.1	4	Syn that it is playnly foly;
F7.1	5	Thoo that ye wolde untill ye dye
F8	4	By dropys of grace that on them down doth rayn;
F11	1	That was my woo is nowe my most gladness;
F11	2	That was my payne is nowe my joyus chaunce;
F11	3	That was my feere is nowe my sykyrness;
F11	4	That was my grefe is now my alegeaunce.
F12	5	Yett more mervell how that I hard the sownde
F13	5	Trustyng sumtyme that she will chaunge her mode
F14	1	Alas, it is I that wote nott what to say,
F14	2	For why I stond as he that is abusyd;
F14	5	But pite it is that trust shulde be mysusyd
F14	7	Wher that is usyd can be no surance.
F15	1	I·am he that hath you dayly servyd,
F17	7	When that they knowe I am sory.
F18.2	2	That women truly
F18.2	4	That cowde nott tell,
F18.2	5	When that ye do lye,
F20	3	Which that passyth my mynde for to express
F20	6	Which that all men knowith, both more and less;
F21	4	To love, thowe I do fere to trace that dawnce,

F21	5	Lest that mysaventure myght fall be chaunce;
F21	7	Hough that evyr it will happ I wote nere I.
F22	4	Absens it is that wolde me wrong;
F23.1	1	That was my joy is now my woo and payne;
F23.1	2	That was my bliss is now my displesaunce;
F23.1	3	That was my trust is now my wanhope playne;
F23.1	4	That was my wele is now my most grevaunce.
F23.1	7	That hath byn your fayre lady and mastress.
F24.4	3	And that gretly
F25.1	7	That of my payne
F27.1	5	Is non of them that lykyth me.'
F27.2	5	That best lykyth me.'
F27.3	1	'On that I love most enterly.'
F27.3	5	Here is not he that plesyth me.'
F27.4	2	'What is his name that thou chosen has?
F27.4	4	'That same is he,
F27.4	5	In hart so fre, that best lykyth me.'
F27.5	5	That day to se it lykyth well me.'
F27.6	2	'Is that your perfytt appetite?'
F27.6b	5	That we three be agrede in oon.'
F28	6	Tyll that I cum tyll her presens,
F29.2	4	That childe wepid alone.
F29.3	2	To save mankynd that was forlorne;
F29.4	2	That men sekyth for to spill,
F29.5	3	For thou art he that hath all wrought,
F30.1	4	Mary, that may,
F30.1	17	That made all thyng
F30.2	14	That is so hye,
F31b	2	That God hymselfe for sole mankynd
F31.1	1	Crist, that was of infynyt myght,
F31.2	1	He that wrought this wordle of nought,
F31.2	2	That made both paynys and joy also,
F31.4	1	'Lo, man, for the that ware onkynd,
F32.1	2	That the Son of God shulde make us fre,
F32.3	5	But blessid be that oure,
F32.3	6	That he suffird that sharpe shoure!
F32.4	3	Remembir thi joys that joyfull aye byn!
F34b	2	Who is that that dothe me call?
F34b	3	'I, a synner that offt doth fall.'
F34b	9	And thynk on this lesson that now I teche the.
F34.5	4	That thi fyve wellis plentuus of fusion,
F36.2	4	That with dispaire for feer and dred I was nere forlore
F36.3	3	He hath to man, to make hym fre that now is thrall.
F37.2	1	Where art thou, Nature, that wont were me to store
F38b	2	And thynk on the paynys that byn in hell.
F38.1	4	That helpis the ever at thi most nede.
F39.1	1	That goodly las,
F40.2	2	To hym that wolde of such recreacion
F40.2	3	That God hath ordent in his first formacion,
F41.4	2	Now have I fownd that I have sought,
F41.4	3	The best chepe flessh that evyr I bought.'

THAT (cont.)

F41.4	4	Yet for his love that all hath wrought
F42.2	1	The fayrest man that best love can,
F45.1	3	Among the flouris that fressh byn.
F45.2	1	In that garden be flouris of hewe:
F45.2	2	The gelofir gent, that she well knewe;
F48b	1	Be hit knowyn to all that byn here
F48b	2	And to all that here-afftir
F48b	4	That I Jhesus off Nazareth
F48.1	7	And that thou be in charite;
F48.1	9	This is that I axe of the,
F48.1	10	That am the cheffe lorde of the fee.
F48.2	2	That I suffird not for the this payne,
F48.2	5	Yet, man, that thou sholdest not be lorne,
F48.2	8	Witness, the son that lost his lyghth,
F48.2	9	Witness, the vale that then did ryve,
F48.2	10	Witness, the bodies that rose from deth to lyve.
F48.3	1	Witness, the erthe that did quake,
F48.3	2	Witness, stonys that all to-brake,
H18	5	Trustyng that dysdayn
H20	1	In May, that lusty sesoun
H22	1	Whoso that wyll hymselff applye
H24	3	That I cannot be prest
H25.2	2	Syth that oure chaunce
H25.6	4	Yet for all that
H25.10	3	From all other that be,
H25.10	6	With her that morneth for me.
H25.11	3	All lovers that trew be,
H25.11	6	My love that mornyth for me.
H27.1	1	A the syghes that cum from my hart
H28	3	Alas, pour hart, tyl that we mete agayne,
H29.4	2	Pytte it war that I shuld be,
H29.5	3	Promyse I mak that know non shall
H31.4	3	Optayne that I do sew,
H31.9	2	That lady gent;
H31.9	4	That day they spent
H34.1	1	Whoso that wyll all feattes optayne,
H35.2	3	I stroke her so that downe she sanke,
H41.3	2	Strangenes that lady hyght.
H47.1	4	Tyl that we mete agayne.
H47.3	4	That I shuld be unkynde.
H47.5	4	Tyll that we mete agayne.
H50.2	5	He provith hymselfe that I sey best,
H50.3	3	In that he doth no camparyng
H50.4	1	My soverayne lorde when that I mete,
H50.4	3	My hart with joe that I be hete
H50.5	2	Ther is none one-lyve that have;
H50.5	5	A vengeance on them that loveth nott best
H50.6	1	The soverayne lorde that is of all,
H51.1	1	Thow that men do call it dotage,
H51.9	2	Thay hynder lovers that wolde be trew.
H62.4	4	That beawtye ys my foo;
H62.6	3	And pray I wyll for them that may,
H63.2	3	My hart ys yours where ever that I go;

THAT (cont.)

H64.2	2	That lovers be
H65.3	4	As well as any that ever I see:
H66.1	1	Though sum saith that yough rulyth me,
H66.1	5	Though sum say that yough rulyth me.
H66.2	1	I pray you all that aged be,
H66.2	5	Though sum sayth [that yough rulyth me.]
H66.3	5	Thow sum saith [that yough rulyth me.]
H66.4	1	Then sone dyscusse that hens we must;
H66.4	3	That all amend; and here an end,
H66.4	5	Though sum [saith that yough rulyth me.]
H75	3	That hath my hart in cure;
H79.1	1	Whoso that wyll for grace sew,
H79.1	4	Els it war pyte that he shuld spede;
H79.1	5	Many oone sayth that love ys yll,
H79.2	2	They wold that other shuld yt dysdayne;
H79.2	4	In that therfor can be non odde,
H82.1	1	Let not us that yong men be
H82.1	3	Thow that age with gret dysdayne
H82.2	4	That which then was most ther joy;
H92.2	4	But follow hys mynd in all that we may.
H92.4	2	Though that dysdaynars wold therin put error,
H92.7	2	That this rude play may well be take,
H92.7	3	And that we may ower fauttes amend,
H97	1	Pray we to God that all may gyde
H97	2	That for our kyng so to provid,
H102.1	1	My lady hath me in that grace
H102.2	2	No love that can be lost;
H103.2	2	To se the paynes that I endure
H105.2	4	This reson that I rede you now, I rede it full ryght
H105.3	2	Save it plesyd me so passyngly that past was my payn
H106.1	4	My lyffe as one that dye would fayne;
H106.3	7	That deth is plesur and nothyng noyus.
H107.4	3	And that gretly
H108	3	But love my fo, that fervent creature
H109b	6	Nay, God forbede! That may not be -
H109.1b	4	That now in the feldes we may us sportt?
H109.1b	5	Nay, God forbede! That may not be;
H109.2	2	That ye gretly move my corage.

THAY (12)

H35.5	1	To the covert bothe thay went,
H41.8	1	Thus how thay dyd we cannot say -
H44.2	2	All ways wherby thay myght it rech;
H51.8	1	Soch lovers though thay take payne
H51.8	2	It were pete thay shuld optayne;
H51.9	2	Thay hynder lovers that wolde be trew.
H62.5	3	Thay stand abak and make it strange;
H79.1	6	But those be thay which can no skyll:
H82.1	6	How thay dyd in ther most lust.
H82.2	1	For yf thay war in lyk case
H82.2	3	Thay may not now than gaynesay

THAY (cont.)
H92.2 3 But I wyll not so whatsoever thay say,

THE (251)
R1.1 3 Y shall hong up my horne by the grenewode spray;
R1.2 1 All the whiles that Y may my bowe bende
R1.2 3 I shall bygge me a boure atte the wodes ende,
R2.1 7 For yet Y am all drowned in the lake
R2.2 1 For sche weche ys of all godely the best
R2.2 6 That she be voyded owte of the grete grevaunce;
R3.3 2 'Be Criste, Y nelle, what ses the man?
R3.3 3 Ye herte my legge agenste the walle;
R3.3 4 Ys this the gentery that ye can?'
R3.3 6 'Now have ye leyde me un the flore,
R3.3 8 Be Criste, Y wolde have schytte the dore!'
R4 2 For of my hert ye have the governaunce;
R5 1 The hye desire that Y have for to se
R5 2 The godely and wommanly bewte
R8 3 From thy servaund, the weche hathe plente
R10.6 3 Turnyng as the wynd,
R11.2 1 The more sorow ys my payn
R12.3 5 The best insew,
R12.3 6 The worst eschew,
R13.2 1 The sterre of Venus which I call her ye,
R15.4 6 And play the wyse.
R15.6 6 The smocke ys hyd."
R16b 1 Come over the burne, Besse,
R16b 3 Come over the burne, Besse, to me!
R16.1 1 The burne ys this worlde blynde
R16.1 6 Cum over the burne, Besse, to me!
R18.4 1 With the seid child, quid faciam?
R19.1 1 Hay how the mavys on a brere!
R19.1 5 The greves among.
R19.3 8 Yll must she the,
F1 1 The farther I go, the more behynde;
F1 2 The more behynde, the nere my wayes ende;
F1 3 The more I sech, the wers can I fynde;
F1 4 The lyghter leefe, the lother for to wende;
F1 5 The trewer I serve, the ferther out of mynde;
F2 3 Nay, nay, nay, nay, I warne the well,
F7.1 1 O my desyre, what eylyth the,
F7.1 8 O my desyre, what eylyth the?
F7.2 8 O my desyre, what aylyth the?
F8 2 Beholde the soveren sede of this rosis twayn,
F10 1 Nowe the lawe is led be clere conciens
F10 6 The pore pepull no tyme hath but ryght
F12 2 Methought the worlde was turnyd up so downe,
F12 3 The son, the moone, had lost ther force and light;
F12 4 The see also drownyd both towre and towne:
F12 5 Yett more mervell how that I hard the sownde
F18.2 7 And thynk the contrary:
F20 5 The bryghtest myrrour and floure of goodlyhed,
F22 5 And thus is the tyme of his song;
F23.2 5 Much the rathir sith my suryd constaunce

THE (cont.)

F24.1	4	The unstedfastness,
F27.4	3	The rose, I suppose? Thyn hart unbrace!'
F27.5	1	'The rose it is a ryall floure.'
F27.5	2	'The red or the white? Shewe his colour!'
F27.6	1	'I love the rose, both red and white.'
F29.1	2	To the grenewode for to play
F29.2	1	As I walkyd undir the grenewode bowe
F29.3	1	'Son,' she sayd, 'I have the borne
F29.3	3	Therfor I pray the, son, no more,
F31.1	2	Egall to the Fathir in deite,
F31.1	3	Inmortal, inpassible, the wordlis lyght,
F31.4	1	'Lo, man, for the that ware onkynd,
F31.4	4	'The to purchace both joy and bliss.'
F32.1	1	Sith it concludid was in the Trinite
F32.1	2	That the Son of God shulde make us fre,
F32.2	4	Thi son was doughti, the fende was adradde;
F32.3	2	The crowne on his hed, the spere at his hart,
F33b	3	For the ran,
F33.1	1	Beholde me, I pray the, with all thi hole reson,
F33.1	7	The Jewis me thretid,
F33.2	2	I love the, then love me; why slepist thou? Awake!
F33.2	3	Remembir my tendir hart-rote for the brake,
F33.3	6	The sturdy nailis bore;
F33.3	8	Than I have done, O man, for the?
F34b	5	'Mercy, Lord, of the I crave.'
F34b	7	'Ye, my maker I call the.'
F34b	8	Than leve thi syn, or I nyll the,
F34b	9	And thynk on this lesson that now I teche the.
F34.1	1	Uppon the cross nailid I was for the,
F34.1	3	Forsake thi syn, man, for the love of me;
F34.2	3	The crowne of thorne, the spere, the nailis thre,
F34.4	5	Whi did I this? To save the from prison.
F36.1	9	To se the sharpe swerde of sorow smert,
F36.1	10	Hough it thirlyd her thoroughoute the hart,
F36.4	1	Unto the cross, handes and feete, nailid he was;
F36.4	2	Full boistusly in the mortess he was downe cast;
F36.4	4	The erth quakyd, the son was dark, whos lyght was past
F37.1	6	Thus trobled am I yet I trust it shalbe for the best
F37.2	2	To lusty plesure? Now lyyng in the flore,
F37.2	5	Thou, Nature, hast lefft me; by the fynd I no rest:
F37.2	6	Thus trobled am I [yet I trust it shalbe for the best
F37.3	6	Thus trobled am I [yet I trust it shalbe for the best
F37.4	1	Now, mercyfull Jhesu, to the make I my mone;
F37.4	3	'Remembir the, my creature, thou must nedis dye, I the ensure.
F37.4	6	Thus trobled am I [yet I trust it shalbe for the best
F38b	1	A, myn hert, remembir the well,
F38b	2	And thynk on the paynys that byn in hell.

F38.1	1	A myn hart, remembir the well
F38.1	4	That helpis the ever at thi most nede.
F40b	4	I shal bere the cost, be swete Sent Denys!
F40.1	4	But it were an angell of the Trinite?
F40.1	6	I shal bere the cost, be swete Sent Denys!]
F40.2	6	I shal bere the cost, be swete Sent Denys!]
F40.3	6	I shal bere the cost, be swete Sent Denys!]
F40.4	6	I shal bere the cost, be swete Sent Denys!]
F41.1	6	Gup, Cristian Clowte, gup, Jak of the Vale,
F41.2	3	Strawe, Jamys foder, ye play the fode;
F41.2	6	Gup, Cristian Clowte, gup, Jak of the Vale,
F41.3	6	Gup, Cristian Clowte, gup, Jak of the Vale,
F41.4	3	The best chepe flessh that evyr I bought.'
F41.4	8	Gup, Cristian Clowte, gup, Jak of the Vale,
F42.1	3	Undir the levys grene?
F42.2	1	The fayrest man that best love can,
F42.2	3	Undir the holy grene.
F43.4	3	And the overplus undir the table of the newe gyse;
F44b	2	Good Lord, preserve the Estrige Fether!
F44.3	2	Pray to thi Son, the secund in Trinite,
F44.3	8	To the we crye and call,
F45.1	3	Among the flouris that fressh byn.
F45.1	5	The lyly-whighte rose methought I sawe,
F45.1	6	The lyly-whighte rose methought I sawe,
F45.2	2	The gelofir gent, that she well knewe;
F45.2	3	The floure-de-luce she did on rewe,
F45.2	4	And said, 'The white rose is most trewe
F45.2	6	The lyly-whighte rose methought I sawe,
F46b	1	Smale pathis to the grenewode,
F46.1	5	So rennyth the chaunce from one to one:
F48b	6	Uppon the crosse with woundis smert
F48.1	2	To the, and thou wilt be repentant;
F48.1	8	Love thi neyboure as I love the!
F48.1	9	This is that I axe of the,
F48.1	10	That am the cheffe lorde of the fee.
F48.2	2	That I suffird not for the this payne,
F48.2	6	In the awter I am offerd my Fader beforne;
F48.2	7	Witness, the daye turnyd to nyghth,
F48.2	8	Witness, the son that lost his lyghth,
F48.2	9	Witness, the vale that then did ryve,
F48.2	10	Witness, the bodies that rose from deth to lyve.
F48.3	1	Witness, the erthe that did quake,
F48.3	7	And, man, for the more sykyrnesse,
F48.3	8	The wounde in my harte the seale it is,
F48.3	9	Iyevyn upon the mownt of Calvary,
F48.3	10	The grete daye of mannys mercy.
F49b	3	'Amende the, man, of thi trespace,
F49.1	3	What paynys I sofferd, I the ensure,
F49.1	4	Where thou were thrall, to make the free.
F49.1	5	Upon the cross with naylis thre
F49.1	7	Therfore remembir the or thou go hence.'
H17	6	Of the red rose and the whyght.
H20	2	To geder the flours down

THE (cont.)

H20	3	By the medows grene;
H20	4	The byrdys sang on every syde
H20	7	The nyghtyngale sang on hie
H20	9	Among the thornys kene.
H22	2	To passe the tyme of youth joly,
H22	3	Avaunce hym to the companye
H23.1	1	The tyme of youthe is to be spent;
H24	1	The thowghtes within my brest,
H25.4	4	The Gode above
H25.7	4	The terys ran down
H27.1	1	A the syghes that cum from my hart
H29.3	1	She doth not waver as the wynde,
H33b	1	Grene growith the holy,
H33b	2	So doth the ive,
H33b	4	Grene growth the holy.
H33.1	1	As the holy grouth grene
H33.2	1	As the holy grouth grene
H34.5	2	To woman also, I thynk, the same.
H34.6	2	Yet never the lesse it ys to moch used.
H35.2	2	The dere shoffe on the mede;
H35.3	2	How she gothe over the playne?
H35.4	3	I bad hym shott and strik the do,
H35.5	1	To the covert bothe thay went,
H35.6	1	I was wery of the game,
H35.6	3	Now the construccyon of the same -
H39	3	My love is to the grenewode gone,
H41b	3	To the grenewode must we go, alas!
H41.1	1	The knyght knokett at the castell gate;
H41.1	2	The lady mervelyd who was therat.
H41.2	1	To call the porter he wold not blyn;
H41.2	2	The lady said he shuld not com in.
H41.3	1	The portres was a lady bryght;
H44.5	1	The faut in whome I cannot sett;
H47.4	1	The daise delectable,
H47.4	2	The violett wan and blo;
H50.1	2	Six coursys at the ryng dyd make,
H50.2	2	As the chefteyne of a waryowere,
H50.2	3	With spere and swerd at the barryoure
H50.2	4	As hardy with the hardyest,
H50.3	5	To have the prayse of all the best;
H50.6	1	The soverayne lorde that is of all,
H51.5	1	The ee doth loke and represent;
H51.7	2	Who love dysdaynyth ys all of the village.
H62.2	2	Upon the grenewod bough,
H62.3	3	The glew is slypt frome the nyk;
H64.1	8	Ys in the dole
H65.1	2	Upon the grenwod bough?
H65.2	2	Opon the grenwode lynde?
H65.3	2	Upon the grenwod tre?
H65.3	3	I can blow the deth of a dere
H65.4	2	Unto the grenwod spray?
H66.4	4	Thus sayth the kyng, the eighth Harry:
H74	1	Deme the best of every dowt

THE (cont.)

H74	2	Tyll the trowth be tryed owt.
H75	5	As the hauke to the lure,
H82.2	5	Wherfor indede the trouth to say
H82.2	6	It ys for yough the metest play.
H96.1	1	Ageynst the Frenchmen in the feld to fyght
H96.1	2	In the quarell of the church and in the ryght,
H97	6	Sent George, graunt hym the victory!
H101.1	3	For all the golde in England
H101.3	2	The age of fifteen yere,
H103.2	2	To se the paynes that I endure
H104.3	1	The tyme passyng
H105.1	1	The moder full manerly and mekly as a mayd,
H105.2	2	Full lovely lookyng on our Lord, the lanterne of lyght
H106.3	4	Of all the sorowes within my hart;
H109b	3	I go to the medowe to mylke my cow.
H109b	4	Than at the medow I wyll you mete
H109b	5	To gather the flowres both fayer and swete.
H109.1b	4	That now in the feldes we may us sportt?
H109.4	2	But the nexte tyme ye must beware
H109.4	3	How in the medow ye mylke your cow.

THEFFE (1)

| F31.3 | 3 | Drawne like a theffe, and for payne swetyng |

THEI (1)

| H82.1 | 5 | In ther myndes consyder thei must |

THEM (20)

F4	7	But them to tell cannott availe.
F8	4	By dropys of grace that on them down doth rayn;
F27.1	5	Is non of them that lykyth me.'
F27.2	4	He pass them all in his degre;
F27.6	3	'To here talke of them is my delite.
F29.4	3	For them to save, it is my will;
F34.2	2	Loke on them well, and have compassion;
F46.2	5	Tyll sum of them begyn to grone:
H23.5	1	Comparysons in them may lawfully be sett,
H41.8	2	We left them ther and went ower way.
H44.4	1	Which puttes them to more and more
H44.5	2	But let them tell which love doth gett.
H44.6	2	Which of ther loves doth get them grace?
H44.7	1	And unto them which doth it know
H50.5	5	A vengeance on them that loveth nott best
H62.6	3	And pray I wyll for them that may,
H66.1	4	Frome them shall I never vary:
H92.4	1	For in them consisteth gret honor,
H92.4	3	For they do sew to get them grace
H96.1	4	Bowys and arows to put them all to flyght:

THEN (24)

| R2.2 | 2 | To myn entent, and so sayeth mo then I, |
| R3.2 | 1 | After asay then may ye wette; |

THEN (cont.)

R12.2	3	Company me thynckyth then best
F3	4	Then be it they that doth me trobill so
F18.2	6	Then speke ye so swetely
F21	3	Then bownden were I such on faythfully
F33.2	2	I love the, then love me; why slepist thou? Awake!
F37.3	1	My voice is so trobled, my seknes then feele I;
F37.3	2	My slepis be so feerfull, I thynk then sure to dye;
F37.4	4	Alas, to dye thou makyst me sure; yet then, good Lord, do thou thi cure
F48.2	3	[Rather then manne sholde be forlorne
F48.2	9	Witness, the vale that then did ryve,
H23.6	1	Vertue it is then youth for to spend
H25.4	3	What sayd sche then to me?
H25.9	1	Then as I ought
H34.3	2	Is wors then deth? Let it be proved!
H44.2	1	Nobyll men then wold suer enserch
H64.1	10	Then helpe must have
H66.4	1	Then sone dyscusse that hens we must;
H79.2	6	Wherfor, then, shuld we yt excho?
H82.2	2	And wold then have goten grace,
H82.2	4	That which then was most ther joy;
H109b	7	I wysse my mother then shall us se!
H109.4	1	Then for this onse I shal you spare,

THER (37)

R1.2	4	Ther to lede my lyffe.
R9	7	Besechyng yeure excuse, ther Y supprise;
R13.2	7	Ther of right I apeyle hyr to be my surgyon.
R15.1	2	Ther founde I Besse
R19.1	6	When Y cam ther
F7.2	7	In whom ther is no remedy;
F8	5	Through whose swete showris now sprong ther is ayen
F10	5	Ther is trewly in every case consolacion
F12	3	The son, the moone, had lost ther force and light;
F14	3	Ther as I trusted I was late cast away,
F16	2	I pray daily ther paynys to asswage
F27.2	1	'Ther is a floure where so he be,
F30.2	15	Ther shall I be,
F36.2	3	Beholdyng ther his lymmys all to-rent and tore,
F39b	3	Ther is non lyke
F47b	2	To strenkyth your comyns in ther ryght.
F47.1	7	To strenkyth your comyns in ther ryght.
F47.2	6	In your person all ther hope is pyght
F47.2	7	To have recover of ther unryght.
H23.2	1	Pastymes ther be I nought treulye
H27.4	3	Ther myght no joys compare with it
H29.5	2	Unto ther lovers trew for to be;
H31.9	5	To ther intent
H35b	2	Ther ys a do in yonder wode; in faith, she woll not dy
H41.7	2	And Pyte said she wold be ther.
H41.8	2	We left them ther and went ower way.
H44.6	2	Which of ther loves doth get them grace?

THER (cont.)
H50.5   2   Ther is none one-lyve that have;
H51.4   2   There is no bote; ther must it be.
H63.1   4   Ther ys none other bote.
H64.2   8   Ther no hart rewith
H82.1   5   In ther myndes consyder thei must
H82.1   6   How thay dyd in ther most lust.
H82.2   4   That which then was most ther joy;
H92.5   3   For withowt ther goode gydaunce
H101.2   3   Thes cowrtyers with ther amorus
H106.4   6   Nay, nay, for why? Ther ys no space.

THERAT (1)
H41.1   2   The lady mervelyd who was therat.

THERBY (1)
H23.5   2   For therby corage is suerly owt fett:

THERE (2)
H35.3   1   There she gothe! Se ye nott,
H51.4   2   There is no bote; ther must it be.

THEREFORE (2)
F32.4   7   Therefore, though deth be nevir so sore,
F48b   9   Therefore I suffird all this payne.

THERFOR (4)
F29.3   3   Therfor I pray the, son, no more,
F29.4   4   Therfor I cum hyther alone.'
F32.2   7   Therfor, thowe deth be never so sore,
H79.2   4   In that therfor can be non odde,

THERFORE (3)
F32.1   6   Therfore, though deth be nevyr so sore,
F32.3   7   Therfore though deth be never so sore,
F49.1   7   Therfore remembir the or thou go hence.'

THERIN (2)
H66.2   4   Therin a wager lay dar I:
H92.4   2   Though that dysdaynars wold therin put error,

THERON (1)
F19   8   To lett itt over pass, and thynk theron no more.

THERTO (3)
F48.3   6   Myn owne seale therto I hyng;
H18   3   And no cause gevyn therto:
H30   3   And trew love lokked therto?

THERUPPON (1)
F36.1   2   And theruppon straynyd he was in every vayne;

THERWYTH (1)
H25.8   3   Therwyth revyved sche,

THERYN (1)
H92.6   4   And vertuus pastaunce must be theryn usyd.

THES (3)
F20   7   Thes vertues byn pryntyd in her doutless.
H92.6   3   Wherfor be thes he must be gydyd
H101.2 3   Thes cowrtyers with ther amorus

THEY (24)
R18.3   3   They wyll me bete cum virgis ac fustibus
F3   4   Then be it they that doth me trobill so
F16   3   And sone to sende where they faynest wolde be,
F17   6   For where I shulde, they be mery,
F17   7   When that they knowe I am sory.
F27.5   4   All on they be;
F32.2   3   They bet him for oure gilt, though he no syn hadd;
F32.3   3   They betyng they broysyng, or liff did depart;
F33.1   8   They mowid, they grynned, they scornyd me,
H20   6   They toyned so clene;
H23.3   1   And they be plesant to God and man,
H24   2   They greve me passyng sore,
H27.1   2   They greve me passyng sore;
H31.9   4   That day they spent
H51.9   1   For often tymes wher they do sewe
H79.2   1   Or else because they may not opteyne,
H79.2   2   They wold that other shuld yt dysdayne;
H92.1   3   For whatsoever they do hym tell,
H92.2   1   For they wold have hym hys libertye refrayne
H92.4   3   For they do sew to get them grace
H101.2 4   They kyndyld my corage.

THI (42)
F12   7   Thi lady hath forgoten to be kynd.'
F30b   3   Kys thi moder, Jhesu,
F31.3   2   As betyng, bobbyng, ye, spettyng on thi face?
F31.4   3   And why, good Lord? Express thi mynd!
F32.2   2   When Jewis with treson to deth thi son ladde;
F32.2   4   Thi son was doughti, the fende was adradde;
F32.2   6   So nowe is knowen thi sonnys myght:
F32.4   2   Lay downe all thi wepyng, let no more be sene!
F32.4   3   Remembir thi joys that joyfull aye byn!
F32.4   4   Thi dere sone is past his trobill and his tene;
F33.1   1   Beholde me, I pray the, with all thi hole reson,
F33.1   3   Sith I for thi sowle sake was slayne in good seson,
F33.3   3   Thus bobbid, thus robbid, thus for thi love ded;
F34b   8   Than leve thi syn, or I nyll the,
F34.1   2   Suffyrd deth to pay thi rawnsum;
F34.1   3   Forsake thi syn, man, for the love of me;
F34.2   5   My hert ryven for thi redempcion.
F34.3   5   Role up this mater; grave it in thi reson:
F34.3   7   My blode best triacle for thi transgression;
F34.4   6   Afore thi hart hang this litell table,
F34.5   3   O Jhesu, graunt of thi benignite
F34.5   4   That thi fyve wellis plentuus of fusion,

THI (cont.)

F34.5	5	Callid thi fyve wondes by computacion,
F34.5	7	Now for thi moders meke mediacion,
F37.4	4	Alas, to dye thou makyst me sure; yet then, good Lord, do thou thi cure
F38.1	4	That helpis the ever at thi most nede.
F44.1	2	Which formyd hast of thi most speciall grace
F44.2	1	Wherfore, good Lord, syth of thi creacion
F44.3	1	Now, good Lady among thi sayntes all,
F44.3	2	Pray to thi Son, the secund in Trinite,
F44.3	4	Be thi servaunt with all his hart so fre.
F47.2	4	And specially hurtis of thi commynalte,
F48b	5	For thi love, man, have suffyrd deth
F48.1	8	Love thi neyboure as I love the!
F49b	3	'Amende the, man, of thi trespace,
H35b	1	Blow thi horne, hunter, and blow thi horne on hye!
H35b	3	Now blow thi horne, hunter, and blow thi horne, joly hunter
H96b	2	Help now thi kyng, thi kyng, and take his part!
H96.1	5	Help now thi king [and take his part!]

THIRLYD (1)

F36.1	10	Hough it thirlyd her thoroughoute the hart,

THIS (75)

R2.1	2	Enforsed me this complaynte for to make,
R2.1	4	Full oghfte or this, Y shall undertake.
R3.1	2	Now thyngke ye this ys a fayre ray?
R3.3	4	Ys this the gentery that ye can?'
R6	1	O blessed lord, how may this be
R7	4	This lyon and lambe was, causyng pyte;
R9	8	Sum love comaundes me this aventure,
R10.2	8	This do I prove.
R10.3	4	This ys my chaunce;
R12.1	4	So God be plecyd, this lyve woll I;
R15.6	1	This young men say
R16.1	1	The burne ys this worlde blynde
R19.3	5	This ys my song:
F1	7	Is it fortune or infortune this I fynde?
F2	4	Thoo that all this yet in vayne be,
F6.2	6	Endure this
F8	2	Beholde the soveren sede of this rosis twayn,
F12	1	Benedicite! Whate dremyd I this nyght?
F23.1	5	What causyth this but only yowre plesaunce
F24.1	5	This wordle beyng
F24.3	5	Lo, in this traunce,
F27.6b	2	This fayre fressh floure full of beaute;
F29.1	1	As I me walkyd this endurs day
F30.1	1	This endurs nyght
F30.1	14	Is in this howse
F31b	1	Jhesu, mercy, how may this be,
F31b	5	Jhesu, mercy, how may this be?
F31.1	5	Jhesu, mercy, [how may this be?]
F31.2	1	He that wrought this wordle of nought,

THIS (cont.)

F31.2	5	Jhesu, mercy, [how may this be?]
F31.3	5	Jhesu, mercy, [how may this be?]
F31.4	2	Gladly suffyrd I all this.'
F31.4	5	[Jhesu, mercy, how may this be?]
F33.1	2	And be not hard-hartid, and for this encheson
F34b	9	And thynk on this lesson that now I teche the.
F34.2	1	My blody wowndes downe railyng be this tre,
F34.2	6	Lett now us twayne in this thyng be tretable:
F34.3	5	Role up this mater; grave it in thi reson:
F34.4	2	Cum to scole; record well this lesson:
F34.4	5	Whi did I this? To save the from prison.
F34.4	6	Afore thi hart hang this litell table,
F37.1	1	A blessid Jhesu, hough fortunyd this?
F39.3	5	'Leve, love, this chance,
F40.4	3	Leve this array! Anothir day
F41.1	2	This wanton clarkis be nyse allway.
F44.2	2	Is this noble prince of riall lynage,
F44.2	7	This eyre of Brytayne,
F44.3	3	For this yong prince, which is and daily shal
F45b	1	This day day dawes,
F45b	2	This gentill day day dawes,
F45b	3	This gentill day dawes,
F45.2	5	This garden to rule be ryghtwis lawe.'
F48b	9	Therefore I suffird all this payne.
F48.1	9	This is that I axe of the,
F48.2	2	That I suffird not for the this payne,
H25.6	2	I tooke this way,
H25.8	1	When I sawe this
H31.1	1	This other day
H35.1	1	Sore this dere strykyn ys,
H35.7	2	Now of this hunter's lore;
H44.6	1	To lovers I put now suer this cace -
H62.5	4	Lo, age ys cause of this;
H92.7	2	That this rude play may well be take,
H97	4	He may acheffe this gret viage:
H97	5	Now let us syng this rownd all thre;
H101.3	3	In all this lond, nowther fre nor bond,
H102.2	3	Alas, alas, what word ys this?
H105.2	1	I mene this by Mary, our Maker's moder of myght,
H105.2	3	Thus saying to our Saviour; this saw I in my syght;
H105.2	4	This reson that I rede you now, I rede it full ryght
H105.3	4	Now, gracious God and goode swete babe, yet ons this game agayne
H107.1	5	This world beyng
H107.3	5	Lo, in this trance,
H109.1	1	Now yn this medow fayer and grene
H109.4	1	Then for this onse I shal you spare,

THO (1)

| F36.1 | 8 | Tho I wept and sore did complayne |

THOF (1)
R15.7   6   Thof he be gon.

THOFF (1)
R4   4   For yeu, dere hert, thoff Y suffere penaunce

THOFTES (1)
R12.2   4   All thoftes and fantyses to dygest.

THOGH (1)
R4   3   And thogh Y wolde, Y koude me noght refrayne

THOO (3)
F1   6   Thoo I go lose, yet am I teyd with a lyne:
F2   4   Thoo that all this yet in vayne be,
F7.1   5   Thoo that ye wolde untill ye dye

THORFFE (1)
R9   9   Thorffe with yeur beute that Y most love and prise.

THORN (1)
R13.2   2   Sharper than thorn, dyamond or steyll,

THORNE (4)
F33.3   1   Off sharpe thorne I have worne a crowne on my hede,
F34.2   3   The crowne of thorne, the spere, the nailis thre,
F36.1   3   A crowne of thorne as nedill sharpe shyfft in his
                  brayne
H103.1   1   A thorne hath percyd my hart ryght sore

THORNYS (1)
H20   9   Among the thornys kene.

THOROUGHOUTE (1)
F36.1   10   Hough it thirlyd her thoroughoute the hart,

THOSE (2)
H23.3   2   Those shuld we covit wyn who can;
H79.1   6   But those be thay which can no skyll:

THOU (30)
R16b   2   Thou lytyll, pretty Besse,
R19.1   9   What doyst thou here?
F27.4   2   'What is his name that thou chosen has?
F29.5   3   For thou art he that hath all wrought,
F31.3   1   A Jhesu, whi suffyrd thou such entretyng,
F32.2   1   Methynkyth in my reson thou owfte to be gladd
F33.1   9   Condemp to deth, as thou maist se;
F33.2   2   I love the, then love me; why slepist thou? Awake!
F33.3   9   Cum when thou lyst, welcum to me!
F34b   4   What woldist thou have?
F34b   6   Why, lovyst thou me?
F34.1   8   Whi art thou froward, syth I am mercyable?
F34.2   8   Why art thou froward sith I am merciable?

THOU (cont.)

F34.3	6	Syth I am kynd, why are thou unstable?
F34.3	8	Be thou not froward syth I am merciable.
F34.4	8	Be thou not affraide sith I am merciable.
F36.2	9	'Yet thou are unkynd, which sleith myn hert,'
F37.2	1	Where art thou, Nature, that wont were me to store
F37.2	5	Thou, Nature, hast lefft me; by the fynd I no rest:
F37.4	3	'Remembir the, my creature, thou must nedis dye, I the ensure.
F37.4	4	Alas, to dye thou makyst me sure; yet then, good Lord, do thou thi cure
F38.1	2	Howgh gretly thou art bownd indede;
F38.1	3	Thou thynkyst on hym nevir a dele
F48.1	2	To the, and thou wilt be repentant;
F48.1	7	And that thou be in charite;
F48.2	5	Yet, man, that thou sholdest not be lorne,
F49b	4	And aske forgeveness or evyr thou dye.'
F49.1	4	Where thou were thrall, to make the free.
F49.1	7	Therfore remembir the or thou go hence.'

THOUGH (12)

F32.1	3	Though deth be bewaylid by waies of pite,
F32.1	6	Therfore, though deth be nevyr so sore,
F32.2	3	They bet him for oure gilt, though he no syn hadd;
F32.3	7	Therfore though deth be never so sore,
F32.4	7	Therefore, though deth be nevir so sore,
H51.8	1	Soch lovers though thay take payne
H66.1	1	Though sum saith that yough rulyth me,
H66.1	5	Though sum say that yough rulyth me.
H66.2	5	Though sum sayth [that yough rulyth me.]
H66.4	5	Though sum [saith that yough rulyth me.]
H92.4	2	Though that dysdaynars wold therin put error,
H109.2	4	Let us make one, though we be twayne!

THOUGHT (11)

R10.3	5	Alas, with thought
F3	5	That be won thought my rest from me doth go.
F3	7	That no thought can reless me of my sore.
F5	2	Which hath byn long plongyng with thought unseyne,
F11	7	Your trewe servant with thought, hart and body.
F29.5	1	'Sone', she sayd, 'let it be in thy thought,
F31.2	3	And suffyr wolde payne as sorowfull thought,
F41.4	5	Wed me or els I dye for thought!
H25.5	1	Alas, thought I,
H47.2	2	Let no thought yow dysmaye!
H106.1	1	My thought oppressed, my mynd in trouble,

THOUGHTIS (3)

F3	1	What causyth me wofull thoughtis to thynk
F3	2	Syn thoughtis byn cheff causers of my woo;
F25.3	4	With thoughtis trew;

THOUSANDE (1)

R9	6	Unly to yeure swete grace a thousande sithe

THOW (8)
R7   1   Thow man, envired with temptacion,
F15   2   Thow I be lytyll in your remembraunce;
H33b   3   Thow wynter blastys blow never so hye,
H47.2   3   Thow ye now parte me fro,
H49.1   3   And thow shal know of myne.
H51.1   1   Thow that men do call it dotage,
H66.3   5   Thow sum saith [that yough rulyth me.]
H82.1   3   Thow that age with gret dysdayne

THOWE (3)
F21   4   To love, thowe I do fere to trace that dawnce,
F25.3   7   Thowe I be shent,
F32.2   7   Therfor, thowe deth be never so sore,

THOWGH (1)
H63.2   1   Thowgh you depart now thus me fro,

THOWGHTES (1)
H24   1   The thowghtes within my brest,

THRALL (2)
F36.3   3   He hath to man, to make hym fre that now is
                  thrall.
F49.1   4   Where thou were thrall, to make the free.

THRE (4)
F27.6   5   Oure prince to se, and rosys thre.'
F34.2   3   The crowne of thorne, the spere, the nailis thre,
F49.1   5   Upon the cross with naylis thre
H97   5   Now let us syng this rownd all thre;

THREE (3)
F27b   5   Yff we three can agre in on.'
F27.4b   5   Yff we three can agre in oon.'
F27.6b   5   That we three be agrede in oon.'

THRETID (1)
F33.1   7   The Jewis me thretid,

THROUGH (1)
F8   5   Through whose swete showris now sprong ther is ayen

THRYLLED (1)
R13.2   3   So depe hath thrylled my hert ynwardly

THUS (41)
R6   2   That Y am thus in heviness?
R10.4   7   Thus evyll Y fare,
R10.5   8   Thus ever fynd I;
R10.6   1   Thus ever y fynd
R11.2   2   So onkyndly thus to be slayn;
R13.1   2   Thus under sylens I do endure,
R15.8   2   Has thus lefte me

THUS (cont.)

F11	5	Thus hath now grace enrychyd my plesaunce,
F18.2	8	Thus knowe we well.
F19	1	Thus musyng in my mynd, gretly mervelyng
F22	5	And thus is the tyme of his song;
F24.5	6	Thus to be shent;
F30.2	4	Thus for to ly,
F33.2	1	Thus nakyd am I nailid, O man, for thy sake;
F33.2	5	Thus toggid to and fro,
F33.2	6	Thus wrappid all in woo,
F33.2	8	Entretid, thus in most cruell wise
F33.3	3	Thus bobbid, thus robbid, thus for thi love ded;
F37.1	6	Thus trobled am I yet I trust it shalbe for the best
F37.2	6	Thus trobled am I [yet I trust it shalbe for the best
F37.3	4	Grete mowntens fallyng over me, thus slepe doth I yn feere
F37.3	6	Thus trobled am I [yet I trust it shalbe for the best
F37.4	2	Nature hath forsakyn me, and lefft me thus alone.
F37.4	6	Thus trobled am I [yet I trust it shalbe for the best
H25.11	1	Thus here an ende;
H28	2	Thus ever to endure;
H41.8	1	Thus how thay dyd we cannot say -
H47.5	3	Thus longe to endure,
H51.6	1	Thus am I fyxed withowt gruge,
H63.2	1	Thowgh you depart now thus me fro,
H66.4	4	Thus sayth the kyng, the eighth Harry:
H75	9	And thus I wyll endure;
H102.1	4	Now sith it ys thus known,
H103.1	3	Thus withowt comfort I am forlore;
H104.4	1	Thus with my care
H105.2	3	Thus saying to our Saviour; this saw I in my syght;
H106.1	6	Thus do I lyve in gret hevenes
H106.4	1	Thus may ye se my wofull chance,
H107.5	6	Thus to be shent;

THY (12)

R7	2	Unto Calvery caste thy mynde.
R8	1	Now helpe, Fortune, of thy godenesse,
R8	2	And onse withdrawe thy adversite
R8	3	From thy servaund, the weche hathe plente
F12	6	Of onys voice sayyng, 'Bere in thy mynd,
F29.5	1	'Sone', she sayd, 'let it be in thy thought,
F29.5	4	And I, thy modir, alone.'
F33.2	1	Thus nakyd am I nailid, O man, for thy sake;
F34.3	2	For-thi contrite of thy contricion;
F34.5	2	Thy deth remembryng of humble afeccion,
H49.1	2	Tel me how thy lemman doth,
H96b	1	Englond, be glad! Pluk up thy lusty hart!

THYN (2)
F27.4   3   The rose, I suppose? Thyn hart unbrace!'
F48.1   3   Hevyn bliss thyn eritage withoute endyng

THYNCKYTH (1)
R12.2   3   Company me thynckyth then best

THYNE (2)
F48b   8   And for I wolde have thyne heritage agayne,
F49.1   6   Fast I was naylyd for thyne offence;

THYNG (7)
F5   6   That I am bownde above all erthly thyng
F30.1   17   That made all thyng
F34.2   6   Lett now us twayne in this thyng be tretable:
F48.3   5   Into witness of which thyng
H31.5   4   Adew, all thyng
H50.3   1   My soverayne lorde in every thyng
H79.2   3   But love us a thyng gevyn by God;

THYNGE (1)
H17   1   Aboffe all thynge

THYNGES (1)
F47.2   3   All mysdone thynges to redress,

THYNGKE (1)
R3.1   2   Now thyngke ye this ys a fayre ray?

THYNK (21)
F2   2   Ye thynk for to discomfort me.
F3   1   What causyth me wofull thoughtis to thynk
F4   6   To thynk my sorows, well may I complayne;
F18.2   7   And thynk the contrary:
F19   8   To lett itt over pass, and thynk theron no more.
F25.2   1   I thynk suerly
F34b   9   And thynk on this lesson that now I teche the.
F34.1   7   Gayne gostly enmys thynk on my passion;
F34.4   1   Thynk agayne, pride, on my humilite;
F34.4   3   Gayne fals envy thynk on my charyte,
F37.3   2   My slepis be so feerfull, I thynk then sure to dye;
F38b   2   And thynk on the paynys that byn in hell.
F38.1   6   To thynk how grevusly I have offend:
F39.1   6   I thynk me bond,
H27.4   1   And I thynk I se her yet,
H34.5   2   To woman also, I thynk, the same.
H35.6   4   What do yow meane or thynk?
H35.7   3   I thynk his bow ys well unbent,
H44.7   2   Better than do I, I thynk it so.
H49.3   1   I cannot thynk such doubylnes
H66.2   3   I thynk sum wars of yche degre;

THYNKE (1)
F2   6   Or else I thynke to be content

THYNKES (1)
H31.3   3   And thynkes with her to rest,

THYNKYST (1)
F38.1   3   Thou thynkyst on hym nevir a dele

THYNKYTH (3)
F7.2   4   Thynkyth my hart can be well payd
F27.6b   3   Most worthy it is, as thynkyth me.
F46.3   2   So it is best, as thynkyth me,

THYS (1)
H92.7   1   Now unto God thys prayer we make,

TIL (1)
R4   5   All for yeure sake, til God me so avaunce

TILL (4)
R2.1   5   Till gode tydinges com my sorwe to slake
R2.2   7   For till she amende Y shall have noght truly
R5   3   Till that Y may in yeure presaunce
F43.3   3   Till his brayne be as wise as a duk;

TO (290)
R1.2   4   Ther to lede my lyffe.
R2.1   2   Enforsed me this complaynte for to make,
R2.1   5   Till gode tydinges com my sorwe to slake
R2.2   2   To myn entent, and so sayeth mo then I,
R3.1   5   'Wene ye that everybody lest to play?'
R3.1   8   Ye will not make to huge a waste.
R3.2   6   Recke ye not to make us shende?
R3.3   5   Take to gev all, and be stille than!
R4   1   Absens of you causeth me to sygh and complayne
R5   1   The hye desire that Y have for to se
R5   4   Prayng to yeure gracius pyte
R5   5   That ye wilde fuchesaffe to have mercy on me
R5   6   And only to be putte to yeure rememoraunce.
R6   4   Ever to plese hym with all myghth,
R9   6   Unly to yeure swete grace a thousande sithe
R10.2   7   To love vaynly;
R10.4   4   To lede my lyf;
R10.6   4   No place to resorte.
R11.2   2   So onkyndly thus to be slayn;
R12.1   9   To my cumfort:
R12.2   4   All thoftes and fantyses to dygest.
R12.3   2   Ys vertu, and vyce to flee;
R12.3   8   Vertu to use,
R12.3   9   Vyce to reffuse,
R13.1   4   To her which ys my yoyus plesure;
R13.2   7   Ther of right I apeyle hyr to be my surgyon.
R13.3   5   And all othyr for hyr sake to eschew,
R13.3   7   And never to chaunge hyr for no new.
R15.3   3   To me alone,
R16b   3   Come over the burne, Besse, to me!

R16.1	6	Cum over the burne, Besse, to me!
R19.1	4	To se her chere
R19.2	4	To a forest wyde
R19.2	9	To take her pray
R20.1	2	To avoyde your custumabyll disdayne;
R20.2	1	Your on-syttyng speche puttyth me to payne
F1	4	The lyghter leefe, the lother for to wende;
F2	2	Ye thynk for to discomfort me.
F2	6	Or else I thynke to be content
F3	1	What causyth me wofull thoughtis to thynk
F4	5	Cannot be well for to be wisht:
F4	6	To thynk my sorows, well may I complayne;
F4	7	But them to tell cannott availe.
F5	3	Full lyk to drowne in wavis of dystres,
F5	7	To love and dred hym as my lord and kyng.
F6.1	5	To complayne
F6.3	7	To be demyd wrongfully.
F6.4	4	For that to mone,
F7.1	3	In willfullness so for to be,
F7.1	7	Butt yff hit be to wissh for one:
F7.2	5	So for to se ye betrayd,
F8	7	All myrthis to maynten, all sorous to subdewe.
F9	7	Her man to be
F12	7	Thi lady hath forgoten to be kynd.'
F13	1	To complayne me, alas, why shulde I so?
F13	4	To her only which is myn yes fode,
F14	1	Alas, it is I that wote nott what to say,
F14	4	And no cause gevyn to be so refusyd;
F15	4	To be put owte of your good governaunce . . .
F16	2	I pray daily ther paynys to asswage
F16	3	And sone to sende where they faynest wolde be,
F18.1	7	To make a belevyng:
F18.2	1	Hit were to grete pite
F19	7	Wherfore I hope to fynd a speciall remedy
F19	8	To lett itt over pass, and thynk theron no more.
F20	3	Which that passyth my mynde for to express
F21	4	To love, thowe I do fere to trace that dawnce,
F21	6	Yet will I me trust to fortune applye;
F22	6	To gett mystrust is his entent
F22	7	To send to her to make me shent.
F24.2	3	Is now to cess
F24.3	2	To my grevaunce
F24.3	8	Willyng to dye.
F24.4	4	To be content,
F24.5	2	To an entent;
F24.5	6	Thus to be shent;
F25.1	6	To you complayne,
F25.2	3	To you gretly
F25.2	5	For to applye
F25.3	6	My lyffe to spente,
F25.3	8	All other to esshewe.
F26	1	O rote of trouth, o princess to my pay,
F26	4	With welth and wordly joy long to endure,

F27.5	5	That day to se it lykyth well me.'
F27.6	3	'To here talke of them is my delite.
F27.6	5	Oure prince to se, and rosys thre.'
F28	3	To love her best and no mo
F29.1	2	To the grenewode for to play
F29.1	3	And all hevyness to put away,
F29.3	2	To save mankynd that was forlorne;
F29.4	2	That men sekyth for to spill;
F29.4	3	For them to save, it is my will;
F30.1	7	To kepe she sought
F30.2	4	Thus for to ly,
F30.2	16	Man to restore,
F31.1	2	Egall to the Fathir in deite,
F31.4	4	'The to purchace both joy and bliss.'
F32.2	1	Methynkyth in my reson thou owfte to be gladd
F32.2	2	When Jewis with treson to deth thi son ladde;
F32.2	5	To joy of every wordlis wight,
F33.1	9	Condemp to deth, as thou maist se;
F33.2	4	With paynys my vaynys constraynyd to crake;
F33.2	5	Thus toggid to and fro,
F33.3	4	Onfaynyd, not deynyd, my blode for to shede:
F33.3	9	Cum when thou lyst, welcum to me!
F34.1	2	Suffyrd deth to pay thi rawnsum;
F34.1	5	To contryte hartes I do remission;
F34.4	2	Cum to scole; record well this lesson:
F34.4	5	Whi did I this? To save the from prison.
F34.5	8	At hir request be to us merciable.
F36.1	1	To Calvery he bare his cross with doulfull payne,
F36.1	9	To se the sharpe swerde of sorow smert,
F36.2	8	Me unto grace for to restore:
F36.3	3	He hath to man, to make hym fre that now is thrall.
F36.3	9	Is by nature constraynyd to smert,
F36.3	11	From deth to lyff he aryse shall.'
F37.1	3	Nature of aquayntance ys turned to a gest,
F37.1	4	So shortly am I bydyn to a grevus fest,
F37.2	1	Where art thou, Nature, that wont were me to store
F37.2	2	To lusty plesure? Now lyyng in the flore,
F37.3	2	My slepis be so feerfull, I thynk then sure to dye;
F37.3	3	My dreme is so mervelous, serpentis semyth me to tere
F37.4	1	Now, mercyfull Jhesu, to the make I my mone;
F37.4	4	Alas, to dye thou makyst me sure; yet then, good Lord, do thou thi cure
F37.4	5	With all good sowlis to cause me lyve in rest.
F38.1	6	To thynk how grevusly I have offend:
F38.2	2	To God above I call and crye;
F38.2	5	Me to amend I will me hye
F39.1	8	To comfort her:
F40.2	2	To hym that wolde of such recreacion
F43.1	3	Save a raggid hode to kover his crowne,
F44.1	3	Arthur oure prynce to us here terrestriall,
F44.1	4	In honor to rayne, Lord, graunt hym tyme and space,

TO (cont.)

F44.1	9	Ryght eyre for to be;
F44.2	4	With joy to rejose his dew enerytaunce,
F44.2	5	His ryght to optayne,
F44.2	6	In honor to rayne,
F44.2	9	Ryght eyre for to be;
F44.3	2	Pray to thi Son, the secund in Trinite,
F44.3	8	To the we crye and call,
F44.3	9	His savegard to be;
F45.2	5	This garden to rule be ryghtwis lawe.'
F46b	1	Smale pathis to the grenewode,
F46.1	1	Love is naturall to every wyght,
F46.1	2	Indyfferent to every creature,
F46.1	5	So rennyth the chaunce from one to one:
F46.2	5	Tyll sum of them begyn to grone:
F46.3	3	To put in one my faithfull trust,
F47b	2	To strenkyth your comyns in ther ryght.
F47.1	2	Whom God hath chose oure gyde to be,
F47.1	7	To strenkyth your comyns in ther ryght.
F47.2	3	All mysdone thynges to redress,
F47.2	7	To have recover of ther unryght.
F48b	1	Be hit knowyn to all that byn here
F48b	2	And to all that here-afftir
F48b	3	To me shal be leffe and dere,
F48.1	2	To the, and thou wilt be repentant;
F48.2	7	Witness, the daye turnyd to nyghth,
F48.2	10	Witness, the bodies that rose from deth to lyve.
F49.1	4	Where thou were thrall, to make the free.
H12	5	To kepe yow me unto?
H18	4	Wherfor to her I me complayn, hey now!
H18	7	And never more to remayne.
H20	2	To geder the flours down
H22	2	To passe the tyme of youth joly,
H22	3	Avaunce hym to the companye
H23.1	1	The tyme of youthe is to be spent;
H23.3	1	And they be plesant to God and man,
H23.6	1	Vertue it is then youth for to spend
H24	4	To serve you evermore.
H25.3	2	To me hart roote
H25.4	3	What sayd sche then to me?
H25.4	6	But styll to morne for me.
H25.5	3	Venus, to blame are ye.
H25.5	6	To helpe my love and me.
H25.6	1	Her for to say
H25.7	2	I to her lept
H25.7	6	It rewyd my hart to se.
H25.9	3	And prayd her to be ble,
H25.9	4	To take comfort
H25.10	5	My hart to go
H27.2	1	Oft to me her godely swet face
H27.2	2	Was wont to cast an nye;
H27.2	3	And now absence to be in place
H27.3	1	I was wont her to behold,
H27.4	2	As wol to God I cowld,

H28	2	Thus ever to endure;
H29.1	1	Iff I had wytt for to endyght
H29.2	3	My hart to have she doth me bynd;
H29.4	1	Yf I to her than war unkynd,
H29.4	3	For she to me ys allway kynd;
H29.5	2	Unto ther lovers trew for to be;
H29.6	2	To by deth departed we be;
H31.3	3	And thynkes with her to rest,
H31.5	5	To god perteynyng,
H31.6	3	To be a lady's pere!'
H31.9	5	To ther intent
H33.3	2	Promyse to her I make,
H33.3	4	To her I me betake.
H34.3	1	Wherfor to love and be not loved
H34.5	1	Love ys gevyn to God and man;
H34.5	2	To woman also, I thynk, the same.
H34.6	2	Yet never the lesse it ys to moch used.
H34.7	1	Grett pyte it ware, love for to compell
H35.3	3	And yf ye lust to have a shott,
H35.4	1	He to go and I to go,
H35.5	1	To the covert bothe thay went,
H35.6	2	I went to tavern to drynk;
H39	3	My love is to the grenewode gone,
H40	2	My love, she is so trew to me.
H40	3	To love her sure whill I am levyng,
H41b	3	To the grenewode must we go, alas!
H41.2	1	To call the porter he wold not blyn;
H41.6	1	He was cownselled to breffe a byll
H44.3	2	And causith lovers owtwardly to refrayne,
H44.4	1	Which puttes them to more and more
H44.6	1	To lovers I put now suer this cace -
H47.5	2	It ys to me gret payne
H47.5	3	Thus longe to endure,
H50.1	5	And of all other for to love best
H50.3	5	To have the prayse of all the best;
H50.4	5	With hart and body to love best
H50.6	5	Off all gode fortunes to send hym best;
H51.3	2	And she to hym most seme most fayre.
H62.3	1	Every bowe for me ys to bygge;
H62.4	2	Owt of her courte to go;
H62.6	1	Now will I take to me my bedes
H64.1	5	To set in one
H64.1	11	Hymselfe to save
H64.1	12	And love to optayne.
H64.2	5	For to procure
H65.2	3	I have strengh to mak it fle
H66.1	2	I trust in age to tarry;
H66.4	2	Pray we to God and Seynt Mary
H67.1	7	To be as yours
H67.2	5	But to endure
H75	5	As the hauke to the lure,
H75	6	So my hart to her I ensure;
H75	8	Glad to do her plesure

H82.1	2	Frome Venus' ways banysht to be;
H82.1	4	Wold have yough love to refrayn,
H82.2	5	Wherfor indede the trouth to say
H92.2	2	And all mery company for to dysdayne;
H92.3	2	But all dysdaynares for to refuse?
H92.4	3	For they do sew to get them grace
H92.4	4	All only reches to purchase.
H92.5	2	Goode Lord, graunt us our mancyon to be!
H92.6	1	For yough ys frayle and prompt to doo,
H92.6	2	As well vices as vertuus to ensew;
H96.1	1	Ageynst the Frenchmen in the feld to fyght
H96.1	4	Bowys and arows to put them all to flyght:
H97	1	Pray we to God that all may gyde
H97	2	That for our kyng so to provid,
H97	3	To send hym power to hys corage
H101.3	1	When I was come to
H102b	2	Why shall not I to my lady
H102.2	4	Her to remember mest
H103.2	2	To se the paynes that I endure
H103.3	3	For which my hart is lyk to brest,
H104b	5	To make me glad
H104.2	4	Me to comfort
H104.3	2	To daunce or syng,
H104.3	3	To swage sumwhat my mone;
H105.2	3	Thus saying to our Saviour; this saw I in my syght;
H105.3	3	Yet softly to her swete sonne methought I hard
		her sayn
H106.3	5	A payne it is, hens to depart,
H106.3	6	Yet my lyfe is to me so grevus
H106.4	3	From all plesure to gret penance;
H106.4	4	Right suere to have no good aventure,
H106.4	5	Good aventure in me to have place:
H107.2	3	Is now to cese
H107.3	2	To my grevance
H107.3	8	Willyng to dye.
H107.4	4	To be content;
H107.5	2	To an entent;
H107.5	6	Thus to be shent;
H109b	3	I go to the medowe to mylke my cow.
H109b	5	To gather the flowres both fayer and swete.

TO-BRAKE (1)

F48.3	2	Witness, stonys that all to-brake,

TO-BREKE (1)

R13.1	3	Unwetyng how myn hert to-breke

TO-RAFF (1)

F36.4	3	His vaynys all and synowis to-raff and brast;

TO-RENT (1)

F36.2	3	Beholdyng ther his lymmys all to-rent and tore,

TO-TORNE (1)
F48.2   4 Yet wold Y eft be all to-torne.]

TOGETHER (1)
F40.3   3 Yff she and I were together alone,

TOGGID (1)
F33.2   5 Thus toggid to and fro,

TOMAS (1)
F34.3   3 Saynt Tomas of Indes, in crudelite

TONG (1)
F43.2   2 His tong rennyth all on buttyrd fyssh,

TOOKE (1)
H25.6   2 I tooke this way,

TORE (1)
F36.2   3 Beholdyng ther his lymmys all to-rent and .tore,

TOWARD (1)
F19   5 As solen, as stately, as strange toward me,

TOWN (1)
R15.6   4 Men tellyth yn town

TOWNE (3)
F10   4 Nethir in towne ne fylde simulacion
F12   4 The see also drownyd both towre and towne:
F43.1   1 Rutterkyn is com unto oure towne

TOWRE (1)
F12   4 The see also drownyd both towre and towne:

TOYNED (1)
H20   6 They toyned so clene;

TRACE (2)
F9   4 In Venus' trace
F21   4 To love, thowe I do fere to trace that dawnce,

TRANCE (1)
H107.3   5 Lo, in this trance,

TRANSGRESSION (1)
F34.3   7 My blode best triacle for thi transgression;

TRAUNCE (1)
F24.3   5 Lo, in this traunce,

TRAYNE (1)
R20.1   3 That ye loth Y love -- wrappe that yn your trayne!

TRE (3)
F30.2   18   Uppon a tre.'
F34.2   1   My blody wowndes downe railyng be this tre,
H65.3   2   Upon the trenwod tre?

TREMLYNG (1)
F36.2   2   With pale visage tremlyng she stode her child
                  before

TRESON (2)
F32.2   2   When Jewis with treson to deth thi son ladde;
F33.1   4   Begylde and betraide by Judas' fals treson;

TRESPACE (1)
F49b   3   'Amende the, man, of thi trespace,

TRESPAS (1)
H31.2   2   Withowt trespas

TRETABLE (1)
F34.2   6   Lett now us twayne in this thyng be tretable:

TREU (1)
R7   3   Remembre how feithefull, how treu, how kynde

TREULYE (1)
H23.2   1   Pastymes ther be I nought treulye

TREUTH (1)
F7.2   1   Treuth nor service nevir so playne

TREW (17)
F25.3   4   With thoughtis trew;
F46.3   4   Forever yff she will trew be,
H25.6   6   So trew of love was sche.
H25.11   3   All lovers that trew be,
H29.2   2   She ys right trew, I do it se.
H29.3   3   But allway trew I do her fynd;
H29.5   2   Unto ther lovers trew for to be;
H30   3   And trew love lokked therto?
H31.3   5   And I so trew,
H33.1   4   Unto my lady trew.
H38   3   I fynde you not trew;
H40   2   My love, she is so trew to me.
H49.3   2   For I fynd women trew;
H51.9   2   Thay hynder lovers that wolde be trew.
H66.3   4   I love trew wher I dyd mary:
H79.1   2   Hys entent must nedys be trew,
H102b   3   Why shall not I be trew?

TREWE (2)
F11   7   Your trewe servant with thought, hart and body.
F45.2   4   And said, 'The white rose is most trewe

TREWER (1)
F1   5   The trewer I serve, the ferther out of mynde;

TREWLY (6)
R10.2   2   A lover trewly,
F10   5   Ther is trewly in every case consolacion
F10   8   Now raynyth trewly in every mannys syght.
H33.4   3   Who hath my hart trewly,
H40   1   I love trewly withowt feynyng;
H107.4 1   Methynk trewly

TREWTH (1)
H50.3   4   But of a trewth he worthyest

TRIACLE (1)
F34.3   7   My blode best triacle for thi transgression;

TRINITE (3)
F32.1   1   Sith it concludid was in the Trinite
F40.1   4   But it were an angell of the Trinite?
F44.3   2   Pray to thi Son, the secund in Trinite,

TRISTYNG (1)
R20.3   2   Y am right glad, tristyng hit woll remanyne;

TROBILL (2)
F3   4   Then be it they that doth me trobill so
F32.4   4   Thi dere sone is past his trobill and his tene;

TROBLED (5)
F37.1   6   Thus trobled am I yet I trust it shalbe for the
                best
F37.2   6   Thus trobled am I [yet I trust it shalbe for the
                best
F37.3   1   My voice is so trobled, my seknes then feele I;
F37.3   6   Thus trobled am I [yet I trust it shalbe for the
                best
F37.4   6   Thus trobled am I [yet I trust it shalbe for the
                best

TROLLY (2)
H39   1   Trolly lolly loly lo,
H39   5   Syng trolly loly lo loly lo!

TROLY (6)
H39   2   Syng troly loly lo!
H75   1   Hey troly loly loly!
H75   4   Hey troly loly loly loly!
H75   7   Hey troly loly loly!
H75   10   Hey troly loly lo!
H109b   1   Hey troly loly lo!

TROUBLE (1)
H106.1 1   My thought oppressed, my mynd in trouble,

TROUTH (5)
  F13   7 Syth for my trouth she nedith no wittness.
  F21   2 In stedfast fayth and trouth with assuraunce;
  F26   1 O rote of trouth, o princess to my pay,
  H82.2   5 Wherfor indede the trouth to say
  H102.2 1 My lady sayth of trouth it ys

TROW (3)
  R3.1   7 Y trow for all youre gret afray
  R11.4   1 I trow on me she wold rewe
  F4   1 So fer I trow from remedy,

TROWTH (1)
  H74   2 Tyll the trowth be tryed owt.

TRULY (3)
  R2.2   7 For till she amende Y shall have noght truly
  F18.2   2 That women truly
  F24.4   1 Methynkyth truly

TRUST (13)
  F4   4 So mekyll dred, so lytyll trust
  F14   5 But pite it is that trust shulde be mysusyd
  F21   6 Yet will I me trust to fortune applye;
  F23.1   3 That was my trust is now my wanhope playne;
  F37.1   6 Thus trobled am I yet I trust it shalbe for the
                best
  F37.2   6 Thus trobled am I [yet I trust it shalbe for the
                best
  F37.3   6 Thus trobled am I [yet I trust it shalbe for the
                best
  F37.4   6 Thus trobled am I [yet I trust it shalbe for the
                best
  F46.3   3 To put in one my faithfull trust,
  H38   2 Hope and trust,
  H56   2 I trust ryght wel of retorn agane.
  H66.1   2 I trust in age to tarry;
  H68   2 I trust we shall mete oftener.

TRUSTED (1)
  F14   3 Ther as I trusted I was late cast away,

TRUSTYNG (2)
  F13   5 Trustyng sumtyme that she will chaunge her mode
  H18   5 Trustyng that dysdayn

TRYED (1)
  H74   2 Tyll the trowth be tryed owt.

TULLY (1)
  F41.1   5 Tully, valy, strawe, let be I say!

TURNED (1)
  F37.1   3 Nature of aquayntance ys turned to a gest,

TURNYD (2)
F12   2   Methought the worlde was turnyd up so downe,
F48.2   7   Witness, the daye turnyd to nyghth,

TURNYNG (1)
R10.6   3   Turnyng as the wynd,

TURNYTH (1)
R20.3   3   But light credens turnyth your love agayne:

TWANE (1)
R20.4   3   Speke or ye smyte, barke or ye byte; holde yowre
                    hondes twane

TWAYN (1)
F8   2   Beholde the soveren sede of this rosis twayn,

TWAYNE (4)
F6.1   6   For with twayne
F34.2   6   Lett now us twa'yne in this thyng be tretable:
H27.3   2   And take in armys twayne;
H109.2   4   Let us make one, though we be twayne!

TWELVE (1)
H101.2   2   Of twelve yere of age,

TWENTY-A-DEVELL (1)
R3.1   4   Leff werke a twenty-a-devell away!

TWEYNE (1)
R2.1   3   Weche Y have songe with wepyng yen tweyne

TWISE (1)
F43.4   2   He will piss a galon-pot full at twise

TWO (1)
H79.2   5   But perfite in dede and betwene two.

TYDE (1)
R19.2   2   And stop a tyde;

TYDINGES (1)
R2.1   5   Till gode tydinges com my sorwe to slake

TYDYNG (1)
R4   6   That Y fro yew may hyre sume gode tydyng,

TYE (1)
H65.4   1   Wherfor shuld I tye up my hownd

TYL (3)
H28   3   Alas, pour hart, tyl that we mete agayne,
H47.1   4   Tyl that we mete agayne.
H108   2   And cannot cesse tyl I sore smart,

TYLL (9)
```
R13.1    6   And so shall contynew tyll I dye,
F2       7   With my desyre tyll I be spent:
F11      6   Wherfor I am and shal be tyll I dye
F22      3   Tyll deth my lyff departe from hens!
F28      6   Tyll that I cum tyll her presens,
F46.2    5   Tyll sum of them begyn to grone:
H47.5    4   Tyll that we mete agayne.
H74      2   Tyll the trowth be tryed owt.
```

TYLLE (1)
```
F25.2    7   Tylle I dye;
```

TYME (8)
```
F7.2     3   Sum tyme is lost and all in vayne
F10      6   The pore pepull no tyme hath but ryght
F22      5   And thus is the tyme of his song;
F44.1    4   In honor to rayne, Lord, graunt hym tyme and space,
H22      2   To passe the tyme of youth joly,
H23.1    1   The tyme of youthe is to be spent;
H104.3   1   The tyme passyng
H109.4   2   But the nexte tyme ye must beware
```

TYMES (3)
```
H50.1    3   Of which four tymes he dyd it take;
H51.9    1   For often tymes wher they do sewe
H67.1    2   All tymes or ours
```

UN (1)
```
R3.3     6   'Now have ye leyde me un the flore,
```

UNBENT (1)
```
H35.7    3   I thynk his bow ys well unbent,
```

UNBRACE (1)
```
F27.4    3   The rose, I suppose? Thyn hart unbrace!'
```

UNCERTEYNE (2)
```
R20b     1   How shall Y plece a creature uncerteyne?
R20.1    4   How sholde Y [plece a creature uncerteyne?]
```

UNCURTESLY (1)
```
F41.3    1   I-wiss, ye dele uncurtesly;
```

UNDER (2)
```
R13.1    2   Thus under sylens I do endure,
H35.2    1   As I stod under a bank
```

UNDERTAKE (1)
```
R2.1     4   Full oghfte or this, Y shall undertake.
```

UNDIR (4)
```
F29.2    1   As I walkyd undir the grenewode bowe
F42.1    3   Undir the levys grene?
```

UNDIR (cont.)
F42.2   3 Undir the holy grene.
F43.4   3 And the overplus undir the table of the newe gyse;

UNDYRTAKE (1)
F6.3   4 I undyrtake

UNKYND (3)
R10.6   2 My lover unkynd,
F36.2   9 'Yet thou are unkynd, which sleith myn hert,'
H29.4   1 Yf I to her than war unkynd,

UNKYNDE (3)
R7   5 And say after me, and be noght unkynde:
H47.3   4 That I shuld be unkynde.
H49.2   1 My lady is unkynde I wis.

UNKYNDLY (3)
R13.3   3 Or els yn feyth unkyndly she doth dele,
F6.3   3 So unkyndly;
F33.1   5 Unkyndly entretid,

UNKYNDNES (3)
H103.3   2 Whos unkyndnes hath me opprest,
H107.2   5 For unkyndnes
H108   4 Whose unkyndnes hath kyld myn hart;

UNKYNDNESS (2)
F23.1   6 Onryghtfully shewyng me unkyndness,
F24.2   5 For unkyndness

UNLAST (1)
H25.8   5 Ful fast unlast

UNLOVED (2)
H108   1 I love unloved; suche is myn aventure,
H108   7 And love unloved; such ys myne adventure.

UNLY (1)
R9   6 Unly to yeure swete grace a thousande sithe

UNNETH (1)
F36.2   11 Unneth on worde cowde she speke more.

UNRYGHT (1)
F47.2   7 To have recover of ther unryght.

UNSEYNE (1)
F5   2 Which hath byn long plongyng with thought unseyne,

UNSTABLE (1)
F34.3   6. Syth I am kynd, why are thou unstable?

288

UNSTEDFASTNES (1)
 H107.1 4 Th'unstedfastnes;

UNSTEDFASTNESS (1)
 F24.1 4 The unstedfastness,

UNTILL (1)
 F7.1   5 Thoo that ye wolde untill ye dye

UNTO (19)
 R7   2 Unto Calvery caste thy mynde.
 R12.1   2 I love and shall unto I dye;
 R13.3   2 And geve me salfe unto my sore?
 F30.1   15 Unto my pay;
 F36.2   8 Me unto grace for to restore:
 F36.4   1 Unto the cross, handes and feete, nailid he was;
 F43.1   1 Rutterkyn is com unto oure towne
 F47.2   5 Which crye and call unto your Majeste.
 F49.1   2 Whome I did make so lyke unto me,
 H12   5 To kepe yow me unto?
 H27.4   4 Unto my hart as now she shuld.
 H29.5   2 Unto ther lovers trew for to be;
 H33.1   4 Unto my lady trew.
 H33.3   1 Now unto my lady
 H44.7   1 And unto them which doth it know
 H65.4   2 Unto the grenwod spray?
 H67.1   6 Unto my pours
 H92.7   1 Now unto God thys prayer we make,
 H105.1   4 Full softly and full soberly unto her swet son
                    she saide

UNTREW (2)
 H31.2   3 Her dere hart was untrew;
 H31.3   1 Seth he untrew

UNTYL (1)
 H16   4 Untyl I dye, alas, alas!

UNTYLL (1)
 H67.1   8 Untyll I dye.

UNWETYNG (1)
 R13.1   3 Unwetyng how myn hert to-breke

UP (10)
 R1.1   3 Y shall hong up my horne by the grenewode spray;
 R18.1   1 Up Y arose in verno tempore
 F12   2 Methought the worlde was turnyd up so downe,
 F34.3   5 Role up this mater; grave it in thi reson:
 F43.3   2 A stoupe of bere up at a pluk,
 H65.1   1 Wherfore shuld I hang up my bow
 H65.2   1 Wherfor shuld I hang up myne arrow
 H65.3   1 Wherfor shuld I hang up my horne
 H65.4   1 Wherfor shuld I tye up my hownd

H96b   1   Englond, be glad! Pluk up thy lusty hart!

UPON (5)
F48.3   9   Iyevyn upon the mownt of Calvary,
F49.1   5   Upon the cross with naylis thre
H62.2   2   Upon the grenewod bough,
H65.1   2   Upon the grenwod bough?
H65.3   2   Upon the grenwod tre?

UPPON (4)
F30.2   18   Uppon a tre.'
F34.1   1   Uppon the cross nailid I was for the,
F36.4   9   Uppon her he cast his dedly loke,
F48b   6   Uppon the crosse with woundis smert

US (22)
R3.2   6   Recke ye not to make us shende?
F32.1   2   That the Son of God shulde make us fre,
F32.4   5   His deth was swete, hit did us goode;
F32.4   6   He bought us with his precious blode:
F34.2   6   Lett now us twayne in this thyng be tretable:
F34.5   6   May washe us all from surfettes reprovable.
F34.5   8   At hir request be to us merciable.
F39.3   7   And let us daunce
F44.1   3   Arthur oure prynce to us here terrestriall,
H17   2   Now lete us synge
H64.1   3   Now let us be;
H64.2   3   Let us now pray
H79.2   3   But love us a thyng gevyn by God;
H82.1   1   Let not us that yong men be
H92.1   1   Lusti yough shuld us ensue,
H92.5   2   Goode Lord, graunt us our mancyon to be!
H97   5   Now let us syng this rownd all thre;
H109b   7   I wysse my mother then shall us se!
H109.1   2   We may us sport and not be sene;
H109.1b   4   That now in the feldes we may us sportt?
H109.1b   6   I wysse my mothyr than shall us se!
H109.2   4   Let us make one, though we be twayne!

USE (4)
R12.3   8   Vertu to use,
R12.3   10   Y shall use me.
H23.2   2   Whych one may use, and vice denye;
H92.3   1   How shuld yough hymselfe best use

USED (1)
H34.6   2   Yet never the lesse it ys to moch used.

USYD (2)
F14   7   Wher that is usyd can be no surance.
H92.6   4   And vertuus pastaunce must be theryn usyd.

UTTER (1)
  H23.4   2   Wherby actyvenesse oon may utter.

VALE (5)
  F41.1   6   Gup, Cristian Clowte, gup, Jak of the Vale,
  F41.2   6   Gup, Cristian Clowte, gup, Jak of the Vale,
  F41.3   6   Gup, Cristian Clowte, gup, Jak of the Vale,
  F41.4   8   Gup, Cristian Clowte, gup, Jak of the Vale,
  F48.2   9   Witness, the vale that then did ryve,

VALY (1)
  F41.1   5   Tully, valy, strawe, let be I say!

VARY (1)
  H66.l   4   Frome them shall I never vary:

VARYABLE (1)
  H47.4   3   Ye ar not varyable;

VARYAUNCE (1)
  F26   2   In whom all vertu is knytt withouten varyaunce,

VAYNE (6)
  R10.5   2   Lovyng yn vayne,
  F2   4   Thoo that all this yet in vayne be,
  F7.2   3   Sum tyme is lost and all in vayne
  F17   2   Syth worde and dede is take in vayne,
  F25.1   3   In every vayne
  F36.1   2   And theruppon straynyd he was in every vayne;

VAYNLY (1)
  R10.2   7   To love vaynly;

VAYNYS (2)
  F33.2   4   With paynys my vaynys constraynyd to crake;
  F36.4   3   His vaynys all and synowis to-raff and brast;

VENGEABLE (1)
  F34.1   6   Be not dispayryd, for I am not vengeable;

VENGEANCE (1)
  H50.5   5   A vengeance on them that loveth nott best

VENUS (4)
  R13.2   1   The sterre of Venus which I call her ye,
  H25.5   3   Venus, to blame are ye.
  H51.2   2   Frome Venus sure he must it fett;
  H62.4   1   Lady Venus hath commaundyd me

VENUS' (2)
  F9   4   In Venus' trace
  H82.1   2   Frome Venus' ways banysht to be;

VERELY (1)
F36.3 10 And yet verely I know in myn hart

VERTU (5)
R12.3 2 Ys vertu, and vyce to flee;
R12.3 8 Vertu to use,
F20   2 With vertu connyng her maner is lede,
F26   2 Endewid with vertu and goodly plesaunce,
F26   3 In whom all vertu is knytt withouten varyaunce,

VERTUE (1)
H23.6 1 Vertue it is then youth for to spend

VERTUES (1)
F20   7 Thes vertues byn pryntyd in her doutless.

VERTUS (1)
H92.3 4 Honest myrth with vertus pastance.

VERTUSE (1)
H50.5 1 So many vertuse gevyn of grace

VERTUUS (2)
H92.6 2 As well vices as vertuus to ensew;
H92.6 4 And vertuus pastaunce must be theryn usyd.

VIAGE (1)
H97   4 He may acheffe this gret viage:

VICE (3)
H23.1 2 But vice in it shuld be forfent.
H23.2 2 Whych one may use, and vice denye;
H34.6 1 But dysdayne ys vice and shuld be refused;

VICES (2)
R12.2 7 Of vices all;
H92.6 2 As well vices as vertuus to ensew;

VICTORY (1)
H97   6 Sent George, graunt hym the victory!

VILLAGE (1)
H51.7 2 Who love dysdaynyth ys all of the village.

VIOLET (1)
F27.2 3 Prymeros, violet, or fressh daysy,

VIOLETT (1)
H47.4 2 The violett wan and blo;

VISAGE (1)
F36.2 2 With pale visage tremlyng she stode her child
                    before

292

VOICE (3)
```
F12      6   Of onys voice sayyng, 'Bere in thy mynd,
F37.3    1   My voice is so trobled, my seknes then feele I;
F49b     2   I harde a voice lowde call and crye
```

VOYDED (1)
```
R2.2     6   That she be voyded owte of the grete grevaunce;
```

VOYDYNG (1)
```
H31.9    3   In voydyng care and mone
```

VYCE (2)
```
R12.3    2   Ys vertu, and vyce to flee;
R12.3    9   Vyce to reffuse,
```

WACH (1)
```
R15.6    3   "Go wach a byrde!
```

WAGER (1)
```
H66.2    4   Therin a wager lay dar I:
```

WAIES (1)
```
F32.1    3   Though deth be bewaylid by waies of pite,
```

WAKYNG (1)
```
F37.3    5   So wakyng ne sleping fynd I no rest:
```

WALKE (1)
```
F41.4    1   'Walke forthe your way, ye cost me nought;
```

WALKYD (2)
```
F29.1    1   As I me walkyd this endurs day
F29.2    1   As I walkyd undir the grenewode bowe
```

WALLE (1)
```
R3.3     3   Ye herte my legge agenste the walle;
```

WALYNG (1)
```
H107.1   6   Of such walyng
```

WAN (2)
```
F33b     5   My body bloo and wan,
H47.4    2   The violett wan and blo;
```

WANHOPE (1)
```
F23.1    3   That was my trust is now my wanhope playne;
```

WANTITH (1)
```
H51.1    2   Who lovyth not wantith corage.
```

WANTON (4)
```
R3.2     3   'Ywisse, wanton, ye shull not yette!
R15.3    1   A wanton chyld
F41.1    2   This wanton clarkis be nyse allway.
```

WANTON (cont.)
H101.2 1 When I was a wanton wench

WAR (7)
H29.4   1 Yf I to her than war unkynd,
H29.4   2 Pytte it war that I shuld be,
H29.5   1 Lernyng it war for women all
H44.1   2 And war rewardit as it hath sene,
H79.1   4 Els it war pyte that he shuld spede;
H82.2   1 For yf thay war in lyk case
H101.1 1 And I war a maydyn,

WARE (2)
F31.4   1 'Lo, man, for the that ware onkynd,
H34.7   1 Grett pyte it ware, love for to compell

WARNE (1)
F2   3 Nay, nay, nay, nay, I warne the well,

WARRANT (1)
H35.3   4 I warrant her barrayne.

WARS (1)
H66.2   3 I thynk sum wars of yche degre;

WARYOWERE (1)
H50.2   2 As the chefteyne of a waryowere,

WAS (59)
R7   4 This lyon and lambe was, causyng pyte;
R10.2   1 Sumtyme was I
R15.2   2 'Y was a mayde
R15.2   5 Y was afrayde
R19.3   1 Whan she was gone
F4   3 Was nevir man saff only I;
F11   1 That was my woo is nowe my most gladness;
F11   2 That was my payne is nowe my joyus chaunce;
F11   3 That was my feere is nowe my sykyrness;
F11   4 That was my grefe is now my alegeaunce.
F12   2 Methought the worlde was turnyd up so downe,
F14   3 Ther as I trusted I was late cast away,
F23.1   1 That was my joy is now my woo and payne;
F23.1   2 That was my bliss is now my displesaunce;
F23.1   3 That was my trust is now my wanhope playne;
F23.1   4 That was my wele is now my most grevaunce.
F24.5   1 My lyff was lent
F29.3   2 To save mankynd that was forlorne;
F31.1   1 Crist, that was of infynyt myght,
F32.1   1 Sith it concludid was in the Trinite
F32.1   4 Yet when oure Laidis Son was slayne
F32.2   4 Thi son was doughti, the fende was adradde;
F32.3   4 All was on red blod withoute any shirt;
F32.4   5 His deth was swete, hit did us goode;
F33.1   3 Sith I for thi sowle sake was slayne in good seson,

WAS (cont.)

F33.2	7	Whereas never man was so
F33.2	9	Was like a lombe offerd in sacrifice:
F34.1	1	Uppon the cross nailid I was for the,
F36.1	2	And theruppon straynyd he was in every vayne;
F36.1	11	So ripe and endles was her payne.
F36.2	4	That with dispaire for feer and dred I was nere forlore
F36.2	6	Her Son was so betraide,
F36.4	1	Unto the cross, handes and feete, nailid he was;
F36.4	2	Full boistusly in the mortess he was downe cast;
F36.4	4	The erth quakyd, the son was dark, whos lyght was past
F36.4	11	And of my dreme was sore agast.
F49b	1	In a slumbir late as I was,
F49.1	6	Fast I was naylyd for thyne offence;
H25.6	6	So trew of love was sche.
H27.2	2	Was wont to cast an nye;
H27.3	1	I was wont her to behold,
H31.1	6	Her hart was full of payne.
H31.2	3	Her dere hart was untrew;
H31.8	3	Her dere hart was full nere
H35.1	4	Lord, I was glad of it!
H35.2	4	But yet she was not dede.
H35.6	1	I was wery of the game,
H41.1	2	The lady mervelyd who was therat.
H41.3	1	The portres was a lady bryght;
H41.4	1	She asked hym what was his name;
H41.6	1	He was cownselled to breffe a byll
H82.2	4	That which then was most ther joy;
H101.2	1	When I was a wanton wench
H101.3	1	When I was come to
H105.3	1	Musyng on her manners, so ny mard was my mayne,
H105.3	2	Save it plesyd me so passyngly that past was my payn
H107.5	1	My lyf was lent

WASHE (1)

F34.5	6	May washe us all from surfettes reprovable.

WASTE (2)

R3.1	8	Ye will not make to huge a waste.
H25.8	4	And her smalle waste

WATCH (1)

F41.2	5	Go watch a bole, your bak is brode.

WATER (1)

F31.3	4	Both water and blode, ye, crucified an hevy case?

WAVER (1)

H29.3	1	She doth not waver as the wynde,

WAVIS (1)
F5   3   Full lyk to drowne in wavis of dystres,

WAY (7)
R19.2   7   And flo her way;
F41.4   1   'Walke forthe your way, ye cost me nought;
H25.2   5   Your love do way
H25.6   2   I tooke this way,
H31.4   2   In no maner a way
H41.8   2   We left them ther and went ower way.
H47.2   1   Do way, dere hart, not so.

WAYES (1)
F1   2   The more behynde, the nere my wayes ende;

WAYLING (1)
F31.2   4   With wepyng, wayling, ye, sownyng for wo.

WAYLYNG (1)
R11.1   2   My mynd also gretly waylyng;

WAYS (2)
H44.2   2   All ways wherby thay myght it rech;
H82.1   2   Frome Venus' ways banysht to be;

WE (37)
F18.2   8   Thus knowe we well.
F27b   5   Yff we three can agre in on.'
F27.4b 5   Yff we three can agre in oon.'
F27.6   4   Joyed may we be
F27.6b 1   'Nowe have we lovyd, and love will we
F27.6b 5   That we three be agrede in oon.'
F40.4   4   We shall both play, when we ar sole:
F44.1   10 Wherfore now syng we:
F44.2   10 Wherefore now syng we:
F44.3   8   To the we crye and call,
F44.3   10 Wherefore now syng we:
H23.3   2   Those shuld we covit wyn who can;
H25.1   5   Sen we depart
H28   3   Alas, pour hart, tyl that we mete agayne,
H29.6   2   To by deth departed we be;
H41b   3   To the grenewode must we go, alas!
H41.8   1   Thus how thay dyd we cannot say -
H41.8   2   We left them ther and went ower way.
H47.1   4   Tyl that we mete agayne.
H47.2   4   We shall mete when we may.
H47.5   4   Tyll that we mete agayne.
H64.2   1   Wherfor now we
H66.4   1   Then sone dyscusse that hens we must;
H66.4   2   Pray we to God and Seynt Mary
H68   2   I trust we shall mete oftener.
H79.2   6   Wherfor, then, shuld we yt excho?
H92.1   4   It ys not for hym we know yt well.
H92.2   4   But follow hys mynd in all that we may.

WE (cont.)
H92.7   1   Now unto God thys prayer we make,
H92.7   3   And that we may ower fauttes amend,
H97   1   Pray we to God that all may gyde
H109.1   2   We may us sport and not be sene;
H109.1b 4   That now in the feldes we may us sportt?
H109.2   4   Let us make one, though we be twayne!

WECHE (4)
R2.1   3   Weche Y have songe with wepyng yen tweyne
R2.2   1   For sche weche ys of all godely the best
R2.2   4   Into gret sekenesse weche holdith hur grevowsly;
R8   3   From thy servaund, the weche hathe plente

WED (1)
F41.4   5   Wed me or els I dye for thought!

WEDDE (1)
R1.2   2   Shall Y wedde no wiffe;

WEL (2)
F40.2   4   Myght wel be calde an conjuracion.
H56   2   I trust ryght wel of retorn agane.

WELCOM (1)
H27.3   4   Farewell, my joe, and welcom payne.

WELCUM (2)
F33.3   9   Cum when thou lyst, welcum to me!
H107.5   4   Welcum, fortune.

WELE (1)
F23.1   4   That was my wele is now my most grevaunce.

WELFARE (2)
H31.5   3   Adew, all my welfare!
H104.4   2   With your welfare,

WELL (30)
F2   1   A, a, my herte, I knowe yow well;
F2   3   Nay, nay, nay, nay, I warne the well,
F4   5   Cannot be well for to be wisht:
F4   6   To thynk my sorows, well may I complayne;
F7.2   4   Thynkyth my hart can be well payd
F18.2   8   Thus knowe we well.
F27b   3   'I love another as well as ye.'
F27.4b   3   'I love anothyr as well as ye.'
F27.5   5   That day to se it lykyth well me.'
F31b   4   My witt nor reson may hit well fynd:
F32.3   1   Well I remember his wowndis were full smert,
F34.2   2   Loke on them well, and have compassion;
F34.4   2   Cum to scole; record well this lesson:
F38b   1   A, myn hert, remembir the well,
F38.1   1   A myn hart, remembir the well

WELL (cont.)

F39b	4	I dare well say,
F45.2	2	The gelofir gent, that she well knewe;
H25.10	4	In well and wo
H29.2	1	I love her well with hart and mynd;
H35.7	3	I thynk his bow ys well unbent,
H49.3	3	In faith my lady lovith me well;
H65b	4	For shote ryght well I may.
H65.1	4	And shot well enough:
H65.3	4	As well as any that ever I see:
H65.4	4	As well as any in May:
H66.2	2	How well dyd ye your yough carry?
H92.1	4	It ys not for hym we know yt well.
H92.6	2	As well vices as vertuus to ensew;
H92.7	2	That this rude play may well be take,
H105.1	3	So pretyly, so pertly, so passingly well apayd,

WELLCUM (1)

F24.5	4	Wellcum, fortune.

WELLIS (1)

F34.5	4	That thi fyve wellis plentuus of fusion,

WELTH (1)

F26	4	With welth and wordly joy long to endure,

WELYNG (1)

F24.1	6	Of such welyng

WENCH (1)

H101.2	1	When I was a wanton wench

WENDE (2)

R3.2	8	My moder cam in, or that ye wende.'
F1	4	The lyghter leefe, the lother for to wende;

WENE (2)

R3.1	5	'Wene ye that everybody lest to play?'
R15.5	5	Men wene I be

WENT (5)

F24.5	5	Yet I ne went
H35.5	1	To the covert bothe thay went,
H35.6	2	I went to tavern to drynk;
H41.8	2	We left them ther and went ower way.
H107.5	5	Yet I ne went

WEPE (6)

R15.7	2	But soore Y wepe
F30.1	6	And sore did wepe.
F32.1	7	Now blessid Lady, wepe no more:
F32.2	8	Now, blessid Lady, wepe [no more:
F32.3	8	Now, blessid Lady, wepe no more:
F32.4	8	Now blessid Lady, wepe no more:

WEPID (1)
F29.2   4   That childe wepid alone.

WEPT (3)
F36.1   4   His modir dere tendirly wept and cowde not
                        refrayne
F36.1   8   Tho I wept and sore did complayne
H25.7   1   At last sche wept;

WEPYNG (5)
R2.1   3   Weche Y have songe with wepyng yen tweyne
F31.2   4   With wepyng, wayling, ye, sownyng for wo.
F32.4   2   Lay downe all thi wepyng, let no more be sene!
F36.4   8   Wepyng and wrang her handes fast.
F38.2   1   With wepyng teris most lamentable

WERE (10)
F18.2   1   Hit were to grete pite
F21   3   Then bownden were I such on faythfully
F25.2   2   Bounden were I
F32.3   1   Well I remember his wowndis were full smert,
F37.2   1   Where art thou, Nature, that wont were me to store
F40.1   4   But it were an angell of the Trinite?
F40.3   3   Yff she and I were together alone,
F46.2   1   One is good, but mo were bettyr
F49.1   4   Where thou were thrall, to make the free.
H51.8   2   It were pete thay shuld optayne;

WERKE (1)
R3.1   4   Leff werke a twenty-a-devell away!

WERS (1)
F1   3   The more I sech, the wers can I fynde;

WERY (1)
H35.6   1   I was wery of the game,

WERYNESS (1)
F5   1   My wofull hart in paynfull weryness,

WETE (1)
H31.6   4   With terys wete

WETHIR (1)
F44b   1   From stormy wyndis and grevous wethir,

WETTE (1)
R3.2   1   After asay then may ye wette;

WHAN (2)
R19.3   1   Whan she was gone
F7.1   2   Whan that desert lakkyth remedy,

WHAT (58)

R3.1	6	Abyde awhile! What have ye haste?
R3.2	5	What do ye here within oure spence?
R3.3	2	'Be Criste, Y nelle, what ses the man?
R10.5	4	What remedy?
R11.1	3	Alas, alas, what remedy?
R11.2	3	Alas, alas, what remedy?
R11.3	3	Alas, alas, [what remedy?
R11.4	3	Alas, alas, what remedy?
R13.3	5	Myn hert and love; what wyll she more?
R18.3	1	Now what shall Y say meis parentibus
R19.1	9	What doyst thou here?
F3	1	What causyth me wofull thoughtis to thynk
F7.1	1	O my desyre, what eylyth the,
F7.1	8	O my desyre, what eylyth the?
F7.2	8	O my desyre, what aylyth the?
F14	1	Alas, it is I that wote nott what to say,
F23.1	5	What causyth this but only yowre plesaunce
F24.1	8	What may I gess?
F27.4	2	'What is his name that thou chosen has?
F30.1	12	Say what ye wolde.'
F33.3	7	What myght I suffir more
F34b	4	What woldist thou have?
F40b	3	Alak, good Jhoane, what may you please?
F40.1	5	Alak, good Jhoone, [what may you please?
F40.2	5	Alak, good [Jhoone, what may you please?
F40.3	2	What shulde I say? My mynde is gone.
F40.3	5	Alak, good Jhoan, [what may you please?
F40.4	5	Alak, good Jhoan, [what may you please?
F41.1	4	What, will ye do nothing but play?
F41.3	2	What, wolde ye frompill me now? fy, fy!
F41.3	3	'What, and ye shal be my piggesnye?'
F49.1	3	What paynys I sofferd, I the ensure,
H12	1	Alas, what shall I do for love,
H12	2	For love, alasse, what shall I do,
H25.4	3	What sayd sche then to me?
H25.5	2	What remedy?
H29.6	3	Happe what wyll happ, fall what shall,
H30	1	Alac, alac, what shall I do,
H35.6	4	What do yow meane or thynk?
H41.4	1	She asked hym what was his name;
H41.5	1	She said, 'Desyre, what do ye here?'
H64.2	11	What remedy?
H102.2	3	Alas, alas, what word ys this?
H103b	1	What remedy, what remedy?
H103b	2	Such is fortune! What remedy?
H103.1	4	What remedy, what remedy?
H103.1	5	Such is fortune! What remedy?
H103.2	4	What remedy, what remedy?
H103.2	5	Such is fortune! What remedy?
H103.3	4	What remedy, what remedy?
H103.3	5	Such is fortune! What remedy?
H107.1	8	What may I gesse?
H109.3	1	Ye have my hert; sey what ye wyll.

WHATE (1)
F12   1   Benedicite! Whate dremyd I this nyght?

WHATSOEVER (2)
H92.1   3   For whatsoever they do hym tell,
H92.2   3   But I wyll not so whatsoever thay say,

WHELE (1)
R13.2   5   And no help but Fortunys whele,

WHEN (27)
R3.3   7   But hadde Y wyste when ye bygan,
R15.6   5   When clothis be downe
R19.1   6   When Y cam ther
R20.3   1   When Y fynde you stedfast and certayne,
F3   3   For when nature wold oft that I shulde wynk,
F17   7   When that they knowe I am sory.
F18.2   5   When that ye do lye,
F32.1   4   Yet when oure Laidis Son was slayne
F32.2   2   When Jewis with treson to deth thi son ladde;
F33.3   9   Cum when thou lyst, welcum to me!
F36.1   6   When I sawe hym so spilt,
F36.4   5   When he lamentable
F39.1   2   When she me bas,
F40.4   4   We shall both play, when we ar sole:
F43.4   1   When rutterkyn from borde will ryse
H25.8   1   When I sawe this
H33.2   3   When flowerys cannot be sene,
H47.2   4   We shall mete when we may.
H47.3   1   When I remembyr me
H50.4   1   My soverayne lorde when that I mete,
H62.3   4   When I shuld shoote I myse;
H62.5   2   When I shulde maydyns kysse,
H64.1   7   For when one sole
H101.2   1   When I was a wanton wench
H101.3   1   When I was come to
H104.1   4   But when ye mysse,
H104.2   1   When ye be hens,

WHER (8)
R10.5   5   Wher Y wold fayn,
F14   7   Wher that is usyd can be no surance.
H31.7   5   Wher I shall dwell,
H35.5   2   For I fownd wher she lay;
H51.9   1   For often tymes wher they do sewe
H64.2   7   Wher love so sewith,
H66.3   4   I love trew wher I dyd mary:
H104b   1   Wher be ye

WHERAS (1)
R10.3   1   Wheras I sought,

WHERBY (2)
H23.4   2   Wherby actyvenesse oon may utter.

WHERBY (cont.)
H44.2   2   All ways wherby thay myght it rech;

WHERE (9)
F16   3   And sone to sende where they faynest wolde be,
F17   5   I wote nott where I may complayn;
F17   6   For where I shulde, they be mery,
F27.2   1   'Ther is a floure where so he be,
F37.2   1   Where art thou, Nature, that wont were me to store
F39.1   4   I wote not where
F49.1   4   Where thou were thrall, to make the free.
H63.2   3   My hart ys yours where ever that I go;
H104b   3   And where be ye gone?

WHEREAS (2)
F33.2   7   Whereas never man was so
F37.1   5   Whereas I am ybid with bodily rest;

WHEREEVER (1)
F46.3   5   And love her only whereever she gone:

WHEREFOR (1)
F2   8   Wherefor, my hart, lett be, lett be!

WHEREFORE (3)
F44.2   10   Wherefore now syng we:
F44.3   10   Wherefore now syng we:
H15   4   And know no cause wherefore.

WHEREVER (1)
R19.3   9   Wherever she be

WHEREVYR (1)
F28   1   Complayne I may wherevyr I go,

WHEREWITH (1)
F36.2   10   Wherewith she fell downe with paynys so smert;

WHERFOR (11)
F11   6   Wherfor I am and shal be tyll I dye
H18   4   Wherfor to her I me complayn, hey now!
H34.3   1   Wherfor to love and be not loved
H50.1   4   Wherfor my hart I hym beqwest,
H64.2   1   Wherfor now we
H65.2   1   Wherfor shuld I hang up myne arrow
H65.3   1   Wherfor shuld I hang up my horne
H65.4   1   Wherfor shuld I tye up my hownd
H79.2   6   Wherfor, then, shuld we yt excho?
H82.2   5   Wherfor indede the trouth to say
H92.6   3   Wherfor be thes he must be gydyd

WHERFORE (8)
F19   7   Wherfore I hope to fynd a speciall remedy
F23.2   3   Wherfore of ryght ye shuld my greffe complayne,

WHERFORE (cont.)
```
F44.1    10  Wherfore now syng we:
F44.2     1  Wherfore, good Lord, syth of thi creacion
H25.3     4  Wherfore, swete hart,
H31.3     6  Wherfore my hart will brest.
H65.1     1  Wherfore shuld I hang up my bow
H109.3    2  Wherfore ye muste my mynde fulfyll,
```

WHERTO (1)
```
H47.1     1  Wherto shuld I expresse
```

WHERWITH (1)
```
F36.4    10  Wherwith sodenly anon I awoke,
```

WHETHER (1)
```
H109b     2  Mayde, whether go you?
```

WHI (6)
```
F31.3     1  A Jhesu, whi suffyrd thou such entretyng,
F32b      1  Affraid, alas, and whi so sodenli?
F32b      2  Whi so dismaid?
F32b      3  Whi shuld she hevy be?
F34.1     8  Whi art thou froward, syth I am mercyable?
F34.4     5  Whi did I this? To save the from prison.
```

WHICH (24)
```
R13.1     4  To her which ys my yoyus plesure;
R13.2     1  The sterre of Venus which I call her ye,
R13.2     6  And only she which my wound begunne;
F5        2  Which hath byn long plongyng with thought unseyne,
F13       4  To her only which is myn yes fode,
F20       3  Which that passyth my mynde for to express
F20       6  Which that all men knowith, both more and less;
F36.2     9  'Yet thou are unkynd, which sleith myn hert,'
F44.1     2  Which formyd hast of thi most speciall grace
F44.1     5  Which of aliaunce
F44.3     3  For this yong prince, which is and daily shal
F47.2     5  Which crye and call unto your Majeste.
F48.3     5  Into witness of which thyng
H44.4     1  Which puttes them to more and more
H44.5     2  But let them tell which love doth gett.
H44.6     2  Which of ther loves doth get them grace?
H44.7     1  And unto them which doth it know
H50.1     3  Of which four tymes he dyd it take;
H51.3     1  Or elles from her which is her hayre;
H79.1     6  But those be thay which can no skyll:
H82.2     4  That which then was most ther joy;
H103.1    2  Which dayly encressith more and more;
H103.3    3  For which my hart is lyk to brest,
H106.2    2  Exilide for ever which is my payne;
```

WHILE (2)
```
F25.2     4  While I endure,
F38.2     3  I will axe grace while I am able,
```

WHILES (1)
R1.2   1   All the whiles that Y may my bowe bende

WHILL (2)
H29.5   4   Whill I leve her name for me.
H40   3   To love her sure whill I am levyng,

WHILLES (1)
H50b   1   Whilles lyve or breth is in my brest

WHITE (3)
F27.5   2   'The red or the white? Shewe his colour!'
F27.6   1   'I love the rose, both red and white.'
F45.2   4   And said, 'The white rose is most trewe

WHO (14)
R12.1   10   Who shall me lett?
R12.2   8   Than who can say
F34b   2   Who is that that dothe me call?
F40.1   2   Good Lord, who may a goodlyer be
F42.1   1   Who shall have my fayre lady?
F42.1   2   Who but I, who but I, who but I,
H23.3   2   Those shuld we covit wyn who can;
H33.4   3   Who hath my hart trewly,
H41.1   2   The lady mervelyd who was therat.
H51.1   2   Who lovyth not wantith corage.
H51.7   2   Who love dysdaynyth ys all of the village.
H51.10 2   Chaunge who so wyll, I wyll be none.

WHOM (7)
F7.2   7   In whom ther is no remedy;
F22   2   Whom I serve and shall as long,
F26   3   In whom all vertu is knytt withouten varyaunce,
F27b   1   'I love, I love, and whom love ye?'
F27.4b 1   'Now have I lovyd, and whom love ye?'
F39b   2   Whom I now seke
F47.1   2   Whom God hath chose oure gyde to be,

WHOME (3)
F49.1   2   Whome I did make so lyke unto me,
H44.5   1   The faut in whome I cannot sett;
H103.3 1   O my swet hart, whome I love best,

WHOS (2)
F36.4   4   The erth quakyd, the son was dark, whos lyght was
                 past
H103.3 2   Whos unkyndnes hath me opprest,

WHOSE (2)
F8   5   Through whose swete showris now sprong ther is ayen
H108   4   Whose unkyndnes hath kyld myn hart;

WHOSO (4)
H22   1   Whoso that wyll hymselff applye

WHOSO (cont.)
H34.1   1   Whoso that wyll all feattes optayne,
H51.10   1   For whoso lovith shuld love butt oone;
H79.1   1   Whoso that wyll for grace sew,

WHOSOEVER (1)
H51.2   1   And whosoever may love gete,

WHY (23)
R3.2   2   Why blame ye me withoute offence?
R10.1   4   Alas, why so?
R13.3   1   She hath me hurt; why shold she not hele,
F6.1   3   And wote not why
F13   1   To complayne me, alas, why shulde I so?
F14   2   For why I stond as he that is abusyd;
F17   1   But why am I so abusyd?
F18.1   4   And wote ye why?
F31.4   3   And why, good Lord? Express thi mynd!
F33.2   2   I love the, then love me; why slepist thou? Awake!
F34b   6   Why, lovyst thou me?
F34.2   8   Why art thou froward sith I am merciable?
F34.3   6   Syth I am kynd, why are thou unstable?
F36.3   5   'Why than so depe morne ye?'
H49.2   2   Alac, why is she so?
H102b   1   Why shall not I?
H102b   2   Why shall not I to my lady
H102b   3   Why shall not I be trew?
H102b   4   Why shall not I?
H102.1   5   Why shall not I?
H102.2   5   Why shall not I?
H106.4   6   Nay, nay, for why? Ther ys no space.
H109.1b 3   Why, wyll ye nott geve me no comfortt,

WHYCH (3)
R10.1   7   Whych causyth my mone;
H23.2   2   Whych one may use, and vice denye;
H23.6   2   In goode dysporttys whych it dothe fend.

WHYGHT (1)
H17   6   Of the red rose and the whyght.

WHYLE (1)
H63.1   3   Frome yow a whyle must I depart;

WHYLS (2)
H67.2   7   Whyls lyf endur,
H108   6   But leve in payne whyls I endure

WHYTT (1)
H35.1   2   And yet she bledes no whytt;

WIFF (1)
F30.1   10   Joseph seyd, 'Wiff,

WIFFE (1)
R1.2   2   Shall Y wedde no wiffe;

WIGHT (1)
F32.2   5   To joy of every wordlis wight,

WILDE (1)
R5   5   That ye wilde fuchesaffe to have mercy on me

WILL (32)
R3.1   8   Ye will not make to huge a waste.
F13   5   Trustyng sumtyme that she will chaunge her mode
F19   4   And so sodenly will chaunge in every degre;
F21   6   Yet will I me trust to fortune applye;
F21   7   Hough that evyr it will happ I wote nere I.
F27.6b   1   'Nowe have we lovyd, and love will we
F28   5   I-wiss yet will I not me complayne
F29.4   3   For them to save, it is my will;
F30.2   6   My Fadir's will.
F34b   10 'A, I will, I will, gentyll Jhesu'.
F38.1   7   I crye God mercy, I will amend.
F38.2   3   I will axe grace while I am able,
F38.2   5   Me to amend I will me hye
F38.2   7   I crye God mercy, I will amend.
F40.1   3   In favoure and in facion (lo, will ye se?)
F40.3   4   I-wis, she will not gyve me a bone:
F41.1   4   What, will ye do nothing but play?
F41.3   5   I will not be japed bodely.
F43.4   1   When rutterkyn from borde will ryse
F43.4   2   He will piss a galon-pot full at twise
F46b   2   Will I love and shall I love,
F46b   3   Will I love and shall I love
F46.3   1   But I will do as I saide furst,
F46.3   4   Forever yff she will trew be,
F48.2   1   If any man will say here agayne
H31.3   4   And will not rew,
H31.3   6   Wherfore my hart will brest.
H49.2   4   And yet she will say no.
H49.3   4   She will change for no new.
H62.6   1   Now will I take to me my bedes
H65b   3   And foster will I be styll

WILLFULLNESS (1)
F7.1   3   In willfullness so for to be,

WILLFULLY (1)
F36.3   2   He willfully doth suffir for love speciall

WILLYNG (2)
F24.3   8   Willyng to dye.
H107.3   8   Willyng to dye.

WILT (1)
F48.1   2   To the, and thou wilt be repentant;

306

WIS (2)
F6.2   5   That I wis
H49.2   1   My lady is unkynde I wis.

WISDOME (1)
F47.2   2   Wisdome with strenkyth and soveraynte

WISE (5)
R9   3   Arested hathe my herte in sodeyn wise,
F23.2   6   Wolde in no wise for joy nor hevyness
F33.2   8   Entretid, thus in most cruell wise
F37.1   2   My mode is changid in every wise,
F43.3   3   Till his brayne be as wise as a duk;

WISHT (1)
F4   5   Cannot be well for to be wisht:

WISSH (1)
F7.1   7   Butt yff hit be to wissh for one:

WITH (97)
R2.1   3   Weche Y have songe with wepyng yen tweyne
R6   4   Ever to plese hym with all myghth,
R7   1   Thow man, envired with temptacion,
R9   2   That with yeure beute and fresche plesaunce pure
R9   9   Thorffe with yeur beute that Y most love and prise.
R10.3   5   Alas, with thought
R12.1   1   Passetyme with good cumpanye
R12.3   1   Cumpany with honeste
R14.1   3   With a dulfull chere here I make my mone,
R14.2   3   With a dulfull chere [here I make my mone,
R15.3   5   Goten with child
R15.4   3   With gode devyse,
R15.4   5   With sorow allso,
R15.5   3   With hert onfayn;
R18.2   2   Full oft with you solebam ludere;
R18.2   4   With right goed cause incipeo flere.
R18.3   2   Bycause Y lay with quidam clericus?
R18.4   1   With the seid child, quid faciam?
R19.1   2   She satt and sang with notes clere;
R19.3   4   With sorowfull grone,
R20.2   3   With hert Y wyll you plece and your love attayne:
F1   6   Thoo I go lose, yet am I teyd with a lyne:
F2   7   With my desyre tyll I be spent:
F5   2   Which hath byn long plongyng with thought unseyne,
F6.1   6   For with twayne
F8   6   A rose most riall with levis fressh of hew,
F11   7   Your trewe servant with thought, hart and body.
F18.1   2   With doubyll delyng
F18.1   5   For ye with your faynyng
F20   2   With vertu connyng her maner is lede,
F21   2   In stedfast fayth and trouth with assuraunce;
F23.2   2   My hart is yours with gret assuraunce.
F23.2   4   And with pite have me in remembraunce

WITH (cont.)

F24.3	1	With displesaunce
F25.1	4	With wofulness;
F25.2	6	With hart, body,
F25.3	2	With good entent,
F25.3	4	With thoughtis trew;
F26	2	Endewid with vertu and goodly plesaunce,
F26	4	With welth and wordly joy long to endure,
F30b	4	With a lawghyng chere.'
F31.2	4	With wepyng, wayling, ye, sownyng for wo.
F32.2	2	When Jewis with treson to deth thi son ladde;
F32.4	6	He bought us with his precious blode:
F33.1	1	Beholde me, I pray the, with all thi hole reson,
F33.1	6	With sharpe corde sore fretid,
F33.2	4	With paynys my vaynys constraynyd to crake;
F36.1	1	To Calvery he bare his cross with doulfull payne,
F36.2	2	With pale visage tremlyng she stode her child before
F36.2	4	That with dispaire for feer and dred I was nere forlore
F36.2	7	With wondis sore araid,
F36.2	10	Wherewith she fell downe with paynys so smert;
F37.1	5	Whereas I am ybid with bodily rest;
F37.4	5	With all good sowlis to cause me lyve in rest.
F38.2	1	With wepyng teris most lamentable
F40.2	1	Her contynaunce with her lynyacion,
F41.1	7	With manerly Margery, milk and ale.
F41.2	7	With manerly [Margery, milk and ale.]
F41.3	7	With manerly Margery, [milke and ale.]
F41.4	7	With manerly Margery, milke and ale.
F41.4	9	With manerly Margery, [milke and ale.]
F43.2	3	Besmerde with grece abowte his disshe,
F44.2	4	With joy to rejose his dew enerytaunce,
F44.3	4	Be thi servaunt with all his hart so fre.
F47.1	3	With gyfftes grete and evydent
F47.1	6	Enforcyng yourselfe with all your myght
F47.2	2	Wisdome with strenkyth and soveraynte
F48b	6	Upon the crosse with woundis smert
F49.1	5	Upon the cross with naylis thre
H25.10	6	With her that morneth for me.
H27.3	3	And now with syghs manyfold,
H27.4	3	Ther myght no joys compare with it
H28	1	With sorowfull syghs and grevos payne
H29.2	1	I love her well with hart and mynd;
H31.3	3	And thynkes with her to rest,
H31.6	4	With terys wete
H33.2	2	With ive all alone
H34.7	2	With dysdayne bothe falce and subtell.
H40	4	My hart with her ever shall be.
H44.3	1	Butt envy reynyth with such dysdayne,
H50.2	3	With spere and swerd at the barryoure
H50.2	4	As hardy with the hardyest,
H50.4	3	My hart with joe that I be hete
H50.4	5	With hart and body to love best

WITH (cont.)
H51.5   2   But mynd afformyth with full consent.
H51.6   2   Myne ey with hart doth me so juge.
H82.1   3   Thow that age with gret dysdayne
H92.3   4   Honest myrth with vertus pastance.
H92.5   1   With goode order, councell and equite,
H96.1   3   With spers and sheldys on goodly horsys lyght,
H101.2   3   Thes cowrtyers with ther amorus
H104.2   2   With your absence
H104.4   1   Thus with my care
H104.4   2   With your welfare,
H106.2   3   My payne with hope hath me begyled;
H107.3   1   With dysplesance
H109.1b 1   Nay, in good feyth, I wyll not melle with you;

WITHDRAWE (1)
R8   2   And onse withdrawe thy adversite

WITHIN (3)
R3.2   5   What do ye here within oure spence?
H24   1   The thowghtes within my brest,
H106.3   4   Of all the sorowes within my hart;

WITHOUTE (7)
R3.2   2   Why blame ye me withoute offence?
R15.5   2   Withoute a frynd
F6.2   2   Withoute offens,
F16   4   Withoute disease or adversyte.
F32.3   4   All was on red blod withoute any shirt;
F43.1   2   In a cloke withoute cote or gowne,
F48.1   3   Hevyn bliss thyn eritage withoute endyng

WITHOUTEN (2)
F24.2   6   Withouten less
F26   3   In whom all vertu is knytt withouten varyaunce,

WITHOUTYN (1)
F26   5   I pray God hartely, withoutyn mysaventure.

WITHOWT (13)
R20.2   2   Withowt cause, Gode knowyth; Y do not fayne.
H31.1   5   Withowt denay
H31.2   2   Withowt trespas
H31.4   5   Withowt denay,
H34.1   2   In love he must be withowt dysdayne,
H40   1   I love trewly withowt feynyng;
H51.6   1   Thus am I fyxed withowt gruge,
H64.1   1   Withowt dyscord
H64.2   6   Withowt denay.
H92.5   3   For withowt ther goode gydaunce
H103.1   3   Thus withowt comfort I am forlore;
H103.2   3   Insaciently withowt recure;
H106.2   7   Endure, alas, withowt hope of recure.

WITHOWTE (1)
H106.1 7 Withowte hope or comfort off redresse.

WITHOWTYN (1)
H107.2 6 Withowtyn les

WITHSTONE (1)
F29.5 2 For mannys gilt is not withstone,

WITNESS (9)
F39.2   7   Sis is witness
F48.2   7   Witness, the daye turnyd to nyghth,
F48.2   8   Witness, the son that lost his lyghth,
F48.2   9   Witness, the vale that then did ryve,
F48.2 10   Witness, the bodies that rose from deth to lyve.
F48.3   1   Witness, the erthe that did quake,
F48.3   2   Witness, stonys that all to-brake,
F48.3   3   Witness, Mari, wittness, Seynt Jhon,
F48.3   5   Into witness of which thyng

WITT (1)
F31b   4 My witt nor reson may hit well fynd:

WITTNESS (3)
F13   7 Syth for my trouth she nedith no wittness.
F48.3   3 Witness, Mari, wittness, Seynt Jhon,
F48.3   4 And othir wittness, many one;

WO (3)
F31.2   4 With wepyng, wayling, ye, sownyng for wo.
H25.10 4 In well and wo
H27.2   4 Alas, for wo I dye, I dye.

WODE (1)
H35b   2 Ther ys a do in yonder wode; in faith, she woll
              not dy

WODES (1)
R1.2   3 I shall bygge me a boure atte the wodes ende,

WOE (2)
R11.4   2 Iff my sorow and woe she knew:
R15.4   2 Lefe of my woe

WOFFULL (1)
F39.3   4 Woffull am I.

WOFFULLY (5)
F33b   1   Woffully araid,
F33b   6   Woffully araide.
F33.1 10   Woffully araid.
F33.2 10   Woffully arayd.
F33.3 10   Woffully araide.

WOFULL (7)
R2.1   1   My wofull hert of all gladnesse baryeyne
F3   1   What causyth me wofull thoughtis to thynk
F5   1   My wofull hart in paynfull weryness,
F24.2   4   My wofull chaunce;
F36.3   7   I must nedis wofull be,
H106.4   1   Thus may ye se my wofull chance,
H107.2   4   My wofull chance;

WOFULNESS (1)
F25.1   4   With wofulness;

WOL (1)
H27.4   2   As wol to God I cowld,

WOLD (16)
R10.5   5   Wher Y wold fayn,
R11.4   1   I trow on me she wold rewe
F3   3   For when nature wold oft that I shulde wynk,
F48.2   4   Yet wold Y eft be all to-torne.]
H25.6   5   Stynt wold sche not,
H29.1   3   Of her godnes than wold I wryght;
H41.2   1   To call the porter he wold not blyn;
H41.7   1   Kyndnes said she wold yt bere,
H41.7   2   And Pyte said she wold be ther.
H44.2   1   Nobyll men then wold suer enserch
H79.2   2   They wold that other shuld yt dysdayne;
H82.1   4   Wold have yough love to refrayn,
H82.2   2   And wold then have goten grace,
H92.2   1   For they wold have hym hys libertye refrayne
H92.4   2   Though that dysdaynars wold therin put error,
H101.1   4   I wold not do amysse.

WOLDE (22)
R3.2   7   Y wolde not yette for furty pence
R3.3   8   Be Criste, Y wolde have schytte the dore!'
R4   3   And thogh Y wolde, Y koude me noght refrayne
R19.2   8   She wolde assay
F6.3   5   It wolde me make
F7.1   5   Thoo that ye wolde untill ye dye
F9   1   Love fayne wolde I;
F9   6   I wolde bynde me
F16   3   And sone to sende where they faynest wolde be,
F21   1   I love, loved, and loved wolde I be
F22   4   Absens it is that wolde me wrong;
F23.2   1   Nor nought cowde have, wolde I nevyr so fayne!
F23.2   6   Wolde in no wise for joy nor hevyness
F25.1   5   I wolde full fayne
F30.1   12   Say what ye wolde.'
F31b   3   Wolde take on Hym humanite?
F31.1   4   And wolde so take mortalite!
F31.2   3   And suffyr wolde payne as sorowfull thought,
F40.2   2   To hym that wolde of such recreacion
F41.3   2   What, wolde ye frompill me now? fy, fy!

311

WOLDE (cont.)
F48b   8 And for I wolde have thyne heritage agayne,
H51.9   2 Thay hynder lovers that wolde be trew.

WOLDIST (1)
F34b   4 What woldist thou have?

WOLL (7)
R1.1   4 Foster woll Y be no more.
R12.1   3 Grugge so woll, but noon denye;
R12.1   4 So God be plecyd, this lyve woll I;
R12.2   1 Yowth woll have nedes dalyaunce,
R19.3   7 That away woll flee,
R20.3   2 Y am right glad, tristyng hit woll remanyne;
H35b   2 Ther ys a do in yonder wode; in faith, she woll
               not dy

WOMAN (2)
F36.3   8 As a woman terrestriall
H34.5   2 To woman also, I thynk, the same.

WOMANHODE (1)
F20   4 Of her bounte, beaute and womanhode;

WOMEN (3)
F18.2   2 That women truly
H29.5   1 Lernyng it war for women all
H49.3   2 For I fynd women trew;

WOMMANLY (2)
R5   2 The godely and wommanly bewte
R9   1 Fayre and discrete, fresche wommanly figure,

WON (1)
F3   5 That be won thought my rest from me doth go.

WONDES (1)
F34.5   5 Callid thi fyve wondes by computacion,

WONDIS (1)
F36.2   7 With wondis sore araid,

WONDYD (1)
R13.2   4 That wondyd soere myself Y fele,

WONE (2)
F24.5   8 Such is her wone.
H107.5   8 Such ys her wone!

WONT (3)
F37.2   1 Where art thou, Nature, that wont were me to store
H27.2   2 Was wont to cast an nye;
H27.3   1 I was wont her to behold,

WOO (5)
```
  F3      2   Syn thoughtis byn cheff causers of my woo;
  F11     1   That was my woo is nowe my most gladness;
  F13     3   But be constraynt, now must I shew my woo
  F23.1   1   That was my joy is now my woo and payne;
  F33.2   6   Thus wrappid all in woo,
```

WORD (1)
```
  H102.2  3   Alas, alas, what word ys this?
```

WORDE (2)
```
  F17     2   Syth worde and dede is take in vayne,
  F36.2  11   Unneth on worde cowde she speke more.
```

WORDES (1)
```
  R15.3   2   Spake wordes myld
```

WORDLE (2)
```
  F24.1   5   This wordle beyng
  F31.2   1   He that wrought this wordle of nought,
```

WORDLIS (2)
```
  F31.1   3   Inmortal, inpassible, the wordlis lyght,
  F32.2   5   To joy of every wordlis wight,
```

WORDLY (1)
```
  F26     4   With welth and wordly joy long to endure,
```

WORLD (1)
```
  H107.1  5   This world beyng
```

WORLDE (2)
```
  R16.1   1   The burne ys this worlde blynde
  F12     2   Methought the worlde was turnyd up so downe,
```

WORNE (2)
```
  F33.3   1   Off sharpe thorne I have worne a crowne on my hede,
  H62.3   2   Myne arow ny worne ys;
```

WORS (1)
```
  H34.3   2   Is wors then deth? Let it be proved!
```

WORST (1)
```
  R12.3   6   The worst eschew,
```

WORTHY (1)
```
  F27.6b  3   Most worthy it is, as thynkyth me.
```

WORTHYEST (1)
```
  H50.3   4   But of a trewth he worthyest
```

WOT (1)
```
  H31.2   5   I wot he hace
```

WOTE (7)
F6.1   3 And wote not why
F14   1 Alas, it is I that wote nott what to say,
F17   5 I wote nott where I may complayn;
F18.1   4 And wote ye why?
F21   7 Hough that evyr it will happ I wote nere I.
F39.1   4 I wote not where
H62.5   1 My berd ys so hard, God wote,

WOULD (1)
H106.1 4 My lyffe as one that dye would fayne;

WOUND (1)
R13.2   6 And only she which my wound begunne;

WOUNDE (1)
F48.3   8 The wounde in my harte the seale it is,

WOUNDIS (1)
F48b   6 Uppon the crosse with woundis smert

WOWND (1)
F30.2 11 Many a wownd

WOWNDES (1)
F34.2   1 My blody wowndes downe railyng be this tre,

WOWNDIS (1)
F32.3   1 Well I remember his wowndis were full smert,

WRANG (1)
F36.4   8 Wepyng and wrang her handes fast.

WRAPPE (1)
R20.1   3 That ye loth Y love -- wrappe that yn your trayne!

WRAPPID (1)
F33.2   6 Thus wrappid all in woo,

WRONG (3)
R19.1 10 Hyt ys grete wrong.'
F22   4 Absens it is that wolde me wrong;
H66.3   3 I hurt no man, I do no wrong;

WRONGFULLY (8)
F6.1   1 Demyd wrongfully
F6.1   7 Demyd wrongfully.
F6.2   1 Demyd wrongfully
F6.2   7 Demyd wrongfully.
F6.3   1 Demyd wrongfully
F6.3   7 To be demyd wrongfully.
F6.4   1 Demyd wrongfully
F6.4   7 Demyd wrongfully.

WROUGHT (3)
  F29.5   3   For thou art he that hath all wrought,
  F31.2   1   He that wrought this wordle of nought,
  F41.4   4   Yet for his love that all hath wrought

WRY (2)
  F24.4   6   Fortune doth wry
  H107.4   6   Fortune doth wry

WRYGHT (1)
  H29.1   3   Of her godnes than wold I wryght;

WYDE (1)
  R19.2   4   To a forest wyde

WYGHT (1)
  F46.1   1   Love is naturall to every wyght,

WYL (2)
  H62.1   3   Foster wyl I be no more
  H62.2   1   Hange I wyl my nobyl bow

WYLDERNES (3)
  R15.1   1   In wyldernes
  R15.8   4   In wyldernes,
  H31.9   6   In wyldernes alone.

WYLL (19)
  R13.3   5   Myn hert and love; what wyll she more?
  R18.3   3   They wyll me bete cum virgis ac fustibus
  R20.2   3   With hert Y wyll you plece and your love attayne:
  H22   1   Whoso that wyll hymselff applye
  H29.6   3   Happe what wyll happ, fall what shall,
  H34.1   1   Whoso that wyll all feattes optayne,
  H39   4   Now after wyll I go;
  H41.6   2   And shew my lady hys oune wyll.
  H51.10   2   Chaunge who so wyll, I wyll be none.
  H62.6   3   And pray I wyll for them that may,
  H75   9   And thus I wyll endure;
  H79.1   1   Whoso that wyll for grace sew,
  H92.2   3   But I wyll not so whatsoever thay say,
  H109b   4   Than at the medow I wyll you mete
  H109.1   3   And yf ye wyll, I shall consent;
  H109.1b   1   Nay, in good feyth, I wyll not melle with you;
  H109.1b   3   Why, wyll ye nott geve me no comfortt,
  H109.3   1   Ye have my hert; sey what ye wyll.

WYN (1)
  H23.3   2   Those shuld we covit wyn who can;

WYND (2)
  R10.6   3   Turnyng as the wynd,
  R15.5   1   Now may I wynd

WYNDE (1)
H29.3   1   She doth not waver as the wynde,

WYNDIS (1)
F44b   1   From stormy wyndis and grevous wethir,

WYNK (1)
F3   3   For when nature wold oft that I shulde wynk,

WYNTER (1)
H33b   3   Thow wynter blastys blow never so hye,

WYSE (2)
R15.4   6   And play the wyse.
H47.3   3   It may in no wyse agre

WYSSE (2)
H109b   7   I wysse my mother then shall us se!
H109.1b 6   I wysse my mothyr than shall us se!

WYSTE (1)
R3.3   7   But hadde Y wyste when ye bygan,

WYTH (2)
H16   3   Wyth dowbyl sorow complayn I must
H51.4   1   Wyth ee and mynd doth both agre;

WYTT (1)
H29.1   1   Iff I had wytt for to endyght

Y (57)
R1.1   1   Y have ben a foster long and meney day;
R1.1   3   Y shall hong up my horne by the grenewode spray;
R1.1   4   Foster woll Y be no more.
R1.2   1   All the whiles that Y may my bowe bende
R1.2   2   Shall Y wedde no wiffe;
R2.1   3   Weche Y have songe with wepyng yen tweyne
R2.1   4   Full oghfte or this, Y shall undertake.
R2.1   6   Y most obey fortuneys ordynaunce,
R2.1   7   For yet Y am all drowned in the lake
R2.2   5   Now Y pray God and that righth hertily
R2.2   7   For till she amende Y shall have noght truly
R3.1   3   'Let go Y say, straw for yeur tale!'
R3.1   7   Y trow for all youre gret afray
R3.2   7   Y wolde not yette for furty pence
R3.3   2   'Be Criste, Y nelle, what ses the man?
R3.3   7   But hadde Y wyste when ye bygan,
R3.3   8   Be Criste, Y wolde have schytte the dore!'
R4   3   And thogh Y wolde, Y koude me noght refrayne
R4   4   For yeu, dere hert, thoff Y suffere penaunce
R4   6   That Y fro yew may hyre sume gode tydyng,
R5   1   The hye desire that Y have for to se
R5   3   Till that Y may in yeure presaunce
R6   2   That Y am thus in heviness?

Y (cont.)

R6	3	And yet Y have do my besynesse
R9	4	Y recommaunde my symple service sure,
R9	7	Besechyng yeure excuse, ther Y supprise;
R9	9	Thorffe with yeur beute that Y most love and prise.
R10.4	2	For Y am bare
R10.4	7	Thus evyll Y fare,
R10.5	5	Wher Y wold fayn,
R10.6	1	Thus ever y fynd
R12.3	10	Y shall use me.
R13.2	4	That wondyd soere myself Y fele,
R14.1	2	Here Y am mysylf alone;
R15.2	2	'Y was a mayde
R15.2	5	Y was afrayde
R15.7	2	But soore Y wepe
R18.1	1	Up Y arose in verno tempore
R18.1	4	Sayng, 'Y fele puerum movere;
R18.3	1	Now what shall Y say meis parentibus
R18.3	2	Bycause Y lay with quidam clericus?
R18.4	2	Shall Y hyt kepe vel interficiam?
R18.4	3	Yf Y sley hyt, quo loco fugiam?
R19.1	6	When Y cam ther
R19.3	2	And Y alone,
R20b	1	How shall Y plece a creature uncerteyne?
R20.1	3	That ye loth Y love -- wrappe that yn your trayne!
R20.1	4	How sholde Y [plece a creature uncerteyne?]
R20.2	2	Withowt cause, Gode knowyth; Y do not fayne.
R20.2	3	With hert Y wyll you plece and your love attayne:
R20.2	4	How sholde Y plece a creature oncertayne?
R20.3	1	When Y fynde you stedfast and certayne,
R20.3	2	Y am right glad, tristyng hit woll remanyne;
R20.3	4	How sholde Y plece a creature oncerteyne?
R20.4	4	How sholde Y plece a creature oncertayne?
F48.2	4	Yet wold Y eft be all to-torne.]

YBID (1)

F37.1	5	Whereas I am ybid with bodily rest;

YCHE (1)

H66.2	3	I thynk sum wars of yche degre;

YE (82)

R3.1	1	'Be pes, ye make me spille my ale!'
R3.1	2	Now thyngke ye this ys a fayre ray?
R3.1	5	'Wene ye that everybody lest to play?'
R3.1	6	Abyde awhile! What have ye haste?
R3.1	8	Ye will not make to huge a waste.
R3.2	1	After asay then may ye wette;
R3.2	2	Why blame ye me withoute offence?
R3.2	3	'Ywisse, wanton, ye shull not yette!
R3.2	4	A, kan ye that? Nou, gode, go hens!
R3.2	5	What do ye here within oure spence?
R3.2	6	Recke ye not to make us shende?
R3.2	8	My moder cam in, or that ye wende.'

R3.3	1	Cum kys me! 'Nay!' Be God, ye shall!
R3.3	3	Ye herte my legge agenste the walle;
R3.3	4	Ys this the gentery that ye can?'
R3.3	6	'Now have ye leyde me un the flore,
R3.3	7	But hadde Y wyste when ye bygan,
R4	2	For of my hert ye have the governaunce;
R5	5	That ye wilde fuchesaffe to have mercy on me
R13.2	1	The sterre of Venus which I call her ye,
R20.1	3	That ye loth Y love -- wrappe that yn your trayne!
R20.4	3	Speke or ye smyte, barke or ye byte; holde yowre hondes twane
F2	2	Ye thynk for to discomfort me.
F7.1	5	Thoo that ye wolde untill ye dye
F7.1	6	Yet other grace can ye gett non
F7.2	5	So for to se ye betrayd,
F8	1	Lett serch your myndis ye of hie consideracion!
F18.1	4	And wote ye why?
F18.1	5	For ye with your faynyng
F18.2	5	When that ye do lye,
F18.2	6	Then speke ye so swetely
F23.2	3	Wherfor of ryght ye shuld my greffe complayne,
F25.1	2	Ye me retayne
F25.1	8	Ye myght redress.
F27b	1	'I love, I love, and whom love ye?'
F27b	3	'I love another as well as ye.'
F27.4b	1	'Now have I lovyd, and whom love ye?'
F27.4b	3	'I love anothyr as well as ye.'
F30.1	12	Say what ye wolde.'
F31.2	4	With wepyng, wayling, ye, sownyng for wo.
F31.3	2	As betyng, bobbyng, ye, spettyng on thi face?
F31.3	4	Both water and blode, ye, crucified an hevy case?
F34b	7	'Ye, my maker I call the.'
F36.3	5	'Why than so depe morne ye?'
F40.1	3	In favoure and in facion (lo, will ye se?)
F41.1	4	What, will ye do nothing but play?
F41.2	1	'Be Gad, ye be a pretty pode,
F41.2	3	Strawe, Jamys foder, ye play the fode;
F41.3	1	I-wiss, ye dele uncurtesly;
F41.3	2	What, wolde ye frompill me now? fy, fy!
F41.3	3	'What, and ye shal be my piggesnye?'
F41.3	4	Be Crist, ye shal not! No, no, hardely!
F41.4	1	'Walke forthe your way, ye cost me nought;
H25.1	6	Morne ye no more for me.
H25.5	3	Venus, to blame are ye.
H27.1	3	Sen ye must nedes from me depart,
H28	4	Joy shall I never ye may be sure.
H35.3	1	There she gothe! Se ye nott,
H35.3	3	And yf ye lust to have a shott,
H41.5	1	She said, 'Desyre, what do ye here?'
H47.2	3	Thow ye now parte me fro,
H47.4	3	Ye ar not varyable;
H66.2	2	How well dyd ye your yough carry?
H67.2	6	Ye may be sure,

YE (cont.)
H104b	1	Wher be ye
H104b	3	And where be ye gone?
H104.1	4	But when ye mysse,
H104.2	1	When ye be hens,
H106.4	1	Thus may ye se my wofull chance,
H109.1	3	And yf ye wyll, I shall consent;
H109.1	4	How sey ye, mayde? Be ye content?
H109.1b	3	Why, wyll ye nott geve me no comfortt,
H109.2	1	Ye be so nyce and so mete of age
H109.2	2	That ye gretly move my corage.
H109.3	1	Ye have my hert; sey what ye wyll.
H109.3	2	Wherfore ye muste my mynde fulfyll,
H109.4	2	But the nexte tyme ye must beware
H109.4	3	How in the medow ye mylke your cow.

YEN (1)
| R2.1 | 3 | Weche Y have songe with wepyng yen tweyne |

YERE (2)
| H101.2 | 2 | Of twelve yere of age, |
| H101.3 | 2 | The age of fifteen yere, |

YERNE (1)
| F36.1 | 5 | Myn hart can yerne and mylt |

YES (5)
F13	4	To her only which is myn yes fode,
F37.2	4	My face disfygurid, myn yes full daslyng;
F39.2	2	Her yes most clere,
H31.6	5	And yes replete
H106.1	5	Myn yes for sorow salt ters doth rayne:

YET (41)
R2.1	7	For yet Y am all drowned in the lake
R6	3	And yet Y have do my besynesse
F1	6	Thoo I go lose, yet am I teyd with a lyne:
F2	4	Thoo that all this yet in vayne be,
F3	6	And yet mythynkyth hit grevith me moche more
F6.2	4	Yet reson is
F7.1	6	Yet other grace can ye gett non
F17	4	Yet moreovyr a gretter payne,
F21	6	Yet will I me trust to fortune applye;
F24.5	5	Yet I ne went
F27.2	2	And shall not yet be namyd for me;
F28	5	I-wiss yet will I not me complayne
F32.1	4	Yet when oure Laidis Son was slayne
F36.2	9	'Yet thou are unkynd, which sleith myn hert,'
F36.3	10	And yet verely I know in myn hart
F37.1	6	Thus trobled am I yet I trust it shalbe for the best
F37.2	6	Thus trobled am I [yet I trust it shalbe for the best

YET (cont.)

F37.3	6	Thus trobled am I [yet I trust it shalbe for the best
F37.4	4	Alas, to dye thou makyst me sure; yet then, good Lord, do thou thi cure
F37.4	6	Thus trobled am I [yet I trust it shalbe for the best
F41.4	4	Yet for his love that all hath wrought
F48.2	4	Yet wold Y eft be all to-torne.]
F48.2	5	Yet, man, that thou sholdest not be lorne,
H25.6	4	Yet for all that
H27.4	1	And I thynk I se her yet,
H34.6	2	Yet never the lesse it ys to moch used.
H35.1	2	And yet she bledes no whytt;
H35.2	4	But yet she was not dede.
H49.2	4	And yet she will say no.
H62.1	5	Yet have I bene a foster.
H62.2	5	Yet have I [bene a foster.]
H62.3	5	Yet have [I bene a foster.]
H62.4	5	Yet have I bene [a foster.]
H62.5	5	Yet have [I bene a foster.]
H62.6	5	Yet have [I bene a foster.]
H67.2	4	Nor yet retayne;
H105.3	3	Yet softly to her swete sonne methought I hard her sayn
H105.3	4	Now, gracious God and goode swete babe, yet ons this game agayne
H106.2	5	Refrayne I must yet in dysdayne,
H106.3	6	Yet my lyfe is to me so grevus
H107.5	5	Yet I ne went

YETT (2)

| F12 | 5 | Yett more mervell how that I hard the sownde |
| H62.2 | 4 | Nor yett in rough; |

YETTE (2)

| R3.2 | 3 | 'Ywisse, wanton, ye shull not yette! |
| R3.2 | 7 | Y wolde not yette for furty pence |

YEU (1)

| R4 | 4 | For yeu, dere hert, thoff Y suffere penaunce |

YEUR (2)

| R3.1 | 3 | 'Let go Y say, straw for yeur tale!' |
| R9 | 9 | Thorffe with yeur beute that Y most love and prise. |

YEURE (7)

R4	5	All for yeure sake, til God me so avaunce
R5	3	Till that Y may in yeure presaunce
R5	4	Prayng to yeure gracius pyte
R5	6	And only to be putte to yeure rememoraunce.
R9	2	That with yeure beute and fresche plesaunce pure
R9	6	Unly to yeure swete grace a thousande sithe
R9	7	Besechyng yeure excuse, ther Y supprise;

YEVYN (1)
F48.1   1   A, man, I have yevyn and made a graunt

YEW (1)
R4   6   That Y fro yew may hyre sume gode tydyng,

YF (6)
R18.4   3   Yf Y sley hyt, *quo loco fugiam?*
H29.4   1   Yf I to her than war unkynd,
H35.3   3   And yf ye lust to have a shott,
H64.2   10   Yf contrarye,
H82.2   1   For yf thay war in lyk case
H109.1   3   And yf ye wyll, I shall consent;

YFF (6)
F7.1   7   Butt yff hit be to wissh for one:
F9   2   Yff I coude spye
F27b   5   Yff we three can agre in on.'
F27.4b   5   Yff we three can agre in oon.'
F40.3   3   Yff she and I were together alone,
F46.3   4   Forever yff she will trew be,

YLL (4)
R12.2   2   Of good or yll some pastaunce;
R12.3   3   Cumpany ys gode or yll,
R19.3   8   Yll must she the,
H79.1   5   Many oone sayth that love ys yll,

YN (19)
R10.3   8   Yn lovys daunce.
R10.4   3   Of yoy, yn care
R10.4   5   Takyn yn a snare
R10.4   8   Lyving yn stryf;
R10.5   1   Lyving yn payn,
R10.5   2   Lovyng yn vayne,
R10.5   3   Hade yn dysdayn;
R11.1   1   My herte ys yn grete mournyng,
R11.3   2   Dame Petyles yn every place over all;
R13.1   1   So put yn fere I dare not speke;
R13.1   7   Abydyng your grace yn hope of mercy.
R13.3   3   Or els yn feyth unkyndly she doth dele,
R15.6   2   Yn sport and play,
R15.6   4   Men tellyth yn town
R19.1   7   She stode yn fere
R19.3   10   Yn castell strong.'
R20.1   3   That ye loth Y love -- wrappe that yn your trayne!
F37.3   4   Grete mowntens fallyng over me, thus slepe doth I
                 yn feere
H109.1   1   Now yn this medow fayer and grene

YNGLOND (1)
F44.1   8   Of Ynglond and Fraunce

YNWARDLY (1)
R13.2   3   So depe hath thrylled my hert ynwardly

YONDER (1)
H35b   2   Ther ys a do in yonder wode; in faith, she woll
                 not dy

YONG (2)
F44.3   3   For this yong prince, which is and daily shal
H82.1   1   Let not us that yong men be

YOU (36)
R4   1   Absens of you causeth me to sygh and complayne
R18.2   2   Full oft with you solebam ludere;
R20.2   3   With hert Y wyll you plece and your love attayne:
R20.3   1   When Y fynde you stedfast and certayne,
F15   1   I am he that hath you dayly servyd,
F25.1   6   To you complayne,
F25.2   3   To you gretly
F25.2   8   I you ensure.
F40b   3   Alak, good Jhoane, what may you please?
F40.1   5   Alak, good Jhoone, [what may you please?
F40.2   5   Alak, good [Jhoone, what may you please?
F40.3   5   Alak, good Jhoan, [what may you please?
F40.4   5   Alak, good Jhoan, [what may you please?
F41.2   2   And I love you an hole cart-lode.'
F43.3   1   Rutterkyn shall bryng you all good luk;
F47.2   1   God hath gyff you of his goodness
H24   4   To serve you evermore.
H38   3   I fynde you not trew;
H47.4   4   I love you and no mo.
H47.5   1   I make you fast and sure;
H63.2   1   Thowgh you depart now thus me fro,
H66.2   1   I pray you all that aged be,
H67.2   1   And make you sure
H104b   6   Yt is but you, my love, alone.
H104.1   6   But you, my love, alone.
H104.2   6   But you, my love, alone.
H104.4   3   Crist kepe you from your fone;
H104.4   6   For you have myne alone.
H105.2   4   This reson that I rede you now, I rede it full
                 ryght
H109b   2   Mayde, whether go you?
H109b   4   Than at the medow I wyll you mete
H109.1b 1   Nay, in good feyth, I wyll not melle with you;
H109.1b 2   I pray you, sir, lett me go mylke my cow!
H109.2   3   Syth I love you, love me agayne;
H109.3   4   Or elles I shall for you be ded.
H109.4   1   Then for this onse I shal you spare,

YOUGH (14)
H66.1   1   Though sum saith that yough rulyth me,
H66.1   5   Though sum say that yough rulyth me.
H66.2   2   How well dyd ye your yough carry?

YOUGH (cont.)

H66.2	5	Though sum sayth [that yough rulyth me.]
H66.3	1	Pastymes of yough sumtyme among,
H66.3	5	Thow sum saith [that yough rulyth me.]
H66.4	5	Though sum [saith that yough rulyth me.]
H82.1	4	Wold have yough love to refrayn,
H82.2	6	It ys for yough the metest play.
H92.1	1	Lusti yough shuld us ensue,
H92.3	1	How shuld yough hymselfe best use
H92.3	3	Yough has as chef assurans
H92.5	4	Yough shuld fall in grett myschaunce;
H92.6	1	For yough ys frayle and prompt to doo,

YOUNG (1)

| R15.6 | 1 | This young men say |

YOUR (39)

R13.1	7	Abydyng your grace yn hope of mercy.
R20.1	1	Your light grevans shall not me constrayne
R20.1	2	To avoyde your custumabyll disdayne;
R20.1	3	That ye loth Y love -- wrappe that yn your trayne!
R20.2	1	Your on-syttyng speche puttyth me to payne
R20.2	3	With hert Y wyll you plece and your love attayne:
R20.3	3	But light credens turnyth your love agayne:
F6.3	2	In your mynd
F8	1	Lett serch your myndis ye of hie consideracion!
F11	7	Your trewe servant with thought, hart and body.
F15	2	Thow I be lytyll in your remembraunce;
F15	4	To be put owte of your good governaunce . . .
F18.1	5	For ye with your faynyng
F23.1	7	That hath byn your fayre lady and mastress.
F27.6	2	'Is that your pure perfytt appetite?'
F30.2	2	Amend your chere,
F39.3	6	Your chere avaunce,
F41.2	4	I am no hakney for your rode;
F41.2	5	Go watch a bole, your bak is brode.
F41.4	1	'Walke forthe your way, ye cost me nought;
F41.4	6	Gup, Cristian Clowte, your breth is stale,
F47b	2	To strenkyth your comyns in ther ryght.
F47.1	5	Sith it is so, now let your labour be
F47.1	6	Enforcyng yourselfe with all your myght
F47.1	7	To strenkyth your comyns in ther ryght.
F47.2	5	Which crye and call unto your Majeste.
F47.2	6	In your person all ther hope is pyght
H25.2	5	Your love do way
H25.3	5	Your mynde revert
H41.4	2	He said, 'Desyre, your man, madame.'
H41.5	2	He said, 'Madame, as your prisoner.'
H47.3	2	Of your most gentyll mynde,
H66.2	2	How well dyd ye your yough carry?
H104.2	2	With your absence
H104.4	2	With your welfare,
H104.4	3	Crist kepe you from your fone;
H104.4	5	Kepe your love

YOUR (cont.)
H109.3 3 And graunte me here your maydynhed,
H109.4 3 How in the medow ye mylke your cow.

YOURE (1)
R3.1 7 Y trow for all youre gret afray

YOURS (3)
F23.2 2 My hart is yours with gret assuraunce.
H63.2 3 My hart ys yours where ever that I go;
H67.1 7 To be as yours

YOURSELFE (3)
F23.2 7 Have but yourselfe, fayre lady and mastres.
F47b 1 Enforce yourselfe as Goddis knyght
F47.1 6 Enforcyng yourselfe with all your myght

YOUTH (2)
H22 2 To passe the tyme of youth joly,
H23.6 1 Vertue it is then youth for to spend

YOUTHE (1)
H23.1 1 The tyme of youthe is to be spent;

YOW (16)
F2 1 A, a, my herte, I knowe yow well;
F25.3 1 I have yow lent
F41.1 1 Ay, besherewe yow! Be my fay
F46.1 4 As fortune fallyth, I yow ensure;
H12 4 I do yow fynde
H12 5 To kepe yow me unto?
H31.5 6 Cryst kepe yow frome all care.
H35.6 4 What do yow meane or thynk?
H41b 1 Yow and I and Amyas,
H41b 2 Amyas and yow and I,
H41b 4 Yow and I, my lyff, and Amyas.
H47.2 2 Let no thought yow dysmaye!
H63.1 3 Frome yow a whyle must I depart;
H63.2 4 For yow do I mone.
H67.1 4 Ower Lord yow gy;
H104.3 6 But yow, my love, alone.

YOWER (1)
H104.1 1 Yower company

YOWRE (3)
R20.4 3 Speke or ye smyte, barke or ye byte; holde yowre
                  hondes twane
F18.1 1 Yowre counturfetyng
F23.1 5 What causyth this but only yowre plesaunce

YOWTH (1)
R12.2 1 Yowth woll have nedes dalyaunce,

324

YOY (1)
R10.4   3   Of yoy, yn care

YOYUS (1)
R13.1   4   To her which ys my yoyus plesure;

YS (58)
R2.2	1	For sche weche ys of all godely the best
R2.2	3	Ys full but late oute of hur kyndely rest
R3.1	2	Now thyngke ye this ys a fayre ray?
R3.3	4	Ys this the gentery that ye can?'
R10.1	5	My myrth ys gon
R10.1	8	Fortune ys my fo.
R10.2	6	Hyt ys foly
R10.3	4	This ys my chaunce;
R10.3	6	My hert ys braught
R10.6	6	As man that ys blynd,
R10.6	8	Alone ys no cumfort.
R11.1	1	My herte ys yn grete mournyng,
R11.2	1	The more sorow ys my payn
R12.1	7	My hert ys sett
R12.2	6	Ys cheff mastres
R12.2	10	Ys best of all?
R12.3	2	Ys vertu, and vyce to flee;
R12.3	3	Cumpany ys gode or yll,
R13.1	4	To her which ys my yoyus plesure;
R14.2	1	My blossum bright ys gone,
R15.3	6	And now ys gone.
R15.4	1	Now hit ys so,
R15.6	6	The smocke ys hyd."
R16.1	1	The burne ys this worlde blynde
R16.1	2	And Besse ys mankynde;
R19.1	10	Hyt ys grete wrong.'
R19.3	5	This ys my song:
F37.1	3	Nature of aquayntance ys turned to a gest,
H29.2	2	She ys right trew, I do it se.
H29.4	3	For she to me ys allway kynd;
H34.5	1	Love ys gevyn to God and man;
H34.6	1	But dysdayne ys vice and shuld be refused;
H34.6	2	Yet never the lesse it ys to moch used.
H35b	2	Ther ys a do in yonder wode; in faith, she woll not dy
H35.1	1	Sore this dere strykyn ys,
H35.7	3	I thynk his bow ys well unbent,
H47.5	2	It ys to me gret payne
H51.7	2	Who love dysdaynyth ys all of the village.
H62.3	1	Every bowe for me ys to bygge;
H62.3	2	Myne arow ny worne ys;
H62.4	4	That beawtye ys my foo;
H62.5	1	My berd ys so hard, God wote,
H62.5	4	Lo, age ys cause of this;
H63.1	4	Ther ys none other bote.
H63.2	3	My hart ys yours where ever that I go;
H64.1	8	Ys in the dole

YS (cont.)
H79.1	5	Many oone sayth that love ys yll,
H82.2	6	It ys for yough the metest play.
H92.1	4	It ys not for hym we know yt well.
H92.6	1	For yough ys frayle and prompt to doo,
H101.1	2	As many one ys,
H102.1	4	Now sith it ys thus known,
H102.2	1	My lady sayth of trouth it ys
H102.2	3	Alas, alas, what word ys this?
H106.3	3	For death ys endar principall
H106.4	6	Nay, nay, for why? Ther ys no space.
H107.5	8	Such ys her wone!
H108	7	And love unloved; such ys myne adventure.

YT (6)
H41.7	1	Kyndnes said she wold yt bere,
H64.2	12	God yt amen.
H79.2	2	They wold that other shuld yt dysdayne;
H79.2	6	Wherfor, then, shuld we yt excho?
H92.1	4	It ys not for hym we know yt well.
H104b	6	Yt is but you, my love, alone.

YWISSE (1)
| R3.2 | 3 | 'Ywisse, wanton, ye shull not yette! |

CONCORDANCE OF
FOREIGN GRAPHIC FORMS

AC (1)
  R18.3   3 They wyll me bete <u>cum</u> <u>virgis</u> <u>ac</u> <u>fustibus</u>

ADEW (3)
  H31.7   2 Adew la bell,
  H68   1 Adew, adew, le company,

AMEN (1)
  H92.7   4 An blysse opteyne at ower last end. Amen.

ANTIQUO (1)
  R18.2   1 Adew, plesers <u>antiquo</u> <u>tempore</u>!

ARBORE (1)
  R18.1   2 And found a maydyn <u>sub</u> <u>quadam</u> <u>arbore</u>

BA (2)
  H105b   2 <u>Mater</u> <u>dulcissima</u> <u>ba</u> <u>ba</u>.

BELL (1)
  H31.7   2 Adew la bell,

CLERICUS (1)
  R18.3   2 Bycause Y lay with <u>quidam</u> <u>clericus</u>?

COMPANY (1)
  H68   1 Adew, adew, le company,

CORAM (1)
  R18.3   4 And me sore chast <u>coram</u> <u>omnibus</u>.

CUM (1)
  R18.3   3 They wyll me bete <u>cum</u> <u>virgis</u> <u>ac</u> <u>fustibus</u>

D'AMOURS (1)
  H67.1   1 <u>Madame</u> <u>d'amours</u>,

DA (2)
  H105b   4 <u>Michi</u> <u>plausus</u> <u>oscula</u> <u>da</u> <u>da</u>!

DERIDERE (1)
  R18.2   3 But for my mysse <u>michi</u> <u>deridere</u>;

DOMINO (4)
  F37.1   7 <u>Sicut</u> <u>domino</u> <u>placuit</u>, <u>ita</u> <u>factum</u> <u>est</u>.
  F37.2   7 <u>Sicut</u> <u>domino</u> <u>placuit</u>, <u>ita</u> <u>factum</u> <u>est</u>.]
  F37.3   7 <u>Sicut</u> <u>domino</u> <u>placuit</u>, <u>ita</u> <u>factum</u> <u>est</u>.]
  F37.4   7 <u>Sicut</u> <u>domino</u> <u>placuit</u>, <u>ita</u> <u>factum</u> <u>est</u>.]

DULCISSIMA (1)
  H105b   2 <u>Mater</u> <u>dulcissima</u> <u>ba</u> <u>ba</u>.

EST (4)
  F37.1   7 <u>Sicut</u> <u>domino</u> <u>placuit</u>, <u>ita</u> <u>factum</u> <u>est</u>.

329

EST (cont.)
F37.2   7   Sicut domino placuit, ita factum est.]
F37.3   7   Sicut domino placuit, ita factum est.]
F37.4   7   Sicut domino placuit, ita factum est.]

ET (2)
R18.4   4   I shall lose God et vitam eternam.'
H68   3   Vive le Katerine et noble Henry!

ETERNAM (1)
R18.4   4   I shall lose God et vitam eternam.'

FACIAM (1)
R18.4   1   With the seid child, quid faciam?

FACTUM (4)
F37.1   7   Sicut domino placuit, ita factum est.
F37.2   7   Sicut domino placuit, ita factum est.]
F37.3   7   Sicut domino placuit, ita factum est.]
F37.4   7   Sicut domino placuit, ita factum est.]

FILI (1)
H105b   3   O pater, O fili?

FILY (1)
H105b   1   Quid petis, o fily?

FLERE (1)
R18.2   4   With right goed cause incipeo flere.

FUGIAM (1)
R18.4   3   Yf Y sley hyt, quo loco fugiam?

FUSTIBUS (1)
R18.3   3   They wyll me bete cum virgis ac fustibus

HENRY (1)
H68   3   Vive le Katerine et noble Henry!

HELY (3)
F36.4   6   Cried, 'Hely, hely, hely!'

IN (2)
R18.1   1   Up Y arose in verno tempore
R18.1   3   That dyd complayne in suo pectore,

INCIPEO (1)
R18.2   4   With right goed cause incipeo flere.

INTERFICIAM (1)
R18.4   2   Shall Y hyt kepe vel interficiam?

ITA (4)
F37.1   7   Sicut domino placuit, ita factum est.

330

ITA (cont.)
```
F37.2    7   Sicut domino placuit, ita factum est.]
F37.3    7   Sicut domino placuit, ita factum est.]
F37.4    7   Sicut domino placuit, ita factum est.]
```

KATERINE (1)
```
H68      3   Vive le Katerine et noble Henry!
```

LA (1)
```
H31.7    2   Adew la bell,
```

LE (4)
```
H68      1   Adew, adew, le company,
H68      3   Vive le Katerine et noble Henry!
H68      4   Vive le prince, le infant rosary!
```

LOCO (1)
```
R18.4    3   Yf Y sley hyt, quo loco fugiam?
```

LUDERE (1)
```
R18.2    2   Full oft with you solebam ludere;
```

MADAME (1)
```
H67.1    1   Madame d'amours,
```

MATER (1)
```
H105b    2   Mater dulcissima ba ba.
```

MEIS (1)
```
R18.3    1   Now what shall Y say meis parentibus
```

MICHI (2)
```
R18.2    3   But for my mysse michi deridere;
H105b    4   Michi plausus oscula da da!
```

MORI (1)
```
R7       6   Paratus sum semper mori pro te.
```

MOVERE (1)
```
R18.1    4   Saying, 'Y fele puerum movere;
```

NOBLE (1)
```
H68      3   Vive le Katerine et noble Henry!
```

O (3)
```
H105b    1   Quid petis, o fily?
H105b    3   O pater, O fili?
```

OMNIBUS (1)
```
R18.3    4   And me sore chast coram omnibus.
```

OSCULA (1)
```
H105b    4   Michi plausus oscula da da!
```

PARATUS (1)
R7   6   Paratus sum semper mori pro te.

PARENTIBUS (1)
R18.3   1   Now what shall Y say meis parentibus

PATER (1)
H105b   3   O pater, O fili?

PECTORE (1)
R18.1   3   That dyd complayne in suo pectore,

PETIS (1)
H105b   1   Quid petis, o fily?

PLACUIT (4)
F37.1   7   Sicut domino placuit, ita factum est.
F37.2   7   Sicut domino placuit, ita factum est.]
F37.3   7   Sicut domino placuit, ita factum est.]
F37.4   7   Sicut domino placuit, ita factum est.]

PLAUSUS (1)
H105b   4   Michi plausus oscula da da!

PRINCE (1)
H68   4   Vive le prince, le infant rosary!

PRO (1)
R7   6   Paratus sum semper mori pro te.

PUERUM (1)
R18.1   4   Sayng, 'Y fele puerum movere;

QUADAM (1)
R18.1   2   And found a maydyn sub quadam arbore,

QUID (2)
R18.4   1   With the seid child, quid faciam?
H105b   1   Quid petis, o fily?

QUIDAM (1)
R18.3   2   Bycause Y lay with quidam clericus?

QUO (1)
R18.4   3   Yf Y sley hyt, quo loco fugiam?

ROSARY (1)
H68   4   Vive le prince, le infant rosary!

SEMPER (1)
R7   6   Paratus sum semper mori pro te.

SICUT (4)
F37.1   7   Sicut domino placuit, ita factum est.

SICUT (cont.)
F37.2   7   Sicut domino placuit, ita factum est.]
F37.3   7   Sicut domino placuit, ita factum est.]
F37.4   7   Sicut domino placuit, ita factum est.]

SOLEBAM (1)
R18.2   2   Full oft with you solebam ludere;

SUB (1)
R18.1   2   And found a maydyn sub quadam arbore,

SUM (1)
R7   6   Paratus sum semper mori pro te.

SUO (1)
R18.1   3   That dyd complayne in suo pectore,

TE (1)
R7   6   Paratus sum semper mori pro te.

TEMPORE (2)
R18.1   1   Up Y arose in verno tempore
R18.2   1   Adew, plesers antiquo tempore!

VEL (1)
R18.4   2   Shall Y hyt kepe vel interficiam?

VERNO (1)
R18.1   1   Up Y arose in verno tempore

VIRGIS (1)
R18.3   3   They wyll me bete cum virgis ac fustibus

VITAM (1)
R18.4   4   I shall lose God et vitam eternam.'

VIVE (2)
H68   3   Vive le Katerine et noble Henry!
H68   4   Vive le prince, le infant rosary!

333

REVERSE INDEX OF
ENGLISH GRAPHIC FORMS

TH'	JOYED	AND
JUDAS'	TRYED	HAND
VENUS'	DISMAID	ENGLAND
A	NAID	STAND
HOYDA	ARAID	END
ALAC	AFFRAID	BEND
BAD	SAID	CONDYSCEND
GAD	BOBBID	FEND
HAD	ROBBID	DEFFEND
GLAD	YBID	OFFEND
SAD	DID	AMEND
HADD	OFFENDID	SPEND
GLADD	CONCLUDID	MYSPEND
DED	SEID	FREND
VOYDED	RAGGID	SEND
AGED	TOGGID	BOND
HED	CHANGID	LOND
MAYDYNHED	BANYSSHID	ENGLOND
GOODLYHED	NAILID	YNGLOND
CRUCIFIED	CALLID	DYAMOND
CRIED	NAYLID	STOND
LOKKED	BEWAYLID	SERVAUND
ASKED	WEPID	SECUND
LED	WRAPPID	FOUND
TROBLED	HOPPID	WOUND
EXILED	DISFYGURID	BOWND
COWNSELLED	BLESSID	FOWND
THRYLLED	FRETID	HOWND
BEGYLED	THRETID	ROWND
GRYNNED	ENTRETID	WOWND
MORNED	HARD-HARTID	BYND
TURNED	GREVID	FYND
DROWNED	PROVID	HYND
TOYNED	DESERVID	BEHYND
GOED	ENDEWID	KYND
JAPED	MOWID	MANKYND
RED	FEELD	ONKYND
DRED	FELD	UNKYND
ENVIRED	CHILD	BLYND
ENFORSED	EXILD	MYND
BLESSED	BOLD	FRYND
OPPRESSED	MANYFOLD	WYND
USED	BEHOLD	GOD
REFUSED	SHOLD	BLOD
DYSPRAYSED	WOLD	GOOD
DEPARTED	WORLD	STOD
ARESTED	SCHULD	GRENEWOD
TRUSTED	SHULD	GRENWOD
LOVED	WOULD	SAVEGARD
UNLOVED	COWLD	HARD
PROVED	KYNDYLD	MARD
REVYVED	CHYLD	INWARD
WED	KYLD	FROWARD
FYXED	MYLD	TOWARD

BERD	SURYD	GYDAUNCE
GADERD	ASSURYD	ALEGEAUNCE
OFFERD	DISPAYRYD	CHAUNCE
SOFFERD	PLESYD	MYSCHAUNCE
SWERD	USYD	ALIAUNCE
SUFFIRD	ABUSYD	SEMBLAUNCE
RECORD	REFUSYD	PENAUNCE
DYSCORD	MYSUSYD	GOVERNAUNCE
LORD	PRYNTYD	ORDYNAUNCE
WORD	LOVYD	CONTYNAUNCE
DISORDYRD	SERVYD	REMEMBRAUNCE
SUFFYRD	REWYD	FRAUNCE
BUTTYRD	BE	REMEMORAUNCE
BUD	BABE	TRAUNCE
LAYD	SHALBE	SURAUNCE
MAYD	LAMBE	ASSURAUNCE
DYSMAYD	LOMBE	PLESAUNCE
PAYD	CACE	DISPLESAUNCE
APAYD	FACE	PRESAUNCE
ARAYD	HACE	PASTAUNCE
PRAYD	PURCHACE	SUBSTAUNCE
BETRAYD	SOLACE	CONSTAUNCE
SAYD	PLACE	ENERYTAUNCE
PLECYD	SPACE	INERYTAUNCE
PERCYD	TRESPACE	AVAUNCE
DYD	UNBRACE	GREVAUNCE
WONDYD	GRACE	DALYAUNCE
COMMAUNDYD	TRACE	VARYAUNCE
GYDYD	PLECE	DAWNCE
SEYD	GRECE	PRYNCE
TEYD	SACRIFICE	FORCE
HYD	VOICE	ENFORCE
ENRYCHYD	VICE	FLOURE-DE-LUCE
NAKYD	SERVICE	NYCE
QUAKYD	FALCE	VYCE
WALKYD	VENGEANCE	BADE
MERVELYD	CHANCE	HADE
THIRLYD	PENANCE	MADE
NAYLYD	CONTENANCE	HADDE
BEGYLYD	TRANCE	LADDE
NAMYD	SURANCE	ADRADDE
DEMYD	DYSPLESANCE	WEDDE
DREMYD	AQUAYNTANCE	ODDE
FORMYD	PASTANCE	FORBEDE
SCORNYD	SUBSTANCE	DEDE
TURNYD	AVANCE	INDEDE
FORTUNYD	GREVANCE	HEDE
DROWNYD	OFFENCE	SHEDE
ONFAYNYD	HENCE	LEDE
PAYNYD	PENCE	BLEDE
STRAYNYD	SPENCE	MEDE
CONSTRAYNYD	ABSENCE	NEDE
DEYNYD	PRINCE	SPEDE
REYNYD	DAUNCE	REDE

338

AGREDE	WOMANHODE	ACHEFFE
SEDE	CART-LODE	THEFFE
MAIDE	BLODE	LEFFE
APAIDE	MODE	BREFFE
ARAIDE	GOODE	GREFFE
AFFRAIDE	PODE	WIFFE
BETRAIDE	RODE	ABOFFE
SAIDE	BRODE	SHOFFE
PERCIDE	STODE	THORFFE
EXILIDE	WODE	LYFFE
PRIDE	GRENEWODE	SALFE
COMFORTIDE	GRENWODE	HYMSELFE
CALDE	HARDE	YOURSELFE
CHILDE	BESMERDE	LYFE
WILDE	PERDE	AGE
OLDE	SWERDE	VIAGE
COLDE	BORDE	VILLAGE
GOLDE	CORDE	PERSONAGE
HOLDE	ACORDE	LYNAGE
BEHOLDE	LORDE	BORAGE
SHOLDE	WORDE	CORAGE
WOLDE	BYRDE	COURAGE
WORLDE	COUDE	VISAGE
SHULDE	KOUDE	ERITAGE
FYLDE	RUDE	HERITAGE
BEGYLDE	MAWDE	DOTAGE
SYLDE	RENEWDE	SWAGE
THOUSANDE	COWDE	ASSWAGE
ENDE	LOWDE	LEGGE
BENDE	MAYDE	GRUGGE
FENDE	AT-A-BRAYDE	BYGGE
SHENDE	AT-ABRAYDE	ESTRIGE
AMENDE	AFRAYDE	HANGE
SENDE	ABYDE	CHANGE
WENDE	LEYDE	STRANGE
RECOMMAUNDE	SEYDE	NOTHINGE
FOUNDE	GYDE	LONGE
WOUNDE	AVOYDE	SONGE
BOWNDE	SYDE	CHAUNGE
FOWNDE	TYDE	SPRYNGYNGE
SOWNDE	WYDE	THYNGE
BYNDE	EE	SYNGE
FYNDE	FEE	GEORGE
BEHYNDE	FLEE	HUGE
KYNDE	KNEE	JUGE
MANKYNDE	FREE	LUGE
UNKYNDE	THREE	GRUGE
LYNDE	SEE	HE
BLYNDE	LEEFE	SPECHE
MYNDE	LEFE	TECHE
WYNDE	GREFE	WECHE
FODE	SAFFE	MOCHE
GODE	FUCHESAFFE	SCHE
HODE	CHEFFE	FRESCHE

339

SUCHE	ASKE	ROLE
YCHE	HAUKE	SOLE
SHE	LYKE	SYMPLE
WASHE	ALE	RULE
SSHE	SEALE	SOWLE
DISSHE	NYGHTYNGALE	FRAYLE
THE	SMALE	AVAYLE
HATHE	PALE	NOBYLE
SITHE	TALE	APEYLE
BOTHE	STALE	WHYLE
DOTHE	VALE	ME
GOTHE	BLE	DAME
ERTHE	ABLE	MADAME
FORTHE	VENGEABLE	GAME
YOUTHE	MERCIABLE	BLAME
HIE	TABLE	NAME
LAKE	DELECTABLE	SAME
SLAKE	TRETABLE	DEME
MAKE	LAMENTABLE	DREME
SPAKE	UNSTABLE	SEME
BRAKE	REPROVABLE	COME
TO-BRAKE	MERCYABLE	WISDOME
CRAKE	VARYABLE	HOME
SAKE	INPASSIBLE	WHOME
FORSAKE	HUMBLE	MAGEROME
TAKE	NOBLE	FROME
BETAKE	TROUBLE	SOME
UNDERTAKE	DOWBLE	SUME
UNDYRTAKE	TRIACLE	BAWME
QUAKE	WORDLE	TYME
AWAKE	DELE	PASSETYME
RECKE	FEELE	OFTYME
SMOCKE	FELE	SUMTYME
MEKE	HELE	NE
SPEKE	WHELE	ANE
TO-BREKE	WELE	CANE
SEKE	FLE	MEANE
THYNGKE	AVAILE	AGANE
LIKE	WHILE	MANE
SIKE	AWHILE	JHOANE
TALKE	CALLE	TWANE
WALKE	SMALLE	BENE
MILKE	WALLE	KENE
MYLKE	MELLE	CLENE
SANKE	NELLE	MENE
THYNKE	SPILLE	GRENE
LOKE	STILLE	SENE
CLOKE	RETAYLLE	TENE
BOOKE	TYLLE	QUENE
TOOKE	BOLE	WENE
STROKE	SCOLE	BETWENE
AWOKE	DOLE	KNE
BARKE	FOLE	MANNE
WERKE	HOLE	SONNE

BEGUNNE	PAYNE	COMPARE
ONE	SPAYNE	SPARE
BONE	RAYNE	WARE
DONE	BRAYNE	BEWARE
MYSDONE	SOVERAYNE	REMEMBRE
FONE	DEFRAYNE	BERE
GONE	REFRAYNE	DERE
EVERYCHONE	BARRAYNE	FEERE
ALONE	TRAYNE	FERE
MONE	CONSTRAYNE	SUFFERE
NONE	RETAYNE	HERE
OONE	OPTAYNE	CHERE
JHOONE	CERTAYNE	THERE
MOONE	ONCERTAYNE	WHERE
GRONE	ATTAYNE	CLERE
SONE	BRYTAYNE	MERE
WITHSTONE	VAYNE	NERE
WONE	TWAYNE	SOERE
SWONE	COLUMBYNE	PERE
WARNE	REYNE	SPERE
LANTERNE	UNSEYNE	BRERE
YERNE	CHEFTEYNE	TERE
BORNE	OPTEYNE	SUERE
BEFORNE	ONCERTEYNE	WERE
HORNE	UNCERTEYNE	WARYOWERE
THORNE	TWEYNE	YERE
LORNE	BARYEYNE	FRE
FORLORNE	THYNE	AGRE
MORNE	LYNE	DEGRE
TO-TORNE	MYNE	THRE
WORNE	REMANYNE	DISPAIRE
BURNE	JOE	DESIRE
OUNE	WOE	BORE
FORTUNE	DEPE	DORE
INFORTUNE	CHEPE	AFORE
DRAWNE	KEPE	BEFORE
OWNE	SLEPE	THEREFORE
DOWNE	WEPE	WHEREFORE
ADOWNE	RIPE	THERFORE
GOWNE	HELPE	WHERFORE
HOWNE	HOPE	HORE
CROWNE	WANHOPE	LORE
DROWNE	HAPPE	FLORE
TOWNE	WRAPPE	FORLORE
DISDAYNE	SHARPE	MORE
DYSDAYNE	STOUPE	EVERMORE
FAYNE	ARE	SOORE
GAYNE	BARE	PORE
AGAYNE	CARE	SORE
PLAYNE	DARE	TORE
COMPLAYNE	FARE	STORE
SLAYNE	WELFARE	RESTORE
MAYNE	HARE	FERRE
REMAYNE	SNARE	STERRE

TRE	WISE	NYSE
CUNTRE	OTHERWISE	RYSE
CURE	TWISE	ARYSE
RECURE	ELSE	DEVYSE
PROCURE	ONSE	WYSE
ENDURE	CHOSE	CATE
YEURE	THOSE	GATE
FIGURE	WHOSE	WHATE
LURE	REJOSE	LATE
DEMURE	LOSE	BETE
OURE	SUPPOSE	FEETE
BOURE	ROSE	FETE
NEYBOURE	AROSE	GETE
SHOURE	COURSE	FORGETE
FLOURE	RELEASSE	HETE
POURE	ALASSE	LETE
FAVOURE	PASSE	REPLETE
SAVOURE	BESSE	METE
YOURE	CESSE	PETE
BARRYOURE	GESSE	DISCRETE
PURE	LESSE	GRETE
SURE	GLADNESSE	STRETE
PLESURE	KYNDNESSE	WETE
ENSURE	GODENESSE	SWETE
CREATURE	SEKENESSE	LEFTE
NATURE	HEVENESSE	OGHFTE
AVENTURE	ACTYVENESSE	OWFTE
MYSAVENTURE	SYKYRNESSE	LYLY-WHIGHTE
ADVENTURE	BESYNESSE	BENEDICITE
DEPARTURE	REDRESSE	DEITE
OWRE	EXPRESSE	PERFITE
TOWRE	YWISSE	WHITE
YOWRE	CROSSE	MORTALITE
FAYRE	DYSCUSSE	DELITE
HAYRE	KYSSE	CRUDELITE
EYRE	BLYSSE	HUMILITE
HYRE	MYSSE	HUMANITE
DESYRE	AMYSSE	BENIGNITE
SE	WYSSE	DYGNITE
CASE	USE	TRINITE
EASE	CAUSE	PITE
PLEASE	BECAUSE	CHARITE
DISEASE	BYCAUSE	CONTRITE
PURCHASE	EXCUSE	ADVERSITE
ESE	REFUSE	DYVERSITE
CESE	REFFUSE	APPETITE
CHESE	SPOUSE	EQUITE
PLESE	VERTUSE	COMMYNALTE
ENCRESE	HOWSE	PLENTE
DAISE	PRAYSE	SPENTE
PRISE	JEBARDYSE	GRAUNTE
EMPRISE	GYSE	HUNTE
SUPPRISE	MYSE	BOUNTE
COVETISE	PROMYSE	FAYNTE

COMPLAYNTE	HAVE	DENYE
SOVERAYNTE	CRAVE	PIGGESNYE
BOTE	GRAVE	JOYE
COTE	SAVE	SPYE
FOTE	GEVE	CONTRARYE
SHOTE	LEVE	CRYE
BOOTE	GREVE	TYE
SHOOTE	IVE	LIBERTYE
ROOTE	TWELVE	BEAWTYE
ROTE	ABOVE	DEWTYE
HART-ROTE	LOVE	CHEF
WOTE	MOVE	TO-RAFF
HARTE	PROVE	SAFF
PARTE	SERVE	CHEFF
DEPARTE	PRESERVE	LEFF
HERTE	FYVE	IFF
RESORTE	GYVE	LIFF
COURTE	LYVE	WIFF
CASTE	ONE-LYVE	HALFF
HASTE	RYVE	HYMSELFF
WASTE	WE	OFF
MAJESTE	LAWE	THOFF
HONESTE	WITHDRAWE	YFF
CRISTE	STRAWE	GYFF
AGENSTE	SAWE	LYFF
MUSTE	SUBDEWE	IF
WYSTE	HEWE	MYSELF
ATTE	SHEWE	SYLF
WETTE	ESSHEWE	MYSYLF
YETTE	NEWE	OF
PUTTE	KNEWE	THOF
SCHYTTE	REWE	YF
PYTTE	BESHEREWE	LYF
BEAUTE	TREWE	STRYF
BEUTE	SEWE	HANG
OUTE	BOWE	WRANG
THOROUGHOUTE	MEDOWE	SANG
WITHOUTE	THOWE	NOTHING
SUTE	NOWE	KING
BEAWTE	KNOWE	WAYLING
BEWTE	SORWE	SLEPING
OWTE	AXE	COMFORTING
ABOWTE	YE	LYVING
WITHOWTE	AYE	SAYING
CLOWTE	DAYE	HONG
NEXTE	DYSMAYE	LONG
BYTE	DYE	AMONG
SMYTE	HYE	SPRONG
PYTE	LYE	STRONG
CHARYTE	APPLYE	WRONG
CONTRYTE	TREULYE	SONG
ADVERSYTE	NYE	TONG
ENSUE	COMPANYE	YONG
VERTUE	CUMPANYE	YOUNG

343

PRAYNG	CONSIDERYNG	SYGH
SAYNG	SYNG	JOSEPH
BOBBYNG	PASSYNG	FLESSH
ENFORCYNG	CAUSYNG	FRESSH
BEHOLDYNG	MUSYNG	ENGLISSH
ENDYNG	BROYSYNG	FOLISSH
ABYDYNG	BETYNG	WISSH
VOYDYNG	COUNTURFETYNG	FYSSH
TYDYNG	ENTRETYNG	DEATH
BEYNG	COVETYNG	HATH
SEYNG	UNWETYNG	DETH
PLONGYNG	SWETYNG	UNNETH
CHAUNGYNG	TRISTYNG	MORNETH
HYNG	TRUSTYNG	NAZARETH
BESECHYNG	SPETTYNG	BRETH
LAUGHYNG	SWETTYNG	SETH
LAWGHYNG	SYTTYNG	CAUSETH
LANGUISSHYNG	ON-SYTTYNG	CONSISTETH
THYNG	BEHAVYNG	LOVETH
NOTHYNG	LEVYNG	SAYETH
KYNG	BELEVYNG	EIGHTH
MAKYNG	LOVYNG	RIGHTH
WAKYNG	SHEWYNG	LYGHTH
LOKYNG	SAYYNG	MYGHTH
LOOKYNG	LYYNG	NYGHTH
WALYNG	CONTRARYYNG	FAITH
DELYNG	WACH	SAITH
KNELYNG	RECH	NEDITH
MERVELYNG	SECH	HOLDITH
WELYNG	WHICH	SLEITH
RAILYNG	HANCH	ENCORAGITH
FALLYNG	WENCH	MAKITH
WILLYNG	MOCH	SITH
TREMLYNG	SOCH	ENCRESSITH
DERLYNG	SERCH	CAUSITH
DASLYNG	ENSERCH	WANTITH
WAYLYNG	CHURCH	GREVITH
DEMYNG	ANGUYSCH	LOVITH
MORENYNG	WATCH	PROVITH
CONNYNG	MUCH	WITH
LERNYNG	SUCH	SHEWITH
MORNYNG	WHYCH	REWITH
MOURNYNG	STRENGH	WHEREWITH
TURNYNG	THOGH	SEWITH
SOWNYNG	BOUGH	KNOWITH
FAYNYNG	HOUGH	GROWITH
FEYNYNG	THOUGH	WHERWITH
PERTEYNYNG	LOUGH	WELTH
WEPYNG	ENOUGH	BOTH
RYNG	ROUGH	DOTH
CAMPARYNG	THROUGH	LOTH
CONTRARYNG	YOUGH	FORSOTH
BRYNG	HOWGH	ERTH
REMEMBRYNG	THOWGH	MYRTH

TREUTH	THI	COUNCELL
GROUTH	FOR-THI	FELL
TROUTH	WHI	ANGELL
YOUTH	SODENLI	HELL
TREWTH	MARI	COMPELL
GROWTH	DOUGHTI	QUARELL
TROWTH	LUSTI	TELL
YOWTH	BAK	SUBTELL
FAYTH	ABAK	LITELL
SAYTH	JAK	CASTELL
ENFORCYTH	LAK	LYTELL
FEYTH	ALAK	CRUELL
CHAUNGYTH	MAK	TWENTY-A-DEVELL
MAKYTH	STRIK	MERVELL
TAKYTH	MILK	WELL
THYNCKYTH	BANK	DWELL
SEKYTH	THYNK	FAREWELL
LAKKYTH	METHYNK	ILL
STRENKYTH	DRYNK	TROBILL
THYNKYTH	WYNK	NEDILL
METHYNKYTH	DARK	WHILL
MYTHYNKYTH	HERK	FROMPILL
LYKYTH	ASK	SPILL
LYTH	DUK	TILL
FALLYTH	LUK	GENTILL
TELLYTH	PLUK	UNTILL
RULYTH	LYK	STILL
AYLYTH	NYK	LYTILL
AVAYLYTH	SHAL	WILL
EYLYTH	INMORTAL	WOLL
SEMYTH	TEL	FULL
AFFORMYTH	WEL	FEITHEFULL
RENNYTH	TIL	PAYNEFULL
MORNYTH	ALL	WOFFULL
TURNYTH	CALL	FAITHFULL
DYSDAYNYTH	FALL	DULFULL
RAYNYTH	EGALL	DOULFULL
REYNYTH	SCHALL	PAYNFULL
MAYNTEYNYTH	SHALL	SYNFULL
SYTH	SPECIALL	WOFULL
PLESYTH	MARSHIALL	FEERFULL
PASSYTH	RIALL	CHERFULL
CAUSYTH	TERRESTRIALL	SORFULL
ABATTYTH	CELESTIALL	RUFULL
SETTYTH	INFERNALL	SOROWFULL
PUTTYTH	MATERNALL	MERCYFULL
GREVYTH	PRINCIPALL	JOYFULL
LOVYTH	THRALL	SHULL
WYTH	NATURALL	PEPULL
KNOWYTH	INMORTALL	YLL
THERWYTH	SPECYALL	FAYLL
I	ESPECYALL	BEWAYLL
LADI	LOYALL	BYLL
THEI	RYALL	CUSTUMABYLL

345

NOBYLL	RAN	CONVENCION
DOUBYLL	WAN	REDEMPCION
STEYLL	BEN	DERISION
FULFYLL	BOUNDEN	PASSION
KYLL	BOWNDEN	COMPASSION
MEKYLL	GARDEN	CONFESSION
SKYLL	FIFTEEN	TRANSGRESSION
CAMAMYLL	THEN	REMISSION
NYLL	WHEN	FUSION
TYLL	MAWDLEN	NON
GENTYLL	SOLEN	ANON
UNTYLL	MEN	OON
STYLL	AMEN	MOON
LYTYLL	FRENCHMEN	NOON
EVYLL	WOMEN	APON
WYLL	SOVEREN	OPON
FREWYLL	SEN	UPPON
WOL	CHOSEN	THERUPPON
FUL	OFTEN	UPON
NOBYL	MAYNTEN	THERON
DOWBYL	GOTEN	SON
TYL	FORGOTEN	REASON
GENTYL	WITHOUTEN	ENCHESON
UNTYL	RYVEN	RESON
WYL	KNOWEN	TRESON
AM	YEN	SESON
CAM	AYEN	PRISON
MADAM	IN	PERSON
THEM	WITHIN	LESSON
HIM	RUTTERKIN	POYSON
COM	THERIN	WANTON
WELCOM	ON	WON
WHOM	BOWNDON	CONSTRUCCYON
FROM	GON	MANCYON
CUM	JHON	SURGYON
WELCUM	CREACION	LYON
WELLCUM	RECREACION	TAVERN
SUM	FACION	THORN
RAWNSUM	MEDIACION	RETORN
BLOSSUM	DISTILLACION	UN
BUXUM	CONSOLACION	SESOUN
HYM	ADULACION	OWN
AN	SIMULACION	DOWN
CAN	FORMACION	KNOWN
DAN	INDIGNACION	TOWN
BYGAN	DOMINACION	YN
THAN	CONSIDERACION	DYSDAYN
WHAN	CONJURACION	FAYN
CRISTIAN	TEMPTACION	ONFAYN
KAN	COMPUTACION	AGAYN
MAN	PRESERVACION	COMPLAYN
LEMMAN	LYNYACION	SLAYN
WOMAN	AFECCION	PAYN
JHOAN	CONTRICION	RAYN

SOVERAYN	WHERTO	AFTER
REFRAYN	WO	AFFTER
SAYN	TWO	LYGHTER
TWAYN	LAP	HUNTER
BYN	HELP	WYNTER
ROBYN	CONDEMP	PORTER
MAYDYN	STOP	FOSTER
BYDYN	HAPP	BETTER
SODEYN	UP	FETTER
BEGYN	GUP	GRETTER
THYN	AR	SWETTER
FORSAKYN	DAR	UTTER
TAKYN	ENDAR	RUTTER
RUTTERKYN	FAR	AWTER
STRYKYN	WAR	SUER
BLYN	REMEMBER	WAVER
MYN	FADER	EVER
THERYN	GEDER	WHEREEVER
SYN	YONDER	NEVER
WITHOUTYN	UNDER	WHOSOEVER
WITHOWTYN	HYNDER	WHATSOEVER
GEVYN	FODER	WHEREVER
HEVYN	MODER	FOREVER
YEVYN	ORDER	OVER
IYEVYN	CONSYDER	RECOVER
WYN	FEER	KOVER
KNOWYN	FER	LOVER
O	WAGER	TREWER
DO	LENGER	OWER
FO	HER	POWER
GO	THER	YOWER
EXCHO	GATHER	FAYER
THO	RATHER	PRAYER
WHO	FETHER	GOODLYER
LO	TOGETHER	REMEMBIR
BLO	WHETHER	SLUMBIR
FLO	OTHER	TENDIR
MO	LOTHER	UNDIR
NO	MOTHER	MODIR
DOO	ANOTHER	SUFFIR
FOO	FARTHER	GELOFIR
GOO	FERTHER	HIR
THOO	NOWTHER	FATHIR
BLOO	HYTHER	RATHIR
WOO	WHER	NETHIR
FRO	MAKER	WETHIR
SO	MANER	OTHIR
ALSO	OFTENER	ANOTHIR
ALLSO	SYNNER	SIR
WHOSO	PRISONER	HERE-AFFTIR
TO	SHARPER	NEVIR
INTO	FAYRER	OR
UNTO	MATER	FOR
THERTO	WATER	WHEREFOR

THERFOR	WHERAS	GENTYLNES
WHERFOR	MASTRAS	WYLDERNES
NOR	WAS	UNSTEDFASTNES
HONOR	AMYAS	FORTUNES
ERROR	BES	PAYNES
FAVOR	VICES	HEVYNES
ENDUR	DAUNCES	PES
YEUR	BEDES	DYSDAYNARES
HUR	BLEDES	PORTRES
ARTHUR	NEDES	MASTRES
SOLUR	FELDES	DYSTRES
OUR	HANDES	FLOWRES
LABOUR	INDES	SES
LAVENDOUR	HONDES	FANTYSES
ODOUR	STONDES	GYFFTES
FOUR	WONDES	THOFTES
SAVIOUR	COMAUNDES	THOWGHTES
FLOUR	WOWNDES	SANTES
COLOUR	MYNDES	COMPLAYNTES
POUR	WODES	SAYNTES
MYRROUR	WORDES	NOTES
FLAVOUR	DYSCORAGES	HARTES
YOUR	TYDINGES	FEATTES
PLESUR	THYNGES	SURFETTES
CREATUR	RECHES	FAUTTES
PETUR	SYGHES	PUTTES
REMEMBYR	THES	VERTUES
MODYR	LYFF-DAIES	GREVES
SUFFYR	WAIES	LOVES
GELOFYR	BODIES	LYVES
HYR	MAKES	DAWES
OTHYR	TAKES	SOROWES
MOTHYR	LOCKES	YES
ANOTHYR	THYNKES	WAYES
PROPYR	LES	JOYES
BETTYR	ENDLES	SYGHS
EVYR	WHILES	IS
HOUGHEVYR	ELLES	GODDIS
NEVYR	WHILLES	NEDIS
WHEREVYR	CARLES	LAIDIS
MOREOVYR	DOUTLES	GOLDIS
JHOON'S	REMEDYLES	HANDIS
MAKER'S	PETYLES	WONDIS
HUNTER'S	TYMES	WOUNDIS
FADIR'S	PASTYMES	WOWNDIS
LADY'S	ANES	MYNDIS
AS	KYNDNES	WYNDIS
BAS	UNKYNDNES	HIS
WHEREAS	GODNES	THIS
HAS	STRANGENES	PATHIS
LAS	HEVENES	CLOTHIS
ALAS	SEKNES	MYRTHIS
TOMAS	IDELNES	CLARKIS
TRESPAS	DOUBYLNES	WORDLIS

DELIS	TERS	MERVELOUS
NAILIS	LOVERS	SOROUS
WELLIS	DYVERS	GREVOUS
SOWLIS	WERS	AMORUS
NAYLIS	COWRTYERS	JHESUS
SLEPIS	WORS	VERTUS
HELPIS	ENDURS	PLENTUUS
TERIS	OURS	VERTUUS
FLOURIS	SOCOURS	GREVUS
SHOWRIS	FLOURS	JOYUS
SIS	DOLOURS	NOYUS
ROSIS	POURS	YOYUS
THOUGHTIS	YOURS	MEDOWS
SERPENTIS	PASS	AROWS
HARTIS	CESS	SOROWS
HERTIS	PRINCESS	YS
HURTIS	GESS	WAYS
WAVIS	LESS	BLODDYS
LEVIS	RELESS	NEDYS
WIS	GUERDONLESS	SHELDYS
I-WIS	CAUSLESS	BYRDYS
JEWIS	DOUTLESS	FORTUNEYS
SYNOWIS	REMEDYLESS	HYS
RYGHTWIS	GLADNESS	THYS
FALS	UNKYNDNESS	KYS
ELS	GOODNESS	MYS
WHYLS	FORGEVENESS	JAMYS
ASSURANS	HEVINESS	LYMMYS
GREVANS	WILLFULLNESS	ENMYS
CREDENS	WOFULNESS	ARMYS
RESIDENS	SYKYRNESS	DENYS
OFFENS	WITNESS	MANNYS
HENS	STEDFASTNESS	SONNYS
CONCIENS	UNSTEDFASTNESS	ONYS
SYLENS	WITTNESS	STONYS
SENS	WERYNESS	THORNYS
ABSENS	HEVYNESS	FORTUNYS
PRESENS	REDRESS	PAYNYS
MOWNTENS	EXPRESS	VAYNYS
ONS	MASTRESS	MAYDYNYS
COMPARYSONS	MORTESS	JOYS
MAYDYNS	BLISS	LEPYS
COMYNS	PISS	CLEPYS
WHOS	I-WISS	DROPYS
PRYMEROS	CROSS	TERYS
GREVOS	US	FLOWERYS
DYSDAYNARS	THUS	ROSYS
WARS	GRACIUS	HORSYS
MODERS	GLORIUS	COURSYS
OTHERS	OVERPLUS	FEATYS
MANNERS	VENUS	BLASTYS
SPERS	GRACIOUS	DYSPORTTYS
PLESERS	PRECIOUS	MAVYS
CAUSERS	CONTRARIOUS	LEVYS

LOVYS	WYGHT	HOT
BOWYS	WISHT	SHOT
AT	BANYSHT	NOT
THAT	IT	CANNOT
WHAT	REWARDIT	GALON-POT
SUMWHAT	HIT	WOT
THERAT	MARGARIT	LEPT
BET	COVIT	WEPT
GET	SALT	PROMPT
LET	GILT	SLYPT
VIOLET	SPILT	ART
MARGARET	WILT	HART
SECRET	BOLT	SMART
GRET	MYLT	PART
SET	INFANT	DEPART
SWET	WARRANT	HERT
YET	PLESANT	SMERT
EFT	PUSANT	DESERT
LEFT	REPENTANT	STERT
LEFFT	SERVANT	REVERT
OFFT	UNBENT	COVERT
SHYFFT	ORDENT	SHIRT
OFT	EVYDENT	COMFORT
LIGHT	FORFENT	DISCOMFORT
RIGHT	GENT	CUMFORT
BRIGHT	HENT	REPORT
WIGHT	SHENT	SPORT
NOGHT	OBEDIENT	RESORT
BRAUGHT	LENT	HURT
OUGHT	EXCELLENT	CAST
BOUGHT	MENT	FAST
FORFOUGHT	JUGEMENT	STEDFAST
THOUGHT	SPENT	AGAST
BETHOUGHT	TO-RENT	HAST
METHOUGHT	INDYFFERENT	CHAST
NOUGHT	SENT	LAST
WROUGHT	ABSENT	UNLAST
SOUGHT	REPRESENT	PAST
NOWGHT	CONSENT	BRAST
ENDYGHT	ENTENT	TAST
FYGHT	INTENT	BEST
HYGHT	CONTENT	SHOLDEST
WHYGHT	AVENT	FEST
LYGHT	FERVENT	GEST
FLYGHT	WENT	DYGEST
MYGHT	WONT	LEST
NYGHT	GRAUNT	MEST
KNYGHT	PLESAUNT	HONEST
PYGHT	SERVAUNT	FAYNEST
RYGHT	MOWNT	REST
BRYGHT	CONSTRAYNT	BREST
UNRYGHT	SAYNT	FOREST
WRYGHT	SEYNT	PREST
SYGHT	STYNT	OPPREST

350

FAYREST	FAUT	YOW
METEST	BUT	SIX
BRYGHTEST	OUT	Y
REQUEST	PUT	AY
BEQWEST	OWT	DAY
HARDYEST	DOWT	PASSE-THE-DAY
WORTHYEST	WITHOWT	FAY
GODLYEST	NEXT	POPAGAY
MAIST	YT	HAY
WOLDIST	HYT	THAY
FRESSHIST	INFYNYT	LAY
SLEPIST	TREU	LULLAY
CRIST	YEU	PLAY
AGEYNST	THOU	MAY
COST	NOU	NAY
LOST	YOU	DENAY
MOST	JHESU	PAY
ALLMOST	VERTU	RAY
FIRST	GEV	BRAY
WORST	DRAW	AFRAY
FURST	STRAW	PRAY
JUST	SAW	SPRAY
LUST	DEW	ARRAY
MUST	ADEW	SAY
TRUST	HEW	ASAY
MYSTRUST	ESCHEW	GAYNESAY
MAKYST	SHEW	ASSAY
THYNKYST	GLEW	WAY
LYST	NEW	AWAY
DOYST	KNEW	ALLWAY
CRYST	CONTYNEW	BY
LOVYST	REW	THERBY
SATT	DREW	WHERBY
FETT	TREW	MERCY
GETT	UNTREW	DY
KNOKETT	SEW	LADY
LETT	ENSEW	REMEDY
VIOLETT	INSEW	BODY
GRETT	YEW	EVERYBODY
SETT	BOW	BLODY
YETT	COW	HARDY
ITT	MEDOW	·STURDY
WITT	HOW	EY
SHOTT	THOW	OBEY
NOTT	LOW	HEY
CANNOTT	BLOW	THEY
COMFORTT	FOLLOW	SLEY
SPORTT	NOW	MENEY
BUTT	INOW	HAKNEY
PERFYTT	KNOW	SEY
WHYTT	AROW	FY
KNYTT	SOROW	GY
SYTT	ARROW	THY
WYTT	TROW	WORTHY

351

WHY	COMLY	STORMY
LY	PLANLY	NY
VALY	WOMMANLY	ANY
GLADLY	SODENLY	MANY
DEDLY	CERTENLY	COMPANY
ONKYNDLY	ONLY	CUMPANY
UNKYNDLY	UNLY	DENY
GOODLY	PLAYNLY	NONY
INWARDLY	VAYNLY	JOY
YNWARDLY	FOLY	YOY
OWTWARDLY	HOLY	MARY
WORDLY	JOLY	ROSEMARY
KYNDELY	LOLY	CONTRARY
BODELY	TROLY	NECESSARY
GODELY	ERLY	VARY
HARDELY	SOBERLY	CALVARY
SOTHELY	MODERLY	DOWNBERY
MERELY	MANERLY	MARGERY
VERELY	ENTERLY	MERY
PRATELY	SUERLY	GENTERY
STATELY	DANDIRLY	SAVERY
SWETELY	TENDIRLY	EVERY
HARTELY	CURTESLY	CALVERY
LOVELY	UNCURTESLY	WERY
PASSINGLY	PETEUSLY	CHEVALRY
PASSYNGLY	PYTEUSLY	SORY
ERTHLY	BOISTUSLY	VICTORY
DAILY	GREVUSLY	CARRY
BODILY	GREVOWSLY	HARRY
HERTILY	GRETLY	TARRY
MEKLY	SOFTLY	WRY
SPECIALLY	INSACIENTLY	FANTASY
LOLLY	PERTLY	BESY
TROLLY	SHORTLY	DAYSY
WOFFULLY	GOSTLY	PRATY
WRONGFULLY	INFYNYTLY	FETY
FAYTHFULLY	TRULY	PRETY
WILLFULLY	TREWLY	FURTY
ONRYGHTFULLY	DAYLY	HASTY
RUFULLY	MERYLY	LUSTY
LAWFULLY	PRETYLY	HEVY
JOYFULLY	MY	ENVY
TULLY		

REVERSE INDEX OF
FOREIGN GRAPHIC FORMS

BA	MORI	QUO
DA	VEL	ANTIQUO
LA	BELL	SUO
OSCULA	SOLEBAM	SEMPER
DULCISSIMA	QUADAM	MATER
ITA	QUIDAM	PATER
SUB	FACIAM	MEIS
AC	INTERFICIAM	VIRGIS
QUID	FUGIAM	PLAUSIS
PRINCE	ETERNAM	PETIS
LE	CORAM	D'AMOURS
NOBLE	VITAM	OMNIBUS
MADAME	CUM	PARENTIBUS
KATERINE	PUERUM	FUSTIBUS
DERIDERE	SUM	CLERICUS
LUDERE	FACTUM	PARATUS
FLERE	AMEN	ET
MOVERE	IN	PLACUIT
ARBORE	O	EST
TEMPORE	LOCO	ADEW
PECTORE	INCIPEO	HELY
TE	DOMINO	FILY
VIVE	VERNO	ROSARY
MICHI	PRO	HENRY
FILI		

INDEX OF RHYMES

```
-ABLE [see -Y] (15)
  ABLE (1)
    lamentable, able (F38.2 1,3)
  DELECTABLE (1)
    delectable, varyable (H47.4 1,3)
  LAMENTABLE (2)
    lamentable, hely, rufully (F36.4 5,6,7)
    lamentable, able (F38.2 1,3)
  MERCIABLE (4)
    tretable, merciable (F34.2 6,8)
    unstable, merciable (F34.3 6,8)
    table, merciable (F34.4 6,8)
    reprovable, merciable (F34.5 6,8)
  MERCYABLE (1)
    vengeable, mercyable (F34.1 6,8)
  REPROVABLE (1)
    reprovable, merciable (F34.5 6,8)
  TABLE (1)
    table, merciable (F34.4 6,8)
  TRETABLE (1)
    tretable, merciable (F34.2 6,8)
  UNSTABLE (1)
    unstable, merciable (F34.3 6,8)
  VARYABLE (1)
    delectable, varyable (H47.4 1,3)
  VENGEABLE (1)
    vengeable, mercyable (F34.1 6,8)

-ACE [see -AS, -ASE] (24)
  CACE (1)
    cace, grace (H44.6 1,2)
  FACE (4)
    face, has, unbrace (F27.4 1,2,3)
    face, case (F31.3 2,4)
    face, place (H27.2 1,3)
    grace, face (H50.5 1,3)
  GRACE (7)
    grace, space (F44.1 2,4)
    grace, purchase (H25.5 4,5)
    cace, grace (H44.6 1,2)
    grace, face (H50.5 1,3)
    case, grace (H82.2 1,2)
    grace, purchase (H92.4 3,4)
    grace, place (H102.1 1,3)
  HACE (1)
    alas, trespas, place, hace (H31.2 1,2,4,5)
  PLACE (4)
    face, place (H27.2 1,3)
    alas, trespas, place, hace (H31.2 1,2,4,5)
    grace, place (H102.1 1,3)
    place, space (H106.4 5,6)
  SOLACE (1)
    solace, alas (H16 2,4)
```

-ACE (cont.)
  SPACE (3)
    trace, space (F9 4,8)
    grace, space (F44.1 2,4)
    place, space (H106.4 5,6)
  TRACE (1)
    trace, space (F9 4,8)
  TRESPACE (1)
    was, trespace (F49b 1,3)
  UNBRACE (1)
    face, has, unbrace (F27.4 1,2,3)

-AD (2)
  GLAD (1)
    sad, glad (H104b 4,5)
  SAD (1)
    sad, glad (H104b 4,5)

-ADD [see -ADDE] (2)
  GLADD (1)
    gladd, ladde, hadd, adradde (F32.2 1,2,3,4)
  HADD (1)
    gladd, ladde, hadd, adradde (F32.2 1,2,3,4)

-ADDE [see -ADD] (2)
  ADRADDE (1)
    gladd, ladde, hadd, adradde (F32.2 1,2,3,4)
  LADDE (1)
    gladd, ladde, hadd, adradde (F32.2 1,2,3,4)

-AGE (10)
  AGE (2)
    age, corage (H101.2 2,4)
    age, corage (H109.2 1,2)
  CORAGE (4)
    dotage, corage (H51.1 1,2)
    corage, viage (H97 3,4)
    age, corage (H101.2 2,4)
    age, corage (H109.2 1,2)
  COURAGE (1)
    courage, village (H51.7 1,2)
  DOTAGE (1)
    dotage, corage (H51.1 1,2)
  VIAGE (1)
    corage, viage (H97 3,4)
  VILLAGE (1)
    courage, village (H51.7 1,2)

-AY [see -AYE] (63)
  AFRAY (1)
    ray, away, play, afray (R3.1 2,4,5,7)
  ALLWAY (3)
    say, allway (F39b 4,8)
    fay, allway, popagay, play, say (F41.1 1,2,3,4,5)

358

-AY (cont.)
  ALLWAY (cont.)
    day, may, allway, denay (H31.1 1,2,4,5)
  ARRAY (1)
    array, day, play (F40.4 3,3,4)
  ASSAY (1)
    nay, way, assay, pray (R19.2 6,7,8,9)
  AWAY (3)
    ray, away, play, afray (R3.1 2,4,5,7)
    say, away (F14 1,3)
    day, play, away (F29.1 1,2,3)
  AY (1)
    may, way, ay, denay (H31.4 1,2,4,5)
  BRAY (1)
    lay, bray (H35.5 2,4)
  DAY (6)
    day, spray (R1.1 1,3)
    day, play, away (F29.1 1,2,3)
    array, day, play (F40.4 3,3,4)
    day, may, allway, denay (H31.1 1,2,4,5)
    day, may (H62.1 2,4)
    day, may (H65b 2,4)
  DENAY (3)
    day, may, allway, denay (H31.1 1,2,4,5)
    may, way, ay, denay (H31.4 1,2,4,5)
    pray, denay (H64.2 3,6)
  FAY (1)
    fay, allway, popagay, play, say (F41.1 1,2,3,4,5)
  GAYNESAY (1)
    gaynesay, say, play (H82.2 3,5,6)
  HAY (1)
    pay, hay (F30.1 15,18)
  LAY (1)
    lay, bray (H35.5 2,4)
  LULLAY (1)
    may, lullay (F30.1 4,5)
  MAY (8)
    may, lullay (F30.1 4,5)
    day, may, allway, denay (H31.1 1,2,4,5)
    may, way, ay, denay (H31.4 1,2,4,5)
    dysmaye, may (H47.2 2,4)
    day, may (H62.1 2,4)
    day, may (H65b 2,4)
    spray, May (H65.4 2,4)
    say, may (H92.2 3,4)
  NAY (1)
    nay, way, assay, pray (R19.2 6,7,8,9)
  PASSE-THE-DAY (1)
    say, passe-the-day (R12.2 8,9)
  PAY (1)
    pay, hay (F30.1 15,18)
  PLAY (6)
    ray, away, play, afray (R3.1 2,4,5,7)
    say, play (R15.6 1,2)

-AY (cont.)
  PLAY (cont.)
    day, play, away (F29.1 1,2,3)
    array, day, play (F40.4 3,3,4)
    fay, allway, popagay, play, say (F41.1 1,2,3,4,5)
    gaynesay, say, play (H82.2 3,5,6)
  POPAGAY (1)
    fay, allway, popagay, play, say (F41.1 1,2,3,4,5)
  PRAY (2)
    nay, way, assay, pray (R19.2 6,7,8,9)
    pray, denay (H64.2 3,6)
  RAY (1)
    ray, away, play, afray (R3.1 2,4,5,7)
  SAY (10)
    say, passe-the-day (R12.2 8,9)
    say, play (R15.6 1,2)
    say, away (F14 1,3)
    say, allway (F39b 4,8)
    fay, allway, popagay, play, say (F41.1 1,2,3,4,5)
    say, way (H25.2 4,5)
    say, way (H25.6 1,2)
    say, way (H41.8 1,2)
    gaynesay, say, play (H82.2 3,5,6)
    say, may (H92.2 3,4)
  SPRAY (2)
    day, spray (R1.1 1,3)
    spray, May (H65.4 2,4)
  WAY (5)
    nay, way, assay, pray (R19.2 6,7,8,9)
    say, way (H25.2 4,5)
    say, way (H25.6 1,2)
    may, way, ay, denay (H31.4 1,2,4,5)
    say, way (H41.8 1,2)

-AID [see -AYD, -AIDE, -AYDE] (6)
  ARAID (2)
    araid, naid, araide (F33b 1,4,6)
    said, betraide, araid (F36.2 5,6,7)
  DISMAID (1)
    dismaid, apaide (F32b 2,4)
  NAID (1)
    araid, naid, araide (F33b 1,4,6)
  SAID (2)
    said, betraide, araid (F36.2 5,6,7)
    said, at-abrayde, mayde, dysmayd (H31.8 1,2,4,5)

-AYD [see -AID, -AIDE, -AYDE] (7)
  APAYD (1)
    mayd, layd, apayd, saide (H105.1 1,2,3,4)
  BETRAYD (1)
    sayd, payd, betrayd (F7.2 2,4,5)
  DYSMAYD (1)
    said, at-abrayde, mayde, dysmayd (H31.8 1,2,4,5)

-AYD (cont.)
  LAYD (1)
    mayd, layd, apayd, saide (H105.1 1,2,3,4)
  MAYD (1)
    mayd, layd, apayd, saide (H105.1 1,2,3,4)
  PAYD (1)
    sayd, payd, betrayd (F7.2 2,4,5)
  SAYD (1)
    sayd, payd, betrayd (F7.2 2,4,5)

-AIDE [see -AID, -AYD] (4)
  APAIDE (1)
    dismaid, apaide (F32b 2,4)
  ARAIDE (1)
    araid, naid, araide (F33b 1,4,6)
  BETRAIDE (1)
    said, betraide, araid (F36.2 5,6,7)
  SAIDE (1)
    mayd, layd, apayd, saide (H105.1 1,2,3,4)

-AYDE [see -AID, -AYD, -EYD] (5)
  AFRAYDE (1)
    seyd, mayde, at-a-brayde, afrayde (R15.2 1,2,4,5)
  AT-A-BRAYDE (1)
    seyd, mayde, at-a-brayde, afrayde (R15.2 1,2,4,5)
  AT-ABRAYDE (1)
    said, at-abrayde, mayde, dysmayd (H31.8 1,2,4,5)
  MAYDE (2)
    seyd, mayde, at-a-brayde, afrayde (R15.2 1,2,4,5)
    said, at-abrayde, mayde, dysmayd (H31.8 1,2,4,5)

-AYE [see -AY] (1)
  DYSMAYE (1)
    dysmaye, may (H47.2 2,4)

-AYLL [see -AYLLE] (1)
  FAYLL (1)
    fayll, retaylle (H25.10 1,2)

-AYLLE [see -AYLL] (1)
  RETAYLLE (1)
    fayll, retaylle (H25.10 1,2)

-AYN [see -AYNE, -EN] (19)
  AGAYN (2)
    payn, vayne, dysdayn, fayn, refrayn, agayn
        (R10.5 1,2,3,5,6,7)
    onfayn, agayn (R15.5 3,6)
  COMPLAYN (2)
    vayne, payne, complayn (F17 2,4,5)
    complayn, dysdayn, slayne, remayne (H18 4,5,6,7)
  DYSDAYN (2)
    payn, vayne, dysdayn, fayn, refrayn, agayn
        (R10.5 1,2,3,5,6,7)

361

-AYN (cont.)
  DYSDAYN (cont.)
    complayn, dysdayn, slayne, remayne (H18 4,5,6,7)
  FAYN (2)
    payn, vayne, dysdayn, fayn, refrayn, agayn
        (R10.5 1,2,3,5,6,7)
    fayn, agayne (H47.1 3,4)
  ONFAYN (1)
    onfayn, agayn (R15.5 3,6)
  PAYN (4)
    payn, vayne, dysdayn, fayn, refrayn, agayn
        (R10.5 1,2,3,5,6,7)
    payn, slayn (R11.2 1,2)
    mayne, payn, sayn, agayne (H105.3 1,2,3,4)
    payn, fayne, rayne (H106.1 2,4,5)
  RAYN (1)
    twayn, rayn, ayen (F8 2,4,5)
  REFRAYN (2)
    payn, vayne, dysdayn, fayn, refrayn, agayn
        (R10.5 1,2,3,5,6,7)
    dysdayne, refrayn (H82.1 3,4)
  SAYN (1)
    mayne, payn, sayn, agayne (H105.3 1,2,3,4)
  SLAYN (1)
    payn, slayn (R11.2 1,2)
  TWAYN (1)
    twayn, rayn, ayen (F8 2,4,5)

-AYNE [see -EYNE, -AYN, -ANE] (89)
  AGAYNE (10)
    certayne, remanyne, agayne, oncerteyne (R20.3 1,2,3,4)
    unseyne, soverayne, agayne (F5 2,4,5)
    slayne, agayne (F32.1 4,5)
    agayne, payne (F48b 8,9)
    agayne, payne (F48.2 1,2)
    payne, agayne (H28 1,3)
    fayn, agayne (H47.1 3,4)
    payne, agayne (H47.5 2,4)
    mayne, payn, sayn, agayne (H105.3 1,2,3,4)
    agayne, twayne (H109.2 3,4)
  ATTAYNE (1)
    payne, fayne, attayne, oncertayne (R20.1 1,2,3,4)
  BARRAYNE (1)
    payne, vayne, brayne, refrayne, complayne, payne
        (F36.1 1,2,3,4,8,11)
  BRAYNE (1)
    playne, barrayne (H35.3 2,4)
  BRYTAYNE (1)
    optayne, rayne, Brytayne, Spayne (F44.2 5,6,7,8)
  CERTAYNE (1)
    certayne, remanyne, agayne, oncerteyne (R20.3 1,2,3,4)
  COMPLAYNE (7)
    complayne, refrayne (R4 1,3)
    payne, complayne, twayne (F6.1 4,5,6)

  COMPLAYNE (cont.)
    fayne, complayne (F23.2 1,3)
    defrayne, retayne, vayne, fayne, complayne, payne
        (F25.1 1,2,3,5,6,7)
    payne, disdayne, complayne (F28 2,4,5)
    payne, vayne, brayne, refrayne, complayne, payne
        (F36.1 1,2,3,4,8,11)
    complayne, payne (H31.1 3,6)
  CONSTRAYNE (1)
    constrayne, disdayne, trayne, uncerteyne (R20.1 1,2,3,4)
  DEFRAYNE (1)
    defrayne, retayne, vayne, fayne, complayne, payne
        (F25.1 1,2,3,5,6,7)
  DISDAYNE (2)
    constrayne, disdayne, trayne, uncerteyne (R20.1 1,2,3,4)
    payne, disdayne, complayne (F28 2,4,5)
  DYSDAYNE (6)
    optayne, dysdayne (H34.1 1,2)
    dysdayne, refrayne (H44.3 1,2)
    opteyne, dysdayne (H79.2 1,2)
    dysdayne, refrayn (H82.1 3,4)
    refrayne, dysdayne (H92.2 1,2)
    payne, refrayne, dysdayne (H106.2 2,4,5)
  FAYNE (4)
    payne, fayne, attayne, oncertayne (R20.1 1,2,3,4)
    fayne, complayne (F23.2 1,3)
    defrayne, retayne, vayne, fayne, complayne, payne
        (F25.1 1,2,3,5,6,7)
    payn, fayne, rayne (H106.1 2,4,5)
  MAYNE (1)
    mayne, payn, sayn, agayne (H105.3 1,2,3,4)
  ONCERTAYNE (2)
    payne, fayne, attayne, oncertayne (R20.1 1,2,3,4)
    slayne, reyne, twane, oncertayne (R20.4 1,2,3,4)
  OPTAYNE (4)
    optayne, rayne, Brytayne, Spayne (F44.2 5,6,7,8)
    optayne, dysdayne (H34.1 1,2)
    payne, optayne (H51.8 1,2)
    payne, optayne (H64.1 9,12)
  PAYNE (18)
    payne, fayne, attayne, oncertayne (R20.1 1,2,3,4)
    payne, complayne, twayne (F6.1 4,5,6)
    vayne, payne, complayn (F17 2,4,5)
    payne, playne (F23.1 1,3)
    defrayne, retayne, vayne, fayne, complayne, payne
        (F25.1 1,2,3,5,6,7)
    payne, disdayne, complayne (F28 2,4,5)
    payne, vayne, brayne, refrayne, complayne, payne
        (F36.1 1,2,3,4,8,11)
    agayne, payne (F48b 8,9)
    agayne, payne (F48.2 1,2)
    twayne, payne (H27.3 2,4)
    payne, agayne (H28 1,3)

PAYNE (cont.)
  complayne, payne (H31.1 3,6)
  payne, agayne (H47.5 2,4)
  payne, optayne (H51.8 1,2)
  payne, agane (H56 1,2)
  payne, optayne (H64.1 9,12)
  payne, refrayne, dysdayne (H106.2 2,4,5)
PLAYNE (4)
  playne, vayne (F7.2 1,3)
  payne, playne (F23.1 1,3)
  playne, barrayne (H35.3 2,4)
  retayne, playne (H67.2 4,8)
RAYNE (2)
  optayne, rayne, Brytayne, Spayne (F44.2 5,6,7,8)
  payn, fayne, rayne (H106.1 2,4,5)
REFRAYNE (5)
  complayne, refrayne (R4 1,3)
  payne, vayne, brayne, refrayne, complayne, payne
    (F36.1 1,2,3,4,8,11)
  dysdayne, refrayne (H44.3 1,2)
  refrayne, dysdayne (H92.2 1,2)
  payne, refrayne, dysdayne (H106.2 2,4,5)
REMAYNE (1)
  complayn, dysdayn, slayne, remayne (H18 4,5,6,7)
RETAYNE (2)
  defrayne, retayne, vayne, fayne, complayne, payne
    (F25.1 1,2,3,5,6,7)
  retayne, playne (H67.2 4,8)
SLAYNE (3)
  slayne, reyne, twane, oncertayne (R20.4 1,2,3,4)
  slayne, agayne (F32.1 4,5)
  complayn, dysdayn, slayne, remayne (H18 4,5,6,7)
SOVERAYNE (1)
  unseyne, soverayne, agayne (F5 2,4,5)
SPAYNE (1)
  optayne, rayne, Brytayne, Spayne (F44.2 5,6,7,8)
TRAYNE (1)
  constrayne, disdayne, trayne, uncerteyne (R20.1 1,2,3,4)
TWAYNE (3)
  payne, complayne, twayne (F6.1 4,5,6)
  twayne, payne (H27.3 2,4)
  agayne, twayne (H109.2 3,4)
VAYNE (5)
  payn, vayne, dysdayn, fayn, refrayn, agayn
    (R10.5 1,2,3,5,6,7)
  playne, vayne (F7.2 1,3)
  vayne, payne, complayn (F17 2,4,5)
  defrayne, retayne, vayne, fayne, complayne, payne
    (F25.1 1,2,3,5,6,7)
  payne, vayne, brayne, refrayne, complayne, payne
    (F36.1 1,2,3,4,8,11)

-AYRE (2)
  FAYRE (1)
    hayre, fayre (H51.3 1,2)
  HAYRE (1)
    hayre, fayre (H51.3 1,2)

-AKE (20)
  AWAKE (1)
    sake, awake, brake, crake (F33.2 1,2,3,4)
  BETAKE (1)
    make, betake (H33.3 2,4)
  BRAKE (1)
    sake, awake, brake, crake (F33.2 1,2,3,4)
  CRAKE (1)
    sake, awake, brake, crake (F33.2 1,2,3,4)
  FORSAKE (1)
    undyrtake, make, forsake (F6.3 4,5,6)
  LAKE (1)
    make, undertake, slake, lake (R2.1 2,4,5,7)
  MAKE (5)
    make, undertake, slake, lake (R2.1 2,4,5,7)
    undyrtake, make, forsake (F6.3 4,5,6)
    make, betake (H33.3 2,4)
    sake, make, take (H50.1 1,2,3)
    make, take (H92.7 1,2)
  QUAKE (1)
    quake, to-brake (F48.3 1,2)
  SAKE (2)
    sake, awake, brake, crake (F33.2 1,2,3,4)
    sake, make, take (H50.1 1,2,3)
  SLAKE (1)
    make, undertake, slake, lake (R2.1 2,4,5,7)
  TAKE (2)
    sake, make, take (H50.1 1,2,3)
    make, take (H92.7 1,2)
  TO-BRAKE (1)
    quake, to-brake (F48.3 1,2)
  UNDERTAKE (1)
    make, undertake, slake, lake (R2.1 2,4,5,7)
  UNDYRTAKE (1)
    undyrtake, make, forsake (F6.3 4,5,6)

-AL [see -ALL] (1)
  SHAL (1)
    all, shal (F44.3 1,3)

-ALE (10)
  ALE (5)
    ale, tale (R3.1 1,3)
    Vale, ale (F41.1 6,7)
    Vale, ale (F41.2 6,7)
    Vale, ale (F41.3 6,7)
    Vale, ale (F41.4 6,7)

-ALE (cont.)
  TALE (1)
    ale, tale (R3.1 1,3)
  VALE (4)
    Vale, ale (F41.1 6,7)
    Vale, ale (F41.2 6,7)
    Vale, ale (F41.3 6,7)
    Vale, ale (F41.4 6,7)

-ALL [see -ALLE, -AL] (32)
  ALL (8)
    calle, all (R11.3 1,2)
    all, all (R12.2 7,10)
    all, speciall, thrall, inmortall, terrestriall, shall
        (F36.3 1,2,3,4,8,11)
    all, shal (F44.3 1,3)
    especyall, all (H25.11 4,5)
    all, shall (H29.5 1,3)
    all, principall, shall (H50.6 1,2,3)
  CALL (3)
    call, fall (F34b 2,3)
    celestiall, maternall, infernall, call (F44.3 5,6,7,8)
    call, principall (H106.3 1,3)
  CELESTIALL (2)
    celestiall, terrestriall (F44.1 1,3)
    celestiall, maternall, infernall, call (F44.3 5,6,7,8)
  ESPECYALL (1)
    especyall, all (H25.11 4,5)
  FALL (1)
    call, fall (F34b 2,3)
  INFERNALL (1)
    celestiall, maternall, infernall, call (F44.3 5,6,7,8)
  INMORTALL (1)
    all, speciall, thrall, inmortall, terrestriall, shall
        (F36.3 1,2,3,4,8,11)
  MATERNALL (1)
    celestiall, maternall, infernall, call (F44.3 5,6,7,8)
  PRINCIPALL (2)
    all, principall, shall (H50.6 1,2,3)
    call, principall (H106.3 1,3)
  SHALL (7)
    shall, walle (R3.3 1,3)
    all, speciall, thrall, inmortall, terrestriall, shall
        (F36.3 1,2,3,4,8,11)
    all, shall (H29.5 1,3)
    shall, shall (H29.6 1,3)
    specyall, shall (H33.4 2,4)
    all, principall, shall (H50.6 1,2,3)
  SPECIALL (1)
    all, speciall, thrall, inmortall, terrestriall, shall
        (F36.3 1,2,3,4,8,11)
  SPECYALL (1)
    specyall, shall (H33.4 2,4)

-ALL (cont.)
  TERRESTRIALL (2)
    all, speciall, thrall, inmortall, terrestriall, shall
        (F36.3 1,2,3,4,8,11)
    celestiall, terrestriall (F44.1 1,3)
  THRALL (1)
    all, speciall, thrall, inmortall, terrestriall, shall
        (F36.3 1,2,3,4,8,11)

-ALLE [see -ALL] (2)
  CALLE (1)
    calle, all (R11.3 1,2)
  WALLE (1)
    shall, walle (R3.3 1,3)

-AME [see -AN] (5)
  GAME (1)
    game, same (H35.6 1,3)
  MADAME (1)
    name, madame (H41.4 1,2)
  NAME (1)
    name, madame (H41.4 1,2)
  SAME (2)
    man, same (H34.5 1,2)
    game, same (H35.6 1,3)

-AN [see -AME] (12)
  BYGAN (1)
    man, can, than, bygan (R3.3 2,4,5,7)
  CAN (3)
    man, can, than, bygan (R3.3 2,4,5,7)
    can, dan (F42b 4,5)
    man, can (H23.3 1,2)
  DAN (1)
    can, dan (F42b 4,5)
  MAN (4)
    man, can, than, bygan (R3.3 2,4,5,7)
    man, ran, wan (F33b 2,3,5)
    man, can (H23.3 1,2)
    man, same (H34.5 1,2)
  RAN (1)
    man, ran, wan (F33b 2,3,5)
  THAN (1)
    man, can, than, bygan (R3.3 2,4,5,7)
  WAN (1)
    man, ran, wan (F33b 2,3,5)

-ANCE [see -ANS, -AUNCE] (13)
  AVANCE (1)
    chance, avance (H107.2 4,8)
  CHANCE (4)
    chance, avaunce, daunce (F39.3 5,6,7)

-ANCE (cont.)
  CHANCE (cont.)
    chance, penance (H106.4 1,3)
    chance, avance (H107.2 4,8)
    dysplesance, grevance, surance, trance, substance, chance
        (H107.3 1,2,3,5,6,7)
  DYSPLESANCE (1)
    dysplesance, grevance, surance, trance, substance, chance
        (H107.3 1,2,3,5,6,7)
  GREVANCE (1)
    dysplesance, grevance, surance, trance, substance, chance
        (H107.3 1,2,3,5,6,7)
  PASTANCE (1)
    assurans, pastance (H92.3 3,4)
  PENANCE (1)
    chance, penance (H106.4 1,3)
  SUBSTANCE (1)
    dysplesance, grevance, surance, trance, substance, chance
        (H107.3 1,2,3,5,6,7)
  SURANCE (2)
    semblaunce, surance (F14 6,7)
    dysplesance, grevance, surance, trance, substance, chance
        (H107.3 1,2,3,5,6,7)
  TRANCE (1)
    dysplesance, grevance, surance, trance, substance, chance
        (H107.3 1,2,3,5,6,7)

-ANE [see -AYEN, -EYNE] (2)
  AGANE (1)
    payne, agane (H56 1,2)
  TWANE (1)
    slayne, reyne, twane, oncertayne (R20.4 1,2,3,4)

-ANYNE [see -AYNE, -EYNE] (1)
  REMANYNE (1)
    certayne, remanyne, agayne, oncerteyne (R20.3 1,2,3,4)

-ANK [see -ANKE] (1)
  BANK (1)
    bank, sanke (H35.2 1,3)

-ANKE [see -ANK] (1)
  SANKE (1)
    bank, sanke (H35.2 1,3)

-ANS [see -ANCE] (1)
  ASSURANS (1)
    assurans, pastance (H92.3 3,4)

-ANT [see -AUNT] (1)
  REPENTANT (1)
    graunt, repentant (F48.1 1,2)

-ARE (12)
  BARE (1)
    beware, bare, care, snare, hare, fare (R10.4 1,2,3,5,6,7)
  BEWARE (2)
    beware, bare, care, snare, hare, fare (R10.4 1,2,3,5,6,7)
    spare, beware (H109.4 1,2)
  CARE (3)
    beware, bare, care, snare, hare, fare (R10.4 1,2,3,5,6,7)
    welfare, care (H31.5 3,6)
    care, welfare (H104.4 1,2)
  FARE (1)
    beware, bare, care, snare, hare, fare (R10.4 1,2,3,5,6,7)
  HARE (1)
    beware, bare, care, snare, hare, fare (R10.4 1,2,3,5,6,7)
  SNARE (1)
    beware, bare, care, snare, hare, fare (R10.4 1,2,3,5,6,7)
  SPARE (1)
    spare, beware (H109.4 1,2)
  WELFARE (2)
    welfare, care (H31.5 3,6)
    care, welfare (H104.4 1,2)

-ART [see -ERT, -IRT] (21)
  DEPART (6)
    smert, hart, depart, shirt (F32.3 1,2,3,4)
    hart, depart (H15 1,3)
    hart, depart (H25.1 4,5)
    hart, depart (H27.1 1,3)
    hart, depart (H63.1 1,3)
    smert, hart, depart (H106.3 2,4,5)
  HART (13)
    smert, hart, depart, shirt (F32.3 1,2,3,4)
    smert, hart (F36.1 9,10)
    smert, hart (F36.3 9,10)
    smert, hart (F48b 6,7)
    smert, hart (F48.1 5,6)
    hart, depart (H15 1,3)
    hart, depart (H25.1 4,5)
    hart, revert (H25.3 4,5)
    hart, depart (H27.1 1,3)
    hart, depart (H63.1 1,3)
    hart, part (H96b 1,2)
    smert, hart, depart (H106.3 2,4,5)
    smert, hart, revert (H108 2,4,5)
  PART (1)
    hart, part (H96b 1,2)
  SMART (1)
    smart, hart, revert (H108 2,4,5)

-AS [see -ACE, -AST] (12)
  ALAS (4)
    las, bas, alas (F39.1 1,2,3)
    solace, alas (H16 2,4)
    alas, trespas, place, hace (H31.2 1,2,4,5)

-AS (cont.)
  ALAS (cont.)
    Amyas, alas, Amyas (H41b 1,3,4)
  AMYAS (2)
    Amyas, alas, Amyas (H41b 1,3,4)
  BAS (1)
    las, bas, alas (F39.1 1,2,3)
  HAS (1)
    face, has, unbrace (F27.4 1,2,3)
  LAS (1)
    las, bas, alas (F39.1 1,2,3)
  TRESPAS (1)
    alas, trespas, place, hace (H31.2 1,2,4,5)
  WAS (2)
    was, cast, brast, past, fast, agast (F36.4 1,2,3,4,8,11)
    was, trespace (F49b 1,3)

-ASE [see -ACE] (4)
  CASE (2)
    face, case (F31.3 2,4)
    case, grace (H82.2 1,2)
  PURCHASE (2)
    grace, purchase (H25.5 4,5)
    grace, purchase (H92.4 3,4)

-AST [see -AS, -ASTE] (6)
  AGAST (1)
    was, cast, brast, past, fast, agast (F36.4 1,2,3,4,8,11)
  BRAST (1)
    was, cast, brast, past, fast, agast (F36.4 1,2,3,4,8,11)
  CAST (1)
    was, cast, brast, past, fast, agast (F36.4 1,2,3,4,8,11)
  FAST (1)
    was, cast, brast, past, fast, agast (F36.4 1,2,3,4,8,11)
  PAST (1)
    was, cast, brast, past, fast, agast (F36.4 1,2,3,4,8,11)
  UNLAST (1)
    waste, unlast (H25.8 4,5)

-ASTE [see -AST] (3)
  HASTE (1)
    haste, waste (R3.1 6,8)
  WASTE (2)
    haste, waste (R3.1 6,8)
    waste, unlast (H25.8 4,5)

-AT [see -ATE, -OT] (2)
  THAT (1)
    that, not (H25.6 4,5)
  THERAT (1)
    gate, therat (H41.1 1,2)

-ATE [see -AT] (1)
  GATE (1)
    gate, therat (H41.1 1,2)

-AUGHT [see -OUGHT] (1)
  BRAUGHT (1)
    sought, bought, nought, thought, braught, forfought
      (R10.3 1,2,3,5,6,7)

-AUNCE [see -ANCE, -AWNCE] (49)
  ALEGEAUNCE (1)
    chaunce, alegeaunce, plesaunce (F11 2,4,5)
  ALIAUNCE (1)
    aliaunce, plesaunce, inerytaunce, Fraunce (F44.1 5,6,7,8)
  ASSURAUNCE (2)
    assuraunce, dawnce, chaunce (F21 2,4,5)
    assuraunce, remembraunce, constaunce (F23.2 2,4,5)
  AVAUNCE (3)
    governaunce, penaunce, avaunce (R4 2,4,5)
    chaunce, avaunce (F24.2 4,8)
    chance, avaunce, daunce (F39.3 5,6,7)
  CHAUNCE (5)
    chaunce, daunce (R10.3 4,8)
    chaunce, alegeaunce, plesaunce (F11 2,4,5)
    assuraunce, dawnce, chaunce (F21 2,4,5)
    chaunce, avaunce (F24.2 4,8)
    daunce, chaunce (H25.2 1,2)
  CONSTAUNCE (1)
    assuraunce, remembraunce, constaunce (F23.2 2,4,5)
  DALYAUNCE (1)
    dalyaunce, pastaunce (R12.2 1,2)
  DAUNCE (5)
    chaunce, daunce (R10.3 4,8)
    pastaunce, daunce (R12.1 5,6)
    displesaunce, grevaunce, suraunce, traunce, substaunce,
      daunce (F24.3 1,2,3,5,6,7)
    chance, avaunce, daunce (F39.3 5,6,7)
    daunce, chaunce (H25.2 1,2)
  DISPLESAUNCE (2)
    displesaunce, grevaunce, plesaunce (F23.1 2,4,5)
    displesaunce, grevaunce, suraunce, traunce, substaunce,
      daunce (F24.3 1,2,3,5,6,7)
  FRAUNCE (1)
    aliaunce, plesaunce, inerytaunce, Fraunce (F44.1 5,6,7,8)
  GOVERNAUNCE (2)
    governaunce, penaunce, avaunce (R4 2,4,5)
    remembraunce, governaunce (F15 2,4)
  GREVAUNCE (3)
    grevaunce, plesaunce (R2.2 6,8)
    displesaunce, grevaunce, plesaunce (F23.1 2,4,5)
    displesaunce, grevaunce, suraunce, traunce, substaunce,
      daunce (F24.3 1,2,3,5,6,7)
  GYDAUNCE (1)
    gydaunce, myschaunce (H92.5 3,4)

371

-AUNCE (cont.)
  INERYTAUNCE (1)
    aliaunce, plesaunce, inerytaunce, Fraunce (F44.1 5,6,7,8)
  MYSCHAUNCE (1)
    gydaunce, myschaunce (H92.5 3,4)
  ORDYNAUNCE (1)
    ordynaunce, plesaunce (R2.1 6,8)
  PASTAUNCE (2)
    pastaunce, daunce (R12.1 5,6)
    dalyaunce, pastaunce (R12.2 1,2)
  PENAUNCE (1)
    governaunce, penaunce, avaunce (R4 2,4,5)
  PLESAUNCE (6)
    ordynaunce, plesaunce (R2.1 6,8)
    grevaunce, plesaunce (R2.2 6,8)
    chaunce, alegeaunce, plesaunce (F11 2,4,5)
    displesaunce, grevaunce, plesaunce (F23.1 2,4,5)
    plesaunce, varyaunce (F26 2,3)
    aliaunce, plesaunce, inerytaunce, Fraunce (F44.1 5,6,7,8)
  PRESAUNCE (1)
    presaunce, rememoraunce (R5 3,6)
  REMEMBRAUNCE (2)
    remembraunce, governaunce (F15 2,4)
    assuraunce, remembraunce, constaunce (F23.2 2,4,5)
  REMEMORAUNCE (1)
    presaunce, rememoraunce (R5 3,6)
  SEMBLAUNCE (1)
    semblaunce, surance (F14 6,7)
  SUBSTAUNCE (1)
    displesaunce, grevaunce, suraunce, traunce, substaunce,
        daunce (F24.3 1,2,3,5,6,7)
  SURAUNCE (1)
    displesaunce, grevaunce, suraunce, traunce, substaunce,
        daunce (F24.3 1,2,3,5,6,7)
  TRAUNCE (1)
    displesaunce, grevaunce, suraunce, traunce, substaunce,
        daunce (F24.3 1,2,3,5,6,7)
  VARYAUNCE (1)
    plesaunce, varyaunce (F26 2,3)

-AUNT [see -ANT] (1)
  GRAUNT (1)
    graunt, repentant (F48.1 1,2)

-AVE (4)
  CRAVE (1)
    have, crave (F34b 4,5)
  HAVE (2)
    have, crave (F34b 4,5)
    have, save (H64.1 10,11)
  SAVE (1)
    have, save (H64.1 10,11)

```
-AWE (2)
  LAWE (1)
    lawe, sawe (F45.2 5,6)
  SAWE (1)
    lawe, sawe (F45.2 5,6)

-AWNCE [see -AUNCE] (1)
  DAWNCE (1)
    assuraunce, dawnce, chaunce (F21 2,4,5)

-E [see -ABLE, -EE, -ESSE, -I, -Y, -YE] (186)
  ADVERSITE (1)
    adversite, plente (R8 2,3)
  ADVERSYTE (1)
    be, adversyte (F16 3,4)
  AGRE (2)
    me, agre (H47.3 1,3)
    agre, be (H51.4 1,2)
  BE (43)
    be, me (R12.3 7,10)
    be, pyteusly (R15.2 3,6)
    cuntre, be (R15.5 4,5)
    she, flee, the, be (R19.3 6,7,8,9)
    me, be, perde, be (F2 2,4,5,8)
    the, be, the (F7.1 1,3,8)
    I, spye, prately, fre, me, be (F9 1,2,3,5,6,7)
    be, adversyte (F16 3,4)
    be, degre, me, remedy (F19 2,4,5,7)
    be, faythfully (F21 1,3)
    be, me (F27.1 4,5)
    be, me, daysy (F27.2 1,2,3)
    be, me (F27.5 4,5)
    be, thre (F27.6 4,5)
    be, tre (F30.2 15,18)
    be, humanite, be (F31b 1,3,5)
    sodenli, be (F32b 1,3)
    ye, pete, be (F36.3 5,6,7)
    degre, be, se, Trinite (F40.1 1,2,3,4)
    be, we (F44.1 9,10)
    be, we (F44.2 9,10)
    be, we (F44.3 9,10)
    me, be (F46.3 2,4)
    be, dygnite, be (F47.1 2,4,5)
    be, me (H25.2 3,6)
    be, me (H25.10 3,6)
    be, me (H25.11 3,6)
    be, me (H29.4 2,4)
    be, me (H29.5 2,4)
    be, me (H29.6 2,4)
    me, be (H40 2,4)
    agre, be (H51.4 1,2)
    be, me (H64.1 3,6)
    we, be (H64.2 1,2)
    be, degre, me (H66.2 1,3,5)
```

-E (cont.)
  BE (cont.)
    be, be (H82.1 1,2)
    equite, be (H92.5 1,2)
    be, se (H109b 6,7)
    be, se (H109.1 9,10)
  BEAUTE (4)
    ye, beaute, ye (F27b 1,2,3)
    ye, beaute, ye (F27.4 6,7,8)
    we, beaute, me (F27.6 6,7,8)
    beaute, fety (F39.2 4,8)
  BEAWTE (1)
    beawte, sche (H25.6 3,6)
  BENIGNITE (1)
    kne, benignite (F34.5 1,3)
  BESSE (2)
    Besse, Besse, me (R16b 1,2,3)
  BEWTE (1)
    se, bewte, pyte, me (R5 1,2,4,5)
  BLE (1)
    ble, me (H25.9 3,6)
  CHARITE (1)
    charite, the, the, fee (F48.1 7,8,9,10)
  CHARYTE (1)
    humilite, charyte (F34.4 1,3)
  COMMYNALTE (1)
    soveraynte, commynalte, Majeste (F47.2 2,4,5)
  CRUDELITE (1)
    pyte, crudelite (F34.3 1,3)
  CUNTRE (1)
    cuntre, be (R15.5 4,5)
  DEGRE (4)
    be, degre, me, remedy (F19 2,4,5,7)
    degre, me (F27.2 4,5)
    degre, be, se, Trinite (F40.1 1,2,3,4)
    be, degre, me (H66.2 1,3,5)
  DEITE (1)
    deite, moralite (F31.1 2,4)
  DYGNITE (1)
    be, dygnite, be (F47.1 2,4,5)
  EQUITE (1)
    equite, be (H92.5 1,2)
  FRE (4)
    I, spye, prately, fre, me, be (F9 1,2,3,5,6,7)
    Trinite, fre, pite (F32.1 1,2,3)
    Trinite, fre (F44.3 2,4)
    fre, me (H29.1 2,4)
  HE (2)
    he, me (R15.8 1,2)
    he, me (F27.4 4,5)
  HONESTE (1)
    honeste, flee (R12.3 1,2)
  HUMANITE (1)
    be, humanite, be (F31b 1,3,5)

-E (cont.)
  HUMILITE (1)
    humilite, charyte (F34.4 1,3)
  IVE (1)
    holy, ive, hye, holy (H33b 1,2,3,4)
  KNE (1)
    kne, benignite (F34.5 1,3)
  MAJESTE (1)
    soveraynte, commynalte, Majeste (F47.2 2,4,5)
  ME (48)
    se, bewte, pyte, me (R5 1,2,4,5)
    remedy, me (R11.1 3,4)
    remedy, me (R11.2 3,4)
    remedy, me (R11.3 3,4)
    remedy, me (R11.4 3,4)
    be, me (R12.3 7,10)
    he, me (R15.8 1,2)
    Besse, Besse, me (R16b 1,2,3)
    she, me (R16.1 3,6)
    me, be, perde, be (F2 2,4,5,8)
    I, spye, prately, fre, me, be (F9 1,2,3,5,6,7)
    be, degre, me, remedy (F19 2,4,5,7)
    be, me (F27.1 4,5)
    be, me, daysy (F27.2 1,2,3)
    degre, me (F27.2 4,5)
    certenly, me (F27.3 4,5)
    he, me (F27.4 4,5)
    be, me (F27.5 4,5)
    we, beaute, me (F27.6 6,7,8)
    me, se (F33.1 8,9)
    the, me (F33.3 8,9)
    me, the (F34b 6,7)
    the, me (F34.1 1,3)
    me, be (F46.3 2,4)
    me, free, thre (F49.1 2,4,5)
    me, me (H25.1 3,6)
    be, me (H25.2 3,6)
    pete, me (H25.3 3,6)
    me, me (H25.4 3,6)
    ye, me (H25.5 3,6)
    sche, me (H25.8 3,6)
    ble, me (H25.9 3,6)
    be, me (H25.10 3,6)
    be, me (H25.11 3,6)
    fre, me (H29.1 2,4)
    se, me (H29.2 2,4)
    she, me (H29.3 2,4)
    be, me (H29.4 2,4)
    be, me (H29.5 2,4)
    be, me (H29.6 2,4)
    me, be (H40 2,4)
    me, agre (H47.3 1,3)
    be, me (H64.1 3,6)
    me, dewtye, me (H66.1 1,3,5)

-E (cont.)
  ME (cont.)
    be, degre, me (H66.2 1,3,5)
  MORALITE (1)
    deite, moralite (F31.1 2,4)
  PERDE (1)
    me, be, perde, be (F2 2,4,5,8)
  PETE (2)
    ye, pete, be (F36.3 5,6,7)
    pete, me (H25.3 3,6)
  PITE (2)
    pite, truly, foly, lye, swetely, contrary
          (F18.2 1,2,3,5,6,7)
    Trinite, fre, pite (F32.1 1,2,3)
  PLENTE (1)
    adversite, plente (R8 2,3)
  PYTE (3)
    se, bewte, pyte, me (R5 1,2,4,5)
    pyte, te (R7 4,6)
    pyte, crudelite (F34.3 1,3)
  SCHE (2)
    beawte, sche (H25.6 3,6)
    sche, me (H25.8 3,6)
  SE (7)
    se, bewte, pyte, me (R5 1,2,4,5)
    me, se (F33.1 8,9)
    degre, be, se, Trinite (F40.1 1,2,3,4)
    knee, se (H25.7 3,6)
    se, me (H29.2 2,4)
    be, se (H109b 6,7)
    be, se (H109.1 9,10)
  SHE (3)
    she, me (R16.1 3,6)
    she, flee, the, be (R19.3 6,7,8,9)
    she, me (H29.3 2,4)
  SOVERAYNTE (1)
    soveraynte, commynalte, Majeste (F47.2 2,4,5)
  TE (1)
    pyte, te (R7 4,6)
  THE (11)
    she, flee, the, be (R19.3 6,7,8,9)
    the, be, the (F7.1 1,3,8)
    fantasy, remedy, the (F7.2 6,7,8)
    the, me (F33.3 8,9)
    me, the (F34b 6,7)
    the, the (F34b 8,9)
    the, me (F34.1 1,3)
    charite, the, the, fee (F48.1 7,8,9,10)
  THRE (4)
    be, thre (F27.6 4,5)
    tre, thre (F34.2 1,3)
    me, free, thre (F49.1 2,4,5)
    thre, victory (H97 5,6)

-E (cont.)
  TRE (3)
    be, tre (F30.2 15,18)
    tre, thre (F34.2 1,3)
    tre, see (H65.3 2,4)
  TRINITE (3)
    Trinite, fre, pite (F32.1 1,2,3)
    degre, be, se, Trinite (F40.1 1,2,3,4)
    Trinite, fre (F44.3 2,4)
  WE (5)
    we, beaute, me (F27.6 6,7,8)
    be, we (F44.1 9,10)
    be, we (F44.2 9,10)
    be, we (F44.3 9,10)
    we, be (H64.2 1,2)
  YE (7)
    ye, ynwardly (R13.2 1,3)
    ye, beaute, ye (F27b 1,2,3)
    ye, beaute, ye (F27.4 6,7,8)
    ye, pete, be (F36.3 5,6,7)
    ye, me (H25.5 3,6)

-EASE [see -YS] (7)
  DISEASE (1)
    ease, disease, please, Denys (F40b 1,2,3,4)
  EASE (1)
    ease, disease, please, Denys (F40b 1,2,3,4)
  PLEASE (5)
    ease, disease, please, Denys (F40b 1,2,3,4)
    please, Denys (F40.1 5,6)
    please, Denys (F40.2 5,6)
    please, Denys (F40.3 5,6)
    please, Denys (F40.4 5,6)

-ECH [see -ERCH] (1)
  RECH (1)
    enserch, rech (H44.2 1,2)

-ED [see -EDE, -ODE] (5)
  DED (2)
    hede, red, ded, shede (F33.3 1,2,3,4)
    maydynhed, ded (H109.3 3,4)
  GOODLYHED (1)
    lede, womanhode, goodlyhed (F20 2,4,5)
  MAYDYNHED (1)
    maydynhed, ded (H109.3 3,4)
  RED (1)
    hede, red, ded, shede (F33.3 1,2,3,4)

-EDE [see -ED, -ODE] (10)
  BLEDE (1)
    indede, nede, blede (F38.1 3,4,5)
  DEDE (2)
    mede, dede (H35.2 2,4)

377

-EDE (cont.)
  DEDE (cont.)
    dede, spede (H79.1 3,4)
  HEDE (1)
    hede, red, ded, shede (F33.3 1,2,3,4)
  INDEDE (1)
    indede, nede, blede (F38.1 2,4,5)
  LEDE (1)
    lede, womanhode, goodlyhed (F20 2,4,5)
  MEDE (1)
    mede, dede (H35.2 2,4)
  NEDE (1)
    indede, nede, blede (F38.1 2,4,5)
  SHEDE (1)
    hede, red, ded, shede (F33.3 1,2,3,4)
  SPEDE (1)
    dede, spede (H79.1 3,4)

-EE [see -E] (6)
  FEE (1)
    charite, the, the, fee (F48.1 7,8,9,10)
  FLEE (2)
    honeste, flee (R12.3 1,2)
    she, flee, the, be (R19.3 6,7,8,9)
  FREE (1)
    me, free, thre (F49.1 2,4,5)
  KNEE (1)
    knee, se (H25.7 3,6)
  SEE (1)
    tre, see (H65.3 2,4)

-EERE [see -ERE] (1)
  FEERE (1)
    tere, feere (F37.3 3,4)

-EFF [see -IFF] (1)
  LEFF (1)
    wiff, leff (F30.1 10,11)

-EYD [see -AYDE] (1)
  SEYD (1)
    seyd, mayde, at-a-brayde, afrayde (R15.2 1,2,4,5)

-EYLL [see -ELE] (1)
  STEYLL (1)
    steyll, fele, whele (R13.2 2,4,5)

-EYNE [see -AYNE, -ANE] (7)
  BARYEYNE (1)
    baryeyne, tweyne (R2.1 1,3)
  ONCERTEYNE (1)
    certayne, remanyne, agayne, oncerteyne (R20.3 1,2,3,4)
  OPTEYNE (1)
    opteyne, dysdayne (H79.2 1,2)

-EYNE (cont.)
  REYNE (1)
    slayne, reyne, twane, oncertayne (R20.4 1,2,3,4)
  TWEYNE (1)
    baryeyne, tweyne (R2.1 1,3)
  UNCERTEYNE (1)
    constrayne, disdayne, trayne, uncerteyne (R20.1 1,2,3,4)
  UNSEYNE (1)
    unseyne, soverayne, agayne (F5 2,4,5)

-EKE [see -YKE] (4)
  MEKE (1)
    meke, seke, lyke (F39b 1,2,3)
  SEKE (1)
    meke, seke, lyke (F39b 1,2,3)
  SPEKE (1)
    speke, to-breke (R13.1 1,3)
  TO-BREKE (1)
    speke, to-breke (R13.1 1,3)

-ELE [see -EYLL, -ELL] (5)
  DELE (2)
    hele, dele (R13.3 1,3)
    well, dele (F38.1 1,3)
  FELE (1)
    steyll, fele, whele (R13.2 2,4,5)
  HELE (1)
    hele, dele (R13.3 1,3)
  WHELE (1)
    steyll, fele, whele (R13.2 2,4,5)

-ELL [see -ELE] (15)
  BELL (1)
    farewell, bell, tell, dwell (H31.7 1,2,4,5)
  COMPELL (1)
    compell, subtell (H34.7 1,2)
  DWELL (1)
    farewell, bell, tell, dwell (H31.7 1,2,4,5)
  FAREWELL (1)
    farewell, bell, tell, dwell (H31.7 1,2,4,5)
  HELL (1)
    well, hell (F38b 1,2)
  SUBTELL (1)
    compell, subtell (H34.7 1,2)
  TELL (3)
    tell, well (F18.2 4,8)
    farewell, bell, tell, dwell (H31.7 1,2,4,5)
    tell, well (H92.1 3,4)
  WELL (6)
    well, well (F2 1,3)
    tell, well (F18.2 4,8)
    well, hell (F38b 1,2)
    well, dele (F38.1 1,3)
    tell, well (H92.1 3,4)

379

-EN [see -AYN, -END] (2)
  AMEN (1)
    condyscend, amen (H64.2 9,12)
  AYEN (1)
    twayn, rayn, ayen (F8 2,4,5)

-ENCE [see -ENS] (6)
  ABSENCE (1)
    hens, absence (H104.2 1,2)
  HENCE (1)
    offence, hence (F49.1 6,7)
  OFFENCE (2)
    offence, hens, spence, pence (R3.2 2,4,5,7)
    offence, hence (F49.1 6,7)
  PENCE (1)
    offence, hens, spence, pence (R3.2 2,4,5,7)
  SPENCE (1)
    offence, hens, spence, pence (R3.2 2,4,5,7)

-END [see -EN, -ENDE, -ENT] (13)
  AMEND (4)
    offend, amend (F38.1 6,7)
    myspend, amend (F38.2 6,7)
    amend, end (H66.4 3,3)
    amend, end (H92.8 3,4)
  CONDYSCEND (1)
    condyscend, amen (H64.2 9,12)
  DEFFEND (1)
    ende, deffend (H25.11 1,2)
  END (3)
    end, unbent (H35.7 1,3)
    amend, end (H66.4 3,3)
    amend, end (H92.8 3,4)
  FEND (1)
    spend, fend (H23.6 1,2)
  MYSPEND (1)
    myspend, amend (F38.2 6,7)
  OFFEND (1)
    offend, amend (F38.1 6,7)
  SPEND (1)
    spend, fend (H23.6 1,2)

-ENDE [see -END] (7)
  BENDE (1)
    bende, ende (R1.2 1,3)
  ENDE (3)
    bende, ende (R1.2 1,3)
    ende, wende (F1 2,4)
    ende, deffend (H25.11 1,2)
  SHENDE (1)
    shende, wende (R3.2 6,8)
  WENDE (2)
    shende, wende (R3.2 6,8)
    ende, wende (F1 2,4)

-ENE [see -YN] (19)
  BENE (2)
    grene, bene (H33.1 1,3)
    bene, sene (H44.1 1,2)
  BETWENE (1)
    grene, quene, byn, betwene (F45.1 1,2,3,4)
  CLENE (1)
    grene, clene, kene (H20 3,6,9)
  GRENE (7)
    grene, grene (F42b 3,6)
    grene, quene, byn, betwene (F45.1 1,2,3,4)
    grene, clene, kene (H20 3,6,9)
    grene, bene (H33.1 1,3)
    grene, sene (H33.2 1,3)
    grene, sene (H109.1 1,2)
  KENE (1)
    grene, clene, kene (H20 3,6,9)
  QUENE (2)
    quene, sene, byn, tene (F32.4 1,2,3,4)
    grene, quene, byn, betwene (F45.1 1,2,3,4)
  SENE (4)
    quene, sene, byn, tene (F32.4 1,2,3,4)
    grene, sene (H33.2 1,3)
    bene, sene (H44.1 1,2)
    grene, sene (H109.1 1,2)
  TENE (1)
    quene, sene, byn, tene (F32.4 1,2,3,4)

-ENS [see -ENCE] (8)
  CONCIENS (1)
    conciens, residens (F10 1,3)
  HENS (3)
    offence, hens, spence, pence (R3.2 2,4,5,7)
    presens, hens (F22 1,3)
    hens, absence (H104.2 1,2)
  OFFENS (1)
    presens, offens (F28 6,7)
  PRESENS (2)
    presens, hens (F22 1,3)
    presens, offens (F28 6,7)
  RESIDENS (1)
    conciens, residens (F10 1,3)

-ENT [see -END, -ENTE] (42)
  CONSENT (2)
    represent, consent (H51.5 1,2)
    consent, content (H109.1 3,4)
  CONTENT (5)
    content, spent (F2 6,7)
    content, entent (F24.4 4,8)
    lent, entent, ment, content, spente, shent
        (F25.3 1,2,3,5,6,7)
    content, entent (H107.4 4,8)
    consent, content (H109.1 3,4)

381

-ENT (cont.)
ENTENT (6)
  entent, shent (F22 6,7)
  content, entent (F24.4 4,8)
  lent, entent, spent, went, shent, ment (F24.5 1,2,3,5,6,7)
  lent, entent, ment, content, spente, shent
      (F25.3 1,2,3,5,6,7)
  content, entent (H107.4 4,8)
  lent, entent, spent, went, shent, ment (H107.5 1,2,3,5,6,7)
EVYDENT (1)
  excellent, evydent (F47.1 1,3)
EXCELLENT (1)
  excellent, evydent (F47.1 1,3)
FORFENT (1)
  spent, forfent (H23.1 1,2)
GENT (1)
  hent, gent, spent, intent (H31.9 1,2,4,5)
HENT (2)
  hent, gent, spent, intent (H31.9 1,2,4,5)
  went, hent (H35.5 1,3)
INTENT (1)
  hent, gent, spent, intent (H31.9 1,2,4,5)
JUGEMENT (1)
  jugement, obedient (F46.2 2,4)
LENT (3)
  lent, entent, spent, went, shent, ment (F24.5 1,2,3,5,6,7)
  lent, entent, ment, content, spente, shent
      (F25.3 1,2,3,5,6,7)
  lent, entent, spent, went, shent, ment (H107.5 1,2,3,5,6,7)
MENT (3)
  lent, entent, spent, went, shent, ment (F24.5 1,2,3,5,6,7)
  lent, entent, ment, content, spente, shent
      (F25.3 1,2,3,5,6,7)
  lent, entent, spent, went, shent, ment (H107.5 1,2,3,5,6,7)
OBEDIENT (1)
  jugement, obedient (F46.2 2,4)
REPRESENT (1)
  represent, consent (H51.5 1,2)
SHENT (4)
  entent, shent (F22 6,7)
  lent, entent, spent, went, shent, ment (F24.5 1,2,3,5,6,7)
  lent, entent, ment, content, spente, shent
      (F25.3 1,2,3,5,6,7)
  lent, entent, spent, went, shent, ment (H107.5 1,2,3,5,6,7)
SPENT (5)
  content, spent (F22 6,7)
  lent, entent, spent, went, shent, ment (F24.5 1,2,3,5,6,7)
  spent, forfent (H23.1 1,2)
  hent, gent, spent, intent (H31.9 1,2,4,5)
  lent, entent, spent, went, shent, ment (H107.5 1,2,3,5,6,7)
UNBENT (1)
  end, unbent (H35.7 1,3)
WENT (3)
  lent, entent, spent, went, shent, ment (F24.5 1,2,3,5,6,7)

```
-ENT (cont.)
  WENT (cont.)
    went, hent (H35.5 1,3)
    lent, entent, spent, went, shent, ment (H107.5 1,2,3,5,6,7)

-ENTE [see -ENT] (1)
  SPENTE (1)
    lent, entent, ment, content, spente, shent
          (F25.3 1,2,3,5,6,7)

-EPE (4)
  KEPE (1)
    kepe, wepe (R15.7 1,2)
  SLEPE (1)
    slepe, wepe (F30.1 3,6)
  WEPE (2)
    kepe, wepe (R15.7 1,2)
    slepe, wepe (F30.1 3,6)

-EPT (2)
  LEPT (1)
    wept, lept (H25.7 1,2)
  WEPT (1)
    wept, lept (H25.7 1,2)

-ER [see -ERE] (6)
  HER (1)
    where, her (F39.1 4,8)
  OTHER (1)
    other, utter (H23.4 1,2)
  PRISONER (1)
    here, prisoner (H41.5 1,2)
  THER (2)
    ther, fere, nere, here (R19.1 6,7,8,9)
    bere, ther (H41.7 1,2)
  UTTER (1)
    other, utter (H23.4 1,2)

-ERCH [see -ECH] (1)
  ENSERCH (1)
    enserch, rech (H44.2 1,2)

-ERE [see -EER, -ER, -IR, -ORE, -OURE, -URE] (28)
  BERE (1)
    bere, ther (H41.7 1,2)
  BRERE (1)
    brere, clere, nere, chere (R19.1 1,2,3,4)
  CHERE (4)
    brere, clere, nere, chere (R19.1 1,2,3,4)
    dere, chere (F30b 2,4)
    dere, chere (F30.2 1,2)
    chere, clere, pere (F39.2 1,2,3)
  CLERE (2)
    brere, clere, nere, chere (R19.1 1,2,3,4)
```

-ERE (cont.)
  CLERE (cont.)
    chere, clere, pere (R39.2 1,2,3)
  DERE (5)
    dere, chere (F30b 2,4)
    dere, chere (F30.2 1,2)
    here, here-afftir, dere (F48b 1,2,3)
    pere, dere (H31.6 3,6)
    nere, dere (H31.8 3,6)
  FERE (1)
    ther, fere, nere, here (R19.1 6,7,8,9)
  HERE (3)
    ther, fere, nere, here (R19.1 6,7,8,9)
    here, here-afftir, dere (F48b 1,2,3)
    here, prisoner (H41.5 1,2)
  MERE (1)
    afore, mere (H35.4 2,4)
  NERE (3)
    brere, clere, nere, chere (R19.1 1,2,3,4)
    ther, fere, nere, here (R19.1 6,7,8,9)
    nere, dere (H31.8 3,6)
  PERE (3)
    chere, clere, pere (F39.2 1,2,3)
    pere, dere (H31.6 3,6)
    yere, pere (H101.3 2,4)
  TERE (1)
    tere, feere (F37.3 3,4)
  WARYOWERE (1)
    pure, waryowere, barryoure (H50.2 1,2,3)
  WHERE (1)
    where, her (F39.1 4,8)
  YERE (1)
    yere, pere (H101.3 2,4)

-ERT [see -ART, -IRT] (12)
  HERT (2)
    hert, stert (R15.7 4,5)
    hert, smert (F36.2 9,10)
  REVERT (2)
    hart, revert (H25.3 4,5)
    smart, hart, revert (H108 2,4,5)
  SMERT (7)
    smert, hart, depart, shirt (F32.3 1,2,3,4)
    smert, hart (F36.1 9,10)
    hert, smert (F36.2 9,10)
    smert, hart (F36.3 9,10)
    smert, hart (F48b 6,7)
    smert, hart (F48.1 5,6)
    smert, hart, depart (H106.3 2,4,5)
  STERT (1)
    hert, stert (R15.7 4,5)

-ERVID [see -ERVYD] (1)
  DESERVID (1)
    servyd, deservid (F15 1,3)

-ERVYD [see -ERVID] (1)
  SERVYD (1)
    servyd, deservid (F15 1,3)

-ES [see -ESE, -ESS, -ESSE] (19)
  ANES (1)
    Bes, Anes, witness (F39.2 5,6,7)
  BES (1)
    Bes, Anes, witness (F39.2 5,6,7)
  DOUTLES (1)
    doutles, remedyles, cese, unkyndnes, les, redresse
        (H107.2 1,2,3,5,6,7)
  DYSTRES (2)
    wyldernes, Besse, dystres, remedyles (R15.1 1,2,4,5)
    weryness, dystres (F5 1,3)
  GENTYLNES (1)
    kyndnesse, gentylnes (H25.4 1,2)
  HEVENES (1)
    hevenes, redresse (H106.1 6,7)
  HEVYNES (1)
    expresse, hevynes (H47.1 1,2)
  IDELNES (1)
    idelnes, mastres (R12.2 5,6)
  LES (1)
    doutles, remedyles, cese, unkyndnes, les, redresse
        (H107.2 1,2,3,5,6,7)
  MASTRES (2)
    idelnes, mastres (R12.2 5,6)
    hevyness, mastres (F23.2 6,7)
  REMEDYLES (3)
    wyldernes, Besse, dystres, remedyles (R15.1 1,2,4,5)
    wyldernes, remedyles (R15.8 4,5)
    doutles, remedyles, cese, unkyndnes, les, redresse
        (H107.2 1,2,3,5,6,7)
  UNKYNDNES (1)
    doutles, remedyles, cese, unkyndnes, les, redresse
        (H107.2 1,2,3,5,6,7)
  UNSTEDFASTNES (1)
    unstedfastnes, gesse (H107.1 4,8)
  WYLDERNES (2)
    wyldernes, Besse, dystres, remedyles (R15.1 1,2,4,5)
    wyldernes, remedyles (R15.8 4,5)

-ESE [see -ES, -ESSE] (1)
  CESE (1)
    doutles, remedyles, cese, unkyndnes, les, redresse
        (H107.2 1,2,3,5,6,7)

-ESS [see -ES, -ESSE] (26)
  CESS (1)
    doutless, remedyless, cess, unkyndness, less, redress
        (F24.2 1,2,3,5,6,7)
  DOUTLESS (2)
    less, doutless (F20 6,7)
    doutless, remedyless, cess, unkyndness, less, redress
        (F24.2 1,2,3,5,6,7)
  EXPRESS (1)
    stedfastness, express (F20 1,3)
  GESS (1)
    unstedfastness, gess (F24.1 4,8)
  GLADNESS (1)
    gladness, sykyrness (F11 1,3)
  GOODNESS (1)
    goodness, redress (F47.2 1,3)
  GUERDONLESS (1)
    guerdonless, wittness (F13 6,7)
  HEVINESS (1)
    heviness, besynesse (R6 2,3)
  HEVYNESS (1)
    hevyness, mastres (F23.2 6,7)
  LESS (2)
    less, doutless (F20 6,7)
    doutless, remedyless, cess, unkyndness, less, redress
        (F24.2 1,2,3,5,6,7)
  MASTRESS (1)
    unkyndness, mastress (F23.1 6,7)
  REDRESS (3)
    doutless, remedyless, cess, unkyndness, less, redress
        (F24.2 1,2,3,5,6,7)
    wofulness, redress (F25.1 4,8)
    goodness, redress (F47.2 1,3)
  REMEDYLESS (1)
    doutless, remedyless, cess, unkyndness, less, redress
        (F24.2 1,2,3,5,6,7)
  STEDFASTNESS (1)
    stedfastness, express (F20 1,3)
  SYKYRNESS (1)
    gladness, sykyrness (F11 1,3)
  UNKYNDNESS (2)
    unkyndness, mastress (F23.1 6,7)
    doutless, remedyless, cess, unkyndness, less, redress
        (F24.2 1,2,3,5,6,7)
  UNSTEDFASTNESS (1)
    unstedfastness, gess (F24.1 4,8)
  WERYNESS (1)
    weryness, dystres (F5 1,3)
  WITNESS (1)
    Bes, Anes, witness (F39.2 5,6,7)
  WITTNESS (1)
    guerdonless, wittness (F13 6,7)
  WOFULNESS (1)
    wofulness, redress (F25.1 4,8)

386

-ESSE [see -E, -ES, -ESE, -ESS, -IS] (10)
  BESSE (1)
    wyldernes, Besse, dystres, remedyles (R15.1 1,2,4,5)
  BESYNESSE (1)
    heviness, besynesse (R6 2,3)
  EXPRESSE (1)
    expresse, hevynes (H47.1 1,2)
  GESSE (1)
    unstedfastnes, gesse (H107.1 4,8)
  GODENESSE (1)
    godenesse, hevenesse (R8 1,4)
  HEVENESSE (1)
    godenesse, hevenesse (R8 1,4)
  KYNDNESSE (1)
    kyndnesse, gentylnes (H25.4 1,2)
  REDRESSE (2)
    hevenes, redresse (H106.1 6,7)
    doutles, remedyles, cese, unkyndnes, les, redresse
        (H107.2 1,2,3,5,6,7)
  SYKYRNESSE (1)
    sykyrnesse, is (F48.3 7,8)

-EST [see -OST] (40)
  BEQWEST (1)
    beqwest, best (H50.1 4,5)
  BEST (14)
    best, rest (R2.2 1,3)
    best, dygest (R12.2 3,4)
    gest, fest, rest, best, est (F37.1 3,4,5,6,7)
    rest, best, est (F37.2 5,6,7)
    rest, best, est (F37.3 5,6,7)
    rest, best, est (F37 4 5,6,7)
    brest, best (H50b 1,2)
    beqwest, best (H50.1 4,5)
    hardyest, best (H50.2 4,5)
    worthyest, best (H50.3 4,5)
    prest, best (H50.4 4,5)
    godlyest, best (H50.5 4,5)
    request, best (H50.6 4,5)
    best, opprest, brest (H103 3 1,2,3)
  BREST (4)
    brest, prest (H24 1,3)
    rest, brest (H31.3 3,6)
    brest, best (H50b 1,2)
    best, opprest, brest (H103.3 1,2,3)
  DYGEST (1)
    best, dygest (R12.2 3,4)
  EST (4)
    gest, fest, rest, best, est (F37.1 3,4,5,6,7)
    rest, best, est (F37.2 5,6,7)
    rest, best, est (F37.3 5,6,7)
    rest, best, est (F37.4 5,6,7)
  FEST (1)
    gest, fest, rest, best, est (F37.1 3,4,5,6,7)

-EST (cont.)
  GEST (1)
    gest, fest, rest, best, est (F37.1 3,4,5,6,7)
  GODLYEST (1)
    godlyest, best (H50.5 4,5)
  HARDYEST (1)
    hardyest, best (H50.2 4,5)
  MEST (1)
    lost, mest (H102.2 2,4)
  OPPREST (1)
    best, opprest, brest (H103.3 1,2,3)
  PREST (2)
    brest, prest (H24 1,3)
    prest, best (H50.4 4,5)
  REQUEST (1)
    request, best (H50.6 4,5)
  REST (6)
    best, rest (R2.2 1,3)
    gest, fest, rest, best, est (F37.1 3,4,5,6,7)
    rest, best, est (F37.2 5,6,7)
    rest, best, est (F37.3 5,6,7)
    rest, best, est (F37.4 5,6,7)
    rest, brest (H31.3 3,6)
  WORTHYEST (1)
    worthyest, best (H50.3 4,5)

-ET [see -IT] (1)
  YET (1)
    yet, it‾ (H27.4 1,3)

-ETE [see -ETT, -IT] (12)
  GETE (1)
    gete, fett (H51.2 1,2)
  HETE (1)
    mete, replete, hete (H50.4 1,2,3)
  METE (4)
    Margarit, mete, strete (F39.3 1,2,3)
    swete, mete, wete, replete (H31.6 1,2,4,5)
    mete, replete, hete (H50.4 1,2,3)
    mete, swete (H109b 4,5)
  REPLETE (2)
    swete, mete, wete, replete (H31.6 1,2,4,5)
    mete, replete, hete (H50.4 1,2,3)
  STRETE (1)
    Margarit, mete, strete (F39.3 1,2,3)
  SWETE (2)
    swete, mete, wete, replete (H31.6 1,2,4,5)
    mete, swete (H109b 4,5)
  WETE (1)
    swete, mete, wete, replete (H31.6 1,2,4,5)

-ETH (2)
  DETH (1)
    Nazareth, deth (F48b 4,5)

```
-ETH (cont.)
  NAZARETH (1)
    Nazareth, deth (F48b 4,5)

-ETHER [see -ETHIR] (1)
  FETHER (1)
    wethir, fether (F44b 1,2)

-ETHIR [see -ETHER] (1)
  WETHIR (1)
    wethir, fether (F44b 1,2)

-ETID (3)
  ENTRETID (1)
    entretid, fretid, thretid (F33.1 5,6,7)
  FRETID (1)
    entretid, fretid, thretid (F33.1 5,6,7)
  THRETID (1)
    entretid, fretid, thretid (F33.1 5,6,7)

-ETT [see -ETE] (7)
  FETT (2)
    sett, fett (H23.5 1,2)
    gete, fett (H51.2 1,2)
  GETT (1)
    sett, gett (H44.5 1,2)
  LETT (1)
    sett, lett (R12.1 7,10)
  SETT (3)
    sett, lett (R12.1 7,10)
    sett, fett (H23.5 1,2)
    sett, gett (H44.5 1,2)

-ETTE (2)
  WETTE (1)
    wette, yette (R3.2 1,3)
  YETTE (1)
    wette, yette (R3.2 1,3)

-ETTER [see -ETTYR] (1)
  FETTER (1)
    bettyr, fetter (F46.2 1,3)

-EW [see -EWE, -OO, -UE] (27)
  ADEW (3)
    sew, adew (H31.4 3,6)
    adew, trew, adew (H38 1,3,4)
  ENSEW (1)
    doo, ensew (H92.6 1,2)
  ESCHEW (2)
    insew, eschew (R12.3 5,6)
    eschew, new (R13.3 6,7)
  HEW (2)
    hew, subdewe (F8 6,7)
```

-EW (cont.)
  HEW (cont.)
    hew, trew (H33.1 2,4)
  INSEW (1)
    insew, eschew (R12.3 5,6)
  KNEW (1)
    rewe, knew (R11.4 1,2)
  NEW (4)
    eschew, new (R13.3 6,7)
    untrew, new (H31.2 3,6)
    untrew, new, rew, trew (H31.3 1,2,4,5)
    trew, new (H49.3 2,4)
  REW (2)
    untrew, new, rew, trew (H31.3 1,2,4,5)
    ensue, rew (H92.1 1,2)
  SEW (2)
    sew, adew (H31.4 3,6)
    sew, trew (H79.1 1,2)
  TREW (7)
    trew, esshewe (F25.3 4,8)
    untrew, new, rew, trew (H31.3 1,2,4,5)
    hew, trew (H33.1 2,4)
    adew, trew, adew (H38 1,3,4)
    trew, new (H49.3 2,4)
    sewe, trew (H51.9 1,2)
    sew, trew (H79.1 1,2)
  UNTREW (2)
    untrew, new (H31.2 3,6)
    untrew, new, rew, trew (H31.3 1,2,4,5)

-EWE [see -EW] (8)
  ESSHEWE (1)
    trew, esshewe (F25.3 4,8)
  HEWE (1)
    hewe, knewe, rewe, trewe (F45.2 1,2,3,4)
  KNEWE (1)
    hewe, knewe, rewe, trewe (F45.2 1,2,3,4)
  REWE (2)
    rewe, knew (R11.4 1,2)
    hewe, knewe, rewe, trewe (F45.2 1,2,3,4)
  SEWE (1)
    sewe, trew (H51.9 1,2)
  SUBDEWE (1)
    hew, subdewe (F8 6,7)
  TREWE (1)
    hewe, knewe, rewe, trewe (F45.2 1,2,3,4)

-EWITH (2)
  REWITH (1)
    sewith, rewith (H64.2 7,8)
  SEWITH (1)
    sewith, rewith (H64.2 7,8)

390

-I [see -E, -Y, -YE] (20)
  I (19)
    I, grevowsly, hertily, truly (R2.2 2,4,5,7)
    I, trewly, fy, deny, foly, vaynly (F10.2 1,2,3,5,6,7)
    remedy, I (R10.5 4,8)
    denye, I (R12.2 3,4)
    remedy, I (F4 1,3)
    wrongfully, I, wrongfully (F6.2 1,3,7)
    I, spye, prately, fre, me, be (F9 1,2,3,5,6,7)
    applye, I (F21 6,7)
    truly, I, gretly, playnly, wry, contrary
        (F24.4 1,2,3,5,6,7)
    suerly, I, gretly, applye, body, dye (F25.2 1,2,3,5,6,7)
    infynytly, I (F30.2 9,12)
    I, dye (F36b 1,2)
    I, dye (F37.3 1,2)
    I, lady (F39.3 4,8)
    lady, I (F42b 1,2)
    I, remedy (H25.5 1,2)
    carry, I (H66.2 2,4)
    I, lady (H102b 1,2)
    trewly, I, gretly, planly, wry, contrary
        (H107.4 1,2,3,5,6,7)
  SODENLI (1)
    sodenli, be (F32b 1,3)

-Y [see -E, -I, -YE] (110)
  BODELY (1)
    uncurtesly, fy, piggesnye, hardely, bodely
        (F41.3 1,2,3,4,5)
  BODY (2)
    dye, body (F11 6,7)
    suerly, I, gretly, applye, body, dye (F25.2 1,2,3,5,6,7)
  BY (1)
    wrongfully, by, wrongfully (F6.4 1,3,7)
  CALVARY (1)
    Calvary, mercy (F48.3 9,10)
  CALVERY (1)
    Calvery, hye (F30.2 13,14)
  CARRY (1)
    carry, I (H66.2 2,4)
  CERTENLY (1)
    certenly, me (F27.3 4,5)
  CHEVALRY (1)
    applye, joly, companye, chevalry (H22 1,2,3,4)
  COMPANY (2)
    company, Henry, rosary (H68 1,3,4)
    company, mery (H104.1 1,2)
  CONTRARY (3)
    pite, truly, foly, lye, swetely, contrary
        (F18.2 1,2,3,5,6,7)
    truly, I, gretly, playnly, wry, contrary
        (F24.4 1,2,3,5,6,7)

391

-Y (cont.)
  CONTRARY (cont.)
    trewly, I, gretly, planly, wry, contrary
        (H107.4 1,2,3,5,6,7)
  CURTESLY (1)
    manerly, curtesly, prately (F39b 5,6,7)
  DAYSY (1)
    be, me, daysy (F27.2 1,2,3)
  DENY (1)
    I, trewly, fy, deny, foly, vaynly (R10.2 1,2,3,5,6,7)
  DY (1)
    hye, dy (H35b 1,2)
  ENTERLY (1)
    enterly, rosemary, savery (F27.3 1,2,3)
  FANTASY (1)
    fantasy, remedy, the.(F7.2 6,7,8)
  FAYTHFULLY (1)
    be, faythfully (F21 1,3)
  FETY (1)
    beaute, fety (F39.2 4,8)
  FOLY (3)
    I, trewly, fy, deny, foly, vaynly (R10.2 1,2,3,5,6,7)
    remedy, foly, dye (F7 2,4,5)
    pite, truly, foly, lye, swetely, contrary
        (F18.2 1,2,3,5,6,7)
  FY (2)
    I, trewly, fy, deny, foly, vaynly (R10.2 1,2,3,5,6,7)
    uncurtesly, fy, piggesnye, hardely, bodely
        (F41.3 1,2,3,4,5)
  GRETLY (3)
    truly, I, gretly, playnly, wry, contrary
        (F24.4 1,2,3,5,6,7)
    suerly, I, gretly, applye, body, dye
        (F25.2 1,2,3,5,6,7)
    trewly, I, gretly, planly, wry, contrary
        (H107.4 1,2,3,5,6,7)
  GREVOWSLY (1)
    I, grevowsly, hertily, truly (R2.2 2,4,5,7)
  GREVUSLY (1)
    crye, grevusly, hye (F38.2 2,4,5)
  GY (1)
    gy, dye (H67.1 4,8)
  HARDELY (2)
    why, hardely (F18.1 4,8)
    uncurtesly, fy, piggesnye, hardely, bodely
        (F41.3 1,2,3,4,5)
  HARRY (1)
    Mary, Harry (H66.4 2,4)
  HELY (1)
    lamentable, hely, rufully (F36.4 5,6,7)
  HENRY (1)
    company, Henry, rosary (H68 1,3,4)
  HERTILY (1)
    I, grevowsly, hertily, truly (R2.2 2,4,5,7)

392

-Y (cont.)
  HOLY (2)
    holy, ive, hye, holy (H33b 1,2,3,4)
  INFYNYTLY (1)
    infynytly, I (F30.2 9,12)
  JOLY (1)
    applye, joly, companye, chevalry (H22 1,2,3,4)
  LADY (5)
    I, lady (F39.3 4,8)
    lady, I (F42b 1,2)
    lady, only (H33.3 1,3)
    lady, trewly (H33.4 1,3)
    I, lady (H102b 1,2)
  LY (1)
    ly, sothely (F30.2 4,5)
  MANERLY (1)
    manerly, curtesly, prately (F39b 5,6,7)
  MARY (2)
    necessary, mary (H66.3 2,4)
    Mary, Harry (H66.4 2,4)
  MERCY (2)
    dye, mercy (R13.1 6,7)
    Calvary, mercy (F48.3 9,10)
  MERELY (1)
    hie, merely (H20 7,8)
  MERY (2)
    mery, sory (F17 6,7)
    company, mery (H104.1 1,2)
  NECESSARY (1)
    necessary, mary (H66.3 2,4)
  ONLY (1)
    lady, only (H33.3 1,3)
  PLANLY (1)
    trewly, I, gretly, planly, wry, contrary
        (H107.4 1,2,3,5,6,7)
  PLAYNLY (1)
    truly, I, gretly, playnly, wry, contrary
        (F24.4 1,2,3,5,6,7)
  PRATELY (2)
    I, spye, prately, fre, me, be (F9 1,2,3,5,6,7)
    manerly, curtesly, prately (F39b 5,6,7)
  PYTEUSLY (1)
    be, pyteusly (R15.2 3,6)
  REMEDY (13)
    remedy, I (R10.5 4,8)
    remedy, me (R11.1 3,4)
    remedy, me (R11.2 3,4)
    remedy, me (R11.3 3,4)
    remedy, me (R11.4 3,4)
    remedy, I (F4 1,3)
    remedy, foly, dye (F7 2,4,5)
    fantasy, remedy, the (F7.2 6,7,8)
    be, degre, me, remedy (F19 2,4,5,7)
    remedy, dye (F24.3 4,8)

-Y (cont.)
  REMEDY (cont.)
    I, remedy (H25.5 1,2)
    contrarye, remedy (H64.2 10,11)
    remedy, dye (H107.3 4,8)
  ROSARY (1)
    company, Henry, rosary (H68 1,3,4)
  ROSEMARY (1)
    enterly, rosemary, savery (F27.3 1,2,3)
  RUFULLY (1)
    lamentable, hely, rufully (F36.4 5,6,7)
  SAVERY (1)
    enterly, rosemary, savery (F27.3 1,2,3)
  SORY (1)
    mery, sory (F17 6,7)
  SOTHELY (1)
    ly, sothely (F30.2 4,5)
  SUERLY (1)
    suerly, I, gretly, applye, body, dye (F25.2 1,2,3,5,6,7)
  SWETELY (1)
    pite, truly, foly, lye, swetely, contrary
      (F18.2 1,2,3,5,6,7)
  TARRY (1)
    tarry, vary (H66.1 2,4)
  TREWLY (3)
    I, trewly, fy, deny, foly, vaynly (R10.2 1,2,3,5,6,7)
    lady, trewly (H33.4 1,3)
    trewly, I, gretly, planly, wry, contrary
      (H107.4 1,2,3,5,6,7)
  TRULY (3)
    I, grevowsly, hertily, truly (R2.2 2,4,5,7)
    pite, truly, foly, lye, swetely, contrary
      (F18.2 1,2,3,5,6,7)
    truly, I, gretly, playnly, wry, contrary
      (F24.4 1,2,3,5,6,7)
  UNCURTESLY (1)
    uncurtesly, fy, piggesnye, hardely, bodely
      (F41.3 1,2,3,4,5)
  UNKYNDLY (1)
    wrongfully, unkyndly, wrongfully (F6.3 1,3,7)
  VARY (1)
    tarry, vary (H66.1 2,4)
  VAYNLY (1)
    I, trewly, fy, deny, foly, vaynly (R10.2 1,2,3,5,6,7)
  VICTORY (1)
    thre, victory (H97 5,6)
  WHY (2)
    wrongfully, why, wrongfully (F6.1 1,3,7)
    why, hardely (F18.1 4,8)
  WRONGFULLY (8)
    wrongfully, why, wrongfully (F6.1 1,3,7)
    wrongfully, I, wrongfully (F6.2 1,3,7)
    wrongfully, unkyndly, wrongfully (F6.3 1,3,7)
    wrongfully, by, wrongfully (F6.4 1,3,7)

-Y (cont.)
  WRY (2)
    truly, I, gretly, playnly, wry, contrary
        (F24.4 1,2,3,5,6,7)
    trewly, I, gretly, planly, wry, contrary
        (H107.4 1,2,3,5,6,7)
  YNWARDLY (1)
    ye, ynwardly (R13.2 1,3)

-ICE [see -ISE] (1)
  SACRIFICE (1)
    wise, sacrifice (F33.2 8,9)

-ID [see -YDE] (1)
  PROVID (1)
    gyde, provid (H97 1,2)

-YD [see -YRDE, -USYD] (2)
  GYDYD (1)
    gydyd, usyd (H92.6 3,4)
  HYD (1)
    byrde, hyd (R15.6 3,6)

-YDE [see -ID] (5)
  ABYDE (1)
    abyde, tyde, gyde, wyde (R19.2 1,2,3,4)
  GYDE (2)
    abyde, tyde, gyde, wyde (R19.2 1,2,3,4)
    gyde, provid (H97 1,2)
  TYDE (1)
    abyde, tyde, gyde, wyde (R19.2 1,2,3,4)
  WYDE (1)
    abyde, tyde, gyde, wyde (R19.2 1,2,3,4)

-IE [see -Y] (1)
  HIE (1)
    hie, merely (H20 7,8)

-YE [see -E, -I, -Y] (32)
  APPLYE (3)
    applye, I (F21 6,7)
    suerly, I, gretly, applye, body, dye (F25.2 1,2,3,5,6,7)
    applye, joly, companye, chevalry (H22 1,2,3,4)
  COMPANYE (1)
    applye, joly, companye, chevalry (H22 1,2,3,4)
  CONTRARYE (1)
    contrarye, remedy (H64.2 10,11)
  CRYE (2)
    crye, grevusly, hye (F38.2 2,4,5)
    crye, dye (F49b 2,4)
  CUMPANYE (1)
    cumpanye, dye (R12.1 1,2)
  DENYE (2)
    denye, I (R12.2 3,4)

395

-YE (cont.)
  DENYE (cont.)
    treulye, denye (H23.2 1,2)
  DEWTYE (1)
    me, dewtye, me (H66.1 1,3,5)
  DYE (12)
    cumpanye, dye (R12.1 1,2)
    dye, mercy (R13.1 6,7)
    remedy, foly, dye (F7 2,4,5)
    dye, body (F11 6,7)
    remedy, dye (F24.3 4,8)
    suerly, I, gretly, applye, body, dye (F25.2 1,2,3,5,6,7)
    I, dye (F36b 1,2)
    I, dye (F37.3 1,2)
    crye, dye (F49b 2,4)
    nye, dye (H27.2 2,4)
    gy, dye (H67.1 4,8)
    remedy, dye (H107.3 4,8)
  HYE (4)
    calvery, hye (F30.2 13,14)
    crye, grevusly, hye (F38.2 2,4,5)
    holy, ive, hye, holy (H33b 1,2,3,4)
    hye, dy (H35b 1,2)
  LYE (1)
    pite, truly, foly, lye, swetely, contrary
        (F18.2 1,2,3,5,6,7)
  NYE (1)
    nye, dye (H27.2 2,4)
  PIGGESNYE (1)
    uncurtesly, fy, piggesnye, hardely, bodely
        (F41.3 1,2,3,4,5)
  SPYE (1)
    I, spye, prately, fre, me, be (F9 1,2,3,5,6,7)
  TREULYE (1)
    treulye, denye (H23.2 1,2)

-YF (2)
  LYF (1)
    lyf, stryf (R10.4 4,8)
  STRYF (1)
    lyf, stryf (R10.4 4,8)

-IFF [see -EFF] (1)
  WIFF (1)
    wiff, leff (F30.1 10,11)

-IFFE [see -YFFE] (1)
  WIFFE (1)
    wiffe, lyffe (R1.2 2,4)

-YFFE [see -IFFE] (1)
  LYFFE (1)
    wiffe, lyffe (R1.2 2,4)

-IGHT [see -YGHT] (2)
  LIGHT (1)
    nyght, light (F12 1,3)
  WIGHT (1)
    wight, myght (F32.2 5,6)

-YGHT [see -IGHT] (30)
  BRYGHT (1)
    bryght, hyght (H41.3 1,2)
  ENDYGHT (1)
    endyght, wryght (H29.1 1,3)
  FLYGHT (1)
    fyght, ryght, lyght, flyght (H96.1 1,2,3,4)
  FYGHT (1)
    fyght, ryght, lyght, flyght (H96.1 1,2,3,4)
  HYGHT (1)
    bryght, hyght (H41.3 1,2)
  KNYGHT (1)
    knyght, ryght (F47b 1,2)
  LYGHT (4)
    myght, lyght (F31.1 1,3)
    wyght, lyght (F46.1 1,3)
    fyght, ryght, lyght, flyght (H96.1 1,2,3,4)
    myght, lyght, syght, ryght (H105.2 1,2,3,4)
  MYGHT (4)
    myght, lyght (F31.1 1,3)
    wight, myght (F32.2 5,6)
    myght, ryght (F47.1 6,7)
    myght, lyght, syght, ryght (H105.2 1,2,3,4)
  NYGHT (3)
    nyght, light (F12 1,3)
    nyght, syght (F30.1 1,2)
    nyght, whyght (H17 3,6)
  PYGHT (1)
    pyght, unryght (F47.2 6,7)
  RYGHT (5)
    ryght, syght (F10 6,8)
    knyght, ryght (F47b 1,2)
    myght, ryght (F47.1 6,7)
    fyght, ryght, lyght, flyght (H96.1 1,2,3,4)
    myght, lyght, syght, ryght (H105.2 1,2,3,4)
  SYGHT (3)
    ryght, syght (F10 6,8)
    nyght, syght (F30.1 1,2)
    myght, lyght, syght, ryght (H105.2 1,2,3,4)
  UNRYGHT (1)
    pyght, unryght (F47.2 6,7)
  WHYGHT (1)
    nyght, whyght (H17 3,6)
  WRYGHT (1)
    endyght, wryght (H29.1 1,3)
  WYGHT (1)
    wyght, lyght (F46.1 1,3)

-YGHTH (4)
  LYGHTH (1)
    nyghth, lyghth (F48.2 7,8)
  MYGHTH (1)
    myghth, nyghth (R6 4,5)
  NYGHTH (2)
    myghth, nyghth (R6 4,5)
    nyghth, lyghth (F48.2 7,8)

-YKE [see -EKE] (1)
  LYKE (1)
    meke, seke, lyke (F39b 1,2,3)

-ILD [see -YLD, -YLYD] (1)
  CHILD (1)
    chyld, myld, begylyd, child (R15.3 1,2,4,5)

-YLD [see -ILD, -YLYD] (2)
  CHYLD (1)
    chyld, myld, begylyd, child (R15.3 1,2,4,5)
  MYLD (1)
    chyld, myld, begylyd, child (R15.3 1,2,4,5)

-ILED [see -YLED] (1)
  EXILED (1)
    exiled, begyled (H106.2 1,3)

-YLED [see -ILED] (1)
  BEGYLED (1)
    exiled, begyled (H106.2 1,3)

-YLYD [see -ILD] (1)
  BEGYLYD (1)
    chyld, myld, begylyd, child (R15.3 1,2,4,5)

-ILL [see -YLL] (3)
  ILL (1)
    ill, spill, will (F29.4 1,2,3)
  SPILL (1)
    ill, spill, will (F29.4 1,2,3)
  WILL (1)
    ill, spill, will (F29.4 1,2,3)

-YLL [see -ILL] (9)
  BYLL (1)
    byll, wyll (H41.6 1,2)
  FREWYLL (1)
    yll, frewyll (R12.3 3,4)
  FULFYLL (1)
    wyll, fulfyll (H109.3 1,2)
  SKYLL (1)
    yll, skyll (H79.1 5,6)
  STYLL (1)
    styll, will (F30.2 3,6)

398

-YLL (cont.)
  WYLL (2)
    byll, wyll (H41.6 1,2)
    wyll, fulfyll (H109.3 1,2)
  YLL (2)
    yll, frewyll (R12.3 3,4)
    yll, skyll (H79.1 5,6)

-ILT [see -YLT] (2)
  GILT (1)
    mylt, spilt, gilt (F36.1 5,6,7)
  SPILT (1)
    mylt, spilt, gilt (F36.1 5,6,7)

-YLT [see -ILT] (1)
  MYLT (1)
    mylt, spilt, gilt (F36.1 5,6,7)

-IN [see -YN] (1)
  IN (1)
    blyn, in (H41.2 1,2)

-YN [see -ENE, -IN] (4)
  BLYN (1)
    blyn, in (H41.2 1,2)
  BYN (2)
    quene, sene, byn, tene (F32.4 1,2,3,4)
    grene, quene, byn, betwene (F45.1 1,2,3,4)
  ROBYN (1)
    Robyn, myne (H49.1 1,3)

-YND [see -YNDE] (22)
  BEHYND (1)
    fynd, unkynd, wynd, behynd, blynd, mynde
        (R10.6 1,2,3,5,6,7)
  BLYND (1)
    fynd, unkynd, wynd, behynd, blynd, mynde
        (R10.6 1,2,3,5,6,7)
  BYND (1)
    mynd, bynd (H29.2 1,3)
  FRYND (1)
    wynd, frynd (R15.5 1,2)
  FYND (3)
    fynd, unkynd, wynd, behynd, blynd, mynde
        (R10.6 1,2,3,5,6,7)
    mankynd, fynd (F31b 2,4)
    wynde, fynd (H29.3 1,3)
  HYND (1)
    lynde, hynd (H65.2 2,4)
  KYND (4)
    mynd, kynd (F12 6,7)
    kynd, fynde (H12 3,4)
    unkynd, kynd (H29.4 1,3)
    kynd, mynd (H34.2 1,2)

399

-YND (cont.)
  MANKYND (1)
    mankynd, fynd (F31b 2,4)
  MYND (4)
    mynd, kynd (F12 6,7)
    onkynd, mynd (F31.4 1,3)
    mynd, bynd (H29.2 1,3)
    kynd, mynd (H34.2 1,2)
  ONKYND (1)
    onkynd, mynd (F31.4 1,3)
  UNKYND (2)
    fynd, unkynd, wynd, behynd, blynd, mynde
        (R10.6 1,2,3,5,6,7)
    unkynd, kynd (H29.4 1,3)
  WYND (2)
    fynd, unkynd, wynd, behynd, blynd, mynde
        (R10.6 1,2,3,5,6,7)
    wynd, frynd (R15.5 1,2)

-YNDE [see -YND, -YNE] (15)
  BEHYNDE (1)
    behynde, fynde, mynde, lyne, fynde (F1 1,3,5,6,7)
  BLYNDE (1)
    blynde, mankynde (R16.1 1,2)
  FYNDE (3)
    behynde, fynde, mynde, lyne, fynde (F1 1,3,5,6,7)
    kynd, fynde (H12 3,4)
  KYNDE (1)
    mynde, kynde, unkynde (R7 2,3,5)
  LYNDE (1)
    lynde, hynd (H65.2 2,4)
  MANKYNDE (1)
    blynde, mankynde (R16.1 1,2)
  MYNDE (4)
    mynde, kynde, unkynde (R7 2,3,5)
    fynd, unkynd, wynd, behind, blynd, mynde
        (R10.6 1,2,3,5,6,7)
    behynde, fynde, mynde, lyne, fynde (F1 1,3,5,6,7)
    mynde, unkynde (H47.3 2,4)
  UNKYNDE (2)
    mynde, kynde, unkynde (R7 2,3,5)
    mynde, unkynde (H47.3 2,4)
  WYNDE (1)
    wynde, fynd (H29.3 1,3)

-YNE [see -YN, -YNDE] (2)
  LYNE (1)
    behynde, fynde, mynde, lyne, fynde (F1 1,3,5,6,7)
  MYNE (1)
    Robyn, myne (H49.1 1,3)

-ING (2)
  COMFORTING (1)
    nothing, comforting (H104.3 4,5)

-ING (cont.)
  NOTHING (1)
    nothing, comforting (H104.3 4,5)

-YNG [see -YNGE] (47)
  BEHAVYNG (1)
    mervelyng, behavyng (F19 1,3)
  BELEVYNG (1)
    counturfetyng, delyng, nothyng, faynyng, demyng, belevyng
      (F18.1 1,2,3,5,6,7)
  BEYNG (2)
    musyng, morenyng, remembryng, beyng, welyng, contraryyng
      (F24.1 1,2,3,5,6,7)
    musyng, mornyng, remembryng, beyng, walyng, contraryng
      (H107.1 1,2,3,5,6,7)
  BRYNG (1)
    tydyng, bryng (R4 6,7)
  COMPARYNG (1)
    thyng, kyng, comparyng (H50.3 1,2,3)
  CONTRARYNG (1)
    musyng, mornyng, remembryng, beyng, walyng, contraryng
      (H107.1 1,2,3,5,6,7)
  CONTRARYYNG (1)
    musyng, morenyng, remembryng, beyng, welyng, contraryyng
      (F24.1 1,2,3,5,6,7)
  COUNTURFETYNG (1)
    counturfetyng, delyng, nothyng, faynyng, demyng, belevyng
      (F18.1 1,2,3,5,6,7)
  DASLYNG (1)
    passyng, daslyng (F37.2 3,4)
  DELYNG (1)
    counturfetyng, delyng, nothyng, faynyng, demyng, belevyng
      (F18.1 1,2,3,5,6,7)
  DEMYNG (1)
    counturfetyng, delyng, nothyng, faynyng, demyng, belevyng
      (F18.1 1,2,3,5,6,7)
  DERLYNG (1)
    derlyng, swettyng, thyng, perteynyng (H31.5 1,2,4,5)
  ENDYNG (1)
    endyng, Kyng (F48.1 3,4)
  ENTRETYNG (1)
    entretyng, swetyng (F31.3 1,3)
  FAYNYNG (1)
    counturfetyng, delyng, nothyng, faynyng, demyng, belevyng
      (F18.1 1,2,3,5,6,7)
  FEYNYNG (1)
    feynyng, levyng (H40 1,3)
  HYNG (1)
    thyng, hyng (F48.3 5,6)
  KYNG (4)
    thyng, kyng (F5 6,7)
    Kyng, thyng (F30.1 16,17)
    endyng, Kyng (F48.1 3,4)
    thyng, kyng, comparyng (H50.3 1,2,3)

-YNG (cont.)
LEVYNG (1)
    feynyng, levyng (H40 1,3)
MERVELYNG (1)
    mervelyng, behavyng (F19 1,3)
MORENYNG (1)
    musyng, morenyng, remembryng, beyng, welyng, contraryyng
       (F24.1 1,2,3,5,6,7)
MORNYNG (2)
    thynge, synge, mornyng, spryngynge (H17 1,2,4,5)
    musyng, mornyng, remembryng, beyng, walyng, contraryng
       (H107.1 1,2,3,5,6,7)
MOURNYNG (1)
    mournyng, waylyng (R11.1 1,2)
MUSYNG (2)
    musyng, morenyng, remembryng, beyng, welyng, contraryyng
       (F24.1 1,2,3,5,6,7)
    musyng, mornyng, remembryng, beyng, walyng, contraryng
       (H107.1 1,2,3,5,6,7)
NOTHYNG (1)
    counturfetyng, delyng, nothyng, faynyng, demyng, belevyng
       (F18.1 1,2,3,5,6,7)
PASSYNG (2)
    passyng, daslyng (F37.2 3,4)
    passyng, syng (H104.3 1,2)
PERTEYNYNG (1)
    derlyng, swettyng, thyng, perteynyng (H31.5 1,2,4,5)
REMEMBRYNG (2)
    musyng, morenyng, remembryng, beyng, welyng, contraryyng
       (F24.1 1,2,3,5,6,7)
    musyng, mornyng, remembryng, beyng, walyng, contraryng
       (H107.1 1,2,3,5,6,7)
SWETTYNG (1)
    derlyng, swettyng, thyng, perteynyng (H31.5 1,2,4,5)
SWETYNG (1)
    entretyng, swetyng (F31.3 1,3)
SYNG (1)
    passyng, syng (H104.3 1,2)
THYNG (5)
    thyng, kyng (F5 6,7)
    Kyng, thyng (F30.1 16,17)
    thyng, hyng (F48.3 5,6)
    derlyng, swettyng, thyng, perteynyng (H31.5 1,2,4,5)
    thyng, kyng, comparyng (H50.3 1,2,3)
TYDYNG (1)
    tydyng, bryng (R4 6,7)
WALYNG (1)
    musyng, mornyng, remembryng, beyng, walyng, contraryng
       (H107.1 1,2,3,5,6,7)
WAYLYNG (1)
    mournyng, waylyng (R11.1 1,2)
WELYNG (1)
    musyng, morenyng, remembryng, beyng, welyng, contraryyng
       (F24.1 1,2,3,5,6,7)

-YNGE [see -YNG] (3)
  THYNGE (1)
    thynge, synge, mornyng, spryngynge (H17 1,2,4,5)
  SPRYNGYNGE (1)
    thynge, synge, mornyng, spryngynge (H17 1,2,4,5)
  SYNGE (1)
    thynge, synge, mornyng, spryngynge (H17 1,2,4,5)

-YNK (4)
  DRYNK (1)
    drynk, thynk (H35.6 2,4)
  THYNK (2)
    thynk, wynk (F3 1,3)
    drynk, thynk (H35.6 2,4)
  WYNK (1)
    thynk, wynk (F3 1,3)

-ION [see -ON, -OWNE, -UM] (28)
  ADULACION (1)
    dominacion, simulacion, consolacion, adulacion
        (F10 2,4,5,7)
  AFECCION (1)
    afeccion, fusion, computacion, mediacion (F34.5 2,4,5,7)
  COMPASSION (1)
    compassion, indignacion, redempcion, convencion
        (F34.2 2,4,5,7)
  COMPUTACION (1)
    afeccion, fusion, computacion, mediacion (F34.5 2,4,5,7)
  CONFESSION (1)
    rawnsum, confession, remission, passion (F34.1 2,4,5,7)
  CONJURACION (1)
    lynyacion, recreacion, formacion, conjuracion
        (F40.2 1,2,3,4)
  CONSIDERACION (1)
    consideracion, consolacion (F8 1,3)
  CONSOLACION (2)
    consideracion, consolacion (F8 1,3)
    dominacion, simulacion, consolacion, adulacion
        (F10 2,4,5,7)
  CONTRICION (1)
    contricion, adowne, reson, transgression (F34.3 2,4,5,7)
  CONVENCION (1)
    compassion, indignacion, redempcion, convencion
        (F34.2 2,4,5,7)
  CREACION (1)
    creacion, preservacion (F44.2 1,3)
  DERISION (1)
    derision, passion (F30.2 7,8)
  DISTILLACION (1)
    lesson, distillacion, prison, poyson (F34.4 2,4,5,7)
  DOMINACION (1)
    dominacion, simulacion, consolacion, adulacion
        (F10 2,4,5,7)

403

-ION (cont.)
  FORMACION (1)
    lynyacion, recreacion, formacion, conjuracion
        (F40.2 1,2,3,4)
  FUSION (1)
    afeccion, fusion, computacion, mediacion (F34.5 2,4,5,7)
  INDIGNACION (1)
    compassion, indignacion, redempcion, convencion
        (F34.2 2,4,5,7)
  LYNYACION (1)
    lynyacion, recreacion, formacion, conjuracion
        (F40.2 1,2,3,4)
  MEDIACION (1)
    afeccion, fusion, computacion, mediacion (F34.5 2,4,5,7)
  PASSION (2)
    derision, passion (F30.2 7,8)
    rawnsum, confession, remission, passion (F34.1 2,4,5,7)
  PRESERVACION (1)
    creacion, preservacion (F44.2 1,3)
  RECREACION (1)
    lynyacion, recreacion, formacion, conjuracion
        (F40.2 1,2,3,4)
  REDEMPCION (1)
    compassion, indignacion, redempcion, convencion
        (F34.2 2,4,5,7)
  REMISSION (1)
    rawnsum, confession, remission, passion (F34.1 2,4,5,7)
  SIMULACION (1)
    dominacion, simulacion, consolacion, adulacion
        (F10 2,4,5,7)
  TRANSGRESSION (1)
    contricion, adowne, reson, transgression (F34.3 2,4,5,7)

-IR [see -ERE] (1)
  HERE-AFFTIR (1)
    here, here-afftir, dere (F48b 1,2,3)

-YR [see -ER] (1)
  BETTYR (1)
    bettyr, fetter (F46.2 1,3)

-YRDE [see -YD] (1)
  BYRDE (1)
    byrde, hyd (R15.6 3,6)

-IRT [see -ART, -ERT] (1)
  SHIRT (1)
    smert, hart, depart, shirt (F32.3 1,2,3,4)

-IS [see -ESSE, -YS, -ISE, -ISS, -YSSE] (10)
  IS (3)
    is, wis, this (F6.2 4,5,6)
    sykyrnesse, is (F48.3 7,8)
    mysse, is (H104.1 4,5)

404

-IS (cont.)
  THIS (6)
    is, wis, this (F6.2 4,5,6)
    this, bliss (F31.4 2,4)
    this, wise (F37.1 1,2)
    this, kysse (H25.8 1,2)
    kysse, this (H62.5 2,4)
    ys, this (H102.2 1,3)
  WIS (1)
    is, wis, this (F6.2 4,5,6)

-YS [see -IS, -YSSE] (12)
  CLEPYS (1)
    lepys, clepys (R16.1 4,5)
  DENYS (5)
    ease, disease, please, Denys (F40b 1,2,3,4)
    please, Denys (F40.1 5,6)
    please, Denys (F40.2 5,6)
    please, Denys (F40.3 5,6)
    please, Denys (F40.4 5,6)
  LEPYS (1)
    lepys, clepys (R16.1 4,5)
  MYS (1)
    ys, mys (H35.1 1,3)
  YS (4)   '
    ys, mys (H35.1 1,3)
    ys, myse (H62.3 2,4)
    ys, amysse (H101.1 2,4)
    ys, this (H102.2 1,3)

-ISE [see -ICE, -IS, -YSE] (6)
  PRISE (1)
    wise, supprise, prise (R9 3,7,9)
  SUPPRISE (1)
    wise, supprise, prise (R9 3,7,9)
  TWISE (1)
    ryse, twise, gyse (F43.4 1,2,3)
  WISE (3)
    wise, supprise, prise (R9 3,7,9)
    wise, sacrifice (F33.2 8,9)
    this, wise (F37.1 1,2)

-YSE [see -YS, -ISE] (5)
  DEVYSE (1)
    devyse, wyse (R15.4 3,6)
  GYSE (1)
    ryse, twise, gyse (F43.4 1,2,3)
  MYSE (1)
    ys, myse (H62.3 2,4)
  RYSE (1)
    ryse, twise, gyse (F43.4 1,2,3)
  WYSE (1)
    devyse, wyse (R15.4 3,6)

405

-ISHT [see -YSSHID] (1)
  WISHT (1)
    banysshid, wisht (F4 2,5)

-ISS [see -IS] (1)
  BLISS (1)
    this, bliss (F31.4 2,4)

-YSSE [see -IS, -YS] (4)
  AMYSSE (1)
    ys, amysse (H101.1 2,4)
  KYSSE (2)
    this, kysse (H25.8 1,2)
    kysse, this (H62.5 2,4)
  MYSSE (1)
    mysse, is (H104.1 4,5)

-ISSH [see -YSSH, -ISSHE] (1)
  ENGLISSH (1)
    Englissh, fyssh, disshe (F43.2 1,2,3)

-YSSH [see -ISSH, -ISSHE] (1)
  FYSSH (1)
    Englissh, fyssh, disshe (F43.2 1,2,3)

-ISSHE [see -ISSH, -YSSH] (1)
  DISSHE (1)
    Englissh, fyssh, disshe (F43.2 1,2,3)

-YSSHID [see -ISHT] (1)
  BANYSSHID (1)
    banysshid, wisht (F4 2,5)

-IT [see -ET, -YTT] (3)
  IT (2)
    yet, it (H27.4 1,3)
    whytt, it (H35.1 2,4)
  MARGARIT (1)
    Margarit, mete, strete (F39.3 1,2,3)

-ITE (3)
  APPETITE (1)
    white, appetite, delite (F27.6 1,2,3)
  DELITE (1)
    white, appetite, delite (F27.6 1,2,3)
  WHITE (1)
    white, appetite, delite (F27.6 1,2,3)

-YTT [see -IT] (1)
  WHYTT (1)
    whytt, it (H35.1 2,4)

-YVE (2)
  LYVE (1)
    ryve, lyve (F48.2 9,10)
  RYVE (1)
    ryve, lyve (F48.2 9,10)

-O [see -OE, -OO, -OU, -OW] (41)
  ALLSO (1)
    so, woe, goo, allso (R15.4 1,2,4,5)
  ALSO (1)
    also, wo (F31.2 2,4)
  BLO (1)
    blo, mo (H47.4 2,4)
  DO (3)
    do, unto (H12 2,5)
    do, therto (H30 1,3)
    go, do (H35.4 1,3)
  EXCHO (1)
    two, excho (H79.2 5,6)
  FO (1)
    so, fo (R10.1 4,8)
  FRO (4)
    fro, woo, so (F33.2 5,6,7)
    fro, therto (H18 2,3)
    so, fro (H47.2 1,3)
    fro, go (H63.2 1,3)
  GO (7)
    woo, so, go (F3 2,4,5)
    go, mo (F28 1,3)
    wo, go (H25.10 4,5)
    go, do (H35.4 1,3)
    lo, lo, go, lo (H39 1,2,4,5)
    go, foo (H62.4 2,4)
    fro, go (H63.2 1,3)
  LO (4)
    lo, lo, go, lo (H39 1,2,4,5)
    lo, you, cow (H109b 1,2,3)
  MO (2)
    go, mo (F28 1,3)
    blo, mo (H47.4 2,4)
  NO (1)
    so, no (H49.2 2,4)
  SO (9)
    so, fo (R10.1 4,8)
    so, woe, goo, allso (R15.4 1,2,4,5)
    woo, so, go (F3 2,4,5)
    so, woo (F13 1,3)
    fro, woo, so (F33.2 5,6,7)
    foo, so (H31.7 3,6)
    know, so (H44.7 1,2)
    so, fro (H47.2 1,3)
    so, no (H49.2 2,4)
  THERTO (2)
    fro, therto (H18 2,3)

407

-O (cont.)
　THERTO (cont.)
　　do, therto (H30 1,3)
　TWO (1)
　　two, excho (H79.2 5,6)
　UNTO (1)
　　do, unto (H12 2,5)
　WO (2)
　　also, wo (F31.2 2,4)
　　wo, go (H25.10 4,5)

-OAN [see -ONE] (1)
　JHOAN (1)
　　Jhoan, mone, sone (F40.4 1,1,2)

-OD [see -ODDE] (1)
　GOD (1)
　　God, odde (H79.2 3,4)

-ODDE [see -OD] (1)
　ODDE (1)
　　God, odde (H79.2 3,4)

-ODE [see -ED, -EDE, -OOD, -OODE] (9)
　BLODE (1)
　　goode, blode (F32.4 5,6)
　BRODE (1)
　　pode, cart-lode, fode, rode, brode (F41.2 1,2,3,4,5)
　CART-LODE (1)
　　pode, cart-lode, fode, rode, brode (F41.2 1,2,3,4,5)
　FODE (2)
　　good, fode, mode (F13 2,4,5)
　　pode, cart-lode, fode, rode, brode (F41.2 1,2,3,4,5)
　MODE (1)
　　good, fode, mode (F13 2,4,5)
　PODE (1)
　　pode, cart-lode, fode, rode, brode (F41.2 1,2,3,4,5)
　RODE (1)
　　pode, cart-lode, fode, rode, brode (F41.2 1,2,3,4,5)
　WOMANHODE (1)
　　lede, womanhode, goodlyhed (F20 2,4,5)

-OE [see -O, -OO] (1)
　WOE (1)
　　so, woe, goo, allso (R15.4 1,2,4,5)

-OKE [see -OOKE] (3)
　AWOKE (1)
　　loke, awoke (F36.4 9,10)
　LOKE (2)
　　loke, awoke (F36.4 9,10)
　　booke, loke (H62.6 2,4)

-OLD [see -OLDE] (3)
  BEHOLD (1)
    behold, manyfold (H27.3 1,3)
  BOLD (1)
    bold, colde (H34.4 1,2)
  MANYFOLD (1)
    behold, manyfold (H27.3 1,3)

-OLDE [see -OLD] (3)
  COLDE (2)
    colde, wolde (F30.1 9,12)
    bold, colde (H34.4 1,2)
  WOLDE (1)
    colde, wolde (F30.1 9,12)

-OLE (4)
  DOLE (1)
    sole, dole (H64.1 7,8)
  FOLE (1)
    fole, sole (F40.4 2,4)
  SOLE (2)
    fole, sole (F40.4 2,4)
    sole, dole (H64.1 7,8)

-ON [see -ION, -ONE, -OON, -OONE, -OWNE, -UNNE] (19)
  ANON (3)
    anon, on (F27b 4,5)
    anon, oon (F27.4 9,10)
    anon, oon (F27.6 9,10)
  ENCHESON (1)
    reson, encheson, seson, treson (F33.1 1,2,3,4)
  GON (2)
    alone, alone, one, gon, alone, mone (F10.1 1,2,3,5,6,7)
    oone, gon (R15.7 3,6)
  JHON (1)
    Jhon, one (F48.3 3,4)
  LESSON (1)
    lesson, distillacion, prison, poyson (F34.4 2,4,5,7)
  NON (2)
    alone, mone, non, everychone (F6.4 2,4,5,6)
    non, one (F7 6,7)
  ON (2)
    anon, on (F27b 4,5)
    on, gone, alone, bone (F40.3 1,2,3,4)
  POYSON (1)
    lesson, distillacion, prison, poyson (F34.4 2,4,5,7)
  PRISON (1)
    lesson, distillacion, prison, poyson (F34.4 2,4,5,7)
  RESON (2)
    reson, encheson, seson, treson (F33.1 1,2,3,4)
    contricion, adowne, reson, transgression (F34.3 2,4,5,7)
  SESON (1)
    reson, encheson, seson, treson (F33.1 1,2,3,4)

-ON (cont.)
  SURGYON (1)
    begunne, surgyon (R13.2 6,7)
  TRESON (1)
    reson, encheson, seson, treson (F33.1 1,2,3,4)

-OND (3)
  BOND (1)
    stond, bond, lond (F39.1 5,6,7)
  LOND (1)
    stond, bond, lond (F39.1 5,6,7)
  STOND (1)
    stond, bond, lond (F39.1 5,6,7)

-ONE [see -OAN, -ON, -OON, -OONE, -OWN, -UNE] (64)
  ALONE (27)
    alone, alone, one, gon, alone, mone (F10.1 1,2,3,5,6,7)
    alone, alone, mone, alone (R14.1 1,2,3,4)
    gone, mone, alone (R14.2 1,3,4)
    alone, moone (R15.1 3,6)
    alone, gone (R15.3 3,6)
    alone, moon (R15.8 3,6)
    gone, alone, mone, grone (R19.3 1,2,3,4)
    alone, mone, non, everychone (F6.4 2,4,5,6)
    alone, alone (F29b 1,2)
    withstone, alone (F29.5 2,4)
    mone, alone (F37.4 1,2)
    on, gone, alone, bone (F40.3 1,2,3,4)
    alone, one (H14 1,2)
    mone, alone (H31.9 3,6)
    alone, gone (H33.2 2,4)
    alone, mone (H63.2 2,4)
    alone, one (H64.1 4,5)
    gone, alone (H104b 3,6)
    mone, alone (H104.1 3,6)
    gone, alone (H104.2 3,6)
    mone, alone (H104.3 3,6)
    fone, alone (H104.4 3,6)
  BONE (1)
    on, gone, alone, bone (F40.3 1,2,3,4)
  EVERYCHONE (1)
    alone, mone, non, everychone (F6.4 2,4,5,6)
  FONE (1)
    fone, alone (H104.4 3,6)
  FRONE (1)
    one, one, frone, gone (F46b.4; 1.5; 2.5; 3.5)
  GONE (8)
    gone, mone, alone (R14.2 1,3,4)
    alone, gone (R15.3 3,6)
    gone, alone, mone, grone (R19.3 1,2,3,4)
    on, gone, alone, bone (F40.3 1,2,3,4)
    one, one, frone, gone (F46b.4; 1.5; 2.5; 3.5)
    alone, gone (H33.2 2,4)
    gone, alone (H104b 3,6)

410

-ONE (cont.)
  GONE (cont.)
    gone, alone (H104.2 3,6)
  GRONE (1)
    gone, alone, mone, grone (R19.3 1,2,3,4)
  MONE (11)
    alone, alone, one, gon, alone, mone (R10.1 1,2,3,5,6,7)
    alone, alone, mone, alone (R14.1 1,2,3,4)
    gone, mone, alone (R14.2 1,3,4)
    gone, alone, mone, grone (R19.3 1,2,3,4)
    alone, mone, non, everychone (F6.4 2,4,5,6)
    mone, alone (F37.4 1,2)
    Jhoan, mone, sone (F40.4 1,1,2)
    mone, alone (H31.9 3,6)
    alone, mone (H63.2 2,4)
    mone, alone (H104.1 3,6)
    mone, alone (H104.3 3,6)
  NONE (1)
    oone, none (H51.10 1,2)
  ONE (7)
    alone, alone, one, gon, alone, mone (R10.1 1,2,3,5,6,7)
    non, one (F7 6,7)
    one, one, frone, gone (F46b.4; 1.5; 2.5; 3.5)
    Jhon, one (F48.3 3,4)
    alone, one (H14 1,2)
    alone, one (H64.1 4,5)
  SONE (1)
    Jhoan, mone, sone (F40.4 1,1,2)
  SWONE (1)
    down, swone (H25.7 4,5)
  WITHSTONE (1)
    withstone, alone (F29.5 2,4)
  WONE (2)
    fortune, wone (F24.5 4,8)
    fortune, wone (H107.5 4,8)

-ONG (9)
  AMONG (2)
    among, wrong (R19.1 5,10)
    among, wrong (H66.3 1,3)
  LONG (1)
    long, wrong, song (F22 2,4,5)
  SONG (2)
    song, strong (R19.3 5,10)
    long, wrong, song (F22 2,4,5)
  STRONG (1)
    song, strong (R19.3 5,10)
  WRONG (3)
    among, wrong (R19.1 5,10)
    long, wrong, wong (F22 2,4,5)
    among, wrong (H66.3 1,3)

-OO [see -EW, -O, -OE] (7)
  DOO (1)
    doo, ensew (H92.6 1,2)
  FOO (2)
    foo, so (H31.7 3,6)
    go, foo (H62.4 2,4)
  GOO (1)
    so, woe, goo, allso (R15.4 1,2,4,5)
  WOO (3)
    woo, so, go (F3 2,4,5)
    so, woo (F13 1,3)
    fro, woo, so (F33.2 5,6,7)

-OOD [see -ODE] (1)
  GOOD (1)
    good, fode, mode (F13 2,4,5)

-OODE [see -ODE] (1)
  GOODE (1)
    goode, blode (F32.4 5,6)

-OOKE [see -OKE] (1)
  BOOKE (1)
    booke, loke (H62.6 2,4)

-OON [see -ON, -ONE] (3)
  MOON (1)
    alone, moon (R15.8 3,6)
  OON (2)
    anon, oon (F27.4 9,10)
    anon, oon (F27.6 9,10)

-OONE [see -ON, -ONE] (3)
  MOONE (1)
    alone, moone (R15.1 3,6)
  OONE (2)
    oone, gon (R15.7 3,6)
    oone, none (H51.10 1,2)

-OOTE (2)
  BOOTE (1)
    boote, roote (H25.3 1,2)
  ROOTE (1)
    boote, roote (H25.3 1,2)

-OR (2)
  ERROR (1)
    honor, error (H92.4 1,2)
  HONOR (1)
    honor, error (H92.4 1,2)

-ORD [see -ORDE] (1)
  DYSCORD (1)
    dyscord, acorde (H64.1 1,2)

412

-ORDE [see -ORD] (1)
  ACORDE (1)
    dyscord, acorde (H64.1 1,2)

-ORE [see -ERE, -ORNE] (47)
  AFORE (2)
    afore, more (F19 6,8)
    afore, mere (H35.4 2,4)
  BEFORE (1)
    sore, before, tore, forlore, restore, more
        (F36.2 1,2,3,4,8,11)
  BORE (1)
    sore, bore, more (F33.3 5,6,7)
  DORE (1)
    flore, dore (R3.3 6,8)
  EVERMORE (2)
    sore, evermore (H24 2,4)
    sore, evermore (H27.1 2,4)
  FLORE (2)
    flore, dore (R3.3 6,8)
    store, flore (F37.2 1,2)
  FORLORE (2)
    sore, before, tore, forlore, restore, more
        (F36.2 1,2,3,4,8,11)
    sore, more, forlore (H103.1 1,2,3)
  HORE (1)
    hore, more (R1.1 2,4)
  LORE (1)
    lore, more (H35.7 2,4)
  MORE (14)
    hore, more (R1.1 2,4)
    sore, store, more (R13.3 2,4,5)
    more, sore (F3 6,7)
    afore, more (F19 6,8)
    borne, forlorne, more (F29.3 1,2,3)
    sore, more (F32.1 6,7)
    sore, more (F32.2 7,8)
    sore, more (F32.3 7,8)
    sore, more (F32.4 7,8)
    sore, bore, more (F33.3 5,6,7)
    sore, before, tore, forlore, restore, more
        (F36.2 1,2,3,4,8,11)
    lore, more (H35.7 2,4)
    more, sore (H44.4 1,2)
    sore, more, forlore (H103.1 1,2,3)
  RESTORE (2)
    restore, sore (F30.2 16,17)
    sore, before, tore, forlore, restore, more
        (F36.2 1,2,3,4,8,11)
  SORE (14)
    sore, store, more (R13.3 2,4,5)
    more, sore (F3 6,7)
    restore, sore (F30.2 16,17)
    sore, more (F32.1 6,7)

-ORE (cont.)
  SORE (cont.)
    sore, more (F32.2 7,8)
    sore, more (F32.3 7,8)
    sore, more (F32.4 7,8)
    sore, bore, more (F33.3 5,6,7)
    sore, before, tore, forlore, restore, more
        (F36.2 1,2,3,4,8,11)
    sore, wherefore (H15 2,4)
    sore, evermore (H24 2,4)
    sore, evermore (H27.1 2,4)
    more, sore (H44.4 1,2)
    sore, more, forlore (H103.1 1,2,3)
  STORE (2)
    sore, store, more (R13.3 2,4,5)
    store, flore (F37.2 1,2)
  TORE (1)
    sore, before, tore, forlore, restore, more
        (F36.2 1,2,3,4,8,11)
  WHEREFORE (1)
    sore, wherefore (H15 2,4)

-ORNE [see -ORE] (6)
  BEFORNE (1)
    forlorne, to-torne, lorne, beforne (F48.2 3,4,5,6)
  BORNE (1)
    borne, forlorne, more (F29.3 1,2,3)
  FORLORNE (2)
    borne, forlorne, more (F29.3 1,2,3)
    forlorne, to-torne, lorne, beforne (F48.2 3,4,5,6)
  LORNE (1)
    forlorne, to-torne, lorne, beforne (F48.2 3,4,5,6)
  TO-TORNE (1)
    forlorne, to-torne, lorne, beforne (F48.2 3,4,5,6)

-ORT [see -ORTE] (7)
  COMFORT (2)
    comfort, report (H25.9 4,5)
    comfort, resort (H104.2 4,5)
  CUMFORT (2)
    resorte, cumfort (R10.6 4,8)
    sport, cumfort (R12.1 8,9)
  REPORT (1)
    comfort, report (H25.9 4,5)
  RESORT (1)
    comfort, resort (H104.2 4,5)
  SPORT (1)
    sport, cumfort (R12.1 8,9)

-ORTE [see -ORT] (1)
  RESORTE (1)
    resorte, cumfort (R10.6 4,8)

-ORTT (2)
  COMFORTT (1)
    comfortt, sportt (H109.1 7,8)
  SPORTT (1)
    comfortt, sportt (H109.1 7,8)

-OST [see -EST] (1)
  LOST (1)
    lost, mest (H102.2 2,4)

-OT [see -AT] (1)
  NOT (1)
    that, not (H25.6 4,5)

OTE (2)
  BOTE (1)
    rote, bote (H63.1 2,4)
  ROTE (1)
    rote, bote (H63.1 2,4)

-OTT (2)
  NOTT (1)
    nott, shott (H35.3 1,3)
  SHOTT (1)
    nott, shott (H35.3 1,3)

-OU [see -O, -OW] (2)
  YOU (2)
    lo, you, cow (H109b 1,2,3)
    you, cow (H109.1 5,6)

-OUBLE [see -OWBLE] (1)
  TROUBLE (1)
    trouble, dowble (H106.1 1,3)

-OUGH [see -OW, -OWE] (5)
  BOUGH (2)
    bough, rough (H62.2 2,4)
    bough, enough (H65.1 2,4)
  ENOUGH (1)
    bough, enough (H65.1 2,4)
  LOUGH (1)
    bowe, inow, lough (F29.2 1,2,3)
  ROUGH (1)
    bough, rough (H62.2 2,4)

-OUGHT [see -AUGHT, -OWTE] (17)
  BETHOUGHT (1)
    ought, bethought (H25.9 1,2)
  BOUGHT (2)
    sought, bought, nought, thought, braught, forfought
        (R10.3 1,2,3,5,6,7)
    nougnt, sought, bought, wrought, thought (F41.4 1,2,3,4,5)

415

-OUGHT (cont.)
  FORFOUGHT (1)
    sought, bought, nought, thought, braught, forfought
        (R10.3 1,2,3,5,6,7)
  NOUGHT (3)
    sought, bought, nought, thought, braught, forfought
        (R10.3 1,2,3,5,6,7)
    nought, thought (F31.2 1,3)
    nought, sought, bought, wrought, thought (F41.4 1,2,3,4,5)
  OUGHT (1)
    ought, bethought (H25.9 1,2)
  SOUGHT (3)
    sought, bought, nought, thought, braught, forfought
        (R10.3 1,2,3,5,6,7)
    sought, abowte (F30.1 7,8)
    nought, sought, bought, wrought, thought (F41.4 1,2,3,4,5)
  THOUGHT (4)
    sought, bought, nought, thought, braught, forfought
        (R10.3 1,2,3,5,6,7)
    thought, wrought (F29.5 1,3)
    nought, thought (F31.2 1,3)
    nought, sought, bought, wrought, thought (F41.4 1,2,3,4,5)
  WROUGHT (2)
    thought, wrought (F29.5 1,3)
    nought, sought, bought, wrought, thought (F41.4 1,2,3,4,5)

-OUN [see -OWN] (1)
  SESOUN (1)
    sesoun, down (H20 1,2)

-OUR [see -OURE] (4)
  COLOUR (1)
    floure, colour, savoure (F27.5 1,2,3)
  FLAVOUR (1)
    odour, lavendour, flavour (F27.1 1,2,3)
  LAVENDOUR (1)
    odour, lavendour, flavour (F27.1 1,2,3)
  ODOUR (1)
    odour, lavendour, flavour (F27.1 1,2,3)

-OURE [see -ERE, -OUR] (5)
  BARRYOURE (1)
    pure, waryowere, barryoure (H50.2 1,2,3)
  FLOURE (1)
    floure, colour, savoure (F27.5 1,2,3)
  OURE (1)
    oure, shoure (F32.3 5,6)
  SAVOURE (1)
    floure, colour, savoure (F27.5 1,2,3)
  SHOURE (1)
    oure, shoure (F32.3 5,6)

-OURS (6)
  D'AMOURS (1)
    d'amours, ours, dolours, socours, pours, yours
        (H67.1 1,2,3,5,6,7)
  DOLOURS (1)
    d'amours, ours, dolours, socours, pours, yours
        (H67.1 1,2,3,5,6,7)
  OURS (1)
    d'amours, ours, dolours, socours, pours, yours
        (H67.1 1,2,3,5,6,7)
  POURS (1)
    d'amours, ours, dolours, socours, pours, yours
        (H67.1 1,2,3,5,6,7)
  SOCOURS (1)
    d'amours, ours, dolours, socours, pours, yours
        (H67.1 1,2,3,5,6,7)
  YOURS (1)
    d'amours, ours, dolours, socours, pours, yours
        (H67.1 1,2,3,5,6,7)

-OUSE [see -OWSE] (1)
  SPOUSE (1)
    spouse, howse (F30.1 13,14)

-OVE (6)
  ABOVE (2)
    above, move (H25.4 4,5)
    above, love (H104.4 4,5)
  LOVE (2)
    love, prove (R10.2 4,8)
    above, love (H104.4 4,5)
  MOVE (1)
    above, move (H25.4 4,5)
  PROVE (1)
    love, prove (R10.2 4,8)

-OVED (2)
  LOVED (1)
    loved, proved (H34.3 1,2)
  PROVED (1)
    loved, proved (H34.3 1,2)

-OW [see -O, -OU, -OUGH, -OWE] (6)
  COW (3)
    lo, you, cow (H109b 1,2,3)
    you, cow (H109.1 5,6)
    cow, now (H109.4 3,4)
  INOW (1)
    bowe, inow, lough (F29.2 1,2,3)
  KNOW (1)
    know, so (H44.7 1,2)
  NOW (1)
    cow, now (H109.4 3,4)

417

-OWBLE [see -OUBLE] (1)
  DOWBLE (1)
    trouble, dowble (H106.1 1,3)

-OWE [see -OUGH, -OW] (1)
  BOWE (1)
    bowe, inow, lough (F29.2 1,2,3)

-OWLD [see -ULD] (1)
  COWLD (1)
    cowld, shuld (H27.4 2,4)

-OWN [see *-ONE, -OUN, -OWNE] (4)
  DOWN (2)
    sesoun, down (H20 1,2)
    down, swone (H25.7 4,5)
  KNOWN (1)
    howne, known (H102.1 2,4)
  TOWN (1)
    town, downe (R15.6 4,5)

-OWND [see -OWNDE] (1)
  WOWND (1)
    fownde, wownd (F30.2 10,11)

-OWNDE [see -OWND, -OWNE] (2)
  FOWNDE (1)
    fownde, wownd (F30.2 10,11)
  SOWNDE (1)
    downe, towne, sownde (F12 2,4,5)

-OWNE [see -ION, -ON, -OWN, -OWNDE] (8)
  ADOWNE (1)
    contricion, adowne, reson, transgression (F34.3 2,4,5,7)
  CROWNE (1)
    towne, gowne, crowne (F43.1 1,2,3)
  DOWNE (2)
    town, downe (R15.6 4,5)
    downe, towne, sownde (F12 2,4,5)
  GOWNE (1)
    towne, gowne, crowne (F43.1 1,2,3)
  HOWNE (1)
    howne, known (H102.1 2,4)
  TOWNE (2)
    downe, towne, sownde (F12 2,4,5)
    towne, gowne, crowne (F43.1 1,2,3)

-OWSE [see -OUSE] (1)
  HOWSE (1)
    spouse, howse (F30.1 13,14)

-OWT (2)
  DOWT (1)
    dowt, owt (H74 1,2)

-OWT (cont.)
  OWT (1)
    dowt, owt (H74 1,2)

-OWTE [see -OUGHT] (1)
  ABOWTE (1)
    sought, abowte (F30.1 7,8)

-UE [see -EW] (1)
  ENSUE (1)
    ensue, rew (H92.1 1,2)

-UGE (2)
  GRUGE (1)
    gruge, juge (H51.6 1,2)
  JUGE (1)
    gruge, juge (H51.6 1,2)

-UK (3)
  DUK (1)
    luk, pluk, duk (F43.3 1,2,3)
  LUK (1)
    luk, pluk, duk (F43.3 1,2,3)
  PLUK (1)
    luk, pluk, duk (F43.3 1,2,3)

-ULD [see -OWLD] (1)
  SHULD (1)
    cowld, shuld (H27.4 2,4)

-UM [see -ION] (1)
  RAWNSUM (1)
    rawnsum, confession, remission, passion (F34.1 2,4,5,7)

-UNE [see -ONE] (2)
  FORTUNE (2)
    fortune, wone (F24.5 4,8)
    fortune, wone (H107.5 4,8)

-UNNE [see -ON] (1)
  BEGUNNE (1)
    begunne, surgyon (R13.2 6,7)

-UR [see -URE] (3)
  CREATUR (1)
    sure, creatur, solur, endure, sure, endur
        (H67.2 1,2,3,5,6,7)
  ENDUR (1)
    sure, creatur, solur, endure, sure, endur
        (H67.2 1,2,3,5,6,7)
  SOLUR (1)
    sure, creatur, solur, endure, sure, endur
        (H67.2 1,2,3,5,6,7)

419

-URE [see -ERE, -OURE, -UR] (45)
ADVENTURE (2)
   adventure, endure, recure (H103.2 1,2,3)
   aventure, creature, endure, adventure (H108 1,3,6,7)
AVENTURE (3)
   figure, pure, sure, cure, aventure (R9 1,2,4,5,8)
   plesure, aventure (H106.4 2,4)
   aventure, creature, endure, adventure (H108 1,3,6,7)
CREATURE (3)
   creature, ensure (F46.1 2,4)
   creature, ensure (F49.1 1,3)
   aventure, creature, endure, adventure (H108 1,3,6,7)
CURE (3)
   figure, pure, sure, cure, aventure (R9 1,2,4,5,8)
   ensure, cure (F37.4 3,4) ·
   demure, cure, lure, ensure, plesure, endure
      (H75 2,3,5,6,8,9)
DEMURE (1)
   demure, cure, lure, ensure, plesure, endure
      (H75 2,3,5,6,8,9)
ENDURE (10)
   endure, plesure, sure (R13.1 2,4,5)
   endure, ensure (F25.2 4,8)
   endure, mysaventure (F26 4,5)
   endure, sure (H28 2,4)
   sure, endure (H47.5 1,3)
   sure, creatur, solur, endure, sure, endur
      (H67.2 1,2,3,5,6,7)
   demure, cure, lure, ensure, plesure, endure
      (H75 2,3,5,6,8,9)
   adventure, endure, recure (H103.2 1,2,3)
   endure, recure (H106.2 6,7)
   aventure, creature, endure, adventure (H108 1,3,6,7)
ENSURE (5)
   endure, ensure (F25.2 4,8)
   ensure, cure (F37.4 3,4)
   creature, ensure (F46.1 2,4)
   creature, ensure (F49.1 1,3)
   demure, cure, lure, ensure, plesure, endure
      (H75 2,3,5,6,8,9)
FIGURE (1)
   figure, pure, sure, cure, aventure (R9 1,2,4,5,8)
LURE (1)
   demure, cure, lure, ensure, plesure, endure
      (H75 2,3,5,6,8,9)
MYSAVENTURE (1)
   endure, mysaventure (F26 4,5)
PLESURE (3)
   endure, plesure, sure (R13.1 2,4,5)
   demure, cure, lure, ensure, plesure, endure
      (H75 2,3,5,6,8,9)
   plesure, aventure (H106.4 2,4)
PROCURE (1)
   sure, procure (H64.2 4,5)

-URE (cont.)
  PURE (2)
    figure, pure, sure, cure, aventure (R9 1,2,4,5,8)
    pure, waryowere, barryoure (H50.2 1,2,3)
  RECURE (2)
    adventure, endure, recure (H103.2 1,2,3)
    endure, recure (H106.2 6,7)
  SURE (7)
    figure, pure, sure, cure, aventure (R9 1,2,4,5,8)
    endure, plesure, sure (R13.1 2,4,5)
    endure, sure (H28 2,4)
    sure, endure (H47.5 1,3)
    sure, procure (H64.2 4,5)
    sure, creatur, solur, endure, sure, endur
        (H67.2 1,2,3,5,6,7)

-URST [see -UST] (1)
  FURST (1)
    furst, trust (F46.3 1,3)

-US (2)
  GREVUS (1)
    grevus, noyus (H106.3 6,7)
  NOYUS (1)
    grevus, noyus (H106.3 6,7)

-USE (4)
  REFFUSE (1)
    use, reffuse (R12.3 8,9)
  REFUSE (1)
    use, refuse (H92.3 1,2)
  USE (2)
    use, reffuse (R12.3 8,9)
    use, refuse (H92.3 1,2)

-USED (2)
  REFUSED (1)
    refused, used (H34.6 1,2)
  USED (1)
    refused, used (H34.6 1,2)

-USYD (6)
  ABUSYD (2)
    abusyd, refusyd, mysusyd (F14 2,4,5)
    abusyd, refusyd (F17 1,3)
  MYSUSYD (1)
    abusyd, refusyd, mysusyd (F14 2,4,5)
  REFUSYD (2)
    abusyd, refusyd, mysusyd (F14 2,4,5)
    abusyd, refusyd (F17 1,3)
  USYD (1)
    gydyd, usyd (H92.6 3,4)

-USSE [see -UST] (1)
  DYSCUSSE (1)
    dyscusse, must (H66.4 1,1)

-UST [see -URST, -USSE] (6)
  LUST (2)
    lust, must (H16 1,3)
    must, lust (H82.1 5,6)
  MUST (3)
    lust, must (H16 1,3)
    dyscusse, must (H66.4 1,1)
    must, lust (H82.1 5,6)
  TRUST (1)
    furst, trust (F46.3 1,3)

RANKING LIST OF
FREQUENCIES

1.) 429 (3.663)
I

2.) 347 (2.963)
AND

3.) 290 (2.476)
MY
TO

4.) 251 (2.143)
THE

5.) 199 (1.699)
THAT

6.) 197 (1.682)
BE

7.) 170 (1.452)
FOR

8.) 169 (1.443)
ME

9.) 166 (1.417)
IN

10.) 155 (1.323)
OF

11.) 136 (1.161)
A

12.) 119 (1.016)
SO

13.) 118 (1.008)
IS

14.) 108 (0.922)
LOVE

15.) 107 (0.914)
ALL

16.) 97 (0.828)
WITH

17.) 90 (0.768)
SHE

18.) 86 (0.734)
HER

19.) 82 (0.700)
YE

20.) 78 (0.666)
NO

21.) 77 (0.657)
NOW

22.) 75 (0.640)
THIS

23.) 73 (0.623)
IT

24.) 65 (0.555)
HART
NOT

25.) 64 (0.546)
AS
MAY

26.) 62 (0.529)
BUT
SHALL

27.) 59 (0.504)
WAS

28.) 58 (0.495)
WHAT
YS

29.) 57 (0.487)
Y

30.) 55 (0.470)
HAVE

31.) 50 (0.427)
AM

32.) 48 (0.410)
HE

33.) 44 (0.376)
HIS

34.) 42 (0.359)
ON
THI

35.) 41 (0.350)
THUS
YET

36.) 39 (0.333)
ALONE
YOUR

37.) 38 (0.324)
HATH

38.) 37 (0.316)
THER
WE

39.) 36 (0.307)
YOU

40.) 35 (0.299)
ALAS

41.) 34 (0.290)
DO
MORE

42.) 33 (0.282)
LADY
OR

43.) 32 (0.273)
GOD
WILL

44.) 30 (0.256)
THOU
WELL

45.) 29 (0.248)
DOTH
MAN

46.) 27 (0.231)
FROM
GOOD
HOW
WHEN

47.) 26 (0.222)
BEST
REMEDY

48.) 25 (0.213)
FULL
MAKE

425

49.) 24 (0.205)
PAYNE
THEN
THEY
WHICH

50.) 23 (0.196)
ADEW
CAN
HYM
MUST
SHULD
SORE
WHY

51.) 22 (0.188)
MOST
US
WOLDE

52.) 21 (0.179)
THYNK

53.) 20 (0.171)
GO
HERE
SUCH
THEM

54.) 19 (0.162)
DETH
EVERY
LORD
NAY
UNTO
WYLL
YN

55.) 18 (0.154)
DYE
RYGHT
SAY
SE
THAN

56.) 17 (0.145)
BY
DERE
EVER
GRACE
LET
MYN
O
SWETE

TREW

57.) 16 (0.137)
DAY
FOSTER
HERT
JOY
ONE
WOLD
YOW

58.) 15 (0.128)
SHAL
SON

59.) 14 (0.120)
BOTH
LORDE
SOVERAYNE
WHO
YOUGH

60.) 13 (0.111)
AT
FORTUNE
JHESU
LOLY
MYGHT
OTHER
PRAY
SAID
SURE
TAKE
TRUST
WITHOWT

61.) 12 (0.102)
AN
ENDURE
GRET
KNOW
MERCY
MYND
THAY
THOUGH
THY

62.) 11 (0.094)
AGAYNE
CANNOT
COMPLAYNE
LO
MONE
MYNE

NEVER
OURE
SYTH
THOUGHT
WHERFOR

63.) 10 (0.086)
ALLWAY
CALL
DYSDAYNE
FAYRE
GONE
MANERLY
MEN
METE
ROSE
UP
WERE

64.) 9 (0.077)
BENE
BYN
CREATURE
DID
DYD
FYND
GRENE
GRETE
GUP
HIT
HOPE
MYNDE
NOTT
PLAY
PUT
SCHE
TYLL
WHERE
WITNESS

65.) 8 (0.068)
BERE
CAUSE
CUM
DEMYD
ENTENT
FLOURE
FROME
GODE
GOODE
HEY
HYS
JOLY
KYNG

LETT
LONG
LOVERS
NAME
NONY
NOR
ONLY
SAWE
SHULDE
SONE
SYNG
THOW
TYME
WHER
WHERFORE
WRONGFULLY

66.)   7 (0.060)
CHERE
CORAGE
DEPART
DOWNE
FRE
FRO
GRENEWODE
GRETLY
KEPE
LEVE
LIKE
MANY
METHOUGHT
NON
NOWE
OVER
PAYNYS
PLACE
PLESAUNCE
RESON
REST
SAVE
SITH
SMERT
SOROW
THYNG
WAR
WAY
WHOM
WITHOUTE
WOFULL
WOLL
WOTE
YEURE

67.)   6 (0.051)
AGE
ALE
AMEND
BESSE
BLESSID
BLODE
BLOW
BOTHE
CARE
CHAUNCE
COMFORT
COST
CRYE
DAUNCE
DESYRE
FAREWELL
FAST
FRESSH
FYNDE
HAD
HORNE
HYE
LUSTY
MARY
MODER
MORNE
NATURE
NE
NERE
PLAYNE
PLECE
PLESURE
PYTE
REFRAYNE
REMEMBIR
RIGHT
SANG
SAYD
SENT
SPENT
TREWLY
TROLY
VAYNE
WEPE
WHI
YF
YFF
YT

68.)   5 (0.043)
ABOVE
ALAK
ALSO

AMONG
ART
AWAY
BEAUTE
BODY
CAST
CHANCE
CHAUNGE
CLOWTE
CONTENT
COWDE
CRISTIAN
CROWNE
CURTESLY
DENYS
ENSURE
FACE
FAYNE
FERE
FEYTH
FORSAKYN
GEVYN
GLAD
GRAUNT
HENS
HERTE
HOLY
KYND
LAY
LOST
LYGHT
LYVE
MARGERY
MAYDE
MO
NEVIR
NEW
NONE
NOUGHT
OFF
OPTAYNE
OUR
PLEASE
PRATELY
RED
RULYTH
SAKE
SETT
SEYD
SHARPE
SHOLDE
SPEKE
SYN
TELL

TROBLED	MYRTH	CASTELL
TROUTH	NY	CAUSYTH
UPON	NYGHT	CHILD
VALE	OWER	CHILDE
VERTU	OWNE	COLOUR
WENT	OWT	COM
WEPYNG	PASSYNG	COME
WISE	PAYN	COMPLAYN
WOFFULLY	PITE	CONTRARY
WOO	PRINCE	COW
YES	PROVID	CURE
	RUTTER	DANDIRLY
69.) 4 (0.034)	RUTTERKYN	DAWES
AFFRAIDE	SAIDE	DELE
AGRE	SAYTH	DENAY
ANON	SENE	DEPE
ANY	SEY	DRED
AVAUNCE	SHALBE	DREME
AVENTURE	SHENT	DYSDAYN
BEHOLDE	SLAYNE	DYSTRES
BOW	SUFFYRD	ELS
BREST	SWET	END
BURNE	THERFOR	ENDE
CASE	THORNE	EYRE
CLERE	THRE	FEERE
COMPANY	TILL	FO
CRIST	TWAYNE	FOLY
CROSS	UNDIR	FORSAKE
DEDE	UPPON	FOWND
DEGRE	USE	FROWARD
DELIS	VENUS	GARDEN
DOWN	WANTON	GAYNE
EVYR	WECHE	GETT
FALL	WHOSO	GILT
FALS	YLL	GRENWOD
FY		GREVAUNCE
GENTILL	70.) 3 (0.026)	GREVOUS
GENTYLL	ABSENCE	GYDE
GODELY	AFORE	HADE
GOODLY	AFTER	HANDES
HANG	ALAC	HAS
HARD	AMYAS	HELP
HELPE	APPLYE	HEVY
HYMSELFE	ARAID	HEVYN
HYT	ARE	HIE
JAK	ARMYS	HONOR
LATE	BEN	HOUGH
LOKE	BLISS	HOYDA
LOVYD	BOUGHT	HUNTER
LYFF	BOWE	HYR
LYKYTH	BUTT	INTO
MERCIABLE	CALVERY	JHOAN
MERY	CAM	JHOONE
MUSYNG	CANNOTT	KNOWE

428

KYSSE
LEDE
LENT
LEST
LIGHT
LOVED
LOVYS
LUST
LYF
LYFFE
LYK
LYKE
LYLY-WHIGHTE
LYTYLL
MADE
MAK
MAKYNG
MANNYS
MEDOW
MENT
METHYNKYTH
MILKE
MODIR
MORNETH
MORNYNG
MYLKE
NAILID
NEDES
NEVYR
NOGHT
NOTHYNG
OFFENCE
OFT
OON
OONE
PAST
PASTAUNCE
PAY
PERE
PETE
PLAYNLY
PURE
PYTEUSLY
RAN
RAYNE
REDRESS
REMEDYLES
REMEMBRYNG
ROTE
SAITH
SAME
SEND   .
SERVE
SERVICE

SEW
SHOTE
SHOTT
SOLE
SONG
SOROWFULL
SOUGHT
SPACE
SPECIALL
SPERE
SPORT
STRENKYTH
STYLL
SUERE
SUFFIRD
SUMTYME
SUMWHAT
SYGHT
THERFORE
THERTO
THES
THOO
THOUGHTIS
THOWE
THREE
THYNKYTH
TOWNE
TRE
TRINITE
TROW
TRULY
TYL
TYMES
UNKYND
UNKYNDE
UNKYNDLY
UNKYNDNES
VICE
VOICE
WEPT
WHEREFORE
WHITE
WHOME
WHYCH
WITHIN
WITTNESS
WO
WOMEN
WONT
WRONG
WROUGHT
WYLDERNES
YOURS
YOURSELFE

YOWRE

71.)   2 (0.017)
ABOWTE
ABSENS
ABUSYD
ABYDE
ADVENTURE
AGAYN
ALASSE
AMENDE
ANOTHER
AQUAYNTANCE
AR
ARAIDE
ARROW
ASSURAUNCE
AVENT
AXE
AY
BARE
BEGYLED
BEHYNDE
BETRAIDE
BETTER
BETWENE
BETYNG
BEUTE
BEWARE
BEYNG
BLAME
BLESSED
BOND
BOTE
BOUGH
BOUNDEN
BRAYNE
BRETH
BRYNG
BYCAUSE
BYGGE
CELESTIALL
CHEF
CHEFF
CHOSEN
CLENE
COLDE
COMYNS
CONSENT
CONSOLACION
CONSTRAYNYD
CONTRITE
CRISTE
CUMFORT

429

CUMPANY	GLORIUS	LOVER
DAILY	GON	LOVITH
DARE	GOSTLY	LOVYNG
DAYE	GOTEN	LOVYTH
DAYLY	GOTHE	LYFE
DEATH	GOVERNAUNCE	LYTELL
DED	GRETT	LYVING
DENYE	GREVE	MADAME
DERLYNG	GREVUS	MANER
DISDAYNE	GREVUSLY	MANKYND
DISEASE	GRONE	MASTRES
DISPLESAUNCE	GROUTH	MAYDYN
DOLE	HADDE	MAYDYNS
DONE	HANDIS	MEKE
DOTHE	HAPP	MERVELL
DOUTLESS	HARDELY	MILK
DULFULL	HARTES	MODE
EE	HAST	MOONE
ELLES	HATHE	MORENYNG
ELSE	HAY	MOVE
ENDURS	HED	MYSAVENTURE
ENTRETID	HENT	MYSELF
ENVY	HEVYNES	MYSSE
ERTH	HEVYNESS	MYSYLF
ESCHEW	HEW	NAILIS
EVERMORE	HIR	NEDIS
EVYLL	HOLE	NEDYS
EXPRESS	HUR	NOBLE
EYLYTH	HURT	NOTHING
FAITH	I-WISS	NYGHTH
FAYER	IF	OFFENS
FAYN	IFF	OFFERD
FEERFULL	ILL	ONCERTAYNE
FELE	INDEDE	ONSE
FER	IVE	ONYS
FETE	JEWIS	OPTEYNE
FETT	JHON	OWN
FLE	JOE	OWTE
FLEE	JOYED	PART
FLORE	JOYS	PASS
FLOURIS	KNYGHT	PASSION
FODE	KYS	PASTYMES
FOO	LAMENTABLE	PAYNEFULL
FORBEDE	LAST	PERSON
FORLORE	LAWE	PLESANT
FORLORNE	LEFF	PLUK
FREND	LEFFE	PORE
FRESCHE	LEFFT	POUR
FYVE	LESS	POWER
GAME	LESSON	PRATY
GENT	LEVYS	PRESENS
GENTYL	LOND	PREST
GET	LONGE	PRETY
GEVE	LOSE	PRINCIPALL

430

PROMYSE	STOND	WALKYD
PURCHASE	STORE	WAN
QUENE	STRANGE	WARE
RECURE	STRAWE	WASTE
REDE	STRAYNYD	WAYS
REDRESSE	SUCHE	WEL
REFRAYN	SUER	WELCUM
REFUSYD	SUERLY	WELFARE
REMEMBER	SUFFIR	WENDE
REMEMBRAUNCE	SUFFYR	WENE
RENNYTH	SURANCE	WHAN
REPENTANT	SYDE	WHATSOEVER
REPLETE	SYGH	WHERBY
REQUEST	SYGHS	WHEREAS
RESTORE	SYLF	WHILE
RETAYNE	TABLE	WHILL
REVERT	TAKYN	WHOS
REW	TERRESTRIALL	WHOSE
REWE	TERYS	WHYLS
RIALL	THERE	WILLYNG
ROBYN	THEREFORE	WIS
RUTTERKIN	THERIN	WITHOUTEN
SAW	THOSE	WOE
SAYNG	THRALL	WOMAN
SAYNT	THYN	WOMMANLY
SEALE	THYNE	WONE
SEE	TRACE	WORDE
SEMYTH	TRESON	WORDLE
SEN	TREWE	WORDLIS
SET	TROBILL	WORLDE
SEYNT	TROLLY	WORNE
SHEW	TRUSTYNG	WRY
SHULL	TURNYD	WYL
SLEPE	UNCERTEYNE	WYND
SODENLY	UNDER	WYSE
SOFTLY	UNKYNDNESS	WYSSE
SORFULL	UNLOVED	WYTH
SOROWS	UNTREW	YERE
SORWE	USYD	YETT
SORY	VAYNYS	YETTE
SOWLIS	VENUS '	YEUR
SPRAY	VERTUUS	YONG
STEDFAST	VICES	YOUTH
STODE	VYCE	

RANKING LIST OF
FOREIGN FORMS

1.)   4 (0.034)
   DOMINO
   EST
   FACTUM
   ITA
   LE
   PLACUIT
   SICUT

2.)   3 (0.026)
   ADEW
   HELY
   O

3.)   2 (0.017)
   BA
   DA
   ET
   IN
   MICHI
   QUID
   TEMPORE
   VIVE

4.)   1 (0.009)
   AC
   AMEN
   ANTIQUO

ARBORE
BELL
CLERICUS
CORAM
CUM
D'AMOURS
DERIDERE
DULCISSIMA
ETERNAM
FACIAM
FILI
FILY
FLERE
FUGIAM
FUSTIBUS
HENRY
INCIPEO
INTERFICIAM
KATERINE
LA
LOCO
LUDERE
MADAME
MATER
MEIS
MICHI
MORI

MOVERE
NOBLE
OMNIBUS
OSCULA
PARATUS
PARENTIBUS
PATER
PECTORE
PETIS
PLAUSIS
PRINCE
PRO
PUERUM
QUADAM
QUIDAM
QUO
ROSARY
SEMPER
SOLEBAM
SUB
SUM
SUO
TE
VEL
VERNO
VIRGIS
VITAM